Innovations
in Instructional Technology
Essays in Honor of M. David Merrill

T0386138

Innovations in Instructional Technology

Essays in Honor of M. David Merrill

Edited by

J. Michael Spector
Florida State University

Celestia Ohrazda
Syracuse University

Andrew Van Schaack
David A. Wiley
Utah State University

Psychology Press
Taylor & Francis Group

New York   London

First published by
Lawrence Erlbaum Associates, Inc., Publishers
10 Industrial Avenue
Mahwah, New Jersey 07430

First issued in paperback 2012

This edition published 2012 by Psychology Press

Psychology Press   Psychology Press
Taylor & Francis Group   Taylor & Francis Group
711 Third Avenue   27 Church Road
New York, NY 10017   Hove, East Sussex BN3 2FA

Psychology Press is an imprint of Taylor & Francis, an informa group company

Cover design by Sean Sciarrone

Library of Congress Cataloging-in-Publication Data

Innovations in instructional technology : essays in honor of M. David
    Merrill / edited by J. Michael Spector ... [et al.].
        p. cm.
Includes bibliographical references and index.
ISBN 0-8058-4836-3 (cloth : alk. paper)
ISBN 978-0-415-64856-1 (Paperback)
1. Instructional systems—Design. 2. Educational technol-
    ogy. I. Spector, J. Michael. II. Merrill, M. David, 1931–
LB1028.38.I53 2005
371.33—dc22
                                            2004056395
                                                    CIP

Dedication

M. David Merrill has dedicated more than 40 years of service to the professional instructional design and technology research and development community. One of his
most notable achievements has been in the form of his mentoring of students and colleagues, as we have attempted to represent in this volume. These achievements would
not have been possible without the support of his large and extended family, as is the
case with many who make such significant and sustained contributions to a profession.
We, and many more of those mentored by David, have come to regard ourselves as part
of that extended family. In the context of this mentoring, we therefore dedicate this
volume to all those who have benefited and will benefit from David's mentoring.

Michael Spector, Celestia Ohrazda, Andy Van Schaack, and David Wiley

April 2004

Contents

Foreword

Marcy P. Driscoll
Florida State University

Whenever I am asked to introduce Dave Merrill to an audience, usually at a conference or other such gathering of instructional technology types, my typical response is to ask him what he would like me to say. "Oh, the most important things about me," he would reply, "are my children and my grandchildren." On one level, this modest answer reveals Dave's deep devotion to his family, and anyone who knows him knows how important family is to him. On another level, however, truer words could hardly be spoken. Not only has Merrill's own work had a tremendous impact on the instructional technology field, but so has the work of his students and their students. This volume is proof. It contains innovative work in educational technology and instructional engineering from distinguished scholars who are former students and colleagues of Merrill's. In some chapters, the authors make a direct connection between their work and Merrill's. In others, the connection is less explicit but no less profound.

It is hard to imagine anyone in the field of instructional technology who has not been touched in some way by Dave Merrill's ideas or the man himself. As a graduate student in the 1970s, I knew about his early work with computer-assisted instruction. I cannot say for sure just how I came to become acquainted with this work, because I was studying educational psychology at the time and my program was focused on basic problems in learning rather than practical matters related to instruction or instructional design. I was under the tutelage of someone whose doctorate, like Merrill's, was from the University of Illinois, so perhaps that was the connection. However, what I really wanted to do was instructional design, so I read whatever I could find on the subject. Interestingly, my first job offer as I was finishing my degree came from Courseware, Inc., an instructional development firm in San Diego that was cofounded by Dave Merrill. Although I chose not to accept the position, I came to know Dave anyway and have had the privilege of calling him a friend and professional colleague for some twenty-odd years.

In this collection of essays honoring M. David Merrill, at least three things should become apparent about him. First of all, he is a strong mentor and role model, not only to his own students, but to others of us in the field who look to him for inspiration and guidance. Some years ago, I faced a choice of running for editor of the *ETR&D* Research Section or working with Larry Lipsitz to create a peer-reviewed Research Section in *Educational Technology*. Dave encouraged me to pursue the latter course, which, although riskier and perhaps harder to do, had the potential of establishing some new and interesting directions in the field. Editing a new publication would give me the opportunity to put together an editorial board and seek articles that crossed disciplinary boundaries and showcased alternative research methods. Although the endeavor was not as successful as we might have hoped, lasting five years only, it was worth the effort to publish more empirical research in the magazine. Merrill emphasized even then, as he has throughout his career, I believe, the need for solid, evidence-based research to show the effectiveness of our models, theories, and instructional designs.

A particular note about Merrill as mentor is that he has always welcomed the debate that comes from ideas that diverge from his own. Several of the authors in this volume allude to conversations with him that not only influenced their thinking but spurred Merrill to write a rejoinder to ideas or questions they posed. In the true spirit of open, academic exchange, Merrill cannot resist responding to a challenge, and we are all the more informed as a result.

Second, Merrill's work has been innovative and it has inspired innovation. From TICCIT to ID_2 to Instructional Transaction Theory, Merrill's ideas have led the field. His publications continue to be required reading in our graduate programs, and we encourage our students to attend his presentations to hear his latest thinking.

Finally, Merrill's work has focused on instruction and how to design it so that it is maximally efficient, effective, and appealing, no matter how it is delivered. In reading the contributions to this volume as well as the text of the recent Association for Educational Communications and Technology (AECT) session that focused on Merrill's contributions to the field, I was struck by his singular focus on instruction. While others design learning environments, or develop performance support tools, or investigate the use of learning technologies, Merrill works on problems related to instruction and the design of instruction. This seems to me to be at the very heart of what we do and what the field is all about. Dave Merrill has helped to lay the foundation of the instructional design field, and the chapters in this volume now build on this foundation to advance us in new and promising ways.

Preface

M. David Merrill has been active in the field of instructional technology for almost 40 years. His contributions range from basic instructional principles and instructional design theory to development and implementation of learning environments. The evolution of Merrill's work reflects the growing maturity of the field. His early work reflects the nascent field of computer-assisted instruction. TICCIT (Time-Shared Interactive Computer-Controlled Information Television) is one of the most innovative systems to emerge in the 1970s. Component Display Theory (CDT) encapsulates the lesson-level design theory embedded in TICCIT and guided the development of many instructional computing systems through the 1980s. Merrill continued to elaborate his theories as technology changed and evolved. New computers and networks made it possible to do new things. In order to take full advantage of computers, Merrill saw the need to evolve additional models to support learning at the lesson level as well as a need to address larger instructional issues. These interests led to a revision of CDT. A new perspective called Second Generation Instructional Design (ID_2) emerged in the 1990s from Merrill's research and development along with a new theory that he called Instructional Transaction Theory. Two strands are evident in Merrill's most recent work: foundation principles for instruction, and issues involving learning objects. Indeed, the ability to meaningfully interweave "micro" and "macro" instructional principles is certainly one hallmark of Merrill's distinguished career.

This volume came about as two of the editors of this volume (Mike Spector and Dave Wiley) discussed how much Merrill had influenced the field for so long in so many positive ways. We decided that such significant and sustained contributions deserved special recognition. We thought that a collection of essays written by leading scholars and practitioners who themselves had been inspired by Merrill was one way to accomplish this goal. In the course of our conversations, we agreed that one of Merrill's most outstanding accomplishments had been the quality of mentoring he provided both students and colleagues. We concluded that we should emulate Merrill's commitment to mentoring and invited two doctoral students to join us in creating and editing this volume—Celestia Ohrazda at Syracuse University and Andy Van Schaack at Utah State University. Much of the credit for this volume goes to Celestia and Andy, who kept the process moving while providing their insights and contributions.

Several contributors to this volume along with others whose work has been informed and inspired by Merrill were invited to participate in a special presidential session at the annual meeting of the Association for Educational Communications and Technology (AECT) in October 2003 in Anaheim, CA. Each panelist was invited to make a comment or ask a question about Merrill's considerable body of research and development over the years. Dave then offered a short response to each one. The contributors to this panel included the editors of this volume, Michael Farris, David Jonassen, Kinshuk, Paul Kirschner, Jim L'Allier, Charles Reigeluth, and Robert Reiser. The session was taped and transcribed by Celestia Ohrazda, who then provided the unedited transcript to Dave Merrill to edit. The edited transcription of this AECT 2003 presidential session forms the epilogue for this volume.

Michael Spector   Celestia Ohrazda   Andy Van Schaack   David Wiley

April 2004

Acknowledgments

We wish to thank a number of individuals and organizations for making this volume possible. First of all, we thank M. David Merrill for his many contributions, which inspired this volume. Second, we thank the publisher, Lawrence Erlbaum Associates, Lori Hawver Kelly, our editor, and Sara Scudder, our production editor. Third, we thank the Association for Educational and Communications Technology and the 11 panel participants in the AECT 2003 presidential session entitled "Questioning Merrill," on which the epilogue to this volume is based. Finally, we thank Syracuse University and Utah State University for providing resources in support of the four editors of this volume.

—Michael Spector, Celestia Ohrazda, Andy Van Schaack, and David Wiley

April 2004

About the Authors

Abedi, Jamal
University of California, Los Angeles, CRESST
301 GSE&IS Building
Los Angeles, CA 90095, USA

Jamal Abedi is an adjunct professor at UCLA Graduate School of Education and Information Studies. He received his PhD from George Peabody College of Vanderbilt University with a specialization: in psychology (psychometrics). Dr. Abedi's research interests include psychometrics and test and scale development. His recent work includes validity studies for the National Assessment of Educational Progress (NAEP) focusing on the impact of language background on students' performance He has also developed a culture-free instrument for measuring creativity and is involved in projects with the Center for Research on Evaluation, Standards, and Student Testing (CRESST).

Boot, Eddy W.
Learning Processes
Department of Training and Instruction
TNO Human Factors
Kampweg 5
3769 ZG, Soesterberg, The Netherlands

Eddy W. Boot is a scientific researcher at TNO Human Factors and is involved in research and development projects concerning the application of information and communication technology (ICT) to improve learning processes. He holds a master's degree in instructional technology from the University of Twente, and specializes in applying instructional theories such as case-based learning and problem-based learning by means of advanced learning technology. Much of his research is also related to the integration of work and learning and the standardization of learning technology in the context of military and organizational training. Currently, he is finishing his PhD work on template-based tool support for inexperienced developers of instructional software.

Brewer, Erin K.
Department of Instructional Technology
Utah State University
224 Jones Education Building
Logan, UT 84322, USA

Erin Brewer is currently a doctoral student at Utah State University. Her dissertation is an exploration of how resource sharing supports learning in online self-organizing social systems. She is an academic great-great-grandchild of Dr. Merrill, and has had the privilege of being in the same department with him during her graduate studies.

Chen, Ashley H. I.
Department of Applied Science and Living
Shih-Chen University
70 Ta-Chih Street, Chung-Shan District
Taipei, Taiwan

Ashley H. I. Chen is an adjunct assistant professor in the Department of Applied Science and Living at Shih-Chien University, Taipei, Taiwan. *Dr. Chen received her BS in* Japanese literature and language at Soochow University, Taipei, Taiwan (1993). She obtained her MS (1997) and PhD (2002) in education, both from the University of Southern California. She was honored for the "Best Dissertation of the Year 2002" with the dissertation titled "Relationships of Teamwork Skills with Performance Appraisals and Salary Information in a Taiwanese Organization."

Dijkstra, Sanne
Faculty of Behavioural Science
Department of Instructional Technology (IST), University of Twente
PO Box 217
NL 7500 AE Enschede, The Netherlands

Sanne Dijkstra is professor emeritus of instructional technology in the Faculty of Behavioral Sciences at the University of Twente, the Netherlands. He was professor of education and instructional technology for many years at the University of Twente, where he also served as professor and chair of the Graduate School of Teacher Training. His areas of interest include industrial and educational psychology. Many of his research publications are on problem-based learning and instructional design. His research is both fundamental and applied, with emphasis on studying the effectiveness and efficiency of the instructional models used. He has a strong interest in the psychology of cognition and learning and in the acquisition of knowledge and skills by solving problems.

Foshay, Wellesley R.
Plato Learning
10801 Nesbitt Avenue South
Bloomington, MN 55437, USA

Rob Foshay is vice president for instructional design and quality assurance for PLATO Learning, Inc. Dr. Foshay is responsible for PLATO's instructional design, development methodology, and internal instructional design training, and he manages PLATO's summative evaluation research. His doctorate is in instructional design from Indiana University. He has contributed over 60 articles to research journals and book chapters on a wide variety of topics in instructional design, technology and education. He is coauthor of *Writing Training That Works: How to Teach Anyone to Do Anything*. He currently serves on the editorial boards of three research journals and has served on the board of directors of the International Society for Performance Improvement (ISPI) and the International Board of Standards for Training, Performance and Instruction (IBSTPI), as well as an ANSI/ASQ committee that developed standards for training and education under the ISO 9000 system.

Gibbons, Andrew S.
Department of Instructional Psychology and Technology
Brigham Young University
Provo, UT 84602, USA

Andy Gibbons is Chair of Instructional Psychology and Technology at Brigham Young University. Dr. Gibbons's work has included numerous large-scale training development projects, projects for the re-engineering of instructional design and development processes, computer-based instruction projects, military and commercial aviation training development, and research and development on instructional simulations. He has created innovative systems for low-cost development of simulations and has published on the use of simulation problems combined with modularized instructional techniques. Dr. Gibbons's current research focuses on the architecture of technology-based instructional products. He has published a design theory of model-centered instruction, proposed a general layering theory of instructional designs, and is currently studying the use of design languages in relation to design layers as a means of creating instructional systems that are adaptive, generative, and scaleable.

Hsieh, I-Lin
University of Southern California
3005A La Paz Lane
Diamond Bar, CA 91765, USA

Jonassen, David H.
School of Information Science and Learning Technologies
and Program in Educaional Psychology
University of Missouri
221C Townsend Hall
Columbia, MO 65211, USA

David Jonassen is Distinguished Professor of Education at the University of Missouri, where he teaches in the Learning Technologies and Educational Psychology programs. Since earning his doctorate in educational media and experimental educational psychology from Temple University, Dr. Jonassen has taught at Pennsylvania State University, University of Colorado, University of Twente in the Netherlands, University of North Carolina at Greensboro, and Syracuse University. He has published 23 books and numerous articles, papers, and reports on text design, task analysis, instructional design, computer-based learning, hypermedia, constructivist learning, cognitive tools, and technology in learning. He has consulted with businesses, universities, public schools, and other institutions around the world. His current research focuses on designing learning systems for problem solving.

de Jong, Ton
Faculty of Behavioral Sciences
Department of Instructional Science
University of Twente
PO Box 217
7500 AE Enschede, The Netherlands

Ton de Jong's PhD study at Eindhoven University of Technology was entitled "Problem Solving and Knowledge Representation in Physics for Novice Students." Currently he is Professor of Instructional Technology and Educational Psychology at the University of Twente. His main interests are in problem solving in science, discovery learning environments, learners' cognitive processes, instructional design, and human–machine interface. The simulation authoring tool called SimQuest that he helped create won the European Academic Software Award in 2000. Currently he is on the Executive Committee of the EC 6th Framework Network of Excellence "Kaleidoscope" and is scientific director of the Dutch National Interuniversity Center for Educational Research. Ton de Jong is author and coauthor of over 100 journal papers and book chapters and was the editor of three books. He is associate editor of *Instructional Science* and on the editorial boards of several other academic journals.

van Joolingen, Wouter R.
Instituut voor de Lerarenopleiding
Universiteit van Amsterdam
Wibautstraat 2-4
1091 GM Amsterdam, The Netherlands

Wouter van Joolingen is an associate professor for ICT and education at the Graduate School of Teaching and Learning, University of Amsterdam. He graduated in theoretical physics at Leiden University and earned a PhD in educational science from Eindhoven University of Technology in 1993. His work focuses on discovery learning with computer simulations, and cognitive tools for the support of learning processes. He was one of the main designers of the SimQuest authoring system for simulation-based learning environments that won the 2000 European Academic Software Award. Together with Ton de Jong, he was awarded the EARLI outstanding publication award for a review study on discovery learning with computer simulations in 1998. In 2003 he was a member of the OECD expert panel for the design of the PISA studies for ICT competency. He is member of the executive committee of the International Society for Artificial Intelligence and Education and a reviewer for several scientific journals.

Kinshuk
Advanced Learning Technology Research Centre
Massey University
Private Bag 11-222
Palmerston North, New Zealand

Kinshuk is an associate professor at the Massey University, New Zealand. He is also director of the Advanced Learning Technology Research Centre. He has been involved in large-scale research projects for exploration-based adaptive educational environments and has published over 100 research papers in international refereed journals, conference proceedings and books. He is an active researcher in learning technologies and human–computer interaction. He is currently chair of the IEEE Technical Committee on Learning Technology, New Zealand Chapter of ACM SIGCHI, and the International Forum of Educational Technology & Society. He is also editor of the SSCI journal of *Educational Technology & Society* and *Learning Technology Newsletter.* He is an editorial board member of more than a dozen journals and program committee member for several international conferences in the area of educational technology area every year.

Kuehl, Marcia
University of Southern California
PO Box 7326
Capistrano Beach, CA 92624-7326, USA

Lin, Taiyu
Advanced Learning Technology Research Centre
Massey University
Private Bag 11-222
Palmerston North, New Zealand

Taiyu Lin is a doctoral student at Massey University, New Zealand. He is engaged in research on cognitive profiling of learners in multidiscipline and multiplatform environments. He is also assistant editor of *Educational Technology & Society.*

L'Allier, James J.
NetG
1751 W. Diehl Road, 2nd Floor
Naperville, IL 60563-9099, USA

James J. L'Allier is Chief Learning Officer and Vice President, Research and Development, for Thomson NETg. Since joining NETg in 1993, he has developed an automated instructional design and product development system under the direction of M. David Merrill, John Keller, and Robert Mager. He was the executive sponsor for a Kirkpatrick Level 3 job impact study in which M. David Merrill served as principal external investigator. He was responsible for the development of the NETg Learning Object, NETg Precision Skilling, and NETg Skill Builder, and holds two patents for related learning technologies. He has published numerous articles on learning and technology. His research and development focus has been on the cost-effective application of instructional design theory and practice in a business production environment. He holds a BS (1969) and MA (1973) from the University of Wisconsin and a PhD (1980) in curriculum and instructional systems from the University of Minnesota.

Marshall, Lori C.
24566 Overlake Drive
Lake Forest, CA 92630, USA

Lori C. Marshall runs a consulting company—the HTQ Research Group—focused on training and development for health care, and, more recently, international research collaboration on teamwork. She is also Clinical Manager of Patient Care Services at Children's Hospital, Los Angeles. She obtained her BS in nursing at California State University, Fullerton in1983, her MSc in nursing in 1996 with an emphasis in education at California State University, Dominguez Hills, and she earned a PhD in educational psychology from the University of Southern California in 2003. Dr. Marshall has over twenty-five years of experience in the health care industry. Her recent work, presentations, and publications address health care teams from a model based on a sociocognitive perspective.

van der Meij, Jan
Faculty of Behavioral Sciences
Department of Instructional Science
University of Twente
PO Box 217
7500 AE Enschede, The Netherlands

Jan van der Meij is a PhD student in the Department of Instructional Technology at the University of Twente. Previously he worked at the National Centre for the Innovation of Education and Training in the Department of Educational Software Development, where he worked in the SERVIVE project, in which the simulation-based learning environment SimQuest was developed. He finished teacher training in electronics at Pedagogical Technical Higher Education (PTH), Zwolle, in 1994; he graduated with a master's degree in educational technology from the University of Twente in 1997. His PhD project concerns learning with multiple representations in simulation-based learning environments. He is especially interested in ways to support students' translation between representations.

van Merriënboer, Jeroen
Educational Technology Expertise Center
Open University of the Netherlands
PO Box 2960
6401 DL Heerlen, The Netherlands

Jeroen J. G. van Merriënboer is a professor of educational technology and is Research Program Director at the Educational Technology Expertise Center of the Open University of the Netherlands. He holds a master's degree in psychophysiology from the Free University of Amsterdam (1984) and a PhD in instructional technology from the University of Twente (1990). van Merriënboer specializes in cognitive architectures and instruction, instructional design for complex learning, holistic approaches to instructional design, and adaptive e-learning applications. He has published widely in the area of learning and instruction and serves on the board of several scientific journals. His prize-winning monograph *Training Complex Cognitive Skills* describes his four-component instructional design model for technical training and offers a systematic, research-based approach to designing environments for complex learning.

Ohrazda, Celestia
Instructional Design Development and Evaluation
Syracuse University School Of Education
330 Huntington Hall
Syracuse NY 13244-4100, USA

Celestia Ohrazda is currently pursuing her PhD in instructional design, development and evaluation at Syracuse University. Her research interests include the use of interactive technologies to promote complex problem solving skills. At present, she is working on a NASA grant through the Syracuse University Research Engineering and Technology Institute to develop a virtual learning environment that supports collaborative knowledge building in teaching and learning, and she teaches digital media production.

O'Neil, Harold, Jr.
Rossier School of Education
University of Southern California
600 Waite Phillips Hall, 600E
Los Angeles, CA 90089-0031, USA

Harry O'Neil is a professor of educational psychology and technology at the University of Southern California's Rossier School of Education and a project director at the UCLA National Center for Research on Evaluation, Standards, and Student Testing (CRESST). His research interests include the computer-based assessment of workforce readiness, particularly problem-solving and collaboration skills, the teaching and measurement of self-regulation skills, and the role of motivation in testing. Dr. O'Neil has also conducted cross-cultural research in Japan on the role of test anxiety and performance, and in Taiwan and Korea on the role of self-regulation and achievement. He has also conducted research on the role of financial incentives on low-stakes tests such as NAEP and TIMSS. He knew David Merrill at Courseware, WICAT, and was a colleague for many years with him at USC. In all of O'Neil's research environments, he has looked to David for interesting, creative ideas in instructional design.

Papaila, Dawn

Dawn Papaila is an instructional design consultant with Tata Interactive Systems. She received her MA in educational technology at San Diego State University. She designs performance support strategies including self-paced e-learning modules. Her clients include Fortune 500 companies, global distributors, nonprofit agencies, and the United States military. She is also president of San Diego's ISPI Chapter (2004). David Merrill has been a major influence in her approach to instructional design. Component display theory is a cornerstone of her content analysis and is often used to educate clients and colleagues unfamiliar with our craft. The first time Dawn Papaila met Dr. Merrill was at his presentation called "Pebble in the Pond" at San Diego State University in 2002. She left that session inspired to challenge and enrich her own approach to e-learning design.

Patel, Ashok
Advanced Learning Technology Research Centre
Massey University
Private Bag 11-222
Palmerston North, New Zealand

Ashok Patel is the Director of CAL Research, De Montfort University, Leicester, United Kingdom. He has been designing educational software for more than 10 years. By profession, he is an accountant and teaches management accounting and business systems. He is a coinitiator of the International Forum of Educational Technology & Society, and coeditor of *Educational Technology & Society*. He is also an executive committee member of IEEE Technical Committee on Learning Technology.

Quinn, D. William
Program Evaluation Coordinator, Office of Reading Chicago Public Schools
125 South Clark Street, 11th Floor
Chicago, IL 60603, USA

D. William Quinn is an evaluator in the Chicago Public Schools specializing in evaluating reading and literacy programs. Prior to joining CPS, Dr. Quinn worked for 3 years as an independent evaluator specializing in evaluating technology use for learning and teaching. He received a doctorate in educational evaluation from Western Michigan University in 1978. He recently completed 10 years at the North Central Regional Educational Laboratory as a senior program associate, where he managed the evaluation unit and evaluated technology use in many setting. He has evaluated technology use for the states of Indiana and Virginia, and for school districts in Chicago, Miami-Dade, and Los Angeles County. For 10 years he was on the faculty in the Department of Instructional Science, Brigham Young University, where he taught graduate research methods courses.

Reigeluth, Charles M.
Indiana University
Wright School of Education, Room 2236
201 North Rose Ave.
Bloomington, IN 47405-1006, USA

Charles M. Reigeluth has been a professor in the Instructional Systems Technology Department at Indiana University since 1988. He has a BA in Economics from Harvard University, and a PhD in instructional psychology from Brigham Young University, where Dave Merrill was his mentor. Before going to Indiana University, Dr. Reigeluth spent 10 years on the faculty of the instructional design program at Syracuse University. His primary area of expertise is instructional design and methods and theories of instruction. He is the major developer of several instructional design theories, including elaboration theory (codeveloped with Dave Merrill) and simulation theory. His recent area of research is learning organizations, systems thinking, and systemic change in organizations. He has published eight books and over 100 articles and chapters on these subjects. He has served as an organizational change consultant for state and local education agencies, and as an instructional design consultant in many different contexts.

Richey, Rita C.
Instructional Technology
Wayne State University
381 Education, Detroit, MI 48202, USA

Rita C. Richey is a professor and program coordinator of instructional technology in the College of Education at Wayne State University, where she has been for over 30 years. She is widely published in the area of instructional design and technology. She has written or edited 10 books, including *Instructional Technology: The Definition and Domains of the Field*, which received the 1995 Outstanding Book Award and the 1996 Brown Publication Award from the Association of Educational Communications and Technology. She has published over 30 articles and books chapters. She is a past *ibstpi* vice-president for research and development and past president of AERA's Instructional Technology SIG. She has received four awards from Wayne State University—the President's Award for Excellence in Teaching, a Distinguished Faculty Fellowship, the Outstanding Graduate Mentor Award, and the award for Outstanding Scholarly Achievement by Women Faculty—and AECT's Distinguished Service Award (2000).

Rossett, Allison
San Diego State University
North Education Room 283, Mail Code: 1182
5500 Campanile Drive
San Diego, CA 92182, USA

Allison Rossett, a professor of educational technology at San Diego State University, is the editor of *The ASTD E-Learning Handbook* (2002) and coauthor of *Beyond the Podium: Delivering Training and Performance to a Digital World* (2001). She has written award-winning books about needs assessment, learning technologies, and changing roles for learning professionals. Allison was the vice-president for research and development for the International Society for Performance Improvement and was honored by it as member-for-life. She commenced a 3-year term on ASTD's Board in 2004. Allison Rossett remembers the first time she met Dave Merrill, although he doesn't remember the first time he met her. She was in an audience at an AECT conference several decades ago. Dave was presenting his work. The main message Rossett took home was that she was not yet ready for prime time—not a bad outcome from a conference. She's eternally grateful, especially now, because she counts Dave as a friend.

Seel, Norbert M.
Albert-Ludwig-Universität Freiburg
Institut für Erziehungswissenschaft
Postfach 79085
Freiburg, Germany

Norbert M. Seel is Professor and Chair, Research on Learning and Instructional Design, and Chair, Department of Educational Science, at the Albert-Ludwigs-University of Freiburg. From 1993 through 1997 he was the dean of the Faculty of Educational Sciences at Dresden University of Technology. His research interests include model-based learning and thinking, inductive reasoning and complex problem solving, and the investigation of exploratory learning within technology-enhanced environments and of research-based principles of instructional design. He has met David Merrill at various international conferences and workshops. Much of Dr. Seel's work in the field of instructional design is strongly influenced by Merrill's expertise. Dr. Seel has published 14 books, including *Psychology of Learning*, and more than 100 journal articles and book chapters in the area of cognitive psychology, learning research, and instruction. He serves as editor of *Technology, Instruction, Cognition, and Learning*.

Spector, J. Michael
Learning Systems Institute, Florida State University
C4600 University Center
Tallahassee, FL 32306-2540, USA

J. Michael Spector is associate director of the Learning Systems Institute and a professor of instructional systems at Florida State University, Syracuse. Previously, he was a professor and chair of IDD&E at Syracuse University; professor of information science and director of educational information science and technology at the University of Bergen, Norway; and senior scientist for instructional systems research at the U.S. Air Force Armstrong Research Laboratory, where he worked with Robert M. Gagné, M. David Merrill, and others on tools to automate various aspects of instructional design. He has published many journal articles and book chapters in the area of instructional design research and has edited two volumes on concepts and issues involved in technology-enhanced learning and instruction. He is executive vice president for *ibstpi*, past president of the Design and Development Division of the Association for Educational and Communications Technology (AECT). He is also editor of *ETR&D-Development.*

Tennyson, Robert
Educational Psychology, University of Minnesota
Room 107 BuH 3171, 178 Pillsbury Dr SE
Minneapolis, MN 55455, USA

Robert Tennyson is a professor of educational psychology and technology in the Learning and Cognition Program at the University of Minnesota. Before joining the faculty at Minnesota, he was a professor of educational research and testing at Florida State University. His published works range from basic theoretical articles on human learning to applied books on instructional design and technology. Dr. Tennyson is editor of the scientific journal *Computers in Human Behavior* (published by Elsevier Science and now in its 20th year). His research and publications include topics on learning and complex cognitive processes, intelligent systems, simulations, testing and measurement, instructional design, and advanced learning technologies.

Van Schaack, Andrew
Instructional Technology, Utah State University
2830 Old Main Hill, Logan, UT 84322-2830, USA

Andrew Van Schaack is a doctoral student studying under Dr. David Merrill in the Department of Instructional Technology at Utah State University. His research focuses on the development of effective and efficient instructional technologies based on empirically validated scientific research. He is also interested in bridging the gap between academia and industry through technology transfer. Prior to entering graduate school, he worked for Apple Computer in California and Tokyo and most recently served as chief scientist for Cerego, Inc., a $30 million educational software company formed to commercialize his patented technologies. In 2002, he was named the USU Department of Instructional Technology's Instructor of the Year.

Veermans, Koen
Instructional Technology
University of Twente

Koen Veermans is a member of the Instructional Technology Unit at the University of Twente. He studied social science informatics at the University of Amsterdam, where he did a master's degree in the area of modeling human learning and problem solving. In 1996 he moved to the University of Twente to work on simulation-based discovery learning environments, with an emphasis on learner modeling and learner support, which resulted in a PhD in 2003. During this period he also participated in the research and design of SimQuest, and started teaching courses for the faculties of educational science and technology and psychology.

Wiley, David A.
Department of Instructional Technology
Utah State University
UMC 2830
Logan, UT 84322-2830, USA

David A. Wiley is executive director of the Open Sustainable Learning Opportunity Group at Utah State University and assistant professor of instructional technology. He has been a National Science Foundation CAREER award recipient, design scientist at the Edumetrics Institute, and continues as a consultant to the Institute for Defense Analyses. He has published numerous articles and book chapters in print and online in the areas of learning objects, informal learning communities, and open access. David traces his academic lineage three generations back to Dave Merrill.

Wilson, Brent G.
Information and Learning Technologies
University of Colorado at Denver
UCD Campus Box 106, PO Box 173364
Denver, CO 80217-3364, USA

Brent G. Wilson is professor and coordinator of the information and learning technologies program at the University of Colorado at Denver. He has published four books and more than 100 papers relating to instructional design and learning technologies. His current research relates to how to help instructional designers create good instruction, how to help students, teachers, and workers make good use of learning resources, how to encourage best practices relating to educational technology within organizations, and how to strengthen the instructional-design profession by improved sharing among practitioners and by grounding practice in a broader theory base. As a doctoral student at Brigham Young University, Brent Wilson worked with David Merrill and Charles Reigeluth in the development of elaboration theory and conducted studies in learner control, component display theory, and elaboration theory. He is active in AECT and AERA and serves on editorial and advisory boards for a number of journals.

Innovations in Instructional Technology: An Introduction to This Volume

J. Michael Spector

Florida State University

INNOVATION

The title of this volume suggests that it is a book about innovations in instructional technology. Indeed, the reader will encounter many innovations in instructional technology, including developments in the area of learning objects, new instructional design models, an instructional design language, new approaches to assessment and evaluation, and much more. What counts as an innovation? Why these innovations and not others? Before providing an overview of the various chapters, I attempt brief answers to these questions.

Calling something an innovation implies that it involves something novel or new, but often much more is implied. Most often, three additional aspects of innovation are implied. First, the existence of a prior state of affairs or a predecessor object is implied. Instructional technologies existed prior to any of the contributors of this volume, including the person whom we are honoring, M. David Merrill.

Second, a process of change to previous states or objects or situations is implied. Innovation typically involves much more than simply replacing something old and obsolete with something new. In the area of instructional technology, it is tempting to think of such simple replacements. A narrow conception of technology might incline one to focus on tangible objects such as chalkboards, mainframe terminals, and overhead projectors. One might go on to say that whiteboards replaced chalkboards, personal computers replaced mainframe terminals, and digital projectors replaced overhead projectors. In some settings this may even be true and may only have involved throwing out the old technology and setting up the new technology.

This is not how the contributors to this volume think about instructional technology, however. The process of making changes is emphasized throughout these chapters, not with regard to pieces of equipment but with regard to how designers, developers, teachers, trainers, and evaluators go about the enterprise of improving learning and instruction.

This in fact is the third aspect of innovation—people. Saying that an innovation has occurred implies that there are people involved. Someone, or a team of people, decided that a state of affairs or a particular approach or a product was inadequate and then set out to make things better. All of the contributors to this volume have been involved throughout their careers in efforts to improve instruction. Merrill has devoted more than 40 years to this enterprise of making instruction better, and he has inspired many others to join the campaign to improve learning and instruction.

Collectively, these essays represent what one distinguished innovator in the field of instructional technology—Dave Merrill—has inspired others to do. Summarizing the small sampling of instructional technology innovations represented in this volume, one is inclined to say that those who have been engaged in processes of change based on Merrill's work in the area of instructional technology have made many contributions. These contributions include knowledge about how people learn, how people solve problems, how designers conceptualize learning spaces, how teachers implement learning activities, and how evaluators assess outcomes.

INSTRUCTIONAL TECHNOLOGY

A question of conscience lies behind what each person does. That question, stated simply, is this: "What will come from what I am now doing and choose to do in the future?" This question can be asked about personal matters as well as about professional decisions and activities. In this context, the question arises in the context of the instructional technology professional practitioner—a researcher, a designer, a developer, a teacher, a trainer, a policymaker, an evaluator, or someone else involved in systematic efforts to improve learning and instruction.

Although the question appears to be simple—what will come from what I am doing—the answer for instructional technologists has proven elusive. In one sense, such simple questions of conscience are difficult to answer in any context. The future is somewhat uncertain. There is a complex interconnectedness among things that makes it difficult to predict the effects of making one change as opposed to another. This is especially true in education. Learners have different backgrounds, experiences, and individual situations. Learning spaces vary significantly. Learning cultures vary significantly. Teachers and trainers have different skills and strengths and weaknesses. Some instructors are rich in terms of available resources and others are not. Resources available to students and teachers change.

Nevertheless, there is general agreement with regard to what counts as learning—relatively stable and persisting changes in attitudes, beliefs, mental models, knowledge, and/or skills. There is general agreement that the processes that support intended changes are vital to learning and instruction. There are some relatively well-established principles of instructions, as many of the contributors to this volume note (Dijkstra, 2004; Spector, 2001).

A hallmark of Merrill's contributions is the notion that the enterprise of improving learning and instruction is a principled although complex activity (Merrill, 2002). As such, instructional design ought to proceed on the foundation of principles that can be tested empirically. Without such principles to guide the planning and implementing of support for learning, instructional design becomes a craft with a few notable artisans receiving accolades for their good deeds. The problems and challenges that exist at the many different levels of learning and instruction in all walks of life are far too pervasive and serious to be resolved by a small band of skilled artisans. The need to improve instructional design theories, models, and methods should become evident when one reads the subsequent chapters of this volume.

OVERVIEW OF CHAPTERS

Learning Objects

The first four chapters involve learning objects and the notion of reusable components. David Wiley argues that it is time for instructional technology to move beyond the conventional knowledge of learning objects because they are not very useful to teachers in their current form. Reuse by teachers for learning should be the guiding focus for the future of learning objects. Ton de Jong and his colleagues in The Netherlands describe a simulation authoring system called SimQuest that involves reuse of learning objects; this system is proving usable by and useful to teachers in science and mathematics classrooms. Kinshuk and colleagues contribute what they call the Cognitive Trait Model to support the dynamic construction of learning objects that are customized for individual learning needs. Jeroen van Merriënboer and his colleagues in The Netherlands argue, as did Wiley, that the traditional approach to learning objects has been based on an analytical approach that encounters problems with metadata, combining and sequencing objects, and sharing objects among developers. Van Merriënboer and colleagues explore an alternative holistic approach, and they conclude with an integrative approach that stresses support for things that teachers and designers typically do, such as edit and modify intermediate or partially complete objects and customize them for local situations.

Learning and Instructional Design

These chapters about knowledge and learning objects are followed by three chapters that involve fundamental aspects of learning and the design of instruction. Norbert Seel presents a model-centered approach for the design of learning environments. This approach involves representing things to be learned as models of reality and then constructing additional representations that will facilitate a learner in coming to understand the targeted model of reality. Seel also presents evidence of this model in keeping with Merrill's insistence that instructional design should be an evidence-based enterprise. David Jonassen argues that the focus of much learning is a problem, in line with Merrill's (2002) first principles of instruction. Jonassen goes on to argue that there are different kinds of problem solving that require different kinds of instructional support. He illustrates this problem-oriented approach with troubleshooting problems. Andrew Gibbons extends the discussion of model-centered and problem-centered instruction to the notion of a principled design language for instructional design. Such a design language would be capable of generating the principles used by Seel and Jonassen to design the types of learning environments they describe.

Assessment, Evaluation, and Validation

There are three chapters in this collection that address innovations in the area of assessment, evaluation, and model validation, all of which are explicitly evidence-based enterprises. Lori Marshall, Harold O'Neil, and colleagues in California describe a specific method to assess the acquisition of teamwork skills that is derived from Merrill's first principles (2002). Their process of collecting and analyzing data to determine the outcomes of using a particular instructional environment serves as one model for evidence-based instructional design practice. Another model of evidence-based practice is provided by Rob Foshay and William Quinn, who discuss design science as an enterprise involving different kinds of evaluations. These include the evaluation of a particular instructional technology in the context for which it was designed. They distinguish learning science from design science from the products of technology, and they argue that policymakers should be careful not to rush to the judgment that observed effects are simply due to changes in technology products. Rita Richey provides a discussion of the processes involved in validating instructional design and development models. She distinguishes internal from external validation and identifies five different validation processes: expert reviews, usability analyzes, component investigations, field evaluations, and controlled testing. She argues that a comprehensive model validation process involves all five of these and that the field should be more engaged in validating existing models.

Learning and Instructional Theory

The next three chapters concern theories of learning and instruction. Sanne Dijkstra discusses the connection between a theory of cognition and a theory of instructional design. Once the linkage between cognition and design is established, Dijkstra shows how this leads to the conception of various objects and how these might be integrated into a problem-based instructional design model. Charles Reigeluth argues that there have been massive changes in society that require entirely new instructional theories and strategies. The evolution from an industrial society to a knowledge-based society demands that people acquire new knowledge and skills and, furthermore, that these be acquired in entirely different ways, such as through performance support systems and personal tutor systems that can be seamlessly integrated into a work environment. Robert Tennyson provides a historical discussion for the linking model used by Dijkstra to derive his problem-based instructional design model. Tennyson identifies six components that the linking model provides: a cognitive subsystem, learning goals and objectives, relative learning time, instructional prescriptions, modes of instruction, and assessments. The value of Tennyson's discussion is that it shows that various approaches to instruction can be derived from this underlying model and that one need not abandon the underlying linking model because a particular approach to instruction proves inadequate. Tennyson argues that modern learner-centered approaches are just as compatible with the underlying linking model as were earlier behaviorist approaches.

Instructional Design Practice

There are then four chapters that involve different kinds of conversations about the nature of instructional design. Brent Wilson takes up a discussion about the practice of instructional design that began in the mid 1990s. Wilson argues in favor of an inclusive approach to instructional design—there is rich variety in instructional design practice. Two ideas help ground the community according to Wilson: (a) conditions of learning and associated outcomes, and (b) a systems view of instruction and instructional development. Broadening the conditions and outcomes and really adopting a systemic view of instruction allows the field to grow without losing its history and the contributions of so many. James L'Allier makes this discussion concrete in terms of his own development and the rational eclecticism that he finds commonly practiced in business and corporate settings. L'Allier agrees with Wilson that adherence to an instructional orthodoxy is not healthy for the growth of the field. Allison Rossett and Dawn Papaila discuss why instructional design practitioners receive less than adequate recognition and suggest what might be done to address this anomaly. The chapter by Andrew Van Schaack and Celestia Ohrazda involves an interview with Dave Merrill on the topic of mentoring instructional designers, primarily those who are in academic settings and will go on to academic and professional careers. Van Schaack and Ohrazda probed Merrill about mentoring and elicited a number of gems, including Merrill's remark that "no is not the right answer." This of course does not mean that "yes" is the right answer. It means that if one wishes to contribute and make progress, one must be persistent, especially in the face of adversity.

Epilogue

The final chapter to this volume is perhaps Merrill at his best. A panel of 11 people presented challenges, comments, and questions at an AECT presidential panel session in October 2003. The questions ranged from the notion of initial passions with regard to instructional technology to connections between theory and practice to questions of conscience. It will be obvious to the reader that Merrill does not need someone else to speak for him.

CONCLUSION

What else can be said about this volume and the enterprise of instructional technology? We can do more, we should do more, and Merrill has inspired us to do more, as demonstrated in the following chapters. In a sense, Merrill has helped define the identity of an instructional technologist. Part of that identity is adherence to evidence-based processes that support principled development and lead toward a theory of instructional design and technology (Reigeluth, 1983).

Although there is a rich variety of work to be done by instructional technologists and many different kinds of instructional technologists, the creed of instructional technology might well be a variation of the physician's Hippocratic oath: (a) do nothing to impair learning and instruction; (b) do what you can to improve learning and instruction; (c) base your actions on evidence that you and others have gathered and analyzed; (d) share the principles of instruction that you have learned with others; and (e) respect the individual rights of all those with whom you interact. We can all thank M. David Merrill for having done so much to define the principles of our discipline.

REFERENCES

Dijkstra, S. (2004). Theoretical foundations of learning and instruction and innovations of instructional design and technology. In N. M. Seel & S. Dijkstra (Eds.), *Curriculum, plans and processes of instructional design: International perspectives* (pp. 17–24). Mahwah, NJ: Lawrence Erlbaum Associates.

Merrill, M. D. (2002). First principles of instruction. *Educational Technology, Research and Development, 50*(3), 43–59.

Reigeluth, C. M. (1983). *Instructional-design theories and models: An overview of their current status*. Hillsdale, NJ: Lawrence Erlbaum Associates.

Spector, J. M. (2001). Philosophical implications for the design of instruction. *Instructional Science, 29*, 381–402.

Chapter 1

Learning Objects in Public and Higher Education

David A. Wiley
Utah State University

REUSE IS NOTHING NEW

Reuse of educational materials is not a new idea in education; all teachers are familiar with resource reuse. To varying degrees we reuse journal articles, lecture notes, slides, textbooks, overheads, lesson plans, stories, visual aids, and construction-paper bulletin-board letters in our teaching. Students are more familiar than we might expect with the notion of reuse of educational materials. Occasionally one can be heard to complain that reuse is occurring on too grand a scale ("he's been using the same lecture notes for ten years?!?").

The reason most teachers would prefer to teach a class they've taught several times rather than a class they have never taught before stems solely from the virtues of reuse. If materials exist from a previous version of the course, preparation of the new course can be faster (i.e., development efficiency can increase). Course materials can be better, as existing materials are improved based on experience with their prior use (i.e., development effectiveness can be increased). Additionally, because there are fewer new materials to be developed, more attention can be paid to these new materials (i.e., development effectiveness can be increased further). In short, teachers do not want an entirely new preparation because they have nothing to reuse. Every teacher knows and appreciates the benefits of reuse, so why are teachers excited by the idea of knowledge objects or learning objects?

THE CONVENTIONAL VIEW OF LEARNING OBJECTS

There is a saying in commercial instructional development that those who would contract for the design and creation of educational materials must pick two of the following three contract criteria: cheap, fast, and good. Materials can be developed quickly and with high quality, but only at high cost; materials can also be developed quickly and inexpensively, but only at low quality, and so on.

Learning objects promise to enable the fulfillment of all three criteria simultaneously by making educational resources more reusable. Learning objects are generally defined as educationally useful, completely self-contained chunks of content. The most popular operationalization of this definition is a three-part structure comprised of an educational objective, instructional materials that teach the objective, and an assessment of student mastery of the objective.

Once a collection of such learning objects exists, and has been stored and cataloged in a digital library or other storage and indexing facility, instructional designers may select and aggregate learning objects from within the collection. Intelligent or automated systems may also be designed that select and aggregate learning objects according to given criteria for individual use.

The threefold structure enables a number of innovative uses of learning objects. For example, designers or systems may utilize assessments from the learning object structure to create pretests. For all individual assessments that learners pass, designers or systems may then remove associated instructional materials, lengthening the time and cost of an individual's instructional program. As another example, designers may develop several learning objects that teach to the same educational objective, varying only aesthetic aspects of the objects. Designers, systems, or learners themselves may then choose one of several *instruction-function-equivalent* objects based on preference. This strategy can enable basic learner choice without jeopardizing instructional designers' intents.

There has been significant interest in using intelligent systems together with learning objects in order to address scalability issues relating to instruction. When intelligent systems are used to select and organize media, as well as provide feedback and grading, enrollment bottlenecks due to the perpetuation of conventional teacher-to-student ratios into online environments may be overcome. In previous writing I have called this bottleneck the teacher bandwidth problem (Wiley, 2002). The largest problem with scaling distance education up to thousands or more students is not a bandwidth problem of how much data may be served through scarce Internet connection resources, but rather a bandwidth problem of how many students may be served through scarce teacher resources. Intelligent systems attempt to alleviate this bandwidth problem by replicating teacher functionality in software—for example, automating the grading of student work or the process of assembling educational resources for student use.

Merrill's instructional transaction theory (ITT) and knowledge objects exemplify this idea of intelligent, automated instruction (Merrill, Li, & Jones, 1991). ITT simulations both can be built from reusable components and can automatically teach, coach, and assess learners. The future described in Merrill's (and others') vision is an educational technology "wonderland." It may even be achievable. However, wonderland is quite a conceptual distance from where mainstream educators are right now, and very few have proven willing to jump down the rabbit hole. The next section describes some reasons why.

PROBLEMS WITH THE CONVENTIONAL VIEW

The popular definition of learning objects as educationally useful, completely self-contained chunks of content, together with the three-fold operationalization already described, is problematic in each of its three components.

Educational Usefulness

The educational usefulness of a learning object is not guaranteed by its strictly following a design template (e.g., having an objective linked to instruction and an assessment). Conforming to an architectural standard does not guarantee that an artifact like a learning object will be educationally useful. This would be like implying that a piece of music that conforms to the sonata structure will be good art, and is simply not the case. There are many compositions that conform to the sonata structure which are not particularly artful at all. On the other hand, there are many artful compositions that do not follow the sonata structure at all.

The reader may quickly desire to point out that art is to some extent in the eye of the beholder, and indeed it is so. Likewise, educationally useful "is in the eye of the learner." If a learning object teaches something a learner has already learned, or something a learner has no immediate desire to learn, then the resource will not be educationally useful to the learner despite its structure and organization. However, if a resource relates directly to a topic a learner has an immediate desire to learn, then the resource will likely be educationally useful to the learner, despite its architecture.

Of course, educational usefulness is also "in the eye of the teacher." A digital library full of downloadable sets of weather and geographical information system data will be of little interest to the middle school music teacher. Likewise, an online catalog of song lyrics and guitar accompaniments will not likely satisfy the needs of the graduate chemistry professor.

Complete Self-Containment

Assuming that learning objects are completely self-contained educational resources implies that, aside from their use, nothing else is necessary for student learning—including social interaction. This rejection of the importance of human interaction is extremely problematic for teaching and learning. Collaboration (Nelson, 1999), cooperation (Johnson & Johnson, 1997; Slavin, 1990), communities (Brown, 1994), social negotiation (Driscoll, 1994), and apprenticeship (Rogoff, 1990) are core instructional strategies for achieving a variety of learning outcomes.

If we believe Gagné's (1985) position that different learning outcomes require different instructional conditions, and we believe that Bloom and Krathwohl (1956) identified a useful hierarchy of learning outcomes, then we may combine these two insights in the following way: The family of instructional strategies that will most likely facilitate learning is different for each family of learning outcomes in Bloom's taxonomy.

It seems to me that one of the ways in which the conditions change as one "climbs" Bloom's "ladder" of learning outcomes is that social interaction becomes increasingly important. For example, a learner does not need to engage in small-group negotiation activities to learn (memorize) the capitals of the 50 states. Individual drill and practice exercises will provide effective, efficient mastery. However, we would not expect students to learn to make complex ethical decisions (evaluations) through isolated drilling with flashcards. We would generally imagine this type of outcome being learned in a small-group setting where discussion, argument, and debate played key instructional roles.

It therefore makes sense to believe that learning objects as conventionally understood—completely self-contained educational experiences—will perform well for outcomes at the bottom of Bloom's taxonomy and decrease in efficacy as higher order outcomes are taught. This may be one reason why learning objects have not been used widely in higher education. Higher educators like to believe that their role is to teach problem solving, critical thinking, and complex reasoning skills. Whether or not this occurs in classroom practice is a separate issue. In the many talks and workshops I have given on learning objects, my experience has been that when faculty members first encounter the idea, many intuitively grasp this weakness of the conventional learning objects approach to reuse and balk on grounds that the paradigm does not provide sufficient pedagogical flexibility.

Chunks of Content

The term *learning object* is synonymous with content. However, Merrill's component display theory attempted to steer the field in another direction—toward reusable strategy objects. His analogy went like this: "Think of the to-be-taught content as data for a computer program to operate on, and think of instructional strategies as the algorithms that manipulate data in the computer program." It is an insightful critique of instructional design and technology curricula that while computer science programs always teach data structures and algorithms together, our programs largely exclude detailed instruction in content-specific or domain-specific areas.

Roschelle and colleagues (2000) pointed out that we should not expect to find that learning objects are highly reused, because research has shown that the struc-

tures on which they are modeled—the software objects of object-oriented programming (OOP)—have failed to be significantly reused for decades now.
Although Roschelle accurately called to our attention that significant reuse of educational components is not occurring, this need only be a problem for instructional
technologists if we confine our conception of learning objects to content.

The issues that public school and university educators have with learning objects, like those just described, are in some ways unsurprising. The majority of
work done on learning objects has happened in military and corporate settings, and
the conventions of corporations and the military are not the same as higher and
public education's conventions, although I believe these educational groups have
much more in common than they have that divides them. A great need exists for individuals to step forward and rethink learning objects in terms of the conventions
of public and higher education.

LEARNING OBJECTS IN PUBLIC
AND HIGHER EDUCATION

This section explores potential resolutions to the problems already raised.

Changing the Conventional View of Learning Objects

For public and higher education audiences, we need to at least enable the kind of
reuse that is already occurring in offices around the world. Who would adopt an innovation whose proponents proclaimed, "It doesn't do much yet, but one day soon
this technology will really enable a lot of things you want! I should warn you,
though, that once you adopt it you won't be able to do any of the things you currently do." Until the learning objects paradigm at least speeds up preparing a
course, as described in the introduction to this chapter, no teacher or professor will
want to use it.

Going back to the list from the beginning of the chapter, none of the journal articles, lecture notes, slides, textbooks, overheads, lesson plans, stories, visual aids,
or construction-paper bulletin-board letters are made up of an objective coupled
with instruction coupled with an assessment. Public and higher education need a
definition of learning object that encompasses the types of resources they already
use—not one that excludes them as the conventional definition does. Wiley and
Edwards (2002) suggested another definition for learning object: Any digital resource that can be reused to mediate learning is a learning object. Although teachers may not be currently using digital versions of the resources in the list given
earlier, they could be. There are compelling reasons to encourage them to make
this one change to their practice.

South and Monson (2000) explained why it is important to encourage faculty to get their materials out of their filing cabinets and onto servers—if an individual faculty member gets such great benefit from reusing their materials,
could not another faculty member get similar benefits from those materials?

South and Monson described a nightmare of instructional media stored in a central location on campus that had to be somehow located by the professor, scheduled for use, wheeled across campus on a cart, set up in the classroom, and finally used, only to have the entire process reversed at the end of class. When these resources were digitized and placed on a central university server, location became a matter of Web searching, scheduling, and the cart simply disappeared, and setup became a matter of "bookmarking." Now 15 professors could use the resource at the same time from classrooms where computers and projectors were already installed and configured.

As Wiley and Edwards (2002) suggested, and as Downes (2004) and others have echoed, public and higher education need to move away from the highly foreign notion of learning objects specifically structured per the conventional view of international standards bodies and arrive at something more familiar—a notion of reusable resources, which happen to be digital.

Educational Usefulness

Teachers are not so naive as to assume that because a textbook or journal article has been published and appears in print, it will meet their students' learning needs. We need to help teachers understand that there will be quality learning objects and poor learning objects, just as there are quality books and articles and poor books and articles. The existence of poor-quality learning objects is not a problem with reusable digital resources; it is a problem common to all educational resources. Teachers will need to vigilantly study learning objects to determine their appropriateness for their learners. No group of all-knowing learning-objects reviewers will be able to tell teachers which resources they should use in their courses any more than all-knowing book or article reviewers can tell teachers which books or articles they should use in their courses.

Complete Self-containment

Merrill repeatedly said that "information is not instruction" (see the epilogue to this volume, for example). More recently, his work on the first principles of instructional design elaborated what he believes *is* instruction—activation of prior knowledge, demonstration of information, opportunities for application and practice with feedback, and purposive scaffolding of integration of new knowledge to promote transfer, all of which are wrapped around a real-world problem (Merrill, 2002).

Although these five principles together are significantly better than information dumps, I must argue that there is more to facilitating learning. I have recently been saying that there is a reason why libraries evolved into universities. This evolution did not occur because one day it was discovered that resources, materials, and content became unimportant; indeed, a quality library is a necessary condition for having a quality university—necessary, but not sufficient. There comes a time when, regardless of how much work the designer of the textbook, journal article, overheads, or intelligent system put into anticipating learners' questions, the learner has a learning need which is not met by a particular resource. Take MIT's amazing OpenCourseWare project as an example (see http://ocw.mit.edu/index.html). Even though one has access to the syllabus, schedule of assignments, problem sets, and video of every lecture for an MIT course on linear algebra, there will come a time for serious students of these materials when they will have a question. To whom do users of a library, be it digital or otherwise, turn? Of whom may they ask their question? This need to ask and to be answered—this need to interact—is at the core of why libraries grew into universities.

A view of learning objects more appropriate for public and higher education will retain this value. Learners need to interact to discuss, interpret, and argue over learning objects just as they do journal articles, textbooks, and the other resources teachers traditionally use in the classroom.

Chunks of Content

Merrill's analogy to data and algorithms provides another perspective on why we may not expect to find significant reuse of conventional learning objects occurring. If content is analogous to data, then we should ask ourselves, "Do computer programmers frequently reuse existing data?" My experience in programming (which I believe in this respect is typical) is that I reuse data only infrequently. However, it has also been my experience as a programmer (and I believe this to be typical as well) that I reuse algorithms regularly.

If you were to examine the source code of any but the most trivial programs, you would see the source code begins by making reference to a variety of libraries of programming algorithms—routines for calculating basic math operations, functions for printing to the screen or accepting input from the keyboard, and so on. Almost every programming language has a collection of libraries or modules of reusable functions, which programmers constantly use to speed up and improve the quality of their development. Books with titles like *Numerical Recipes in C* (Press, Flannery, Teukolsky, & Vetterling, 1992) are extremely popular as they show programmers exactly how to implement features that are common across programming projects.

Although a book entitled *Instructional Design Recipes in SCORM Simple Sequencing* (an analogous book for programmers can be found online at http://www.lsal.cmu.edu/lsal/expertise/projects/developersguide/sstemplates/templates-v1p0-20030228.pdf) would be great for hard-core instructional designers, teachers with no instructional design training are frequently incapable of seeing different layers of instructional design (Gibbons, Nelson, & Richards, 2000). For example, some teachers may have trouble seeing where the content of such a book ends and its instructional strategy starts, or what the difference is between the book's layout and its instructional strategy. For the time being, we need a definition and practice of learning objects that realizes that most teachers combine content and strategy (and sometimes even presentations) in one tangled pile, just like the other resources currently used in the classroom.

CONCLUSION

It may be that ideally the field of instructional design and technology would move toward something like the conventional view of learning objects use, in line with Merrill's view of knowledge objects and instructional transactions. However, we cannot get there all at once. A logical next step toward the promised future world of learning objects is not to ask educators to leap from current practice to fully automated instruction built from reusable parts by intelligent systems. The logical next step is to enable and support all of the things teachers already do in a digital form. I can almost hear you ask, "But why go to all the trouble of re-enabling what people already do? Because doing it online is so much cooler?" Of course not. We should enable these things online because changing the size of the pool of resources available for a teacher's reuse from the resources in their own drawer to those in the digital drawers of 10,000 other teachers around the world will help the teacher begin to see what learning objects might eventually be about. If we can create that curiosity in normal public and higher educators, then we have made another simultaneously small step and giant leap toward realizing the potential of instructional technology that Merrill and others have pioneered.

REFERENCES

Bloom B. S., & Krathwohl, D. R. (1956). *Taxonomy of educational objectives: The classification of educational goals. Handbook I: Cognitive domain.* New York: Longmans, Green.

Brown, A. L. (1994). The advancement of learning. *Educational Researcher, 23*(3), 4–12.

Downes, S. (2004). Resource profiles. *Journal of Interactive Multimedia and Education,* 2004(5). Special Issue on the Educational Semantic Web. Available: http://www-jime.open.ac.uk/2004/5

Driscoll, M. P. (1994). *Psychology of learning for instruction.* Boston: Allyn and Bacon.

Gagné, R. M. (1985). *The conditions of learning* (4th ed.). New York: Holt, Rinehart & Winston.

Gibbons, A. S., Nelson, J., & Richards, R. (2000). The nature and origin of instructional objects. In D. A. Wiley (Ed.), *The instructional use of learning objects.* Bloomington, IN: Association for Educational Communications and Technology. Retrieved April 2, 2004, from http://www.reusability.org/read/chapters/gibbons.doc

Johnson, D. W., & Johnson, R. T. (1997). *Joining together: Group theory and group skills* (6th ed.). Boston: Allyn & Bacon.

Merrill, M. D. (2002). First principles of instruction. *Educational Technology Research and Development, 50*(3), 43–59.

Merrill, M.D., Li, Z., & Jones, M. K. (1991). Instructional transaction theory: An introduction. *Educational Technology, 31*(6), 7–12.

Nelson, L. M. (1999). Collaborative problem solving. In C. M. Reigeluth (Ed.), *Instructional-design theories and models: A new paradigm of instructional theory.* (pp. 241–267). Mahwah, NJ: Lawrence Erlbaum Associates.

Press, W. H., Flannery, B. P., Teukolsky, S. A., & Vetterling, W. T. (1992). *Numerical recipes in C: The art of scientific computing* (2nd ed.). Cambridge, MA: Cambridge University Press.

Rogoff, B. (1990). *Apprenticeship in thinking: Cognitive development in social context.* New York: Oxford University Press.

Roschelle, J., DiGiano, C., Chung, M., Repenning, A., Tager, S., & Treinen, M. (2000). *Reusability and interoperability of tools for mathematics learning: Lessons from the ESCOT project.* Retrieved April 2, 2004, from http://www.escot.org/escot/docs/ISA2000-Reusability%20Reprint.pdf

Slavin, R. E. (1990). *Cooperative Learning: Theory, research, and Practice.* Englewood Cliffs, NJ: Prentice-Hall.

South, J., & Monson, D. (2000). A university-wide system for creating, capturing, and delivering learning objects. In D. A. Wiley (Ed.), *The instructional use of learning objects.* Bloomington, IN: Association for Educational Communications and Technology. Retrieved April 2, 2004 from http://reusability.org/read/chapters/south.doc

Wiley, D. A. (2002). *The coming collision between automated instruction and social constructivism.* Retrieved April 2, 2004 from http://wiley.ed.usu.edu/docs/collision_09.doc

Wiley, D. A., & Edwards, E. K. (2002). Online self-organizing social systems: The decentralized future of online learning. *Quarterly Review of Distance Education, 3*(1), 33–46.

Chapter
2

Authoring Discovery Learning Environments: In Search of Reusable Components

Ton de Jong
University of Twente

W. R. van Joolingen
University of Amsterdam

K. Veermans
University of Twente

J. van der Meij
University of Twente

AUTHORING INSTRUCTIONAL SYSTEMS

Authoring (including design and delivery) of information and communication technology (ICT)-based learning environments is difficult and time-consuming. It is difficult because authoring of such learning environments requires a combination of domain expertise, instructional design skills, and technical skills. It is time-consuming because each and every aspect of a learning environment needs to be designed from both a content and an instructional perspective and needs to be implemented in software. Often, estimates of hours devoted to production time in

11

relation to typical learning time are presented. Tannenbaum (2001), for example, asserted that in the early days of computer-based instruction, 100 to 200 of hours of authoring time were required to create 1 hour of instructional time. Merrill and the ID_2 Research Group (1998) mentioned 300 hours of authoring time for 1 hour of instruction. Nowadays, according to Tannenbaum (2001), the costs are as high or even higher due to the more advanced interfaces and multimedia that are available. Although these estimates cannot be regarded as very reliable (they are too dependent on unknown factors such as expertise of the designer, available tools, type of learning environment involved, etc., and for modern learning environments it is hard to speak of hours of instruction time), the estimated production time figures make clear that the design of ICT-based learning environments is very costly. Therefore, it is not surprising to see that there has been a search for tools that help to reduce production time and at the same time maintain or improve the instructional design quality (Merrill, 2002b).

Reuse of existing learning environments is one of the mechanisms to support time efficiency and quality assurance (Murray, 1999). Reuse basically means that existing components are used again in some form in a newly authored learning environment. Reuse may refer to the *content* of a learning environment or to the *instructional design* or to both. When the content and instructional design have been taken into account adequately, reuse may also refer to the *technical realization* of a learning environment. This means that components can be reused more or less directly in an ICT-based learning environment without additional programming.

THE PROCESS OF REUSE

When authors start creating learning environments and want to reuse existing components, they need to be able to *find* the right components. Duncan (2003), for example, described the idea that components can be shared (or traded) so that an author has access to a large set of resources for reuse. Standardization plays an important role to facilitate the search process for appropriate reusable components. There are many different standardization bodies (see http://www.cetis.ac.uk), but they all share the objective of making components accessible. Reuse also implies that a component was *designed for reuse*, meaning that both at technical (implementation and system) and conceptual (pedagogical and content) levels reuse is possible. At a technical level it must be possible to isolate the component from the learning environment for which it was originally designed. At the conceptual level, a component must have some kind of closure, meaning that it can be viewed relatively independent of the context in which it is actually used.

Often, authors have a need to *adapt* the selected components to their own wishes. Reusability and adaptability go hand in hand. Murray (1999) explicitly mentioned customization, extensibility, and scriptability as key characteristics of proficient authoring systems. With respect to *content,* authors and teachers quite often have specific ideas about what should be included in a course or lesson, which creates a demand for adaptability. This adaptability may range from almost complete replacement of the content to the change of specific symbols or other items. Adaptation of instructional design components will, for example, be possible by setting parameters in the component (e.g., for a multiple-choice question the number of alternatives can be set).

Components that are reused may differ in size or granularity, as it is sometimes called. Reused material may be quite global (e.g., overall instructional goals and general domain structures) or fine grained (e.g., specific instructional actions and domain structures).

Finally, the reusable components should be designed in such a way that they can be *combined* in the new learning environment. This means that content needs to be consistent and coherent over the different components, that there should be an overall instructional strategy over the different components, and that the components need to interact smoothly at a technical level.

Until now we have been using the general term *component* to indicate something that can be reused. The more widely used term is *learning object*. One of the earlier definitions of a learning object was given by the IEEE: "Any entity, digital or non-digital, which can be used, reused and referenced during technology-supported learning" (IEEE, 2002). This definition is such a broad one that it is hard to exclude anything from being a learning object (Friesen, 2004). Wiley (2000) also recognized this problem and discussed the different usages of the term *learning object,* and concluded that there is a proliferation of definitions, each taking a different route in making the term more specific. Wiley (2000) came to define a learning object as "any digital resource that can be reused to support learning" (p. 7). He continued by saying:

> This definition includes anything that can be delivered across the network on demand, be it large or small. Examples of smaller reusable digital resources include digital images or photos, live data feeds (like stock tickers), live or prerecorded video or audio snippets, small bits of text, animations, and smaller web-delivered applications, like a Java calculator. Examples of larger reusable digital resources include entire web pages that combine text, images and other media or applications to deliver complete experiences, such as a complete instructional event. (Wiley 2000, p. 7)

What is apparent in Wiley's approach to the term is that it covers all the levels of granularity and does not differentiate between the content, instructional design, and delivery.

In this chapter, we describe how we have designed an object-oriented authoring tool called SimQuest for the design and delivery of simulation-based discovery learning environments. In SimQuest, building blocks are offered as reusable components for simulation-based discovery learning environments. Before describing SimQuest, a short summary is given of Merrill's work on instructional design, which has been one of the inspirations for creating SimQuest.

MERRILL'S VIEW ON INSTRUCTIONAL DESIGN

Merrill's work on instructional design has been an inspiration source for many designers and researchers. In Merrill's work, reuse has a central place. In his component design theory (CDT_2), Merrill (2001a) used a whole set of so-called *knowledge objects* to describe what in the previous section has been indicated with the term *content*. These knowledge objects are grouped by Merrill into four main groups of objects: entities, actions, processes, and properties. In this overview, properties, take a special place, because they give descriptors for the first three types of objects. Placed together in structures, knowledge objects of different kinds can be used to describe complete domains. In Merrill (2002a) these knowledge objects are combined with *instructional strategy components*. Primary instructional strategy components are low-level instructional actions. For example, the instructional strategy component "TELL" simply means that information is presented to a learner. The strategy component "ASK" asks a learner to recall information that was presented. Instructional design combines instructional components together with knowledge objects into instruction. The type and sequence of primary instructional components are determined by the overall instructional strategy chosen. Merrill (1999) called this strategy the instructional transaction shell. Traditionally, the optimal strategy to use is determined from an analysis of the instructional goals and characteristics of the learner (Romiszowski, 1981).

The aspects of reuse that were mentioned in the introductory section can be identified in the work by Merrill. The *content* or *domain* is represented by the *knowledge objects*, and the *instructional design* is represented by the *primary instructional components* and the *instructional transaction shells*. The production (*technical realization*) level is covered by Merrill in his work on ID Expert, an automated instructional development system (Merrill & ID_2 Research Group, 1998). In ID Expert the uncoupling of the domain and the instructional design is realized in a software tool. In ID expert, information in the knowledge base of the system can be linked to an instructional transaction, so that this part of the domain is included in a lesson. Merrill and the ID_2 Research Group (1998) presented a simple example of a lesson in which a map of Europe needs to be learned. New countries to be learned can easily be added in the instruction by creating links to a description of the specific knowledge in the knowledge base. Also, the combination of instructional transactions making up the instructional strategy is included. The instructional transaction shell is "a computer program that promotes a particular set of learner interactions and that we can reuse for different content topics" (Merrill & ID_2 Research Group, 1998, p. 245). In ID Expert, adaptability is covered by changing so-called instructional parameters. For example, in an instructional shell that gives the learner a practice exercise, a parameter value determines the mastery criterion in percentage (Merrill & ID_2 Research Group, 1998).

In our own work we have concentrated on the authoring (design and delivery) of simulation-based learning environments for discovery learning. In Merrill's later work (see, e.g., Merrill, 2003), he also extended his theory and authoring tools to computer simulations (i.e., the Instructional Simulator). In our work we have followed a number of the principles outlined in Merrill's work, but at some points our approach differs from his method. In the following sections an overview is given of the specific characteristics of simulation-based discovery learning. On the basis of this analysis, requirements are listed for simulation-based learning environments. This brings us to present general architectural characteristics for simulation-based learning environments, which are then made concrete by presenting the way this was realized for SimQuest learning environments. This architecture makes object-oriented design a natural approach for the SimQuest authoring tool. Finally, we describe how different actors (authors, teachers, developers, and learners) use the SimQuest approach for reuse of components.

SIMULATION-BASED DISCOVERY LEARNING

The basic idea behind simulation-based discovery learning is to provide learners with an environment in which they indeed can discover the underlying model of a domain (de Jong & van Joolingen, 1998). This type of learning has gained much interest in recent years (Bransford, Brown, & Cocking, 1999). One of the requirements for scientific discovery learning to occur is that learners have a sufficient level of control over the domain in order to perform the experiments they see as needed for discovering the properties of the domain.

Instead of experimenting with a real system, a simulation-based environment offers a simulation thereof, which has several advantages (Allessi & Trollip, 1985; de Jong, 1991). First, simulations have a number of practical advantages. They are *safe*, increase the *availability* of systems that are scarce, use minimal *resources*, are *adjustable*, and allow for *experimentation with systems that normally cannot be physically manipulated*. Second, simulations offer new instructional opportunities. For example, simulations visualize processes that are invisible in natural systems by, for instance, showing animations of probability distributions or graphs of quantities like energy or impulse. In this way, multiple views and multiple representations of the simulated system can be offered (see, e.g., Ainsworth, 1999; van der Meij & de Jong, 2003). These advantages of learning with simulations contribute to their suitability for providing an environment for discovery learning. The freedom that is offered to learners for safe and flexible experimentation provides ample opportunity for discovery of the underlying model and, hence, for genuine knowledge construction. The new instructional opportunities help to provide learners with facilities that support specific discovery learning processes.

However, in spite of the aforementioned advantages, learners have considerable difficulties with simulation-based discovery learning. De Jong and van Joolingen (1998) provided an extensive overview of these problems and indicate how simulations can be extended to help prevent or overcome these problems. The basic idea is to embed the simulation in an instructional environment that supports the processes of discovery learning. In such a supportive environment the behavior of the simulation and that of the instructional support should be tuned. This leads to the concept of *integrated simulation learning environment*. In such an environment, simulations and instructional support measures cooperate to offer timely and adequate support to the learners' learning processes.

The next section introduces the structure of integrated simulation learning environments and the way they can be built out of individual components, providing a basis for reuse.

INTEGRATED SIMULATION LEARNING ENVIRONMENTS

An integrated simulation learning environment consists of: (a) a *simulation model* that can be explored by learners, producing data on the simulated system; (b) a *simulation interface* providing one or more visual representations of the simulation model to control, manipulate, and observe the simulation model; and (c) *instructional support measures* to support the discovery learning process.

Figure 2.1 presents an example of a part of such an integrated learning environment. This is a simulation-based learning environment on the physics topic of dynamics: a mass (box) lying on a slope. In Fig. 2.1 the simulation model is not visible, but the simulation interface and (part of) the instructional measures are shown.

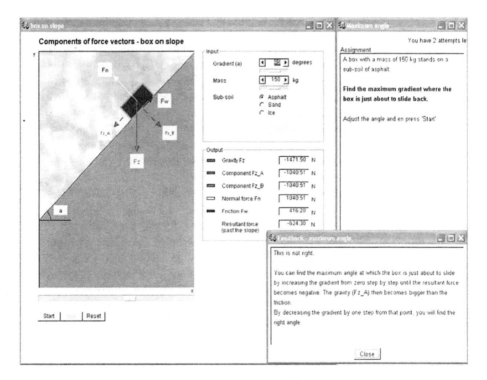

FIG. 2.1.   Example of a part of an integrated learning environment.

The *simulation interface* should allow the learner to control the simulation model, to vary the values of the input variables that are relevant for the domain to be discovered, and to observe the behavior of the simulated phenomenon. The simulation interface must thus provide an accessible interface to relevant variables in the simulation model. In Fig. 2.1 it can been seen that the learner can manipulate various variables, such as the slope and the mass of the box, through the simulation interface. The simulation interface also provides the external representations of the model state. This may include graphs, drawn in real time as the simulation proceeds, and animations that display visual representations of model states. In Fig. 2.1 the output is shown as different force components, both numerically and graphically.

Instructional support measures scaffold learners in the discovery learning processes. Instructional support measures may range from assignments presented to the learner, explanations providing just-in-time information, to electronic tools to help create hypotheses or to monitor the learners' actions. Typically, in a simulation-based discovery environment, different kinds of these measures are available to support the various stages of the learning process and the various learning processes within these stages. In Fig. 2.1, to the right, an example of an assignment is shown. In this case, this is a so-called "optimization assignment" that asks the learner to reach a certain state in the simulation. As a rule, assignments provide the learner with feedback after the assignment has been done.

In the example assignment given in Fig. 2.1, the learner is asked to optimize a certain situation—that is, to adjust the slope so that the box in Fig. 2.1 is just about to start to move (the friction is equal to the force along the slope). This instructional support measure, given to the learner as a practice task, needs to be able to: (a) set the initial conditions in the simulation model to set up the task; (b) monitor the task in real time, as the learner proceeds with the assignment; and (c) interrupt by stopping the simulation model on successful operation, or stop it when a certain constraint for the assignment is broken (e.g., when the box starts to slide). The first of these three requirements is that the instructional support measure controls the simulation model; the second requires that the assignment reads information from the simulation model during run time; and the third requirement implies that the simulation model can control the instructional measure in the learning environment.

Even more complex interaction between the simulation model, the interface, and the instructional support measures is necessary when feedback is given that is based on an analysis of the learners behavior and that is tailored to the needs of the learner. For instance, Veermans, de Jong, and van Joolingen (2000) presented an instructional support measure that provides feedback on the experimental behavior of the learner. The measure selects and orders experiments done by the learner and indicates the extent to which these experiments are capable of testing the current learner's hypothesis. In order to enable this kind of feedback, the instructional support measure must have access to: (a) the set of variables that are present in the simulation model and what kind (input, output, state) they are; (b) the manipulations by the learner on the input and state variables; (c) the results of these manipulations; and

(d) the learner's current hypothesis. The first three of these four items can be extracted from the simulation model; the fourth may come from another instructional measure, for instance, a hypothesis scratchpad on which the learner enters his or her hypothesis (Gijlers & de Jong, submitted; van Joolingen & de Jong, 1991).

THE DESIGN OF SIMQUEST

Merrill's ideas on instructional design provide an interesting basis for design principles for simulation-based learning environments. Merrill (2001b) described the importance of separating content (knowledge objects) and instructional design (instructional strategy components). This principle can be readily applied in simulation-based discovery learning. By defining in a domain independent way, for instance, an optimization assignment (such as the one described for Fig. 2.1), one can strive for reuse of the same *instructional design structures* in different domains. For *knowledge* objects, our approach is somewhat different than Merrill's approach. In SimQuest we define simulation models that can be combined and reused in new learning environments, but the instructional support measures do not get their information automatically from a knowledge representation. Instead, the author fills the instructional measures with content and links them to the simulation model. The same mechanism also applies to the design of the simulation interface.

A major question that we faced was how to realize the level of interaction with the simulation model required by the various instructional support measures. Simulations may differ in model, structure, computational formalism, and many other aspects. In order to facilitate interaction between different parts of the simulation learning environment, the learning environment must represent the relevant information in a format that can be handled by the instructional measures while providing access to simulation commands such as setting the value of a variable and starting or stopping the simulation. Because of the possible variance in simulation models, the necessary access to the simulation model must be abstracted, providing uniform access to the simulation model by different kinds of support measures. For this abstraction the *simulation context* was introduced. The simulation context is a part of the SimQuest architecture that provides access to the necessary details of the simulation in a uniform way. The simulation context, therefore, controls the access to the simulation model, providing the level of interaction with the simulation as needed, without the need for the instructional support measures to know the simulation model's internal details.

At the time of authoring a simulation-based learning environment, the simulation context provides the instructional measures with general information about the simulation model: the names of the variables, as well as other properties, such as unit and value range, the names of possible actions on the simulation, and the static or dynamic nature of the simulation model. In this way the author of the learning environment is able to specify the behavior of the instructional measures, such as which variables the instructional measure should control or watch, or which variables to use in generating feedback to the learner, at an abstract level. At run time, the simulation context feeds the instructional measures with the actual values of the relevant variables and allows for control actions to be executed. In the example of the box on the slope (see Fig. 2.1) this scheme would be implemented as follows. A building block (template) for the assignment (in this case an "optimization assignment") would be drawn from the library of reusable building blocks and added to the appropriate simulation context (see Fig. 2.2). This process of copying a building block and placing it in a simulation context is called instantiation (see van Joolingen & de Jong, 2003).

After having instantiated the building block the author needs to specialize it (see van Joolingen & de Jong, 2003). In this example, this means that the author needs to provide the building block with information on: (a) the state of simulation model when the assignment opens ($mass = 8$, $surface friction = 0.4$); (b) a description of the optimal state to be reached in terms of values for variables (maximum angle); (c) constraints ($maximum velocity = 1$); (d) constraints on the interaction (only the slope may be modified); and (e) how to interact with the simulation to stop the process (stop when a constraint is broken and give related feedback, or when the bottom of the slope is reached). All the information needed to enable the

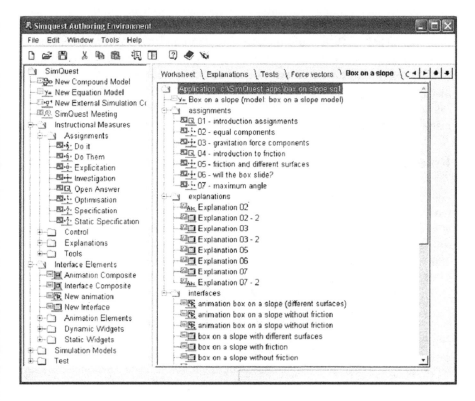

FIG. 2.2.   SimQuest authoring environment.

instructional measure to actually perform its actions at runtime can be supplied by the 'simulation context'. The state might be set in terms of expressions like: $mass = 8$. The optimal state as: $angle = 40°$ and $height = 0$, or $39° < angle < 41°$. Constraints as: 0 $m/s < velocity < 1$ m/s. Breaking the constraint may trigger an instructional action such as *"tell the learner that the box is coming off the slope too fast."* This instructional action is implemented by firing another instructional measure, for instance an explanation. During run time (learner use of the simulation), conditions for success and failure can continually be checked and the learning environment can adapt its behavior to the changing state of the simulation model.

The object-oriented design as realized in SimQuest with the separation between structure and content of instructional support levels provides the basis for reuse in the design of simulation-based learning environments. Reuse becomes possible at a domain independent level. In the next section it is outlined how this works in practice.

REUSE IN SIMQUEST

SimQuest supports a range of reusers. The main target groups of reusers are *authors* and *teachers*. Authors instantiate and specialize SimQuest building blocks to create learning environments, which in turn can be modified by teachers for their special needs. The separation between authors and teachers is not strict; basically, teachers can perform the same activities as authors, but in practice they will show a more restrictive use of the SimQuest reuse facilities. Two other groups of users are distinguished as well. The SimQuest *developers* reuse existing components within and outside SimQuest to build new ones, and *learners* also can reuse SimQuest building blocks.

Reuse by Authors

Authors use the SimQuest authoring environment to build new SimQuest learning environments or to modify existing ones for a large(r) group of teachers or learners. Van Joolingen and de Jong (2003) presented an extensive overview of the SimQuest authoring process. Authors are the primary target users of the SimQuest authoring environment. The author is often a domain expert, who is not necessarily a programmer or an expert in the didactics of discovery learning. To cope with the latter, an author may cooperate with an instructional designer.

Reuse of Building Blocks From the Library.   In the authoring process the author uses a library of building blocks (see Fig. 2.2). Each building block contains a specific template in which the author can specify properties of the building block. In an assignment template the author might, for instance, need to specify a question, possible answers, number of attempts, and the state of the simulation model when the assignment opens. Templates contain open fields (e.g., a question field) and options to choose from (e.g., the number of attempts or the option to play sound when the assignment is started) (see Fig. 2.3).

An author can also reuse an already specified building block, copying it and changing the content where needed. Copied building blocks may be used with the same simulation model, with a different simulation context within the same SimQuest application or even within another SimQuest application. The author may create and maintain his or her own library of (partially) instantiated building blocks. SimQuest automatically takes care of the technical aspects involved with moving building blocks from one simulation context to another.

Reuse of Conglomerates of Building Blocks With the SimQuest Wizard. SimQuest contains a wizard that offers the author specific layouts of interfaces and characteristic sequences of instructional support, consisting of multiple building blocks. These structures are reusable components of a larger grain size than the individual building blocks in the library. For example, the wizard component *experiment* consists of these building blocks: assignment, explanation(s), simulation interface, and, optionally, sound and an image. The experiment component automatically provides a control structure for these building blocks that, for example, automatically opens the simulation interface when the assignment opens, and closes the simulation interface when the assignment closes. Authors can reuse these structures, but also have the freedom to step out of the wizard and adapt the structures to their specific needs.

Reuse of Simulation Models.   SimQuest models can easily be reused and extended. SimQuest simulation models are specified through a text editor as equa-

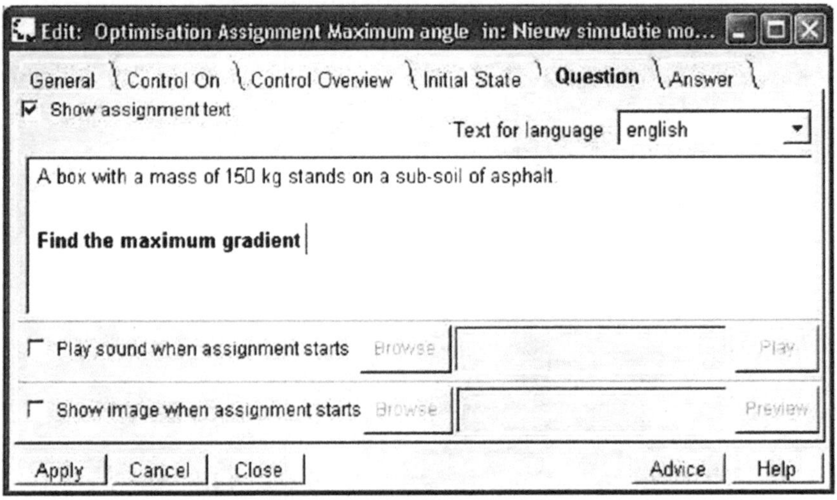

FIG. 2.3.   Example of assignment template.

tions. A syntax help file supports the author in building the simulation model (see Fig. 2.4). This allows the author to reuse almost any simulation model available, inside or outside SimQuest.

Each SimQuest simulation context has its own model or set of models. All SimQuest building blocks within a particular simulation context make use of the simulation model connected to it. Changes in a simulation model are immediately available in all building blocks. Simulation models can easily be reused for other simulation contexts and learning environments.

Reuse by Teachers

Teachers usually do not author completely new SimQuest learning environments. Their reuse typically, but not necessarily, invokes the reuse of a complete environment by adapting it to a specific context. To provide learners with coherent and dedicated instructional material, teachers have to be able to adapt learning environments to their own needs. SimQuest offers teachers the possibility to do this. The SimQuest components that teachers can easily modify are the building blocks, instructional strategies, and visualizations.

Reuse of Instantiated and Specified Building Blocks. When teachers want to modify the instruction, they can do so by modifying the content of assignments or explanations or by adding assignments or explanations. Adapting the content of the environment to specific situations, for instance, includes

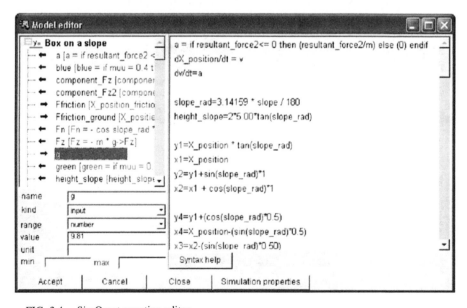

FIG. 2.4.   SimQuest equation editor.

adapting the terminology and symbols used. Changing an assignment or explanation text can be done by selecting the appropriate building block shown in the application view and opening an editor on it (see Fig. 2.3). The text can now easily be changed on the tab sheet labeled Question (assignments) or Explanation (explanations). After saving the assignment and explanation, the new text is immediately ready for use.

Reuse of an Instructional Strategy.   SimQuest allows for implementing an instructional strategy by using a modifiable control mechanism. Changing the control structure of a learning environment changes the way the learner interacts with the system. For example, a teacher can make the choice between opening assignments in a fixed order or leaving this choice to the learner. Strategies as such are not reusable; they are tied to the building blocks. A teacher, however, may adapt a strategy to her or his liking.

Reuse of Visualizations.   The SimQuest library contains several static and dynamic interface elements that can be used for the visualization of the simulation model. Teachers rarely build new interfaces but do make small modifications to existing ones. By copying and then modifying these visualization, easy reuse by teachers is possible. For instance, if an existing interface is too complex for learners, elements from it can be deleted. Conversely, elements can also be added from the library. Most interface elements are directly usable after connecting it to the right variable (see Fig. 2.5). Already specified interface elements can easily be copied and reused for other interfaces.

Reuse by Developers

Developers basically create the building blocks that are subsequently used by SimQuest authors and teachers. At the same time, developers themselves are also reusers. SimQuest itself is a product of reuse. The system reuses visualizations and tools for creating them from Visual Works, the programming platform for Smalltalk in which SimQuest was developed. Also other components in SimQuest are reused, either from other SimQuest components or from external parties.

Reuse of the Design and Implementation of Building Blocks.   The object-oriented design of SimQuest, especially the building blocks that make up the SimQuest library, allows for relatively easy extension of the system with new building blocks based on existing ones. The functionality that is shared with the existing learning object can be reused while new functionality is added. This is especially valuable in cases where the ideas for new building blocks were inspired by already existing ones. We started SimQuest, for example, with four types of assignments. During the development of SimQuest, one additional type of assignment was added, and subsequent project work led to several more. A great deal of the code for editing and execution of assignments is shared by all assignments.

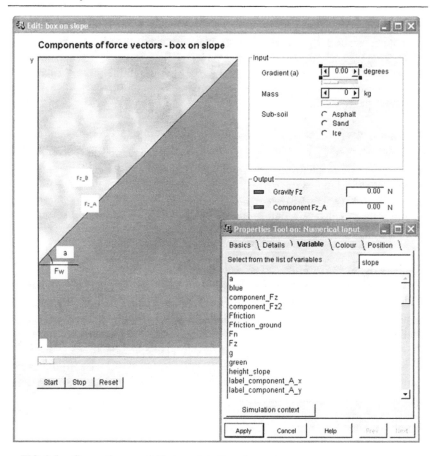

FIG. 2.5.   Connecting a variable to an interface element.

Reuse of External Components.   A recent extension of the building blocks was made for a research project that investigated *collaborative learning* with a simulation-based learning environment (Gijlers & de Jong, in press). This project required two learners to be able to establish a connection between their computers for the collaboration. Once this connection is established, the two learners share one learning environment, can take control over the learning environment, and can communicate through chat. For this purpose, the library has been extended with a new building block, which drew quite extensively on reuse. At the design level, this extension is inspired by theory about collaborative learning, whereas at the implementation level an existing external collaboration tool (Netmeeting) is re-used, which lowered the implementation efforts and costs.

Reuse of External Representations for Modeling.   There has been a growing interest in using modeling as a learning activity (Milrad, Spector, &

Davidsen, 2002). The idea is that by constructing a computer model, learners will gain more understanding about the phenomenon that they are trying to model. The tool used to make simulation models in SimQuest was not suitable for used by learners, and a new tool that allowed learners to design their models (Löhner, van Joolingen, & Savelsbergh, 2003) was developed. This new tool subsequently replaced the old modeling tool for authors as well. This illustrates a form of reuse in which the design and parts of the implementation of a learner tool were reused in the redesign of an author tool.

Reuse by Learners

Learners typically are using learning environments developed specifically for them. Although learners are generally not reusing building blocks, there is an exception. The authoring environment can be used for learning by design (Kafai, 1996). In this type of learning, learners are learning about the domain of the simulation not only by exploration, but also by designing instruction for hypothetical other learners (Vreman-de Olde & de Jong, 2004). The idea is that by thinking about the simulation and about possible assignments for peer learners, learners will engage in self-explanatory activities and, as a consequence, better learning results will be obtained. SimQuest was used in this way by making the instructional building blocks in the library (i.e., the assignments) available to the learners.

CONCLUSION

The main purpose of this chapter was to explore how reusability could be applied in authoring simulation-based discovery environments. For this exploration we have taken the authoring environment SimQuest as an example. In SimQuest, reusability may take place with regard to pedagogical structures, domain (content), and the implementation of these components. All this can be done at different levels of grain size. An important point in reuse is also the adaptability of the components that are reused. We have discussed how this is realized in SimQuest. We have also indicated that the type of reuse may depend on the type of person who is reusing components and in this respect distinguished between an author, a teacher, a developer, and a learner.

The main type of reuse with SimQuest is *reuse of pedagogical structures*. The SimQuest library contains sets of instructional measures that are empty pedagogical structures in which the author has to fill in the content and set specific parameters. With the SimQuest control system the author can lay down the overall pedagogical structure of the learning environment. Our experience is that authors and teachers can very well perform this type of reuse. Although, especially for teachers, designing discovery learning environments is something novel, using the SimQuest reusability features enables them to make this type of learning environments. SimQuest gives teachers further support through a pedagogical advice tool that provides them with background information and examples of good practice.

In SimQuest two types of *reuse of content* can be distinguished. The first type of content is the simulation models in SimQuest. For designing models, the SimQuest library contains a set of reusable building blocks. In addition, SimQuest has a facility to link existing models created simulation models outside SimQuest to a SimQuest simulation context so that they can be used in a learning environment as if they were genuine SimQuest models. The second type of content within SimQuest is the domain information in assignments, feedback, explanations, and so on. Reuse of this type of content was not included in our ideas when setting up SimQuest. At the onset, SimQuest was meant as an authoring system to be used only by teachers. We found, however, that creating sound models and elegant interfaces was often beyond the skills of teachers. This implied that gradually the idea of an authoring system for teachers changed toward a service in which complete learning environments are delivered and teachers used the authoring system to adapt the learning environment. In this case they also receive the content included in the pedagogical structures of SimQuest. In adapting the learning environment they use a subset of the full authoring facilities of SimQuest and adapt small parts of interfaces, the content of explanations, assignments, or other instructional measures.

Reuse of the *technical implementation* is used by all types of users throughout SimQuest. All SimQuest components created in the SimQuest authoring system function technically in the SimQuest learning environments. Although this means a restrictive type of reusability (SimQuest components will not function outside SimQuest), we think that this is a very important aspect of reusability; users never have to worry about the functioning of SimQuest components.

In this chapter we have shown that SimQuest building blocks may vary at the level of granularity. Reusable components can be an assignment, an interface element (so not a complete interface), but they could also be a complete interface, a structure with content (e.g., in a composite), or a structure without content (e.g., in the wizard). At the start of this chapter we criticized the openness of the IEEE definition of learning objects. Merrill (cited in Welsch, 2002) remarked in the same context: "No one seems to know what a learning object is in the first place. One of the absurd definitions I heard was, 'as small as a drop, as wide as the ocean.' In other words, if everything is a learning object, then nothing is a learning object." When we take SimQuest building blocks as being learning objects, we think we have shown that building blocks when taken at a reasonable level of granularity, within a specific context, and with adaptability as a key characteristic may help to create productive authoring systems.

REFERENCES

Ainsworth, S. E. (1999). The functions of multiple representations. *Computers & Education, 33,* 131–152.

Alessi, S. M., & Trollip, S. R. (1985). *Computer based instruction, methods and development*. Englewood Cliffs, NJ: Prentice Hall.

Bransford, J. D., Brown, A. L., & Cocking, R. R. (Eds.). (1999). *How people learn: Brain, mind, experience, and school*. Washington, DC: National Academy Press.

de Jong, T. (1991). Learning and instruction with computer simulations. *Education & Computing, 6*, 217–229.

de Jong, T., & van Joolingen, W. R. (1998). Scientific discovery learning with computer simulations of conceptual domains. *Review of Educational Research, 68*, 179–202.

Duncan, C. (2003) Conceptions of learning objects: Social and educational issues. In A. Littlejohn (Ed.), *Reusing online resources: A sustainable approach to e-Learning* (pp. 12–19). London: Kogan Page.

Friesen, N. (2004). Three objections to building blocks. In R. McGreal (Ed.), *Online education using learning objects* (pp. 59–70). London: Routledge Falmer.

Gijlers, H., & de Jong, T. (submitted). Sharing and confronting propositions in collaborative scientific discovery learning.

Gijlers, H., & de Jong, T. (in press). The relation between prior knowledge and students' collaborative discovery learning processes. *Journal of Research in Science Teaching*.

IEEE. (2002). *IEEE Learning Technology Standards Committee (LTSC) IEEE P1484.12 Learning Object Metadata Working Group; WG12 Home page*. Retrieved April 9, 2004, from http://ltsc.ieee.org/wg12

Kafai, Y. B. (1996). Learning design by making games. Children's development of design strategies in the creation of a complex computational artifact. In Y. B. Kafai & M. Resnick (Eds.), *Constructionism in practice: Designing, thinking, and learning in a digital world* (pp. 71–96). Mahwah, NJ: Lawrence Erlbaum Associates.

Löhner, S., van Joolingen, W. R., & Savelsbergh, E. R. (2003). The effect of external representation on constructing computer models of complex phenomena. *Instructional Science, 31*, 395–418.

Merrill, M. D. (1999). Instructional transaction theory (ITT): Instructional design based on knowledge objects. In C. M. Reigeluth (Ed.), *Instructional design theories and models: a new paradigm of instructional technology* (pp. 397–425). Mahwah, NJ: Lawrence Erlbaum Associates.

Merrill, M. D. (2001a). Knowledge objects and mental models. In D. A. Wiley (Ed.), *The instructional use of building blocks*. Retrieved April 9, 2004, from http://reusability.org/read/chapters/merrill.doc

Merrill, M. D. (2001b). Components of instruction toward a theoretical tool for instructional design. *Instructional Science, 29*, 291–310.

Merrill, M. D. (2002a). Effective use of instructional technology requires educational reform. *Educational Technology, 42*, 13–16.

Merrill, M. D. (2002b). Instructional strategies and learning styles: Which takes precedence? In R. Reiser & J. Dempsey (Eds.), *Trends and Issues in instructional technology* (pp. 83–99). Upper Saddle River, NJ: Prentice Hall.

Merrill, M. D. (2003). Using knowledge objects to design instructional learning environments. In T. Murray, S. Blessing, & S. Ainsworth (Eds.), *Authoring tools for advanced technology educational software: Toward cost-effective production of adaptive, interactive, and intelligent educational software* (pp. 181–204). Dordrecht: Kluwer Academic.

Merrill, M. D., & ID$_2$ Research Group. (1998). ID Expert™: A second generation instructional development system. *Instructional Science, 26*, 243–262.

Milrad, M., Spector, J. M., & Davidsen, P. I. (2002). Model facilitated learning. In S. Naidu (Ed.), *Learning and teaching with technology: Principles and practices* (pp. 13–27). London: Kogan Page.

Murray, T. (1999). Authoring intelligent tutoring systems: Analysis of the state of the art. *International Journal of AI and Education, 10*, 98–129

Romiszowski, A. J. (1981). *Designing instructional systems.* London: Kogan Page.

Tannenbaum, R. S. (2001). Learner interactivity and production complexity in computer-based instructional materials. *Cubiquity, 2.* Retrieved April 9, 2004, from http://www.acm.org/ubiquity/views/r_tannenbaum_4.html

van der Meij, J., & de Jong, T. (2003, August). *Supporting the translation between multiple representations.* Paper presented at the 2003 EARLI conference, Padua, Italy.

van Joolingen, W. R., & de Jong, T. (1991). Supporting hypothesis formation by learners exploring an interactive computer simulation. *Instructional Science, 20*, 389–404.

van Joolingen, W. R., & de Jong, T. (2003). SimQuest: Authoring educational simulations. In T. Murray, S. Blessing, & S. Ainsworth (Eds.), *Authoring tools for advanced technology educational software: Toward cost-effective production of adaptive, interactive, and intelligent educational software* (pp. 1–31). Dordrecht: Kluwer Academic.

Veermans, K. H., de Jong, T., & van Joolingen, W.R. (2000). Promoting self directed learning in simulation based discovery learning environments through intelligent support. *Interactive Learning Environments, 8*, 229–255.

Vreman-de Olde, C., & de Jong, T. (2004). Student-generated assignments about electrical circuits in a computer simulation. *International Journal of Science Education, 26*, 59–73.

Welsch E. (2002). SCORM: Clarity or calamity? *Online Learning*, 2002-07-01.

Wiley, D. A. (2000). Connecting building blocks to instructional design theory: A definition, a metaphor, and a taxonomy. In D. A. Wiley (Ed.), *The instructional use of building blocks*. Retrieved April 9, 2004, from http://reusability.org/read/chapters/wiley.doc

Supporting the Mobility and the Adaptivity of Knowledge Objects by Cognitive Trait Model

Kinshuk
Tai-yu Lin
Massey University

Ashok Patel
De Montfort University

Early instructional systems and their authoring tools were frame-based (Merrill, Li, & Jones, 1991), and they were typically called programmed instruction (Schulmeister, 1997). A major limitation for programmed instructions was the way the domain data had to be tightly bound to the frames. Merrill and colleagues (1991) adopted the approach of separating data and algorithm to allow design emphasis to be placed on the algorithm—a sequence of computations that can be repeated over and over with different data—after the separation. The frame-based approach with branching can also be regarded as one that separates algorithms and data, but it is a very limited one in terms of its ability to provide customized instruction to learners.

This separation of data and algorithm provided the key idea that facilitates the formation of a new wave of instructional design. As the data (domain content) and the algorithm (strategy) for teaching can be constructed separately, researchers can focus on (a) how to design and construct the learning materials so that they can be used in multiple contexts—knowledge objects—and (b) how to design different algorithms for different learners on the same set of data—adaptive instruction. This chapter focuses on adaptive instruction using knowledge objects.

Merrill (1998) defined a knowledge object as "a precise way to describe the subject matter content or knowledge to be taught" (p. 1). A knowledge object provides a framework to organize the subject matter in a way that it can be used in different contexts and can be represented in different forms for presentation. Researchers have recently introduced the term *learning object*, defined in a number of ways with no consensus yet achieved, such as "any digital resource that can be reused to support learning" (Wiley, 2002, p. 7). The main purpose of the learning object concept is reusability, and the origin of this concept is attributed to the work on knowledge objects, as Wiley (2002) noted:

> The first serious theoretical work on the idea of using assemblages of individual digital resources as the basis for instructional design was done by Merrill and his colleagues on the TICCIT project at Brigham Young University when they developed the Component Display Theory (CDT) in the early 1970s. (p. 1)

A learning object may be defined as "any entity, digital or non-digital, that may be used for learning, education or training" (LTSC IEEE, 2002, p. 6). This broad definition of learning object is criticized by Wiley (2000): "The definition (of learning object) is extremely broad, and upon examination fails to exclude any person, place, thing, or idea that has existed at anytime in the history of the universe" (p. 5). Therefore, Merrill's (1998) definition of knowledge object as a reusable instructional material is used throughout this chapter.

CUSTOMIZED EDUCATION AND ADAPTIVITY

In computer-based learning environments, customized education requires adaptivity features provided by the system. Adaptivity can be applied in content presentation, which generates the learning content adaptively to suit the particular learner's aptitude, and in adaptive navigational control, which dynamically modifies the presentation structure of the learning environment in order to prevent overloading the learner's cognitive load. Systems equipped with adaptivity have been proven more effective and efficient than traditional nonadaptive systems (De Bra, Brusilovsky, & Houben, 1999). These adaptive systems use sophisticated student modeling techniques to infer student attributes such as competency level and specific preferences. Most of the existing student modeling approaches focus on representing the domain-dependent student interactions with the system, such as how many units or topics have been completed or which skills a student has acquired. Such student models are called performance-based student models (Anderson & Reiser, 1985; Burton & Brown, 1982; El-Sheikh, 1997; Martin, 1999).

Despite the prevalence of performance-based models, the modeling of individual differences in cognitive processing is one of the areas where the full potential of student modeling has not yet been achieved (Lovett, Daily, & Reder, 2000). Intensive research work on human cognition is carried out to identify the relationship between the educational tasks and various cognitive traits of the learners so that the adaptivity could be provided in learning systems to suit the different requirements raised from each individual's differences. The importance of cognitive traits of the learners relevant to the learning process is discussed next.

COGNITIVE TRAITS

Recent adoption of the term *cognitive capacity* in the field of adaptive instruction (Cooper, 1998; Kashihara, Kinshuk, Oppermann, Rashev, & Simm, 2000; Kinshuk, Oppermann, Patel, & Kashihara, 1999) raised the awareness of the influence of cognitive abilities on the learning process and result. Instead of providing adaptive assistance to the learners based on their subject domain performance, cognitive-oriented approaches support learning with consideration of the differences of learners' cognitive abilities. In a learning context, cognitive abilities of learners are then regarded as their resources for learning. The adaptivity thus provided tries to optimize the learning process based on these resources by (a) not overloading the cognitive capacity of the learner as it discourages the learner and (b) supplementing the learning process as much as the cognitive capacity can afford so that maximum learning result can be obtained.

As opposed to Charles E. Spearman's general factor, which indicates the general intellectual ability, L. L. Thurston claimed that there are seven different primary mental abilities, whereas Raymond Cattell and Philip Vernon sorted the general factor and the primary mental abilities into a hierarchy (The Learning Curve, n.d.). Upon close scrutiny, cognitive capacity can be divided into subcomponents. Learners with a higher cognitive capacity generally learn more rapidly and have better comprehension than those with lower cognitive capacities (Cooper, 1998). The speed of learning is related to how fast the human brain processes incoming information (information processing speed), the ability to integrate new knowledge into existing cognitive structures (associative learning skill), and the ability to work out the underlying rules of the perceived data (inductive reasoning skill). Information processing and information retrieval activities require the resources of working memory. Comprehension of what was perceived is also closely linked with associative learning skills, inductive learning skills, and working memory, as well as the ability to reflect on what was learned.

Therefore, it is obvious that the performance of one's cognitive capacity depends on the performance of it subcomponents. This is analogous to Cattell and Vernon's proposition, mentioned earlier, of the hierarchical structure of human intelligence, with a general factor at the top of the hierarchy and the primary mental abilities at the bottom of the hierarchy. However, the focus of this research work is on the search of a different perspective to provide instructional adaptivity, and

Thurston's seven primary mental abilities are not totally embraced. Instead, this research work attempts to select and address those cognitive abilities that are relevant in a learning context. The *cognitivist* view of learning, which posits that knowledge is represented as mental schema and that learning is a process that involves the reorganization of schema, is adopted here. At the time of this writing, four cognitive abilities have been identified as potentially significant to learning: working memory capacity, inductive reasoning ability, associative learning ability, and information processing speed. These cognitive abilities are traits of one's overall cognitive capacity; therefore, they are called "cognitive traits."

Unlike knowledge or expertise, which are more domain specific and evolve with time and experience, cognitive traits are relatively stable and transferable over different tasks. Thus, the student model obtained in one domain can provide a reliable prediction of the performance of the same student in another domain. Differences of cognitive traits cause differences in quality, efficiency, and overall performance on the learning tasks carried out.

IMPACT OF COGNITIVE TRAITS ON LEARNING

Before discussing the cognitive traits in detail, it is important to consider how they can benefit the learning process. In adaptive learning systems, the adaptive features attempt to modify the learning content and navigational paths to create different versions of the same materials to suit different needs (Kashihara et al., 2000). Various aspects of learning content and navigational paths that are affected by the adaptivity are listed in Table 3.1.

Many modern adaptive learning systems are built using hypermedia technology, in which paths are generally presented as a series of links. The *amount and detail of content* affects the volume of the presentation. The *concreteness* determines the abstract level of the information. The *structure* of information indicates the ordering, arrangement, and sequencing of the information. With regard to structure, elaboration theory (Reigeluth, 1992) suggests that the instruction should be organized in increasing order of complexity for optimal learning. The final category in Table 3.1 is information resources such as text, audio, and graphics. Each type of

TABLE 3.1

Aspects of Learning Content and Navigational Paths

Path	Number Relevance
Content	Amount (detail)
	Concreteness
	Structuredness
Information resources	Number

media has a potentially different impact on each individual's learning. If there is more than one type of media (e.g., a textual explanation and a chart), it could make the information more explanatory and easier for future recall, although there are cases where mixed media creates interference patterns for learners (e.g., synchronizing audio with scrolling text).

In order to illustrate how the consideration of cognitive traits could impact learning, a cognitive trait—working memory capacity—is selected for an exemplary formalization.

STUDY OF WORKING MEMORY CAPACITY

Working memory is the cognitive system that allows us to keep active a limited amount of information (roughly, 7 ± 2 items) for a brief period of time (Miller, 1956). The research on working memory (Huai, 2000; Kearsley, 2001) shows that the speed of learning, the memorization of learned concepts, the effectiveness of skill acquisition, and many other learning abilities are all affected by the capacity of working memory, which is mainly comprised of two components: the limited memory storage system, and the central execution unit carrying out various cognitive operation efforts.

Working memory is also referred to as short-term memory, especially when the focus is on the limited storage aspect rather than on cognitive operations pertaining to that small and transient type of memory. Working memory denotes the memory capable of transient preservation of information and is functionally different from the memory that stores historical information (the long-term memory). Richards-Ward (1996) named it the short-term store (STS) to emphasis its role of temporary storage of recently perceived information. The term *working memory* refers to the same construct as the STS does in terms of the capacity of transient storage. In addition, it also acknowledges that cognitive processes take place in working memory. Baddeley (1992) indicated that the major function of the working memory is to temporarily store the outcomes of intermediate computations when solving a problem, and to allow operations or further computations on these temporary outcomes.

Baddeley (1992) described working memory according to its structure as a control–slave system comprised of the central executive (controlling component), phonological loop (slave component for verbal information), and a visual–spatial sketchpad (slave component for graphical information). The central executive takes the role of monitoring and controlling the output of the two slave systems and selecting what is relevant for potential processing (Richards-Ward, 1996).

In addition to the storage capacity, Atkinson and Shiffrin (1968) defined working memory functionally as the gateway allowing information to be transferred to long-term memory. This definition stresses the ability to channel incoming isolated information (as perceived by our senses) to a semantically networked structure in the long-term memory. This involves a great degree of cognitive effort, such as interpretation, translation, association, memorization, and so on. This functionality is comparable to the central executive already mentioned; essentially, it transforms and transfers messages from the short-term storage system into the long-term one. The transformation process invokes the formation of rules, which are the results of learning according to structural learning theory (Scandura, 1973), from data (may come from sensory perceptions); the transfer process also involves filtering which rules and data are to be stored for long-term and which are to be discarded.

Several studies have shown that age-related performance of young children and old adults compared with young adults can be characterized by the inability to retain information in working memory while simultaneously processing other information (Case, 1995; Salthouse & Babcock, 1991). Deficiencies in working memory capacity result in different performances in a variety of tasks. Examples of tasks affected include natural language use (comprehension, production, etc.), skill acquisition, and so on (Byrne, 1996).

An empirical study by Huai (2000) showed that students with a versatile learning style also have a significantly smaller short-term working memory but have remarkably higher learning results in the long run, whereas students with a serial learning style (highly capable of following and remembering sequentially fixed information) have better short-term working memory capacity but poorer learning results in the long run. This point shows the intricate relationship between innate abilities and different learning styles and how learning styles might be adopted to circumvent deficiencies in those abilities. The navigational strategies adopted by serial learners are linear, whereas holist learners sometimes do better by jumping directly to more complex concepts (Felder, 1988).

FORMALIZING WORKING MEMORY CAPACITY

The effort to facilitate learning with regard to working memory may be realized in an instructional design that facilitates the synchronized operation of the central executive by assisting with the formation of higher order rules, construction of mental models, and, of course, minimizing the work load of working memory. Working memory is analyzed next with respect to learning. The issue here is how different levels of working memory will affect the components of learning systems (as mentioned in Table 3.1), thus triggering the need for adaptivity.

Low Working Memory Capacity

The number of paths and the amount of information should be constrained so as to protect learners from getting lost in the vast amount of information and from overloading working memory with complex hyperspace structures (Kashihara et al., 2000), as well as to allow more time for learners to review essential content as desired. The relevance of the information should be kept high so learners get important information and know its use. The concreteness of the information should be kept high so learners can grasp fundamental rules first and use them to generate higher order rules, as suggested by structural learning theory (Scandura, 1973) and other relevant learning theories. The structure of the information should stay unchanged. The increase of the *structuredness* of information can facilitate the building of mental models and assist in the future recall of information. As Huai (2000) indicated, however, versatile learners tend to have smaller short-term memory (storage aspect of working memory) than serial learners, and the increase of structuredness limits their navigational freedom, which is the primary way they learn. Basically, the net effect of these two tendencies cancels out, so the structure of information is recommended to remain unchanged for learners with low working memory capacity. The number of information resources should be high, so learners can work with the media resources that work best with their aptitudes without increasing the cognitive load on already low working memory capacity (aptitude treatment theory; see Cronbach & Snow, 1989), and allow deeper level of processing of the information and hence deeper understanding on the subject domain (level of processing; see Craik & Lockhart, 1972).

High Working Memory Capacity

The number of paths and the amount of information should be kept high and place less emphasis on the relevance of the information in order to enlarge the exploration and domain space of the learning process. This will enable more knowledge to be available to the learners who process more higher order rules, which "account for creative behavior (unanticipated outcomes) as well as the ability to solve complex problems by making it possible to generate (learn) new rules" (Kearsley, 2001, p. 1). The concreteness of the information should be minimized to avoid boredom resulting from too many similar examples. The structure of the information and the number of information resources should remain unchanged because there are no direct and apparent benefits associated with changes. This discussion is formalized in Table 3.2.

The symbols used in the formalization in Table 3.2 have the following meanings:

- $+ \circledR$ should increase.
- $- \circledR$ should decrease.
- $\backslash + \circledR$ should slightly increase (recommend only), or could increase.
- $\backslash - \circledR$ should slightly decrease (recommend only), or could decrease.

TABLE 3.2
Working Memory Formalization

| | Path | | Content | | | Resource |
Level	Number	Relevance	Amount	Concreteness	Structure	number
Low	–	+	–	+	\	+
High	\+	\–	+	–	\	\

Kinshuk and Lin (2003) provided similar discussions on other cognitive traits. The resulting chart of cognitive traits is shown in Table 3.3.

The discussion so far has covered how instruction can be adapted to suit differences in working memory capacity. However, an urgent question needs to be addressed for the pragmatism of what had been done so far, which is: How can the result of the formalization be implemented in actual instruction or how can existing instruction be reorganized to account for this cognitive trait? Merrill's (1998) knowledge objects bring light to this question. The relationship of knowledge object and cognitive trait formalization is discussed next.

KNOWLEDGE OBJECT
AND COGNITIVE TRAITS FORMALIZATION

The definition of a knowledge object is particularly suitable for the prescription provided by the cognitive traits formalization. A knowledge object can have adaptivity elements as its properties (e.g., the amount of content, the concreteness of content) (Merrill, 1998). There are classes, described by the kinds of knowledge objects, for each of these adaptivity element properties, depending on the require-

TABLE 3.3

Cognitive Traits Formalization

Student attributes	Level	Path		Content			Information resources
		No	Rel	Amt	Con	Str	No
Work memory capacity	Low	1	5	1	5	3	5
	Std	3	3	3	3	3	3
	High	4	2	5	1	4	4
Inductive reasoning skill	Low	4	2	5	5	5	3
	Std	3	3	3	3	3	3
	High	2	3	1	2	3	3
Information processing speed	Low	1	5	1	3	4	3
	Std	3	3	3	3	3	3
	High	5	1	5	3	3	3
Associative learning skill	Low	5	5	3	3	5	5
	Std	3	3	3	3	3	3
	High	2	1	3	3	2	3

Note. No, number; Rel, relevance; Amt, amount; Con, concreteness; Str, structure; Std, standard.

ments of the domain, for example, high or low concreteness of the content. Knowledge objects can have several portrayals each corresponding to those classes. For example, a physics lesson on momentum can have two different portrayals: presenting the lesson in low concreteness, and presenting the lesson in high concreteness. Different portrayals are given according to the learner's requirement for different concreteness to obtain the best learning result.

Therefore, the work on the cognitive traits formalization can be greatly supported by the concept of a knowledge object, which provides the necessary structural tools (components) to construct a curriculum that employs cognitive traits formalization to provide adaptivity. The usability and adaptivity of the concept of knowledge object can be greatly enhanced by cognitive traits formalization, which provides the theoretical tools to achieve adaptivity for those designers who wish to use knowledge objects as the building blocks of a curriculum.

THE COGNITIVE TRAIT MODEL

The ultimate goal of the cognitive trait model (CTM) is to have a student model that can be persistent over a long period of time and consistent across a variety of domains. Thus, the CTM is suitable for those students who aim to proceed in lifelong learning. It is not essential for CTM to be able to predict student behavior or outcomes the very first time it is applied or even the first few times a student uses a learning system constructed according to CTM. Rather, what is required is a student model that can come to represent student abilities, especially lower level learning abilities and associated cognitive traits, very well over time. The CTM can still be applicable and useful after a long period of time due to the more-or-less persistent nature of cognitive traits of human beings, as mentioned earlier. When a student encounters a new learning environment, the learning environment can directly use the CTM of that particular student, and does not need to construct a new model from the same learner taking a different course or sequence of courses from that used in the original construction of that learner's cognitive trait model. In this sense, the CTM is like a learning companion, and can be analogous to those health records that can be carried by people on smart cards.

THE ARCHITECTURE OF THE COGNITIVE TRAIT MODEL

The architecture of the cognitive trait model is represented in Fig. 3.1. The learner interface provides a presentation of the learning environment with which learners will interact. In Web-based systems, the learner interface is generally implemented inside a Web browser. Due to the stateless nature of the HTTP protocol used by Web browsers, it is necessary to embed a mechanism that can monitor events created by a learner's interactions with a learning environment. The mechanism is represented by the interface listener component in Fig. 3.1. Learner interactions are interpreted as a series of learner actions performed on

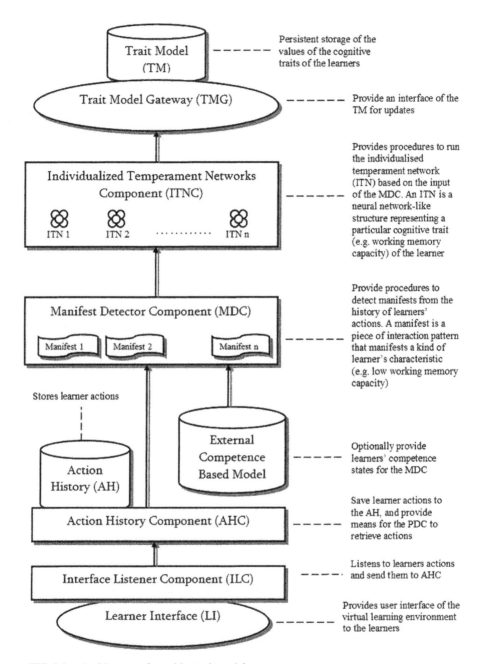

FIG. 3.1.   Architecture of cognitive trait model.

knowledge objects. Actions are the passed on to the action history components and are stored in action history.

The *competence-based model* presents a learner's domain competence and models the problem-solving process that the learner undertakes. Certain information of the competence-based model, such as passing or failing a unit, can be useful for detecting manifests (indications) of some cognitive traits; data in the competence-based model are used as a source by the manifest detector component.

Various manifests are defined on the basis of cognitive traits. Each manifest is a piece of an interaction pattern that manifests a learner characteristic (e.g., low working memory capacity). The manifest detector component has knowledge of a number of manifests and detects those manifests within a series of actions that are requested from the action history component. Each manifest belongs to one of the two groups (low or high) of a particular cognitive trait, and each manifest belongs to only one particular individualized temperament network.

The individualized temperament network component in Fig. 3.1 can have more than one individualized temperament network (ITN). An ITN is a neural network-like structure. Each ITN represents a particular cognitive trait (e.g., working memory capacity) of the learner. Each node in the ITN has a weight and corresponds to a manifest. Once a manifest is detected from the learner's actions, the corresponding node is activated. The execution of the ITN involves polling of all the nodes in the network. One of the two groups (low or high) is selected as the prevailing group that wins in the polling, and the other becomes the recessive group. The weights of the manifests in the prevailing group are increased by the gradient constant, whereas the weights of the manifests in the recessive group are decreased by the gradient constant. The results of the execution of the ITNs are then sent to the trait model gateway, which is responsible for all the transactions to the trait model.

SUMMARY

The idea of separating data from algorithms (Merrill, Li, & Jones, 1991) in instructional design gave rise to two important research fields: knowledge objects and adaptive instruction. Knowledge objects provide a framework within which the teaching materials of a particular skill or concept to be taught are encapsulated as the components of a knowledge object (Merrill, 1998; Merrill, 2001; Merrill & ID2 Research Team, 1996). Components of knowledge objects not only present the data of the knowledge object, but they also provide meaning to the structure of the knowledge object so that automated instructional development is made possible (Merrill & ID2 Research Team, 1996).

The strength of adaptivity in education does not just lie in its novelty. Experimental studies have substantially proven its ability to enhance learning speed, memorization and comprehension (Cooper, 1998; Richards-Ward, 1996); its customizable property makes it a preferable choice for lifelong learning systems.

Adaptivity relies heavily on the ability to infer student attributes correctly and in a timely manner during the learning process. Because most student models are only competence oriented, the adaptation can only be provided in a performance-based manner, which means that the learning environment adapts itself in those areas where the student's performance is identified (or predicted) as suboptimal.

The cognitive trait model (CTM) provides a supplementary module to any existing learning environment that wishes to support adaptation at the cognitive level. The existing competence models can be used for performance-based adaptivity, whereas the CTM can supply the adaptivity that addresses the differences of each individual's cognitive traits.

REFERENCES

Anderson, J. R., & Reiser, B. J. (1985). The LISP tutor. *Byte, 10*, 159–75.

Atkinson, R. C., & Shiffrin, R. M. (1968). Human memory: A proposed system and its control processes. In K. W. Spence & J. T. Spence (Eds.), *The psychology of learning and motivation: Advances in research and theory* (Vol. 2, pp. 89–195). New York: Academic Press.

Baddeley, A. D. (1992). Working memory. *Science, 255*, 556–559.

Burton, R. R., & Brown, J.S. (1982). An investigation of computer coaching for informal learning activities. In D. Sleeman & J. Brown (Eds.), *Intelligent tutoring systems* (pp. 79–98). Orlando, FL: Academic Press.

Byrne, M. (1996). *A computational theory of working memory.* Retrieved April 9, 2004, from http://www.acm.org/sigchi/chi96/proceedings/doctoral/Byrne/mdb_txt.htm

Case, R. (1995). Capacity-based explanations of working memory growth: A brief history and reevaluation. In F. E. Weinert & W. Schneider (Eds.), *Memory performance and competencies: Issues in growth and development* (pp. 23–24). Mahwah, NJ: Lawrence Erlbaum Associates.

Cooper, G. (1998). *Research into cognitive load theory and instructional design at UNSW.* Retrieved April 9, 2004, from http://education.arts.unsw.edu.au/CLT_NET_Aug_97.html

Craik, F., & Lockhart, R. (1972). Levels of processing: A framework for memory research. *Journal of Verbal Learning & Verbal Behavior, 671*–684.

Cronbach, L., & Snow, R. (1989). Aptitude-treatment interaction as a framework for research on individual differences in learning. In P. Ackerman, R. J. Sternberg, & R. Glaser (Eds.), *Learning and individual differences* (pp. 13–60). New York: W. H. Freeman.

De Bra, P., Brusilovsky, P., & Houben, G. J. (1999). Adaptive hypermedia: From systems to framework. *ACM Computing Surveys, 31*(4). Retrieved April 9, 2004, from http://www.cs.brown.edu/memex/ACM_HypertextTestbed/papers/25.html

El-Sheikh, E. (1997). *A functional student model for an ITS.* Retrieved April 9, 2004, from http://www.cse.msu.edu/~elsheikh/cse845/paper.html

Felder, R. M. (1988). Learning and teaching styles in engineering education. *Engineering Education, 78*(7), 674–681.

Huai, H. (2000). *Cognitive style and memory capacity: Effects of concept mapping as a learning method.* Unpublished doctoral dissertation, University of Twente, Enschede: The Netherlands.

Kashihara, A., Kinshuk, Oppermann, R., Rashev, R., & Simm, H. (2000). A cognitive load reduction approach to exploratory learning and its application to an interactive simulation-based learning system. *Journal of Educational Multimedia and Hypermedia, 9*(3), 253–276.

Kearsley, G. P. (2001). *Explorations in learning & instruction: The theory into practice database.* Retrieved April 9, 2004, from http://tip.psychology.org/scandura.html

Kinshuk, & Lin, T. (2003). User exploration based adaptation in adaptive learning systems. *International Journal of Information Systems in Education, 1*(1), 22–31.

Kinshuk, Oppermann, R., Patel, A., & Kashihara, A. (1999). Multiple representation approach in multimedia based intelligent educational systems. In S. P. Lajpie & M. Vivet (Eds.), *Artificial intelligence in education* (pp. 259–266). Amsterdam: ISO Press.

Lovett, M. C., Daily, L. Z., & Reder, L. M. (2000). *A source activation theory of working memory: Cross-task prediction of performance in ACT-R**. Retrieved April 9, 2004, from http://www.psy.cmu.edu/~LAPS/pubs/Lovett00CogSysResearch2.pdf

LTSC IEEE. (2002). *Draft standard for learning object metadata*. Retrieved September 10, 2002, from http://ltsc.ieee.org/doc/wg12LOM_1484_12_1_v1_Final_Draft.pdf

Martin, B. (1999). Constraint-based modeling: Representing student knowledge. *New Zealand Journal of Computing, 7*(2), 30–38. Retrieved April 9, 2004, from http://www.cosc.canterbury.ac.nz/~bim20/paper_nzjc.pdf

Merrill, M. D. (1998, March/April). Knowledge objects. *CBT Solutions*, pp. 1–11.

Merrill, M. D. (2001, January-February). A knowledge object and mental model approach to a physics lesson. *Educational Technology, 41*(1), 36–47.

Merrill, M. D., & ID2 Research Team. (1996). Instructional transaction theory: Instructional design based on knowledge objects. *Educational Technology, 36*(3), 30–37.

Merrill, M. D., Li, Z., & Jones, M. K. (1991). Instructional transaction theory: An introduction. *Educational Technology, 31*(6), 7–12.

Miller, G. (1956). The magic number seven, plus or minus two: Some limit of our capacity for processing information. *Psychology Review, 63*(2), 81–96.

Reigeluth, C. M. (1992). Elaborating the elaboration theory. *Educational Technology Research & Development, 40*(3), 80–86.

Richards-Ward, L. A. (1996). *Investigating the relationship between two approaches to verbal information processing in working memory: An examination of the construct of working memory coupled with an investigation of meta-working memory*. Palmerston North, New Zealand: Massey University.

Salthouse, T. A., & Babcock, R. (1991). Decomposing adult age differences in working memory. *Developmental Psychology, 27*, 763–776.

Scandura, J. M. (1973). *Structural learning I: Theory and research*. London: Gordon & Breach.

Schulmeister, R. (1997). *Hypermedia learning systems. Theory–Didactics–Design* (English version of *Grundlager hypermedialer Lernsysteme. Theorie–Didaktik–Design*). 2. Aktual. Aufl. R. Oldenbourg Verlag: Munchen. Retrieved April 9, 2004, from http://www.izhd.uni-hamburg.de

The Learning Curve. (n.d.). *Intelligence theories*. Retrieved April 9, 2004, from http://library.thinkquest.org/C0005704/content_la_intel_theories.php3

Wiley, D. A. (2000). Connecting learning objects to instructional design theory: A definition, a metaphor, and a taxonomy. In D. A. Wiley (Ed.), *The instructional use of learning objects: Online version*. Retrieved April 9, 2004, from http://reusability.org/read/chapters/wiley.doc

Wiley, D. A. (2002). Learning objects—A definition. In A. Kovalchick & K. Dawson (Eds.), *Educational technology: An encyclopedia*. Santa Barbara, CA: ABC-CLIO. Retrieved April 9, 2004, from http://wiley.ed.usu.edu/docs/encyc.pdf

Chapter
4

A Holistic Pedagogical View of Learning Objects: Future Directions for Reuse

Jeroen J. G. van Merriënboer
Open University of the Netherlands

Eddy Boot
TNO

E-learning is rapidly becoming popular because of its place and time independence and its integrated presentation and communication facilities (Jochems, van Merriënboer, & Koper, 2003; Khan, 2001). However, the wide implementation of e-learning will require large amounts of high-quality learning content. The development of sufficient learning content proves to be extremely difficult, because it requires considerable time, large budgets, and design and development expertise that are only scarcely available (Rosenberg, 2000). Since the spread of computer-based training in the 1980s, there have been many attempts to build computer-based design tools and authoring systems to make the development of high-quality learning materials faster, cheaper, and simpler (Locatis & Al-Nuaim, 1999). This is not an easy task. The tools and systems that are currently available typically lack a firm pedagogical model, seldom accommodate different development styles or levels of expertise, and often enable only simple, straightforward instruction (Boot, Veerman, & van Merriënboer, submitted; for a discussion of tools, see van Merriënboer & Martens, 2002).

This chapter discusses an alternative approach, which focuses on the *reuse* of learning materials. The basic idea is that once made, learning content could be used many times in many different instructional settings. Reuse is based on modularization. If the learning content is divided into small, modular chunks, often called *learning objects*, developers will be able to combine and recombine these objects to create new learning content. Learning technology standards provide the common frameworks to technically enable this type of reuse. The establishment of a *learning object economy*, in which reusable learning objects are widely available and easily applicable for different e-learning systems and different instructional purposes, should reduce the development costs significantly (ADL Technical Team, 2001). Furthermore, there have been proposals to develop intelligent tools that use learning objects to automatically construct learning activities in real time for a particular instructional setting (ADL Technical Team, 2001; Fletcher & Dodds, 2000).

Despite the expected benefits of reusable learning objects, the potential to overcome the developmental bottlenecks has certainly not been realized yet. If learning objects are reused at all, it is mostly at the level of clip art (Wiley, 1999), wherein low-level media components such as graphics and videos are applied in another setting. In this chapter, we analyze causes and propose possible solutions for the general lack of reuse within the instructional technology community. The structure of the chapter is as follows. First, the current technological approach to learning objects is described. This approach is generally consistent with a traditional analytical pedagogical view. Relatively small obstacles for reuse are described with respect to the metadata problem, the arrangement problem, and the exchange problem. Second, a more powerful holistic pedagogical view is described, which is currently dominating the field of instructional design. This view is *not* consistent with the current technological approach. Relatively large obstacles for reuse are described with respect to the context problem, the pedagogical function problem, and the correspondence problem. Third, an integrative approach that stresses re-editing instead of reuse, intermediate instead of final products, templates instead of instantiations, and technical automation of what can be automated is presented as a possible solution to overcome both small and large obstacles to reuse. The chapter ends with a general discussion, stressing the need to reconcile the fields of learning technologies and instructional design.

A TECHNOLOGICAL APPROACH TO LEARNING OBJECTS

The concept of reusable learning objects is intended to satisfy organizational, technical, and economical demands. From an organizational viewpoint, there is a growing need for flexible education, that is, time- and place-independent delivery methods as well as close monitoring of learning processes for pedagogical (assessment and personalization) and financial (billing) reasons. From a technical viewpoint, vendors of e-learning systems and content providers strive for interoperability and portability because their clients demand that investments in e-learning are *future proof*. Thus, it should be possible to interconnect different e-learning systems (i.e., interoperability) and to use the same learning content for different e-learning systems (i.e., portability or interchangeability). From an economic viewpoint, it is believed that an open market for wide exchange of learning content is beneficial for both providers (created once, sold many) and purchasers (bought once, used many).

These organizational, technical, and economical demands, instead of pedagogical requirements, dominate the current field of learning technologies. Learning objects are expected to enable a more cost-effective process of developing, managing, and delivering learning content. This section first describes the characteristics of learning objects according to the technological approach. Second, it is argued that this technological approach is only consistent with a traditional, analytical pedagogical view. Third, the main problems with the use of learning objects within this analytical pedagogical framework are described.

What Are Learning Objects?

Most authors agree that learning objects are digital units of information with an instructional purpose. The main principle underlying learning objects is the building-block method. Each learning object can be combined with every other learning object. This is somewhat similar to the assembling of LEGO bricks and is therefore referred to as the LEGO method (Ackermann, 1996). In a critique of this method, Wiley (2000) cites the same comparison, describing three similarities between properties of learning objects and LEGO bricks. First, LEGO bricks can be combined with any other LEGO bricks, regardless of their size, color, or shape. Second, LEGO bricks can be assembled in any manner desired. Third, combining LEGO bricks is easy, so that everyone is able to create something new. This metaphor illustrates the potential of building blocks to flexibly and easily create new structures. However, it is an overly simplified metaphor, as argued by Wiley (2000) and explained later in this article.

The external structure of learning objects must be standardized in order to be able to use them as true building blocks and reach the desired interoperability and portability. *Learning technology standards* are intended to ensure that learning objects will be developed, organized, and distributed in a uniform manner (Hamel & Ryan-Jones, 2002). There are many organizations and initiatives for the development of learning technology standards, including: (a) official standards bodies such as ISO, CEN/ISSS, ANSI, and NEN; (b) user organizations like the Aviation Industry CBT Committee (AICC) and the IEEE, with a Learning Technology Standards Committee that developed the Learning Object Metadata standard (LOM); (c) government-sponsored initiatives like the Advanced Distributed Learning (ADL) initiative; and (d) consortia of vendors, publishers, and educational organizations such as the IMS Global Learning Consortium and the Dublin Core Metadata Initiative. The standards that have been developed and proposed by these different organizations and initiatives are not really certified yet. They are really specifications that are still under construction and continuously changing.

It is important to note that current standards initiatives focus on learning *content* and, in particular, the following three aspects. First, they prescribe the connecting structure between different learning objects, that is, how they can be (re)combined. Second, they prescribe the communication structure between learning objects and e-learning systems, that is, how a content management system or delivery system should use the learning objects. Third, they prescribe the metadata fields for learning objects, that is, how the objects should be labeled by means of *tags*. Pedagogical issues are hardly dealt with in the standardization of structure, communication, and metadata—often because the claim is made that standardization should be "pedagogically neutral." However, even a neutral approach should offer the opportunity to implement a wide variety of instructional methods in such a way that interoperability and portability is warranted. A first attempt to do this is by describing a generic instructional structure for learning objects by means of an educational modeling language (EML) (Koper, 2003; Koper & Manderveld, 2004), which provided the input for the Learning Design group of the IMS Global Learning Consortium (IMS-LD) (Koper, Olivier, & Anderson, 2002). Although IMS-LD is still pedagogically neutral, it offers possibilities to implement instructional methods in a standardized fashion.

To summarize, learning objects are mainly technical building blocks to create larger structures in a flexible way. Remaining problems deal with the boundaries of definition and the standardization of the technical structure to enable (re)combination of learning objects. For an outsider, it is very hard to determine if learning content is properly standardized because the complexity of standards makes them useful for specialists only; hard test mechanisms are seldom present, and the interrelationships between different standards for different aspects of learning objects are often unclear. More importantly, problems exist with regard to the pedagogical poverty of learning objects. This is further discussed in the next sections.

The Technological Approach Only Fits an Analytical Pedagogical View

The technological approach to learning objects, described in the previous section, is fully consistent with an analytical pedagogical view that has previously been labeled the "world of knowledge" (van Merriënboer & Kirschner, 2001; van Merriënboer, Seel, & Kirschner, 2002) and the *atomistic perspective* (Spector, 2001a). This analytical view is closely associated with instructional design (ID) as originally conceived by Gagné (1965). The common answer to the question "What are we to teach?" lies in taxonomies of learning outcomes, typically referring to particular knowledge elements (e.g., facts, concepts, rules, strategies, etc.). Taxonomies of learning outcomes have a long history, with the taxonomies of Bloom (1956; see also Anderson & Krathwohl, 2001) and Gagné (1965) still in wide use. Gagné (1965) also made clear that specific learning outcomes were typically determined on the basis of some kind of task analysis. He introduced the concept of a *learning hierarchy* as a means of task decomposition. This hierarchy holds that a more complex intellectual skill is at the top of the hierarchy with enabling skills at a lower level. Later instructional design models further refined taxonomies of learning (e.g., Merrill's performance–content matrix, 1983) and detailed the task-analytic procedures necessary for reaching a highly specific description of what to teach in terms of particular learning outcomes (e.g., Leshin, Pollock, & Reigeluth, 1992).

According to the analytic pedagogical view, the common answer to the question "How are we to teach?" rests on Gagné's idea of the *conditions of learning*. Many theories for the design of instruction, which were called first-generation instructional design models by Merrill, Li, and Jones (1990a, 1990b, 1992), presume that the optimal conditions for learning mainly depend on the goal of the learning process. By analyzing these goals, instructional designers can devise the instructional methods that will best achieve them. First-generation instructional design models assume that designers can describe a whole content domain in terms of learning goals and can then develop instruction for each of the learning goals, taking the optimal conditions of learning for each goal into account. For instance, in order to reach the goal of performing a particular procedure, one must describe the steps in the procedure, give one or more demonstrations of the procedure, and then ask the learner to perform the procedure and give immediate feedback on task performance. Goals other than performing a procedure, such as remembering a concept, applying a principle, or memorizing a fact, demand different instructional methods. This approach can easily be applied to the creation of learning objects. A typical example is the reusable learning object (RLO) strategy of CISCO, which explicitly assigns *one* learning goal directly to *one* learning object (CISCO White Paper, 2000). Because each learning object represents a particular, independent piece of instruction, it is possible to create larger instructional arrangements rather flexibly, by arranging and sequencing the learning objects either before learning takes place or in real time as learning activities occur.

In an epistemological sense, the analytic pedagogical view takes a scientific perspective that can be traced back to the publication in 1637 of Descartes's *Discourse on Method* (1637/1960), in which the process of dividing and subdividing a problem until small, immediately understandable parts are found is described (see also Spector, 2001b). But its major strength, namely, its analytic approach, is at the same time its major weakness. As argued by Wilson (1998), "the reduction of each phenomenon to its constituent elements, [is] followed by the use of the elements to *reconstitute* [italics added] the holistic properties of the phenomenon" (p. 146). This process of reconstitution works well for a limited set of elements, but for complex learning situations, instructional designers face extremely large sets of highly integrated knowledge elements (or, learning objects). They need to synthesize many instructional strategies that are all necessary to reach multiple learning goals. Although instructional design models that adhere to an analytical pedagogical view are very helpful for analyzing learning goals and apportioning these goals into their constituent elements, they provide far less guidance for synthesizing the large number of instructional strategies that may help to make learning more effective, efficient, and appealing. In our opinion, a holistic pedagogical view is needed to deal with complex learning situations. But before discussing this holistic view, we take a closer look at the relatively small practical problems that are associated with the use of learning objects within the analytical pedagogical framework.

Small Problems of Reuse

The current technological approach to learning objects nicely fits an analytical pedagogical view and will no doubt facilitate the future reuse of learning materials that adhere to this view. However, from a practical viewpoint there are three problems that need to be solved: (a) the metadata problem, (b) the arrangement problem, and (c) the exchange problem.

The *metadata problem* refers to the fact that it is difficult and extremely labor-intensive to specify metadata for all learning objects. First, there is a lively discussion on the amount of necessary metadata fields. If a developer of an object fills out too few fields, other developers, searching for objects, will probably be overwhelmed with a large amount of possibly relevant learning objects. Morever, using more fields heavily increases the workload associated with the specification of learning objects. Although using many metadata fields may help other developers to find *exactly* what they want, it reduces the chance that they find anything at all because the chance that an object has the features *a, b,* and *c* is smaller than the change that it has only the features *a* and *b*. Furthermore, there is also discussion on the nature of the metadata. For instance, well-defined metadata fields make it difficult or even impossible for individual developers to express their intentions unambiguously, whereas loosely defined fields yield communication problems between developers and, eventually, between e-learning systems.

The *arrangement problem* refers to the fact that combining and sequencing learning objects into larger arrangements is not always easy and self-evident. This can be illustrated by the LEGO metaphor. This analogy only applies to the basic LEGO bricks, which are only appropriate to build simple structures. For building more complex structures, one requires the equivalent of more advanced LEGO bricks, as found in Technical LEGO (e.g., axles, gearwheels, receptors, programmable bricks, etc.). In contrast to basic LEGO bricks, Technical LEGO elements differ in their external structures (i.e., the way they can be attached to each other) and thus *cannot* be combined with every other element. Also, they differ in their internal structures (i.e., the function of the element, like an axle or gearwheel) so that they can only be combined into certain arrangements to form bigger elements. This illustrates that differences between learning objects can prevent valid arrangements. For instance, if two learning objects differ in their external structures because they yield incommensurable assessment information (e.g., one is using American A–B–C grading, the other the European 10-point scale), they cannot easily be combined into a valid arrangement. As an example for difference in internal structure, two learning objects (e.g., an annotated picture and a piece of text) may together yield an invalid arrangement because in one learning object another word is used to refer to the same thing as in the other object (e.g., the word "screen" is used in the annotated figure and the word "monitor" is used in the piece of text), which will make the arrangement very confusing for the learner. With regard to the arrangement problem, it may even be argued that only large instructional arrangements like complete lessons or courses can be reused effectively (Wiley, 2000).

The *exchange problem* refers to the fact that it may be difficult to exchange learning objects between developers and e-learning systems. From a psychological viewpoint, the readiness to share learning objects is not self-evident, as this implies access for others to personal notions and ideas. This raises a psychological threshold for developers to let others reuse their materials. But the other side of the coin is that others do not easily accept objects that were not developed by them, something known as the "not-invented-here" syndrome. Second, organizational factors like security policies (e.g., for military information) and infrastructure (e.g., firewalls that prevent using plug-ins or java applets) may prohibit an effective exchange of learning objects. Third, current regulations concerning intellectual property rights (IPRs) often limit the sharing of learning objects.

The popular opinion in the field of learning objects is that the problems just discussed will be solved in the forthcoming years by new technical solutions, organizational agreements, and juridical clarifications. However, there is a more fundamental issue related to the learning technology standards that define the structure of learning objects. Just as instructional design models have their own ecology (Edmonds, Branch, & Mukherjee, 1994), learning technology standards also have their own ecology, that is, a context within which they are developed and function. Applying learning objects structured according to a particular standard into a new context, without considering contextual differences, can violate this ecology and lead to a mismatch. For example, a standard like ADL-SCORM is developed in a governmental and military setting, and provides a means to package, describe, sequence, and deliver web pages for use by a *single* learner. So one must carefully consider if it is appropriate to apply ADL-SCORM in an academic context that emphasizes collaborative learning, such as is found in many problem-based learning models (Norman & Schmidt, 1992). Such contextual problems with learning objects also play a central role if one takes a holistic pedagogical viewpoint. The next section discusses pedagogical approaches that stress the use of integrative learning tasks and related problems with learning objects.

A HOLISTIC PEDAGOGICAL VIEW ON LEARNING OBJECTS

A technological approach to learning objects is fully consistent with an analytical pedagogical view. However, this analytical pedagogical view has been heavily criticized since the late 1980s. Most recent theories of instruction tend to focus on authentic learning tasks that are based on real-life tasks as the driving force for learning (Merrill, 2002; Reigeluth, 1999). The general assumption is that such authentic tasks help learners to integrate the knowledge, skills, and attitudes necessary for effective task performance; give them the opportunity to learn to coordinate constituent skills that make up complex task performance; and eventually enable them to transfer what is learned to their daily life or work settings. This focus on authentic, whole tasks can be found in practical educational approaches, such as project-based education, the case method, problem-based learning, and competency-based learning, and in theoretical models, such as Collins, Brown, and Newman's (1989) theory of cognitive apprenticeship learning, Jonassen's (1999) theory of constructive learning environments, Nelson's (1999) theory of collaborative problem solving, and Schank's theory of goal-based scenario's (Schank, Berman, & MacPerson, 1999).

All these theories share a holistic pedagogical view. This section first describes this holistic view and contrasts it with the analytic view. Second, the holistic view is illustrated by one particular design theory, namely, van Merriënboer's (1997) four-component instructional design model. Its implications for the conceptualization of learning objects are explored. Finally, the relatively large problems that are associated with the use of learning objects within a holistic pedagogical framework are described.

The Holistic Pedagogical View

The holistic pedagogical view originates from the world of work (van Merriënboer & Kirschner, 2001; van Merriënboer, Seel, & Kirschner, 2002). The common answer to the what-to-teach question lies in a description of real-life or professional tasks. This view is best associated with the social-constructivist paradigm, based on the idea that learners primarily construct knowledge based on their own mental and social activity. Constructivism holds that in order to learn, learning needs to be situated in problem solving in real-life, authentic contexts (Brown, Collins, & Duguid, 1989) where the environment is rich in information and where there are often no answers that are simply right or wrong.

In answering the how-to-teach question, a holistic view on learning assumes that complex knowledge and skills are best learnt through cognitive apprenticeship on the part of the learner in a rich environment (Collins, 1988). Experiences are provided for the learners that mimic the apprenticeship programs of adults in trades, or teachers in internship. Although it is not possible to immerse the learner to the extent that a traditional internship would imply, through the use of simulations and meaningful experiences, the learner would learn the ways of knowing of an expert. Meaning is negotiated through interactions with others where multiple perspectives on reality exist (von Glasersfeld, 1988). Reflexivity is essential and must be nurtured (Barnett, 1997a, 1997b). Finally, all of this is best—and possibly only—achieved when learning takes place in ill-structured domains (Spiro, Coulson, Feltovich, & Anderson, 1988).

The philosophical roots of this pedagogical view can be traced back to holism, which dominated classical Greek philosophy, then became less popular, but reemerged in the last half of the 20th century (e.g., in Forrester's work on system dynamics, 1961). The main problem of a holistic approach is how to deal with complexity. Most authors introduce some notion of "modeling" to attack this problem. For instance, Spector's (2001b) framework for model-facilitated learning (MFL) suggests that there must always be a number of phases in learning, with a graduated progression from concrete experiences toward more abstract reasoning and hypothetical problem solving. Achtenhagen's (2001) notion of "modeling the model" prescribes a two-step approach to pedagogical modeling, namely, modeling reality and then modeling those models of reality from a pedagogical perspective. This modeling of the model for instructional purposes allows the designer to determine which elements of the original model can be omitted, and which elements can be made abundant (not in the original, but introduced for supporting the functions of the model). Van Merriënboer's four-component instructional design model (for short, 4C/ID model; van Merriënboer, 1997; van Merriënboer, Clark, & de Croock, 2002) also offers a range of instructional methods to deal with complexity. This model is described in more detail in the next section.

4C/ID Model and Learning Objects

As an exponent of the holistic view, the 4C/ID model emphasizes whole, meaningful learning tasks as the driving force for learning. Three other components are distinguished in the blueprint for an educational program, resulting in its four components:

1. *Learning tasks.* Concrete, authentic and meaningful whole-task experiences that are provided to learners.
2. *Supportive information.* Information that is helpful to the learning and performance of nonroutine aspects of learning tasks, explaining how a domain is organized and how to approach tasks or problems in this domain.
3. *Procedural information.* Information that is prerequisite to the learning and performance of routine aspects of learning tasks, giving a specification of how to perform those aspects.
4. *Part-task practice.* Additional repetitive practice for routine aspects that need to be performed at a very high level of automaticity after the training.

The 4C/ID model reduces complexity in three ways: (a) with scaffolding, which is related to the learning tasks; (b) with optimal timing of information presentation, which is related to the supportive and procedural information; and (c) by supporting the automation of routine task aspects, which is related to part-task practice (van Merriënboer, Kirschner, & Kester, 2003). With regard to *scaffolding,* a further distinction is made between simple-to-complex sequencing and learner support. The designer uses so-called *task classes* to sequence learning tasks from simple to complex. The first task class contains learning tasks that are representative of the simplest tasks professionals encounter in the real world. Each subsequent task class contains learning tasks of a higher complexity. Learning tasks within the same task class are equally difficult and can be performed on the basis of the same body of knowledge, but these learning tasks vary on the same dimensions that occur in the real world. As in cognitive apprentice-ship learning, learner support will be high for the initial learning tasks in the same task class, but diminish as learners acquire more expertise for this particu-lar category of tasks (Collins et al., 1989). Learner support can be fully inte-grated with the learning tasks (e.g., learners start with studying given solutions or examples, then complete partial solutions, and finally have to solve problems independently) or take the form of external support structures, such as process worksheets that divide the problem-solving process in phases and ask guiding questions that may help to complete each phase.

With regard to the *timing of information presentation*, the basic idea is that performing the learning tasks is simplified if relevant information is presented just in time. Supportive information mainly pertains to models explaining how the content domain is organized (mental-model information) and strategies and heuristics explaining how to approach problems in this domain (cognitive-strat-egy information). It is thus *generalized* information that helps to perform the nonroutine aspects of a set of equivalent learning tasks, or tasks within the same task class. Therefore, supportive information is best presented before learners start to work on the learning tasks belonging to one task class and kept available throughout the training program. For each subsequent task class, additional or elaborated supportive information is presented to enable the learners to perform the more complex version of the whole task. Procedural information, in contrast, is presented just in time to perform the routine aspects of the learning task at hand. It is highly *specific* information that is best presented precisely when learn-ers need it to perform the consistent aspects of the learning task. It preferably takes the form of direct, step-by-step, or how-to instruction and is quickly faded away for subsequent learning tasks.

With regard to the *automation of routine aspects*, part-task practice may also help to simplify the performance of the learning tasks. The whole-task approach that is characteristic of the 4C/ID model implies that routine aspects of perfor-mance are, if possible, not trained separately but only practiced in the context of whole learning tasks. However, if a very high level of automaticity is desired for particular routine aspects, the learning tasks may not provide enough practice to reach this level because the responsible learning process (i.e., strengthening) re-quires large amounts of repetition that is not available. For those aspects, addi-tional part-task practice may be provided—such as children drilling multi-plication tables or musicians practicing musical scales. According to the 4C/ID model, additional part-task practice starts only after the learners have been intro-duced to the routine aspects in the context of the learning tasks, so that part-task practice takes place in a fruitful cognitive context allowing learners to identify the activities that are required to integrate the routine aspects in the whole task. Part-task practice may be beneficial to whole-task learning because it automates routine aspects and frees up processing resources that can subsequently be de-voted to the problem solving and reasoning aspects of the learning tasks (i.e., nonroutine aspects).

Holistic instructional design models, such as the 4C/ID model, result in instructional programs that are made up of a highly interrelated set of elements. Consequently, learning objects can be typified as a learning task, supportive information, a case study, a task class, and so forth. Figure 4.1 provides an overview of the main types of elements or "learning objects" that can be distinguished in a training blueprint developed according to the 4C/ID model (using UML notation; see Arlow & Neustadt, 2002).

It should be clear that such learning objects can only be used in a meaningful way if they are applied within a particular context, if they fulfill the particular pedagogical function they are designed for, and if they are combined with specific other elements. These issues are further discussed in the next section.

Large Problems of Reuse

Although the holistic pedagogical view is dominant in the current field of instructional design (Merrill, 2002; Reigeluth, 1999), it is not yet sufficiently recognized in the field of learning technologies (see Spector & Anderson, 2000, where there is explicit recognition of the holistic view). This is not surprising, because a holistic view causes some fundamental problems for the use of learning objects. At least three problems, which are manageable in the analytical pedagogical view, become urgently problematic in the holistic pedagogical view: (a) the context problem, (b) the pedagogical function problem, and (c) the correspondence problem.

The *context problem* refers to the fact that effective learning objects cannot be created in isolation, without an implicit or explicit instructional setting, target group, and other contextual descriptors. This may seriously hinder reuse. Suppose, for example, that a learning object is created consisting of a picture of a piece of machinery, one part of the machine that is highlighted by color coding, and an explanatory text for this highlighted part. This learning object can be effectively used for a presentation, but not for a test because the explanatory text may not be used as feedback (i.e., another pedagogical purpose); it can be effectively used for individual e-learning but not for teacher-led instruction because the explanatory text may be redundant with the explanation of the teacher and deteriorate learners' performance (i.e., another instructional setting causing the so-called redundancy effect; see Sweller, van Merriënboer, & Paas, 1998), and it can be effectively used for most learners but not for the color-blind because of the color coding (i.e., another target group). In sum, this implies that every learning object has its own context specificity, which makes it hard to apply it in a context other than that for which it was originally created.

The *pedagogical function problem* refers to the fact that it is difficult to express the pedagogical intentions for a learning object by means of technical properties such as metadata, leading to suboptimal reuse. Properties like size or format can be sufficiently described in metadata, but the pedagogical function is hard to specify. First, this is caused by the fact that learning objects can often fulfill different functions. For instance, according to Merrill's component display theory (1983) a pho-

54

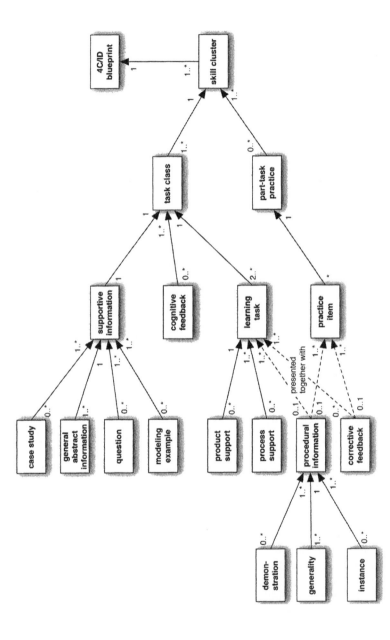

FIG. 4.1.   An overview of the main elements in a training blueprint developed according to the 4C/ID model (the four components are high-lighted). Normal arrows represent part-of relations; the numbers indicate the multiplicities (e.g., a task class may consist of 1 to many learning tasks; a learning task may be part of only 1 task class). Dotted arrows represent other specified relationships.

tograph of an eagle can be used as an *example* or instance of the concept "bird," as a *test item* where learners must classify the bird as an eagle, as an *alternate representation* of a textual description of an eagle, and so on. Furthermore, the pedagogical function of one learning object may require other complimentary learning objects, which may or may not be available to the developer. For instance, the pedagogical function of the photograph of the eagle may be that of an example, but this requires the joint availability of another learning object with the pedagogical function of a generality (i.e., a definition of the concept "bird").

The *correspondence problem* is probably the most obstinate problem we are facing because it touches the heart of the holistic pedagogical view. According to the analytic view, particular learning objects correspond with particular parts of the learning domain, which are often specified by single learning goals (i.e., one-to-one correspondence). An arrangement of learning objects and associated learning goals will always cover the whole domain. In contrast, the holistic view stresses the indivisible nature of the learning domain. Particular learning objects do not correspond with particular parts of the learning domain, but rather evoke actions from the learner to construct an increasingly more complex cognitive representation of this domain. As a rule, different learning objects thus aim at the construction of one and the same representation (i.e., many-to-one correspondence). For instance, cognitive flexibility theory (Spiro, Feltovitch, Jacobson, & Coulson, 1991) stresses that multiple perspectives of the same phenomenon are necessary to reach a rich representation of a domain, which is transferable to new situations. In the same line of reasoning, the 4C/ID model stresses that multiple learning tasks, which vary on dimensions that also vary in the real world, are necessary to reach an effective cognitive representation that allows for the performance of complex tasks. Consequently, a developer working from a holistic viewpoint will typically search not for one particular learning object but for a set of learning objects (e.g., perspectives, learning tasks, models) that is meaningfully interrelated and aimed at the construction of *one* rich cognitive representation.

In summary, the context problem, pedagogical function problem, and correspondence problem block an effective reuse of learning objects in development projects that reflect a holistic pedagogical viewpoint. Although the smaller problems associated with an analytical pedagogical view will probably be solved in the forthcoming years, the larger problems of the holistic pedagogical approach are fundamental and require a major rethinking of the nature of learning objects. The next section discusses an integrative approach to overcome both small and large problems.

SMALL PROBLEMS, LARGE PROBLEMS, AND PRELIMINARY SOLUTIONS

The previous sections discussed a highly divergent set of problems that limit the possible reuse of instructional materials. This section proposes four directions to overcome these problems: (a) Focus on reedit instead of reuse; (b) apply intermediate analysis and design products as learning objects; (c) emphasize templates instead of concrete instantiations; and (d) technically automate what can be automated. As can be seen in Table 4.1, there is not one single solution for all problems. Instead, a multipath solution is proposed, taking several directions to facilitate desired reuse. There is not one direction to solve each problem; each proposed direction solves more than one problem, but all problems will only be solved if several directions are taken simultaneously.

Reedit Instead of Reuse

Too often, reuse is interpreted as simply using a learning object again—without making any changes to it. Alternatively, reuse can be interpreted as changing learning objects in order to meet new requirements. Actually, this is what most teachers do with traditional instructional materials. Teachers gather useful articles, books, graphics, and other learning materials, which they then alter, shorten, annotate, and embellish for use in their own lessons. A focus on such reediting instead of simple reuse may help to solve both small and large problems.

With regard to the small problems, reediting increases the chance that the developer finds something useful, because it becomes less important to find exactly

TABLE 4.1

Small Problems, Large Problems and Proposed Solutions to Facilitate Reuse

	Proposed solutions			
	Reedit Instead of Reuse	Intermediate Instead of Final Products	Templates Instead of Instantiations	Automate What Can Be Automated
Small problems of reuse				
Metadata problem	+			+
Arrangement problem	+	+	+	
Exchange problem	+		+	
Large problems of reuse				
Context problem	+	+	+	+
Pedagogical function problem	+	+		
Correspondence problem		+		

Note. A plus sign indicates that a particular solution is believed to contribute to solving a particular problem.

what is wanted. In other words, reediting diminishes the metadata problem because it makes it easier to reach a match between the metadata of the stored learning object and the reduced set of metadata specified by the developer who is searching for this object. Reediting also affects the arrangement problem because it is possible to change objects in such a way that they agree with each other. For instance, if one object applies the American A–B–C grading and another object the European 10-point scale, one object can be edited to make them both compatible. Finally, reediting simplifies the exchange or *sharing* of learning objects between developers and between e-learning systems. Especially, the not-invented-here syndrome becomes less important because developers have the freedom to make any desired changes and so develop a sense of ownership.

With regard to the large problems, reediting diminishes the context problem because the possibility to reedit the learning object opens the option to make them context specific. For example, a learning object consisting of a picture of a piece of machinery, one part of the machine that is highlighted by color coding, and an explanatory text for this highlighted part can easily be changed in order to make it effective for color-blind learners (e.g., by enhancing the contrast between the highlighted part and its background). Along the same lines, reediting also positively affects the pedagogical function problem. In the preceding example, it would for instance be possible to reedit the learning object that is designed for presentation in such a way that it becomes a test item (e.g., by removing the explanatory text). Summarizing, a focus on reediting instead of simply reusing learning objects may help to solve most of the identified problems. However, a very important condition for taking this direction would be that learning objects are available as *open source code* or *open content*.

Intermediate Instead of Final Products

Although learning objects are generally defined as digital units of information with an instructional purpose, they are typically limited to the final products that can be directly presented to learners. Of course, there are many other information units with an instructional purpose, such as the results of a contextual analysis, target group analysis, or task analysis; descriptions of performance and instructional objectives for a particular lesson or course; a blueprint including learning activities providing the basis for the development of instructional materials; and so forth. These intermediate products contain rich information that describes the final products for which they were made, but they are suitable for reuse as well.

With regard to the small problems, intermediate products may help to solve the arrangement problem because they provide insight in valid arrangements and so guide the selection and sequencing of final products. For example, if the result of a task analysis (i.e., intermediate product) provides an ordered sequence of decision steps, this facilitates the search and arrangement of demonstrations (i.e., final products) for each step. If a list of instructional objectives (i.e., intermediate product) is available for a new educational program, this facilitates the search and arrangement of courses (i.e., final products) that constitute the program.

With regard to the large problems, intermediate products may help to solve the context problem because they provide rich information about the final products, which facilitates the finding of learning objects that exactly fit a new context. Actually, the intermediate products can fulfill the same role as the metadata that are specified for final products, but they are expected to be more effective because they provide more content-related information. For instance, if a developer is searching for a picture of a particular type of milling machine, the result of a task analysis on milling (i.e., intermediate product) will be very helpful for finding the most effective picture (i.e., final product) because it indicates the controls and displays that need to be operated by the learners and, therefore, should be visible in the picture. Typically, this type of information (i.e., which displays and controls are visible on the machine) is *not* part of the picture's metadata. Furthermore, intermediate products may also help to solve the pedagogical function problem because they can provide rich information that helps the developer to determine which pedagogical functions can or cannot be fulfilled by a final product. For instance, if in our example the result from the task analysis allows the developer to determine that *all* controls and displays that are necessary to operate the milling machine are visible on the picture, he or she may decide to use this picture not as an illustration but as a test, in which the learner must describe the steps and simultaneously point out the necessary controls and displays for operating the machine.

Probably the most important added value of intermediate products is that they may help to solve the correspondence problem. According to the holistic pedagogical view, an interrelated set of final products is necessary to evoke multiple actions from the learner that yield one rich cognitive representation of the domain (many-to-one correspondence). The intermediate products enable a better search for *sets* of final products because they specify how the final products are meaningfully interrelated. For example, an intermediate product may be a 4C/ID training blueprint that specifies a sequence of task classes for a complex skill such as searching for literature (see van Merriënboer, Clark, & de Croock, 2002). Each task class precisely specifies the requirements and criteria for learning tasks that fit this task class, and will thus simplify the finding of suitable learning tasks, that is, final products such as cases, concrete problems, or simulation exercises. If, for example, a "searching-for-literature" training program was developed for psychology students, with learning tasks from the psychology domain, this program could relatively easily be adapted to another domain because the domain-independent requirements for the learning tasks are exactly described. Summarizing, a focus on intermediate instead of final products may help to solve particularly the larger problems of reuse. An important condition is that developers carefully document such intermediate products in a digital form, preferably in databases that interrelate intermediate and final products. Computer-based instructional design tools may help to do so (for an example of such a tool based on the 4C/ID model, see de Croock, Paas, Schlanbusch, & van Merriënboer, 2002).

Templates Instead of Instantiations

Teachers not only reedit instructional materials for use in their own lessons, but they also make ample use of implicit or explicit templates. For instance, teachers use templates: for organizing their lessons (e.g., presenting content, providing practice with feedback, discussing results, etc.); for reaching particular types of instructional objectives (e.g., to support learning a procedure, state the general steps of procedure, provide several demonstrations, require learners to perform the procedure, and so on in accordance with component display theory; see Merrill, 1983); and for designing computer screens for their e-learning lessons. A focus on templates instead of instantiations may increase the effectiveness of reuse. A similar orientation on templates can be found in object-oriented programming (OOP), which offers a solution for dealing with highly complex development processes by decomposing the software into independent units that can be easily reused because they abstract away from many details (Booch, 1994).

With regard to small problems, templates may help to solve the arrangement and exchange problem. The arrangement problem is diminished because templates can offer better opportunities than instantiations to make valid combinations of learning objects. For instance, two instantiations of which one uses the American A–B–C grading system and the other uses the European 10-point grading system are difficult to combine in one arrangement. If instead of two instantiations two templates were used, offering the opportunity to specify the required grading system (e.g., by selecting it from a list of possible options), there would be no arrangement problem because one could simply specify the same grading system for each learning object. Furthermore, the exchange problem and, in particular, the not-invented-here syndrome are at least partly solved because developers are expected to specify the instantiations according to their preferences. Like reediting, such specification will help to develop a sense of ownership.

With regard to large problems, templates partly solve the context problem because the context-sensitive information need not be in the template but only in the instantiation of this template. They offer the developer the opportunity to specify the context-sensitive information. For instance, if a developer is using a template for reaching an instructional objective of the type "using a procedure" (i.e., give general steps of procedure, give several demonstrations, ask learner for demonstrations), the developer may specify a demonstration that is explained in English for one context or target group, and a demonstration that is explained in another language for another context or target group. Summarizing, a focus on templates instead of instantiations may help to solve the arrangement, exchange, and context problem. However, an important implication is that templates should contain as little contextual information as possible, so that the developer can specify precisely this context-specific information.

Automate What Can Be Automated

Advancements in information technology may also offer facilities that support reuse of instructional materials. Machines now perform more and more tasks that in the past could only be performed by humans, and this is especially beneficial for processing large amounts of information. With regard to small problems, the best example pertains to metadata creation and exchange. Current research (Boot & Veerman, 2003) aims at the development of algorithms for the automatic analysis of multimedia content and the semantic indexing of this content in metadata fields. Such automation is not only more cost-effective but may also yield more objective metadata than indexing by hand. Another approach is the use of a resource description framework (RDF) to develop different vocabularies of metadata. RDF is an infrastructure that provides the foundation for metadata interoperability across different resource description communities (Miller, 1998). If different metadata vocabularies adhere to RDF, learning objects that are labeled with metadata from one vocabulary can also be found if they are searched for with metadata labels from another vocabulary. OWL, which is developed as a vocabulary extension of RDF, is an example of a semantic web ontology language that enables the sharing of ontologies on the World Wide Web (Bechhofer et al., 2003).

With regard to large problems, one example pertains to automatic translation as a way to diminish the context problem. On the one hand, translations from speech to written text (i.e., speech recognition) and from written text to speech (i.e., speech synthesis) may increase reuse between target groups. On the other hand, translations between different languages may increase reuse between regions.

DISCUSSION

This chapter first discussed the current technological approach to reusable learning objects. This approach is fully consistent with a traditional, analytical pedagogical view resting on the assumption that a learning domain can be described in terms of relatively independent learning goals or pieces of content. Despite some problems pertaining to the specification of metadata and the arrangement and exchange of learning objects, it is concluded that the current technological approach may help to increase the flexibility of education, improve the technical interoperability and interchangeability, and increase the cost-effectiveness of the development process. However, this only seems to work well for relatively simple learning domains that can be decomposed into independent parts. If complex learning is at stake, that is, if learning is directed toward reaching highly integrated sets of learning goals, the technological approach falls short.

A holistic pedagogical view, with a focus on authentic learning tasks as the driving force for learning, currently replaces the analytic view to allow for complex learning. Such a holistic pedagogical view is not sufficiently sustained by the current technological approach to learning objects because it causes additional problems that are very hard to solve. These fundamental problems pertain to the fact that learning objects cannot fully be isolated from their context, are always associated with a particular pedagogical function, and may need corresponding objects to reach one and the same (integrated) learning goal. Consequently, a major rethinking of the nature of reusable learning objects is required. Four future directions were discussed: (a) Focus on reediting instead of on plain reuse of learning objects; (b) emphasize the reuse of intermediate instead of final design products; (c) use templates instead of instantiations as learning objects; and (d) technically automate those aspects of reuse that can be automated. Taken together, these directions may yield a more powerful approach to reuse.

The most important implication of the proposed approach concerns the future relationship between the field of learning technologies and the field of instructional design. In the field of learning technologies, on the one hand, the focus has mostly been on technical, organizational, and economical issues. Proposals for learning objects largely neglected pedagogical issues, claiming the importance of pedagogically neutral standards. However, an undesirable effect is that learning technologies sustain traditional pedagogical models that rest on an analytic approach, but not the more recent pedagogical models that rest on a holistic approach and aim at complex learning. In the field of instructional design, on the other hand, the focus has mostly been on pedagogical issues. The questions of how particular pedagogical models can be technically realized, flexibly applied in different contexts, and developed in a cost-effective way have not been taken seriously enough. Therefore, too many educators and instructional designers view developments in the field of learning technologies as not directly relevant to their own work. They simply assume that their new pedagogical models will be sustained by new learning technologies and standards, but they seem to be unaware of the fact that those learning technologies may, in the worst case, block educational innovations instead of facilitate them.

In our opinion, successful educational innovations require a complete synthesis of instructional design theories and learning technologies. Pedagogical, technical, organizational, and economic factors cannot be isolated from each other but should always be studied in combination (see Jochems et al., 2003). The importance of such an integrated approach to e-learning and learning objects should not be underestimated because there are vital interests for many different stakeholders, and the investments are huge in terms of money, time, and manpower. We hope that the future directions discussed in this chapter promote a holistic pedagogical view on complex learning and at the same time help to close the gap between the fields of learning technologies and instructional design.

ACKNOWLEDGMENTS

The authors thank Marcel de Croock and Peter Sloep for their thought-provoking and helpful comments on earlier drafts of this chapter.

REFERENCES

Achtenhagen, F. (2001). Criteria for the development of complex teaching-learning environments. *Instructional Science, 29,* 361–380.

Ackermann, P. (1996). *Developing object-oriented multimedia software.* Heidelberg, Germany: Verlag fur digitale Technologie GmbH.

ADL Technical Team. (2001). *Sharable Content Object Reference Model (SCORM™) Version 1.2. The SCORM overview.* Retrieved June 16, 2003, from http://www.adlnet.org

Anderson, L. W., & Krathwohl, D. R. (Eds.). (2001). *A taxonomy for learning, teaching and assessing: A revision of Bloom's taxonomy of educational objectives.* New York: Addison Wesley Longman.

Arlow, J., & Neustadt, I. (2002). *UML and the unified process: Practical object-oriented analysis and design.* Edinburgh, UK: Pearson Education.

Barnett, R. (1997a). *Towards a higher education for a new century.* London: University of London, Institute of Education.

Barnett, R. (1997b). *Higher education: A critical business.* Buckingham, UK: Open University Press.

Bechhofer, S., van Harmelen, F., Hendler, J., Horrocks, I., McGuinness, D. L., Patel-Schneider, P. F., & Lynn, A. S. (2003). OWL web ontology language reference. Retrieved October 3, 2003, from http://www.w3.org/TR/owl-ref

Bloom, B. S. (1956). *Taxonomy of educational objectives: Cognitive domain.* New York: David McKay.

Booch, G. (1994). *Object-oriented analysis and design with applications.* Redwood City, CA: Benjamin/Cummings.

Boot, E. W., & Veerman, A. L. (2003). Support tools for e-learning from a user perspective. *Proceedings of the 4th International Conference on Information Technology Based Higher Education,* 7–9 July 2003, Marrakech, Morocco.

Boot, E. W., Veerman, A. L., & van Merriënboer, J. J. G. (submitted). *Instructional development templates for domain experts.*

Brown, J. S., Collins, A., & Duguid, P. (1989). Situated cognition and the culture of learning. *Educational Researcher, 18*(1), 32–42.

CISCO White Paper. (2000). *Reusable learning object strategy: Definition, creation process, and guidelines for building.* Retrieved June 16, 2003, from http://www.digital pipe.com/pdf/dp/white_papers/e_learning/Cisco_rlo_roi.pdf

Collins, A. (1988). *Cognitive apprenticeship and instructional technology* (Tech. Rep. No. 6899). Cambridge, MA: BBN Labs, Inc.

Collins, A., Brown, J. S., & Newman, S. E. (1989). Cognitive apprenticeship: Teaching the craft of reading, writing and mathematics. In L. B. Resnick (Ed.), *Knowing, learning, and instruction: Essays in honor of Robert Glaser* (pp. 453–493). Hillsdale, NJ: Lawrence Erlbaum Associates.

de Croock, M. B. M., Paas, F., Schlanbusch, H., & van Merriënboer, J. J. G. (2002). ADAPTit: Tools for training design and evaluation. *Educational Technology, Research and Development, 50*(4), 47–58.

Descartes, R. (1960). *Discourse on the method for rightly conducting the reason and seeking truth in the sciences* (Trans. L. J. Lafleur). New York: Bobbs-Merrill. (Original work published 1637)

Edmonds, G. S., Branch, R. C., & Mukherjee, P. (1994). A conceptual framework for comparing instructional design models. *Educational Technology, Research and Development, 42*(2), 55–72.

Fletcher, J., & Dodds, P. (2000). *All about ADL*. ASTD Learning Circuits, May 2000. Retrieved June 16, 2003, from http://www.learningcircuits.org/may2000/fletcher.html

Forrester, J. W. (1961). *Industrial dynamics*. Cambridge, MA: MIT Press.

Gagné, R. M. (1965). *The conditions of learning*. New York: Holt, Rinehart, & Winston.

Hamel, C. J., & Ryan-Jones, D. (2002). Designing instruction with learning objects. *International Journal of Educational Technology* [online], *3*(1). Retrieved June 16, 2003, from http://www.ao.uiuc.edu/ijet/v3n1/hamel/index.html

Jochems, W., van Merriënboer, J. J. G., & Koper, E. J. R. (Eds.). (2003). *Integrated E-learning: Implications for pedagogy, technology, and organization*. London: RoutledgeFalmer.

Jonassen, D. H. (1999). Designing constructivist learning environments. In C. M. Reigeluth (Ed.), *Instructional design theories and models: A new paradigm of instructional theory* (Vol. II, pp. 371–396). Mahwah, NJ: Lawrence Erlbaum Associates.

Khan, B. H. (Ed.). (2001). *Web-based training*. Englewood Cliffs, NJ: Educational Technology Publications.

Koper, E. J. R. (2003). Combining re-usable learning resources and services to pedagogical purposeful units of learning. In A. Littlejohn (Ed.), *Reusing online resources: A sustainable approach to eLearning* (pp. 46–59). London: Kogan Page.

Koper, E. J. R., & Manderveld, J. M. (2004). Educational modelling language: Modelling reusable, interoperable, rich and personalised units of learning. *British Journal of Educational Technology, 35*, 537–552.

Koper, E. J. R., Olivier, B., & Anderson, T. (2002). *IMS learning design information model: Final*. Boston: IMS.

Leshin, C. B., Pollock, J., & Reigeluth, C. M. (1992). *Instructional design strategies and tactics*. Englewood Cliffs, NJ: Educational Technology Publications.

Locatis, C., & Al-Nuaim, H. (1999). Interactive technology and authoring tools: A historical review and analysis. *Educational Technology, Research and Development, 47*(3), 63–76.

Merrill, M. D. (1983). Component display theory. In C. M. Reigeluth (Ed.), *Instructional-design theories and models: An overview of their current status* (pp. 278–333). Hillsdale, NJ: Lawrence Erlbaum Associates.

Merrill, M. D. (2002). First principles of instruction. *Educational Technology, Research and Development, 50*(3), 43–59.

Merrill, M. D., Li, Z., & Jones, M. K. (1990a). Limitations of first generation instructional design (ID¹). *Educational Technology, 30*(1), 7–11.

Merrill, M. D., Li, Z., & Jones, M. K. (1990b). Second generation instructional design. *Educational Technology, 30*(2), 7–14.

Merrill, M. D., Li, Z., & Jones, M. K. (1992). An introduction to instructional transaction theory. In S. Dijkstra,, H. P. M. Krammer, & J. J. G. van Merriënboer (Eds.), *Instructional models in computer-based learning environments* (NATO ASI Series F, Vol. 104, pp. 15–41). Berlin, Germany: Springer Verlag.

Miller, E. (1998). An introduction to the Resource Description Framework. *Bulletin of the American Society for Information Science, 25*(1), 15–19.

Nelson, L. M. (1999). Collaborative problem solving. In C. M. Reigeluth (Ed.), *Instructional design theories and models: A new paradigm of instructional theory* (Vol. II, pp. 241–267). Mahwah, NJ: Lawrence Erlbaum Associates.

Norman, G. R., & Schmidt, H. G. (1992). The psychological basis of problem-based learning: A review of the evidence. *Academic Medicine, 67*(9), 557–565.

Reigeluth, C. M. (Ed.). (1999). *Instructional-design theories and models: A new paradigm of instructional theory* (Vol. 2). Mahwah, NJ: Lawrence Erlbaum Associates.

Rosenberg, M. J. (2000). *E-learning, strategies for delivering knowledge in the digital age.* New York: McGraw-Hill.

Schank, R. C., Berman, T. R., & Macpherson, K. A. (1999). Learning by doing. In C. M. Reigeluth (Ed.), *Instructional design theories and models: A new paradigm of instructional theory* (Vol. II, pp. 161–181). Mahwah, NJ: Lawrence Erlbaum Associates.

Spector, J. M. (2001a). Tools and principles for the design of collaborative learning environments for complex domains. *Journal of Structural Learning and Intelligent Systems, 14*(4), 483–510.

Spector, J. M. (2001b). Philosophical implications for the design of instruction. *Instructional Science, 29,* 381–402.

Spector, J. M., & Anderson, T. M. (2000). *Holistic and integrated perspectives on learning, technology, and instruction: Understanding complexity.* Mahwah, NJ: Lawrence Erlbaum Associates.

Spiro, R. J., Coulson, R. L., Feltovich, P. J., & Anderson, D. K. (1988). *Cognitive flexibility theory: Advanced knowledge acquisition in ill-structured domains* (Tech. Rep. No. 441). Champaign: University of Illinois, Center for the Study of Reading.

Spiro, R. J., Feltovich, P. J., Jacobson, M. J., & Coulson, R. L. (1991). Cognitive flexibility, constructivism and hypertext: Random access instruction for advanced knowledge acquisition in ill-structured domains. *Educational Technology, 31*(5), 24–33.

Sweller, J., van Merriënboer, J. J. G., & Paas, F. (1998). Cognitive architecture and instructional design. *Educational Psychology Review, 10*(3), 251–296.

van Merriënboer, J. J. G. (1997). *Training complex cognitive skills.* Englewood Cliffs, NJ: Educational Technology Publications.

van Merriënboer, J. J. G., Clark, R. E., & de Croock, M. B. M. (2002). Blueprints for complex learning: The 4C/ID*-model. *Educational Technology, Research and Development, 50*(2), 39–64.

van Merriënboer, J. J. G., & Kirschner, P. A. (2001). Three worlds of instructional design: State of the art and future directions. *Instructional Science, 29,* 429–441.

van Merriënboer, J. J. G., Kirschner, P. A., & Kester, L. (2003). Taking the load of a learners' mind: Instructional design for complex learning. *Educational Psychologist, 38*(1), 5–13.

van Merriënboer, J. J. G., & Martens, R. (Eds.). (2002). Computer-based tools for instructional design. *Educational Technology, Research and Development, 50*(4), special issue.

van Merriënboer, J. J. G., Seel, N. M., & Kirschner, P. A. (2002). Mental models as a new foundation for instructional design. *Educational Technology, 42*(2), 60–66.

von Glasersfeld, E. (1988). *Cognition, construction of knowledge, and teaching* (ERIC Document Reproduction Service No. ED 294–754).

Wiley, D. A. (1999). *Learning objects and the new CAI: So what do I do with a learning object?* [Online]. Retrieved June 16, 2003, from http://wiley.ed.usu.edu/docs/instruct-arch.pdf

Wiley, D. A. (2000). Connecting learning objects to instructional design theory: A definition, a metaphor, and a taxonomy. In D. A. Wiley (Ed.), *The instructional use of learning objects: Online version.* Retrieved June 16, 2003, from http://reusability.org/read/chapters/wiley.doc

Wilson, E. O. (1998). *Consilience: The unity of knowledge.* New York: Alfred A. Knopf.

Chapter
5

Designing Model-Centered Learning Environments: Hocus-Pocus or the Focus Must Strictly Be on Locus

Norbert M. Seel
Albert-Ludwigs-University of Freiburg

Looking ahead to the year 2000, Gustafson, Tillman, and Childs (1992) suggested that "we shall eventually find ourselves on the path toward a theory of instructional design" (p. 456) if instructional design (ID) is able to expand its intellectual basis in the not too distant future. However, 8 years later, in 2000 in an article in *Training Magazine* (Gordon & Zemke, 2000) the suggestion was made that ID in its current form is as good as dead because its foundation is not suitable for facing new societal and technological demands. The main argument against ID is that education and training must accommodate a diverse, widely distributed set of students who need to learn and transfer complex cognitive skills to an increasingly varied set of real-world contexts and settings. ID in its traditional form is considered by many incapable of meeting these requirements. Another argument against ID is that ID will be subsumed under the broader field of *information design* (Duchastel, 1999).

Actually, several paradigm shifts of psychology as well as new societal and technological demands have challenged ID as both a discipline and a technology in the past two decades. As a result, we can observe a substantial uncertainty in the field of ID with regard to its epistemological, psychological, and technological foundations. Nevertheless, in this same time period ID has continued to evolve, assimilating and advancing theories from psychology, systems theory, and communication technologies. Recent additions have been influenced by constructivism, situated cognition, e-learning approaches to distance education, and information theory. Ritchie and Earnest (1999) pointed out that "with each iteration, we enhance our understanding of how to impact the performance of individuals and organizations" (p. 35). Beyond this, I confess that *we sometimes must go back to the basics in order to go forward into the future*. A good way of demonstrating the effectiveness of such a strategy is provided by the constructivism-objectivism debate of the 1990s. Another example may consist in the discussion of Myers's (1999) rhetorical question, "Is there a place for instructional design in the information age?," initiated by Duchastel's (1999) provocative verdict.

If we reconsider the various trends of ID in the past decades, we can state that theories and models of ID come in different types and concern different worlds. In these different worlds, ideas about "how to help people learn better" lead to different answers to the two basic questions of ID: "what to teach" and "how to teach it" (cf. van Merriënboer, Seel, & Kirschner, 2002). Among others, M. David Merrill has contributed greatly to answering these questions. In this essay, written in honor of David Merrill, I focus on the instructional design of environments that aim at supporting model-centered learning. A central goal of this chapter is to demonstrate that environments that aim at discovery and exploratory learning must be carefully designed, even if they are implemented by means of new information and communication technologies. More specifically, in a first step I take up Duchastel's argument that ID will be subsumed in the future under the field of information design. I go back to the basics of information science in order to describe its basic understanding of the totality of learning processes as the construction of internal models of the environment. In the second section, I demonstrate that this understanding of learning corresponds to a large extent with the *mental model* approach that has evolved from cognitive constructivism and that characterizes my research in the past two decades. Accordingly, in the next section I describe the approach of model-centered learning and teaching for two instructional settings. In the final section I discuss the results of several empirical studies on model-centered learning and teaching with regard to ID.

IS THERE A PLACE FOR ID IN THE INFORMATION AGE?

To answer this question, Myers (1999) compared an ID approach and an information science approach side by side, arguing that information design only focuses on a part of ID. Nevertheless, Duchastel's argumentation can also be taken as a starting point for a look back at the 1960s, when information science evolved in the broader context of cybernetics and its various applications. Actually, in information science of this time we can find interesting ideas concerning learning and teaching that continue to be relevant for the design of learning environments today.

In information science, "information" is defined as a unit of measurement of the uncertainty of a message concerning an event's appearance. If a message is syntactically understood as a sequence of signs, then the *informational content* measures the effort necessary for the classification of the transmitted signs. Accordingly, the information is greater to the extent that the event is surprising. Thus, there is no information when the receiver can attend the signal with certainty. In this restricted sense, the information of a message has nothing to do with its relevance or centrality for the receiver. The two sentences "You have won first prize in the lottery" and "A hedgehog is nesting in the garden" may have the same amount of information, but the first message will be evaluated by the receiver as more important. This example shows that "information" is strongly associated with communication. Three aspects of *informational exchange* can be distinguished in this context:

- A *statistical aspect* of information exchange in the aforementioned sense.
- A *semantic aspect* of communication that culminates in the question of whether the receiver of a message can understand the meaning of the signals.
- A *pragmatic aspect*, associated with the question of whether the receiver of a message shows the (behavioral) change intended by the sender.

Educational and instructional processes are processes of communication. Accordingly, educational science is interested in communication itself, as well as in the resulting changes of consciousness. A basic assumption of information science is that communication primarily occurs by means of phonetic and written language (which also includes mathematical, technical, or other symbols as well as graphic diagrams). The information of a given text (a work of prose, a letter, an e-mail message, or text from a textbook) is to a large extent dependent on the receiver's expectations and knowledge. For example, a telegram with the sentence "Yesterday Peter arrived healthy" will have more information for the telegrapher who does not know anything about Peter than for the receiver who knows that the sender's wife has expected a baby and that the parents had chosen Peter or Karin as name for the baby. This example demonstrates that the (semantic) information of a message depends on the receiver's knowledge about factual relationships of the environment and situational circumstances of the message. This kind of information, called *subjective information*, varies depending on the different degrees of difficulty for learners of differing age, language competence and prior knowledge. This opens a series of relevant issues for ID. In the case where one knows the subjective information of a text, one can quantify the subjective difficulty of the material or of its comprehension. Moreover, on the basis of the subjective information of learning material one can specify the informational content of developed measurements of learning results. Finally, the measurement of subjective information also allows one to assess the cognitive processes occurring in the course of message perception.

In information science, the correlative to educational concepts such as learning material and objectives is related to the semantic level. Educational objectives are not independent. Rather, as we can learn from Merrill's work (Merrill, 1987, 1994, 2000), knowledge about facts, relations, principles, and concepts is a precondition for the formulation of objectives, such as the performance of mathematical operations, the analysis of particular problem classes, the constructive solution of defined tasks, or the application of rules. As a common characteristic of all general definitions of objectives, we can postulate that the acquisition and processing of material is either a transition phase or the desired final state of the teaching and learning process. The material itself is realized by means of text, books, bibliographies, and collections of tasks to be mastered. Usually, *the learning materials are well-prepared parts of very complex—and not necessarily consistent—systems of human knowledge and societal norms.* Even parts of materials are complex systems of findings, relations, and interconnections. The concrete task of instructional planning consists in the measurement of the informational content of any material, for example, concerning the mechanism of an electric motor, the way of life of salmon, or the content of the Potsdam agreement. For a verbalized text from a textbook one can determine the subjective information with regard to a particular group of addressees or students. A text that describes both completely and concisely the whole content of the material is called a *basal text*. From such a text, students can extract the entire content of teaching material—for example in self-study—if the students can apply the appropriate learning techniques.

However, individuals are typically not concerned with basal texts but rather with texts that are redundant and contain diagrams, summaries, and other messages aimed at facilitating its understanding. Typically, the texts students are provided within instruction are designed well to minimize the load of subjective information—that is to say, the effort necessary for understanding. Interestingly, we can currently find similar approaches in cognitive psychology, such as Sweller's "cognitive load theory" (cf. Sweller, Chandler, Tierney, & Cooper, 1990), which considers the mental effort necessary to master learning tasks as a central factor in the structuring of, for example, technical material. Sweller and others argue that "worked-out examples" may be helpful for mastering learning tasks (cf. Renkl, Stark, Gruber, & Mandl, 1998).

This leads to the question of the basic understanding of learning in information science. The focus of information science is evidently on *verbal learning*, which is defined as a process of information exchange between the learner and the environment. This information exchange occurs by means of communication and information processing. Accordingly, in the information science of the early 1960s we already can find the conception of learning as a complex procedure of information processing. Moreover, there were authors, such as Steinbuch (1961), who considered the totality of learning processes as the construction of *internal models* of the environment. They are conceived of as cognitive isomorphisms of the structured domains or elements of the environment. The isomorphism is considered to be a threshold value that can be approached through the internal models of a subject but that must not be reached. The threshold value of such an ideal model is that the elements B_j of the model B correspond with all elements A_j of the environmental domain A. Then, this correspondence must also exist between the relations between each element, making a change of the internal model isomorphic with a change of the environment and vice versa.

However, the construction of internal models should not be overemphasized as the construction of an internal model of the entire environment. Rather, the primary concern here is with the construction of partial models and structures that correspond to particular domains of the environments or its elements. Because internal models are built up they imply a transfer (i.e., transinformation) on the information of the environment. Such models can be deterministic and probabilistic models.

Interestingly, this conception of learning corresponds to a large extent with the approach of mental models that emerged in the early 1980s in cognitive science to capture logical thinking and situated cognition (Seel, 2001). An analysis of the literature indicates different main lines of research on mental models. Although Johnson-Laird (1983) emphasized the specific role of mental models for deductive reasoning and logic, other authors, such as Kluwe and Haider (1990), Moray (1988), and Seel (1991), focused on the construction of *semantic mental models* and their specific role in explaining the physical world. Here, different functions of models, such as *envisioning* and *analogical reasoning,* have been investigated in the fields of text and discourse processing (Rickheit & Habel, 1999) and in the operation of complex systems of physics or economics (Markman, 1998; Seel, Al-Diban, & Blumschein, 2000). Furthermore, there is a tradition of research on model building activities for specific subjects. This research emphasizes design-based modeling in the context of guided discovery and exploratory learning in different subject matter fields, such as mathematics or physics (Lesh & Doerr, 2000; Penner, 2001). All these movements can be subsumed under the broader field of model-centered learning.

WHAT IS MODEL-CENTERED LEARNING?

The idea of model-centered learning (MCL) has a long tradition in 20th-century psychology. Bandura (1971) developed a paradigm for the field of social learning that was based on the imitation of a model's behavior. Craik (1943) introduced the idea of *internal models* to cognitive psychology with the notion of a working model. He argued that an individual who intends to give a rational explanation for something must develop practicable methods in order to generate adequate explanations from knowledge of the world and with limited information-processing capacity. Thus, in order to create situation-specific plausibility the individual constructs a *model* that integrates the relevant semantic knowledge and meets the requirements of the situation to be mastered. This model "works" when it is within the realm of the subject's knowledge as well as the explanatory need with regard to the concrete learning situation to be mastered cognitively. Craik's conception of internal models has been adapted by numerous psychologists who were concerned with the investigation of people's operating of complex technical or physical systems (see, e.g., Hacker, 1977; Veldhuyzen & Stassen, 1977). Nevertheless, the theory of *mental models*, which encompasses situated cognition as well as qualitative reasoning (Gentner & Stevens, 1983; Greeno, 1989; Johnson-Laird, 1983), has proved to be the most influential approach.

The idea of mental models is based on two assumptions: that (a) "the person constructs the reality" (Buss, 1979), and (b) cognition and learning take place through the use of mental representations in which individuals organize symbols of experience or thought in such a way that they effect a systematic representation of this experience or thought as a means of understanding it or of explaining it to others (Seel, 1991). Learning occurs when people actively construct meaningful mental representations from presented information, such as coherent *mental models* that represent and communicate subjective experiences, ideas, thoughts, and feelings (cf. Mayer, Moreno, Boire, & Vagge, 1999).

From both a psychological and an epistemological point of view, models are constructed in accordance with specific intentions of the model-building person in order to "map" the environment in many respects. In order to illustrate this point one can refer to globes that are models of the earth. Naturally, a particular globe is not a little earth, but rather it is constructed and designed to give answers to questions concerning the locations of different places or distances between places. With regard to the chemical composition of the earth, a globe is not relevant. Other examples of modeling can be taken from the field of physics, such as Rutherford's atomic model or Newton's models of gravitation. These examples show that models are always representations of something: They represent natural or artificial objects, so-called originals, which can in their turn be models of something. Accordingly, talking about models implies, first of all, asking for the original to be modeled.

From the formal point of semantics, modeling can be defined as *homomorphisms* between relational systems. This is illustrated as in Fig. 5.1.

A *relational system* $\mathbf{a} = [A, R_1^A, ..., R_n^A]$, that is, the base domain or original, should be mapped on another relational system $\mathbf{b} = [B, S_1^B, ..., S_n^B]$, that is, the target domain, with the aim to explain the target domain with the help of the base domain. In epistemology and cognitive psychology, this mapping is called an *analogy* and presupposes the construction of two internal models of these domains. This can be illustrated through an example given by Holyoak and Thagard (1995):

> Our knowledge of water provides us with a kind of internal model of how it moves. Similarly, our knowledge of sound provides us with a kind of model of how sound is transmitted through the air. Each of these mental models links an internal representation to external reality. But when we consider the analogy between water waves and sound propagation, we are trying to build an isomorphism between two internal models. Implicitly, we are acting as if our model of water waves can be used to modify and improve our model of sound. (p. 33)

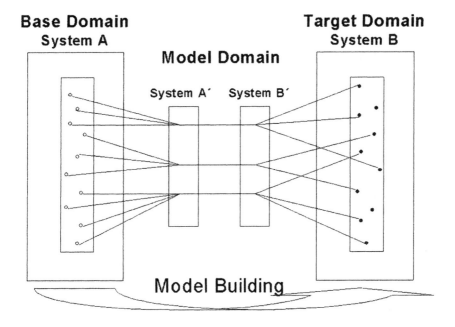

FIG. 5.1.   Semantic model building.

The structural features of model building and the involved homomorphisms and isomorphisms have been described in more detail by Seel (1991). On the basis of these structural features, four functions of model building can be distinguished:

- Models aid in the *simplification* of an investigation to particular and relevant phenomena in a closed domain.
- Models aid in the *envisioning* (or visualization) of a complex structure or system.
- Models aid in the *construction of analogies,* which help to identify the structure of an unknown domain with the help of the structure of a known domain. In this way a well-known explanation (e.g., Rutherford's atomic model) can be mapped onto a phenomenon to be explained (e.g., quantum mechanisms). Such models are called *analogy models.*
- Finally, models may aid in the *simulation* of a system's processes. This occurs when an individual interacts with the objects involved in a situation in order to manipulate them mentally in such a way that the cognitive operations simulate specific transformations of these objects that may occur in real-life situations. These *simulation models* operate as thought experiments that produce qualitative inferences with respect to the situation to be mastered (Greeno, 1989).

According to Stachowiak (1973), there are two main classes of mental models: *perceptual models* and *thought models*. In the vocabulary of Glaser, Lesgold, and Lajoie (1987) and Johnson-Laird (1983), perceptual models are *appearance* or structural *models* that represent the external world in a static manner. This concept of appearance models largely corresponds with the concept of models in information science (Weltner, 1970). *Thought models* include qualitative process models as well as inductively derived artifacts that represent physical systems and their causal relationships in a dynamic manner. However, Norman (1983) pointed out that we must distinguish between our conceptualization of a mental model and the actual mental model we think a person might have. To capture this idea, he conceptually separates "conceptual models" from "mental models." Accordingly, Kluwe and Haider (1990) distinguished between different kinds of models. First, for a (complex) system S of the world there is a subjective internal or *mental model* of S, MM(S), which represents the knowledge a person has or can reconstruct with regard to S. Second, there is an objective model OM(S), developed by scientists on the basis of their subjective mental models. We consider them to be *conceptual models*, CM(S). According to Hestenes (1987), they represent the objective knowledge of a discipline. CM(S) can thus be conceived as the shared knowledge of a scientific community that results from the mental models of scientists. Third, cognitive psychologists develop *psychological models* of the mental models of a system, PM[MM(S)]. These are the conceptual models that Norman (1983) emphasized.

Interestingly, Kluwe and Haider (1990) introduced a fourth kind of model, which is especially important for instructional design: *design and instructional models,* DIM[CM(S)]. I understand these models as instructionally designed conceptual models of a system S, which are used for the construction of interfaces (learning tasks, manuals, and training) in order to guide the learners' construction of mental models. These *designed instructional models* are related to all other types of models. This can be illustrated as in Fig. 5.2 (Seel, 2003).

HOW CAN WE INFLUENCE MODEL-CENTERED LEARNING THROUGH INSTRUCTION?

The question of how we can influence model-centered learning through instruction has long been at the core of various educational approaches (see, e.g., Karplus, 1969), and in the field of research on mental models we can find a strong pedagogical impetus from the very beginning (Seel, 2003). According to Johnson-Laird (1989) and other authors, we can distinguish between several sources for the construction of mental models: (a) the learner's ability to construct models in an inductive manner, either from a set of basic components of world knowledge or from analogous models that the learner already possesses; (b) everyday observations of the outside world associated with the adaptation of cultural models; and (c) other people's explanations. Among these sources the third one seems to be especially relevant for education and instruction.

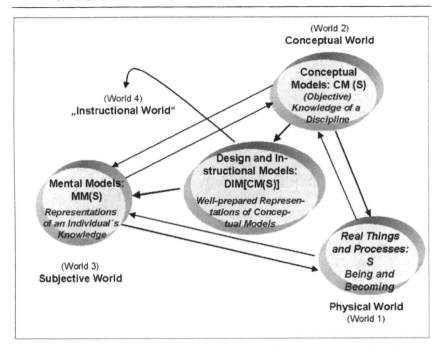

FIG. 5.2.   The interplay of designed instructional models with other kinds of models.

According to Carlson (1991), instruction can be designed to involve the learner in an inquiry process in which facts are gathered from data sources, similarities and differences among facts are noted, and concepts are developed. In this process, the instructional program serves as a facilitator of learning for students who are working to develop their own answers to questions. On the other hand, instructional programs can present clearly defined concepts followed by clear examples. A designed conceptual model may be presented ahead of the learning tasks in order to direct the learner's comprehension of the learning material. More generally, we can distinguish between different paradigms of model-centered instruction according to whether they aim at (a) self-organized discovery and exploratory learning, (b) externally guided discovery learning, and (c) learning oriented toward the imitation of an expert's behavior or the adaptation of teachers' explanations.

Clearly, there might exist environments that can initiate a form of learning based on free exploration by invention, but in instructional contexts we regularly operate with well-prepared and designed learning environments that constrain the student's learning processes to various extents. Accordingly, at the beginning of research on model-centered instruction the focus was on the pedagogical idea as expressed by Mayer (1989), which suggests that "students given model-instruction may be more likely to build mental models of the systems they are studying and to use these models to generate creative solutions to transfer problems" (p. 47). As a consequence, many studies on the learning-dependent progression of mental models focused on the internalization of conceptual models the students were provided with in the course of instruction (Mayer, 1989; Seel, 1995; Seel et al., 2000). This research belongs to the third paradigm—learning oriented toward the imitation of an expert's behavior or the adaptation of teachers' explanations.

An alternative approach emphasizes the role of *discovery learning* for the construction of mental models (Penner, 2001). According to this approach, the learner has to search continuously for information in a given learning environment in order to complete or stabilize an initial mental model that corresponds to an "a priori understanding" of the material to be learned. The goal of instruction is to create microworlds in which objects follow specific sets of rules. One example is a microworld in which balls fall in accordance with Newton's laws of motion (White, 1993). Students explore this model by developing hypotheses and then varying input parameters to investigate how well their conjectures align with the model. In mathematics education the defining characteristic of this kind of discovery learning is that students explore conventional mathematical symbolizations in experientially real settings (Kaput, 1994). More generally, Doerr (1996) stated with regard to the various settings of discovery learning that students have to develop *expressive models* to explain phenomena using a variety of tools. According to Doerr, this model building begins with students' informal understanding and progressively builds on it.

Self-guided learning occurs as a multi-step process of model-building and revision (Penner, 2001). Johnson-Laird (1983) conceived of this process as a "fleshing out" procedure that can be understood as a *reductio ad absurdum* that continuously examines whether or not a model can be replaced with an alternative model (Seel, 1991). Self-guided discovery learning is very ambitious insofar as the learners must have previously achieved adequate problem-solving and metacognitive skills to guide their learning process. Therefore, for beginning students it can be argued that self-organized discovery learning is closely associated with learning by trial and error but not by deep understanding. Incidentally, Briggs (1990) demonstrated in a case study that an instructional strategy aiming at discovery learning may dramatically increase the probability of stabilizing faulty initial mental models. Consequently, a substantial conceptual change does not take place, and relatively stable intermediate states of causal understanding often precede the conceptual mastery intended by instruction.

In sum, self-organized learning aimed at the creation of mental models can indeed be rather pretentious. It is a process that even an expert might sweat over sometimes. In order to be effective, learning environments aiming at model-building activities must be carefully designed.

DESIGNING EFFECTIVE ENVIRONMENTS FOR MCL

Decades ago, Wertheimer (1959) pled to design learning environments in such a way that learners can effectively work on the solution of new problems. In the 1960s and

1970s, several educational psychologists argued in a similar vein in accordance with Piaget's epistemology. For example, Bruner (1966) introduced the idea of guided discovery learning into the educational discussion, whereas Farnham-Diggory (1972) favored "free learning environments," and Stolurow (1973) developed his conception of *transactional instruction*, according to which learning environments should provide opportunities for reflective thinking. These different conceptions agree on the point that learning can be externally supported but not forced. Stolurow, for example, argued that if we want to improve exploratory learning and problem solving we need well-designed environments that provide the learners with optimal conditions for the development of initiatives and reduce external guidance to a minimum. From Stolurow's point of view, learning environments are not given a priori but rather they must be developed and designed. Accordingly, he explicitly pleaded for a program of instructional design as an evolving technology based on theoretical assumptions about psychological dispositions of the learner, learning activities, realistic learning results, and potential effects of learning materials.

We can summarize the different lines of argumentation by stating that successful model-centered instruction presupposes that effective learning environments be designed in accordance with two different conceptions: First, there is a goal-oriented design of learning environments that has to be done by instructional designers and aims at the internalization of well-designed conceptual models (so-called DIM[CM(S)]) with which the students are provided. Second, there are instructional approaches that emphasize the self-organized construction and revision of models by the students in the course of discovery learning. Gibbons (1998) integrated both lines of argumentation:

> The events of instruction, which are the structures we design, serve human learning processes under the ultimate control of the individual. Instruction, therefore, does not *cause* learning but *supports* learning intentions the learner commits…. Some of these processes (such as the initial processing of visual or auditory information) are involuntary, but many of them (focusing attention, finding and selecting associations, etc.) are completely voluntary. (p. 3)

In accordance with this precept, Gibbons formulated seven principles of model-centered instruction around these concepts: (a) experience (i.e., learners should be given maximum opportunity to interact with one or more self-constructed models of systems for learning purposes), (b) problem solving, (c) denaturing, (d) sequence, (e) goal orientation, (f) resourcing, and (g) instructional augmentation. These seven principles are to be considered a fundamental basis for the instructional design of effective learning environments.

From my point of view, several approaches of model-oriented teaching, such as the cognitive apprenticeship approach (for more details see the next section of this chapter) or, more specifically for math education, Gravemeijer's approach (Gravemeijer, Cobb, Bowers, & Whitenack, 2000), correspond with Gibbon's principles. Gravemeijer argued that *emergent models* play a central role in individual students' learning and in the collective mathematical development of the classroom community. The notion of emergent models encompasses some aspects of the exploratory approach insofar as students are encouraged to develop their own models, but do so in situations that are chosen by the teacher to support the realization of a proposed learning trajectory. Thus, it is possible for the designer to lay out a proposed developmental route for the classroom community in which students first model situations in an informal way (this is called a *model of* the situation) and then "mathematize" their informal modeling activity (this produces a *model for* reasoning). Although Gravemeijer's approach can be situated between externally guided and discovery learning, another current movement of instructional research is closely related to the idea of *model-based discovery learning*. Bhatta and Goel (1997) developed an interesting approach called integrated design by analogy and learning (IDeAL) within a theory of adaptive design. Similarly, Smith and Unger (1997) emphasized *conceptual bootstrapping* as a conception of analogy-based learning and problem solving. Both conceptions are based on the assumption that learners create their own designs through the retrieval of and adaptation to known designs.

An in-depth analysis of the various approaches of model-based discovery learning that aim to improve transfer between complex domains indicates that this kind of learning presupposes well-designed learning environments and materials. Bhatta and Goel (1997), for example, emphasized *task-guided learning,* which is dependent on designed learning tasks and the learner's domain-specific prior knowledge. Accordingly, the instructional design of learning tasks are at the core of IDeAL, which encourages students to construct device designs (in the fields of electrics, electronics, and heat exchangers) by having them carry out model-based and similarity-based learning which refers to retrievable knowledge about primitive functions within the known domain. Another approach to design-based modeling has been developed by Erickson and Lehrer (1998). They distinguish between the design-components *planning, transforming, evaluation,* and *revision.* Each of these components involves various model-building activities. For example, *planning* includes defining the nature of the problem (asking questions) and project management (e.g., composition of the learning group, and decision making concerning tasks and roles), whereas *transforming* consists of information search, information extraction, organization, and so on.

In the following section I present two approaches to the design of environments for model-centered learning that correspond with the main lines of argumentation described above.

LESSONS LEARNED FROM RESEARCH

In the following paragraphs I describe two projects of my research group that focused on model-centered learning in various instructional settings. The first project, realized from 1994 until 2001,[1] focused on the *internalization of predesigned conceptual models* the students are provided with in the course of learning. The focus of the second project[2] is on the use of *mental models as devices for discovery learning*. The main characteristic of both projects is the strong orientation toward basic research on the learning-dependent progression of mental models initiated through instruction. More specifically, we designed the learning environments mainly in order to test theoretical hypotheses, with our main interest being the systematic experimental variation of decisive model-building factors.

Research on Providing Model Information

In the first project we conducted a series of replication studies to investigate externally guided model-based learning in a comprehensive multimedia learning environment designed in accordance with principles of the cognitive apprenticeship approach. We started with the development of the multimedia learning environment called dynamic systems of economics. The cognitive apprenticeship approach of Collins, Brown, and Newman (1989) proved to be a promising instructional strategy, providing students with predesigned conceptual models to encourage them to imitate an expert's explanations. Moreover, this instructional approach prescribes in detail what the learner has to do in each sequence of learning in order to achieve particular objectives.

According to the cognitive apprenticeship approach, effective learning environments can be characterized by 18 features in four broad dimensions: *Content, methods, sequencing,* and the *sociology of teaching*. In a first step we separated a fifth dimension emphasizing the important aspects of *motivation* and the corresponding need for the motivational design of learning environments. Because the cognitive apprenticeship is mainly concerned with macro-aspects of planning, we combined it in a next step with the *tetraheder model* of Jenkins (1979), which we consider to be relevant for the micro level of the design of learning tasks. The result of the combination of both approaches can be described as in Table 5.1.

An analysis of the literature indicates that the authors of the cognitive apprenticeship approach considered the distinguished features as "building blocks" of instructional design that could be applied and evaluated separately with regard to their effectiveness. Accordingly, several studies (Farmer, Buckmaster, & Legrand, 1992; Lajoie & Lesgold, 1989; Volet, 1991) focused on selected methods, such as modeling and coaching, whereas Järvelä (1995) investigated the methods model-

[1] I gratefully acknowledge financial support for this research from a generous grant by the Deutsche Forschungsgemeinschaft (the German Research Association) with grant Se 399/4. The research group consisted of Sabine Al-Diban, Susanne Held, Claudia Hess, Wolfram Lutterer, Christoph Nennstiel, Katharina Schenk, Ralph Siegel, and Susan Wilcek.

[2] This project started in March 2002. Again I can gratefully acknowledge financial support for this research from a generous grant by the Deutsche Forschungsgemeinschaft (the German Research Association) with grant Se 399/8. The research group consists of Bettina Couné, Pablo Dummer, Katharina Schenk, and Susanne Steiner, Ulrike Hanke, and Dirk Heuthaler.

TABLE 5.1
Intersection Between the Cognitive Apprenticeship Approach and the Jenkins Tetraheder

Cognitive Apprenticeship	Personal Variables	Jenkins		
		Learning Tasks Materials	Activities of Learning	Results of Learning Criteria
Contents	Declarative knowledge Heuristic knowledge	Curriculum of a subject matter Topic	Acquisition of declarative and procedural knowledge	Schemata Mental Models
Methods	Control strategies Learning styles	Modeling Coaching Scaffolding Articulation Reflection Exploration	Generative procedural learning Metacognition	Rules, principles, proceduralization
Sequencing	Knowledge Organization	Sequencing of learning steps	Increasing complexity and variety	"Learning hierarchies"
Motivation	Instrinsic Motivation	Difficulty of tasks	Need for achievement	Interests Attitudes
Sociology	Cooperation Competition	Authenticity Contextuality	Culture of expert practice Team spirit	Social behaviors and skills Attitudes

ing, scaffolding, and reflection in the course of verbal interactions in the classroom. Casey (1996) investigated all methods of cognitive apprenticeship in the sequence proposed by the theory. Interestingly, Casey also investigated the appropriateness of this approach for the design of multimedia learning environments.

Table 5.1 illustrates how we realized the intersection between the cognitive apprenticeship approach and the Jenkins tetrahederal model (for more details, see Seel et al., 2000; Seel & Schenk, 2003).

In *modeling*, an expert explains the conceptual model economic circuit and the cybernetic model control loop. The students should adapt these *conceptual models* to accomplish the subsequent phases of learning. In *coaching*, the students are supervised and given guidance as they try to find solutions to a given task in an adaptive manner. The guidance given in coaching involves "result-oriented support" that was not difficult to realize, whereas the realization of *scaffolding* proved to be complicated. Actually, the authors of the cognitive apprenticeship approach have not prescribed in detail how to realize this component. Therefore, we referred to Riedel (1973), who effectively applied "process-oriented support" in discovery learning. On the whole, we contrasted the instructional support in coaching and scaffolding as summarized in Table 5.2.

Additionally, in scaffolding, special heuristics for problem solving were taught. These consisted of the decomposition of a complex problem into subproblems and the construction of analogies between the subproblems (Catrambone, 1998). Furthermore, two different instructional strategies for operating with analogies were realized: (a) *subsumption* of analogous learning tasks under a schema of a general problem-solving structure followed by its instantiation through a detailed worked-out example, and (b) *induction* of a more general problem-solving schema from analogous learning tasks by a comparison of different examples in order to extract structural similarities.

Realizing *articulation* and *reflection* within the multimedia program turned out to be a severe problem. Articulation is defined as the process of thinking aloud while working on a task, and reflection is defined as the comparison of the problem solving procedures applied by the learner and the expert respectively. Collins and colleagues (1989) maintained that these methods contribute to the development of reflective thinking and metacognitive control of learning. After an unsuccessful attempt to implement articulation and reflection in a computer-based way, we realized both methods in the form of a teach-back procedure (Sasse, 1991) in a social learning situation. This procedure is based on a constructive interaction between two communication partners who have simi-

TABLE 5.2
Kinds of Instructional Support in Coaching and Scaffolding

Coaching: Result-Oriented Support	Scaffolding: Process-Oriented Support
Subject-oriented organization of learning	Problem-oriented organization of learning
Support finding solutions	*Support for structuring*
Help in form of tasks and prescriptions for acting without taking into account the current problem	Help in stating the current problem more precisely
Help in the identification of relevant task components	Help in analyzing the problem
Help in generalizing the relevant relationships	Help in the formation of hypotheses Help in testing of hypotheses
Help in over-learning	Help in recognizing the essentials of current problems

lar domain-specific knowledge. One of them plays the role of a teacher who explains, for example, the states, functions, and transformations of a complex system to the other.

In the final part of the apprenticeship instruction, *exploration*, learners have to solve transfer tasks—one of them requires a "near transfer" (i.e., the task remains in the same subject-matter domain of economics) and the other one requires a "far transfer" from economics onto ecology. In sum, the methods of cognitive apprenticeship were realized in the sequence illustrated in Fig. 5.3.

The results of five evaluation studies with more than 400 subjects justify the statement that the cognitive apprenticeship approach can be considered a sound framework for the instructional design of environments for constructivist learning. So far these results correspond with observations and empirical results of other studies, such as those of Casey (1996), Chee (1995), and Lajoie and Lesgold (1989), according to which cognitive apprenticeship principles are suitable for the instructional design of learning environments—but with the reservation that it proved difficult to realize the methods of articulation and reflection in a multimedia learning environment (also see the corresponding results of Casey, 1996). Basically, the same holds true with respect to the realization of scaffolding. Nevertheless, empirically well substantiated is the learning effectiveness of the

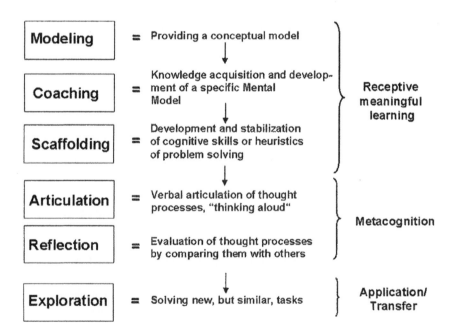

FIG. 5.3.   The methods of cognitive apprenticeship as implemented in the multimedia program (Seel et al., 2000).

multimedia program with regard to apprenticeship methods, which aim at explanatory descriptions as in expository teaching. Interestingly, the sequence of the methods "modeling–coaching–scaffolding–exploration" significantly improved the learning process. With this sequence, learners achieved above-average results in accomplishing the learning tasks and satisfactory results in accomplishing the more complex transfer tasks in exploration. In view of the partially inconsistent argumentation of the authors of the cognitive apprenticeship concerning the sequence of methods, this result has far-reaching significance for the instructional design of model-centered learning environments.

Apart from this, the overall results with regard to the effectiveness of the apprenticeship methods suggest a more detailed analysis of the learning and transfer performances in order to separate the methods' effectiveness (for more details, see Seel & Schenk, 2003). The weak spot of the instruction was evidently scaffolding, seen by the fact that none of our efforts to enable the learners to develop a promising problem-solving strategy (e.g., decomposing a complex problem into subproblems and solving them by analogy) were effective. The significant decrease of performance between coaching and scaffolding that was observable in all replication studies indicates that the learners could not progress from content-oriented to process-oriented learning in the sense of an increasingly self-regulated accomplishment of analogous tasks. Although this finding corresponds with recent research on analogical learning and thinking (Alexander, White, Haensly, & Grimmins-Jeanes, 1987; Newby, Ertmer, & Stepich, 1995), it is not satisfactory from a didactic point of view, especially with regard to the results of the regression analyses, according to which scaffolding did not influence the transfer sought in exploration. Actually, with regard to the accomplishment of transfer tasks the performances in coaching proved to be a significant predictor. To put it in slightly exaggerated terms, the instructional program could abstain from scaffolding without any effect on the performance of the transfer tasks in exploration. Some arguments for this may be found in the fact that the subjects of our studies were constrained by the instructional program and did not receive additional advice by a teacher, as suggested by Palincsar (1986), who considered the dialogue to be a solid basis for effective scaffolding. The multimedia instruction was not capable of adapting the learning tasks to the individual learner. For example, it cannot adapt the difficulty of a learning task to the learners' abilities to compensate for a learner's missing knowledge. Furthermore, the multimedia instruction did not make available appropriate "cognitive tools" to support the learners in accomplishing the learning tasks.

In designing scaffolding, we followed the recommendations of Collins et al. (1989) and the usual procedures of cognitive task analysis (Jonassen, Tessmer, & Hannum, 1999). Accordingly, we explicated the structure of tasks that we considered a precondition to the solution of learning tasks by analogy. We achieved this by providing the learners with an easier learning task that they could solve, and then increased the difficulty of tasks until the learners were no longer able to solve them on their own. Hmelo and Guzdial (1996) saw this organization of tasks as an example of "black-box scaffolding," which may improve the performance in the case of "closed" or well-structured domains but is ineffective in making the intended scaffold transparent for problem solving, especially in complex domains. Obviously, our data confirm this argument. As an alternative, Hmelo and Guzdial considered redesigning learning tasks to support the task performance with the help of a "supplantation" (as defined by Salomon, 1979) of the cognitive operations involved in the task solutions. Moreover, the task performance can be supported by the application of cognitive tools, which give advice to the learners on representing and manipulating a problem (e.g., with the help of graphic diagrams). These forms of scaffolding are taken by Hmelo and Guzdial to be examples of "glass-box scaffolding," as their aim is to help to learners in cases where they cannot master the problems on their own. Thus, the lesson learned is that in the future scaffolding should be primarily oriented toward the idea of glass-box scaffolding, with the aim of expanding the opportunities of learning with appropriate cognitive tools.

MODEL-CENTERED DISCOVERY LEARNING

Parallel to the research inspired by the mental model approach we can find—especially in the fields of mathematics and physics education—various approaches to model-centered instruction. Stewart, Hafner, Johnson, and Finkel (1992) circumscribed the central idea of these instructional approaches, stressing that "a science education should do more than instruct students with respect to the conclusions reached by scientists; it should also encourage students to develop insights about science as an intellectual activity" (p. 318). Accordingly, advocates of this approach argued that "given that we wish to involve students in the practices of scientists, we focus primarily on model building" (Penner, Lehrer, & Schauble, 1998, p. 430). Indeed, in science some of the most important goals of instruction are to help students develop powerful models for making sense of their experiences involving light, gravity, electricity, and magnetism. It has also been obvious that young students invent models of their own and that changing students' ways of thinking must involve challenging and testing these models (Penner, 2001). The model-building approach provides a significant challenge for the understanding of how to nurture, accommodate, and respond to the partial and incomplete models that students are likely to build with regard to phenomena of physics. We find a similar argument with regard to learning mathematics. A major role of algebra education is to develop confidence and facility in using variables und functions to *model* numerical patterns and other quantitative relationships (National Council of Teachers of Mathematics, 1994). Accordingly, Lesh and Doerr (2000) and other authors talked about models that students should develop in attempts to produce mathematical descriptions or explanations of systems of the physical world. These authors argued that helping students to develop powerful models should be among the most important goals of science and mathematics instruction.

My research group is involved in a large project in accordance with these conceptions of *model-based discovery learning.* In 2003 we carried out an initial experiment with a multimedia learning environment—"The Forest as an Ecological System"—that provides students with a complex way of looking at a complex problem to be solved. The students' task is to construct an "explanatory model" of the phenomenon in question. Accordingly, they have to construct an analogical model in which similar functions and relations between system elements can be found. In order to enable the students (15 years of age on average) to construct analogy models, the learning environment provides them with several "tools" for self-organized discovery learning. It consists of several major units:

1. In the *Problem Space,* learners are asked to explain a phenomenon with a model they already know. The known model is the basis model for analogical reasoning. This means that students build two models—one of the basis area and one of the target area.

2. The *Model-Building Kit (MoBuKi)* introduces a tutor to impart knowledge about model building and analogical reasoning. It includes four phases of analogical reasoning:
   • Understanding the phenomenon to be explained (the students build an initial but incomplete mental model of a source domain).
   • Constructing an exploratory model of the target domain.
   • Comparing both models (those of the source and target domain).
   • Evaluating the similarity between both models: Learners generate hypotheses about the behavior of the models they select. They verify these hypotheses.
   Moreover, the *Model Building Kit* also contains a library of analogies realized, and explanations of characteristics and functions of models.

3. The *information archive* <wissen.de> contains documents, pictures, and sound recordings about models from different fields of knowledge, but also additional information about the living space "forest."

4. The *toolbox* "PowerPoint" facilitates model drawing and note taking about the concepts used.

5. The *curriculum unit* "Forest" offers scientific explanations of ecological systems as bits of knowledge. The learners can choose different topics, for example, "photosynthesis" or "food chain." The explanations in this unit do not contain any models. The learners have to pull together all information to build a model.

Figure 5.4 illustrates the component architecture of the learning environment.

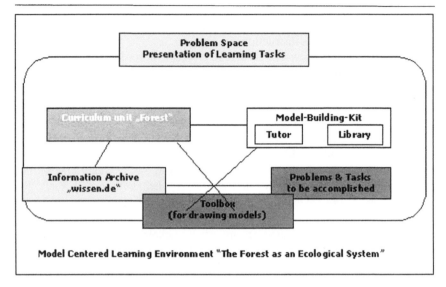

FIG. 5.4.   The architecture of the multimedia environment "The forest as an ecological system."

Design Elements

Beyond this formal structure of the learning environment we have defined the following *design elements* of the environment as supportive for exploratory model building activities.

Representational Formats.   Multimedia allows one to connect digitally represented symbols in a flexible and nonlinear way. We consider multimedia to be an emergent technology, which allows one to integrate independent technologies, such as text, pictures, digital video, sound, animations, and simulations. With this design element we intend for students to learn to operate with the various information technologies in an active and constructive manner and to use them as a means for representation and communication of knowledge.

Context Boundedness.   This design element corresponds with the situated cognition approach, according to which learning is dependent on the context and involves the construction of mental models. It is realized in our learning environment primarily on the basis of case-oriented tasks and problems. Related learning activities aim at the construction and application of mental models in order to effectively represent domain-specific knowledge in multiple but concrete contexts.

Explication of Semantic Depth Structures.   This design element is based on research that indicates that novices often focus on a problem's superficial features and are not able to comprehend the depth structures as experts do. As a consequence, a central goal of the learning environment is to elaborate the structural aspects of knowledge in varying contexts. Therefore, we distinguish three steps:

1. Identification of abstract domain-specific concepts.
2. Elaboration of how structural components of knowledge can be applied in case- and problem-oriented contexts. To realize this, the students are provided with selected cases, with comments concerning the depth-structure in which the abstract concepts are explained.
3. Visualizing of semantic structures by means of causal diagrams (Al-Diban, 2002) or of concept maps that aim at dynamic qualitative representations of the mental models developed by novices and experts.

Scaffolding.   By referring to the studies of Coleman (1998), Riedel (1973), and others, we deliver various hints and advice in the learning environment in order to facilitate discovery learning and problem solving. As in the former project, we distinguish between result- and process-oriented support (see Table 5.2).

Networking by Means of Analogies.   With this design element we intend for analogies to be constructed within and between domains. This idea goes back to the theory of mental models and structure mapping from a source to a target domain (Seel, 1991). We know from research that it is often very difficult for students to create analogies between different domains in order to solve problems (Ross, 1989). Therefore, the learning environment contains links between similar cases of the same domain as well as links between cases from different domains.

With these design elements we aim at different learning activities, such as the active construction of structural knowledge, the step-by-step development of a problem-solving schema, the implantation of new concepts, conceptual networking, and cognitive experimenting (*thought experiments*). The cognitive research of the past decades clearly demonstrates that novices have available a broad range of mental representations (e.g., preconceptions, naive theories, and epistemic beliefs) with regard to the various phenomena of the world, but often these representations contradict scientific explanations. Therefore, a central goal of the model-building kit *MoBuKi* is to motivate students to construct several models for the same phenomenon and then to realize the "fleshing out" procedure (as described by Johnson-Laird, 1983) in order to find the "best" model. Moreover, the students are also provided with models of experts in order to compare them with the self-constructed models.

Currently we are concerned with the implementation of the first experiment, which tests several hypotheses concerning the effectiveness of model-based discovery learning as well as the effectiveness of the designed learning environment.

CONCLUDING REMARKS

Our research on model-centered learning environments corresponds to a large extent with Merrill's late work on "knowledge objects and mental models" as described in Merrill (2000). In this paper, Merrill argued that a major concern of instructional design is the representation and organization of subject matter content to facilitate learning. Moreover, his central thesis was that the analysis of subject matter content (knowledge) can facilitate both the external representation of knowledge for purposes of instruction ("knowledge objects") and the internal representation and use of knowledge by means of the learners' mental models. If a student is taught a concise knowledge representation for different kinds of instructional outcomes, the student can use this representation as a meta-mental model to facilitate acquisition of specific mental models. Interestingly, this argumentation corresponds to a large extent with the research on how students are effectively provided with model information. However, although this research works with broad conceptions of instruction, such as cognitive apprenticeship, Merrill started with the specification of knowledge components (facts, concepts, rules, and higher order rules) and types of knowledge structures (lists, taxonomies, algorithms, causal nets). The central function of mental models is seen in providing the learners with appropriate algorithms or heuristics for manipulating these knowledge components in order to solve problems.

In accordance with his component display theory and its elaborations across several decades, David Merrill (2000) described in this paper knowledge components that are thought to be appropriate and sufficient to precisely describe certain types of knowledge. Furthermore, he described knowledge structures as a form of schema that learners use to represent knowledge. From his point of view, a mental model is a schema plus the cognitive processes for manipulating and modifying the knowledge that can be activated by a schema. Merrill's argument corresponds with the theory of mental models presented here (Seel, 1991) insofar as the suggested processes should enable learners to manipulate the knowledge components of conceptual network knowledge structures for purposes of classification, generalization, and concept elaboration. Beyond this, the suggested processes enable learners to manipulate the knowledge components of process knowledge structures for purposes of explanation, prediction, and troubleshooting. Merrill's central hypothesis is that knowledge components and structures could serve as "meta-mental models" that would enable learners to more easily acquire conceptual and causal networks and their associated processes. The resulting specific mental models would facilitate their ability to solve problems of conceptualization and interpretation.

In sum, Merrill's (2000) paper can be considered a useful elaboration of the mental model approach in the context of instructional design. Its merit is to demonstrate that a careful analysis of subject matter contents ("knowledge") and its structures may serve as a sound basis for the construction of mental models. Beyond this, Merrill demonstrates that the instructional design of model-centered learning is not hocus-pocus but rather its focus must be strictly on locus: the careful analysis of knowledge to be acquired and applied in order to solve problems.

REFERENCES

Al-Diban, S. (2002). *Diagnose mentaler Modelle*. Hamburg: Kovac.

Alexander, P. A., White, C. S., Haensly, P. A., & Grimmins-Jeanes, M. (1987). Training in analogical reasoning. *American Educational Research Journal, 24*, 387–404.

Bandura, A. (1971). *Social learning theory*. New York: General Learning Press.

Bhatta, S. R., & Goel, A. (1997). Learning generic mechanisms for innovative strategies in adaptive design. *Journal of the Learning Sciences, 6*(4), 367–396.

Briggs, P. (1990). The role of the user model in learning as an internally and externally directed activity. In D. Ackermann & M. J. Tauber (Eds.), *Mental models and human–computer interaction 1* (pp. 195–208). Amsterdam: Elsevier.

Bruner, J. S. (1966). *Toward a theory of instruction*. Cambridge, MA: Harvard University Press.

Buss, A. R. (1979). *A dialectical psychology*. New York: Irvington.

Carlson, H. L. (1991). Learning style and program design in interactive multimedia. *Educational Technology Research and Development, 39*(3), 41–48.

Casey, C. (1996). Incorporating cognitive apprenticeship in multimedia. *Educational Technology Research and Development, 44*(1), 71–84.

Catrambone, R. (1998). The subgoal learning model: Creating better examples so that students can solve novel problems. *Journal of Experimental Psychology: General, 127*(4), 355–376.

Chee, Y. S. (1995). Cognitive apprenticeship and its application to the teaching of smalltalk in a multimedia interactive learning environment. *Instructional Science, 23*, 133–161.

Coleman, E. B. (1998). Using explanatory knowledge during collaborative problem solving in science. *Journal of the Learning Sciences, 7*(3 & 4), 387–427.

Collins, A., Brown, J. S., & Newman, S. E. (1989). Cognitive apprenticeship: Teaching the crafts of reading, writing, and mathematics. In L. B. Resnick (Ed.), *Knowing, learning, and instruction* (pp. 453–494). Hillsdale, NJ: Lawrence Erlbaum Associates.

Craik, K. J. W. (1943). *The nature of explanation*. Cambridge: Cambridge University Press.

Doerr, H. M. (1996). Integrating the study of trigonometry, vectors, and force through modeling. *School Science and Mathematics, 96*, 407–418.

Duchastel, P. (1999). *Instructional design in the information age*. IFETS Forum. Paper presented and discussed on IFETS Forum, May 1999. Retrieved April 9, 2004, from http://gmd.de/discussionss/discuss_may99.html

Erickson, J., & Lehrer, R. (1998). The evolution of critical standards as students design hypermedia documents. *Journal of the Learning Sciences, 7*(3 & 4), 351–386.

Farmer, J. A., Buckmaster, A., & Legrand, A. (1992). Cognitive apprenticeship: Implications for continuing professional education. *New Directions for Adult and Continuing Education, 55*, 41–49.

Farnham-Diggory, S. (1972). *Cognitive processes in education: A psychological preparation for teaching and curriculum development*. New York: Harper & Row.

Gentner, D., & Stevens, A. L. (Eds.).(1983). *Mental models*. Hillsdale, NJ: Lawrence Erlbaum Associates.

Gibbons, A. S. (1998, April). *Model-centered instruction*. Paper presented at the Annual Meeting of the American Education Research Association, San Diego, CA.

Glaser, R., Lesgold, A., & Lajoie, S. (1987). Toward a cognitive theory for the measurement of achievement. In R. R. Ronning, J. Glover, J. C. Conoley, & J. C. Witt (Eds.), *The influence of cognitive psychology on testing and measurement* (pp. 41–85). Hillsdale, NJ: Lawrence Erlbaum Associates.

Gordon, I., & Zemke, R. (2000). The attack on ISD: Have we got instructional design all wrong? *Training Magazine, 37*, 43–53.

Gravemeijer, K., Cobb, P., Bowers, J., & Whitenack, J. (2000). Symbolizing, modeling, and instructional design. In P. Cobb, E. Yackel, & K. McClain (Eds.), *Symbolizing and communicating in mathematics classrooms. Perspectives on discourse, tools, and instructional design* (pp. 225–273). Mahwah, NJ: Lawrence Erlbaum Associates.

Greeno, J. G. (1989). Situations, mental models, and generative knowledge. In D. Klahr & K. Kotovsky (Eds.), *Complex information processing* (pp. 285–318). Hillsdale, NJ: Lawrence Erlbaum Associates.

Gustafson, K. L., Tillman, M. H., & Childs, J. W. (1992). The future of instructional design. In L. J. Briggs, K. L. Gustafson, & M. H. Tillman (Eds.), *Instructional design: Principles and applications* (pp. 451–467). Englewood Cliffs, NJ: Educational Technology.

Hacker, W. (1977). Bedeutung und Analyse des Gedächtnisses für die Arbeits- und Ingenieurpsychologie—zu Gedächtnisanforderungen in der psychischen Regulation von Handlungen. In F. Klix & H. Sydow (Eds.), *Zur Psychologie des Gedächtnisses* (pp. 150–174). Bern: Huber.

Hestenes, D. (1987). Toward a modeling theory of physics instruction. *American Journal of Physics, 55*(5), 440–454.

Hmelo, C. E., & Guzdial, M. (1996). Of black and glass boxes: Scaffolding for doing and learning. In *Proceedings of the Second International Conference on the Learning Sciences* (pp. 128–133). Charlottesville, VA: Association for the Advancement of Computers in Education.

Holyoak, K. J., & Thagard, P. (1995). *Mental leaps. Analogy in creative thought.* Cambridge, MA: MIT Press.

Järvelä, S. (1995). The cognitive apprenticeship model in a technologically rich learning environment: Interpreting the learning interaction. *Learning and Instruction, 5*(3), 237–259.

Jenkins, J. J. (1979). Four points to remember: A tetrahedral model of memory experiments. In L. S. Cermak, & F. I. M. Craik (Eds.), *Levels of processing in human memory* (pp. 429–446). Hillsdale, NJ: Lawrence Erlbaum Associates.

Johnson-Laird, P. N. (1983). *Mental models. Towards a cognitive science of language, inference, and consciousness.* Cambridge: Cambridge University Press.

Johnson-Laird, P. N. (1989). Mental models. In M. I. Posner (Ed.), *Foundations of cognitive science* (pp. 469–499). Cambridge, MA: MIT Press.

Jonassen, D. H., Tessmer, M., & Hannum, W. H. (1999). *Task analysis methods for instructional design.* Mahwah, NJ: Lawrence Erlbaum Associates.

Kaput, J. J. (1994). The representational roles of technology in connecting mathematics with authentic experience. In R. Biehler, R.W. Scholz, R. Sträßer, & B. Winkelmann (Eds.), *Didactics of mathematics as a scientific discipline* (pp. 379–397). Dordrecht: Kluwer.

Karplus, R. (1969). *Introductory physics: A model approach.* New York: Benjamins.

Kluwe, R. H., & Haider, H. (1990). Modelle zur internen Repräsentation komplexer technischer Systeme. *Sprache & Kognition, 9*(4), 173–192.

Lajoie, S. P., & Lesgold, A. (1989). Apprenticeship training in the workplace: Computer-coached practice environment as a new form of apprenticeship. *Machine-Mediated Learning, 3*, 7–28.

Lesh, R., & Doerr, H. M. (2000). Symbolizing, communicating, and mathematizing: Key components of models and modeling. In P. Cobb, E. Yackel, & K. McClain (Eds.), *Symbolizing and communicating in mathematics classrooms. Perspectives on discourse, tools, and instructional design* (pp. 361–383). Mahwah, NJ: Lawrence Erlbaum Associates.

Markman, A. B. (1998). *Knowledge representation.* Mahwah, NJ: Lawrence Erlbaum Associates.

Mayer, R. E. (1989). Models for understanding. *Review of Educational Research, 59*(1), 43–64.

Mayer, R. E., Moreno, R., Boire, M., & Vagge, S. (1999). Maximizing constructivist learn-ing from multimedia communication by minimizing cognitive load. *Journal of Educa-tional Psychology, 91*(4), 638–643.

Merrill, M. D. (1987). The new component design theory: Instructional design for courseware authoring. *Instructional Science, 16,* 19–34.

Merrill, M. D. (1994). *Instructional design theory.* Englewood Cliffs, NJ: Educational Technology Publications.

Merrill, M. D. (2000). Knowledge objects and mental models. In D. A. Wiley (Ed.), *The in-structional use of learning objects.* Retrieved April 9, 2004, from http://reusabil-ity.org/read/chapters/merrill.doc

Moray, N. (1988). *A lattice theory of mental models of complex systems.* Urbana-Cham-paign: Engineering Psychology Research Laboratory, University of Illinois.

Myers, K. L. (1999). Is there a place for instructional design in the information age? *Educa-tional Technology, 39*(6), 50–53.

Newby, T. J., Ertmer, P. A., & Stepich, D. A. (1995). Instructional analogies and the learn-ing of concepts. *Educational Technology Research and Development, 43*(1), 5–18.

Norman, D. A. (1983). Some observations on mental models. In D. Gentner & A. L. Stevens (Eds.), *Mental models* (pp. 7–14). Hillsdale, NJ: Lawrence Erlbaum Associates.

Palincsar, A. S. (1986). The role of dialogue in providing scaffolded instruction. *Educa-tional Psychologist, 21*(1 & 2), 73–98.

Penner, D. E. (2001). Cognition, computers, and synthetic science: Building knowledge and meaning through modeling. *Review of Research in Education, 25,* 1–35.

Penner, D. E., Lehrer, R., & Schauble, L. (1998). From physical models to biomechanics: A design-based modeling approach. *Journal of the Learning Sciences, 7*(3 & 4), 429–449.

Renkl, A., Stark, R., Gruber, H., & Mandl, H. (1998). Learning from worked-out examples: The effects of example variability and elicited self-explanations. *Contemporary Educa-tional Psychology, 23,* 90–108.

Rickheit, G., & Habel, C. (Eds.). (1999). *Mental models in discourse processing and rea-soning.* Amsterdam: Elsevier.

Riedel, K. (1973). *Lehrhilfen zum entdeckenden Lernen. Ein experimenteller Beitrag zur Denkerziehung.* Hannover: Schroedel.

Ritchie, D., & Earnest, J. (1999). The future of instructional design: Results of a Delphi study. *Educational Technology, 39*(6), 35–42.

Ross, B. H. (1989). Distinguishing types of superficial similarities: Different effects on the access and use of earlier problems. *Journal of Experimental Psychology: Learning, Memory, and Cognition, 15,* 456–468.

Salomon, G. (1979). *Interaction of media, cognition and learning.* San Francisco: Jossey-Bass.

Sasse, M. (1991). How to t(r)ap users' mental models. In M. J. Tauber, & D. Ackermann (Eds.), *Mental models and human–computer interaction* (Vol. 2, pp. 59–79). Amster-dam: North-Holland.

Seel, N. M. (1991). *Weltwissen und mentale Modelle.* Göttingen: Hogrefe.

Seel, N. M. (1995). Mental models, knowledge transfer, and teaching strategies. *Journal of Structural Learning, 12*(3), 197–213.

Seel, N. M. (2001). Epistemology, situated cognition, and mental models: "Like a bridge over troubled water." *Instructional Science, 29*(4–5), 403–428.

Seel, N. M. (2003). Model-centered learning and instruction. *Technology, Instruction, Cognition, and Learning, 1*(1), 59–85.

Seel, N. M., Al-Diban, S., & Blumschein, P. (2000). Mental models and instructional plan-ning. In J. M. Spector, & T. M. Anderson (Eds.), *Integrated and holistic perspectives on learning, instruction and technology: Understanding complexity* (pp. 129–158). Dordrecht: Kluwer.

Seel, N. M., & Schenk, K. (2003). Multimedia environments as cognitive tools for enhancing model-based learning and problem solving: An evaluation report. *Evaluation and Program Planning, 26*(2), 215–224.

Smith, C., & Unger, C. (1997). What's in dots-per-box? Conceptual bootstrapping with stripped-down visual analogies. *Journal of the Learning Sciences, 6*(2), 143–181.

Stachowiak, H. (1973). *Allgemeine Modelltheorie*. Wien: Springer.

Steinbuch, K. (1961). *Automat und Mensch. Über menschliche und maschinelle Intelligenz*. Berlin: Springer.

Stewart, J., Hafner, R., Johnson, S., & Finkel, E. (1992). Science as model building: Computers and high-school genetics. *Educational Psychologist, 27*(3), 317–336.

Stolurow, L. M. (1973). Lernumwelten oder Gelegenheiten zum Nachdenken. In W. Edelstein, & D. Hopf (Eds.), *Bedingungen des Bildungsprozesses. Psychologische und pädagogische Forschungen zum Lehren und Lernen in der Schule* (pp. 351–398). Stuttgart: Klett.

Sweller, J., Chandler, P., Tierney, P., & Cooper, M. (1990). Cognitive load as a factor in the structuring of technical material. *Journal of Experimental Psychology: General, 119*, 176–192.

van Merriënboer, J. J. G., Seel, N. M., & Kirschner, P. A. (2002). Mental models as a new foundation for instructional design. *Educational Technology, 42*(2), 60–66.

Veldhuyzen, W., & Stassen, H. G. (1977). The internal model concept: An application to modelling human control of large ships. *Human Factors, 19*, 367–380.

Volet, S. E. (1991). Modelling and coaching of relevant, metacognitive strategies for enhancing university students' learning. *Learning and Instruction, 1*(4), 319–336.

Weltner, K. (1970). *Informationstheorie und Erziehungswissenschaft*. Quickborn: Schnelle.

Wertheimer, M. (1959). *Productive thinking* (rev. ed.). New York: Harper & Row.

White, B. (1993). Thinker tools: Causal models, conceptual change, and science education. *Cognition and Instruction, 10*(1), 1–100.

Chapter
6

Problem Solving: The Enterprise

David H. Jonassen
University of Missouri

MICRO-LEVEL INSTRUCTION

Historically, most instructional design models have focused on how to analyze, organize, and teach individual lessons focused on individual instructional objectives. This is especially true for models based on an objectivist epistemology. The most coherent of these objectivist models and methods, I believe, are those developed and communicated by David Merrill and his colleagues, including component display theory[1] (CDT) and ID2 (also known as transaction theory). I have studied those models extensively and have taught them to numerous students. I have also applied and implemented them in a variety of venues.

In this chapter, I claim that Merrill's models and those of Gagné are limited in their ability to support learning a broad range of human activities by their focus on single learning outcomes represented by single objectives. Other scholars may debate the epistemological assumptions of these models; however, the tendency of those claiming to be social and cognitive constructivists has too often been to re-

---

[1] I do not regard most developments in instructional design as theories. I believe that prescriptive theories of instruction as described by Reigeluth (1983b) are actually models that are based on descriptive theories of learning. However, such a dialectic is irrelevant to the purpose of this chapter and therefore is not addressed.

place the objectivist epistemology with a constructivist epistemology as the only legitimate (and therefore unified) theory of learning. Constructivism represents a new paradigm of learning, but it has not replaced, nor should it replace, objectivism. Human learning, as a sufficiently complex and poorly understood phenomenon, is able to accommodate multiple paradigms and resist any unified theory of instructional design (Jonassen, 2003).

After briefly reviewing Merrill's models, including component display theory and ID2, I argue that problem solving, the implicit cognitive outcome of most constructivist learning environments, can provide an appropriate structure for organizing and sequencing micro-level lessons.[2]

Component Display Theory

Component display theory (CDT) is an integrated system of instructional design principles and prescriptions for organizing micro-level instruction. CDT (Merrill, 1983, 1987) evolved from a number of veins of work, including the Instructional Strategy Diagnostic Profile (Merrill, Richards, Schmidt, & Wood, 1977), the Instructional Quality Inventory (Ellis & Wulfeck, 1978; Merrill, Reigeluth, & Faust, 1979; Montague, 1983; Montague & Wulfeck, 1982), and the Author Training Course for the Navy (Courseware, Inc., 1978). From a task description perspective, a major contribution of Merrill's work, vis-à-vis Gagné's learning taxonomy, was the performance–content matrix. CDT, like Gagné's (1977) taxonomy, assumes that different learning outcomes require different instructional conditions. Merrill evolved his own taxonomy of learning over a period of years, using an analysis of school-based learning outcomes (Merrill, 1973; Reigeluth, Merrill, & Bundeson, 1978). He concluded that almost all learning activities involved facts, procedures, concepts, rules, and principles. Although most taxonomies describe learning outcomes on only a single dimension, Merrill's taxonomy describes both the content and the task, that is, what you do with the content. You can remember content, use content (one version [Montague, 1983] distinguishes between use with an aid and use unaided), and (in later versions) find content (discover, generate, or use cognitive strategies). Facts can only be remembered, according to Merrill. Use-level and find-level performances describe the acts of applying or discovering concepts, procedures, rules, or principles in new situations.

Related to each task and content combinations are sets of instructional strategies about the type and sequence of instructional conditions that will facilitate each type of learning performance. These strategies include generalities (statement of a rule or principle, definition of a concept, or listing of steps in a procedure), instances (detailed or actual examples of the generality), and practice performing the skill with feedback.

---

[2]The lack of instructional prescriptions is not a problem for many researchers in the learning sciences field.

Instructional presentations may be made in either an expository or an inquisitory manner. That is, generalities and instances may be presented, told, shown, or demonstrated (expository), or they may be asked of the learner, requiring the learner to state the generality, provide instances, solve problems, or perform the activities (inquisitory). For an expository lesson, the instructor presents the statement, provides examples, and requires practice and a restatement of the generality by the learner. A discovery lesson may start with the inquisitory instances, requiring the learner to induce the generality from the instances. Thus, the expository information would function as feedback. CDT goes on to specify a variety of secondary or supplementary presentation forms, such as elaborations, mnemonics, and forms of feedback.

CDT offers one of the clearest and most comprehensive prescriptions for designing micro-level instructional units. What it does not prescribe is how to sequence multiple objectives of lessons into macro-level designs. That was to come later.

ID2—Transaction Theory

Second-generation instructional design (ID2) represented a conceptual effort to identify and represent course content in larger structures. ID2 was a concept-rich system that analyzed and organized content into frames (entities, activities, or processes) that could be elaborated with attributes, components, abstractions, or associations (Jones, Li, & Merrill, 1990; Merrill, Li, & Jones, 1990). These frames could be combined and linked to form enterprises (described later in this chapter). These frames were later reorganized and redefined as transactions (Merrill, Li, & Jones, 1991, 1992; Merrill, Jones, & Li, 1992). Transactions describe instructional interactions with learners, the elements of which were described in transaction shells. Three classes of instructional transactions were defined: component transactions (identify, execute, and interpret); abstraction transactions (classify, judge, generalize, and transfer); and association transactions (propagate, analogize, substitute, design, and discover). Each transaction was comprised of different combinations of entity, activity, and process frames. For some time, Merrill and his colleagues worked on an automated system for organizing the very complex combinations of transactions, frames, elaborations, and elaborated frame networks, using them to generate instructional transactions.

In an effort to instantiate the use of transaction theory for ourselves, and because we did not have access to Merrill's transaction generator, Woody Wang and I developed our transaction generator in order to experiment with the theory. The first transaction generator used a semantic network (concept mapping program) called SemNet (Fisher, 1991) to represent transactions. The semantic network shells possessed only links to represent the kinds of relationships implied by each kind of transaction. For example, Fig. 6.1 illustrates the different kinds of relationships that can be depicted in a *concept* shell—a kind of abstraction shell. Designers were required to identify the concepts required to fill the transaction shell. Figure 6.2 illustrates a single screen of a *propagate* shell for a lesson on government security. The network includes several other screens that elaborate the entire shell.

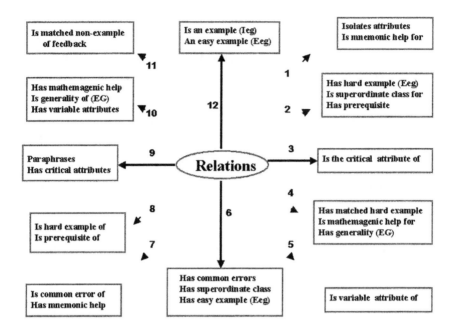

FIG. 6.1.   Relationships in a concept shell.

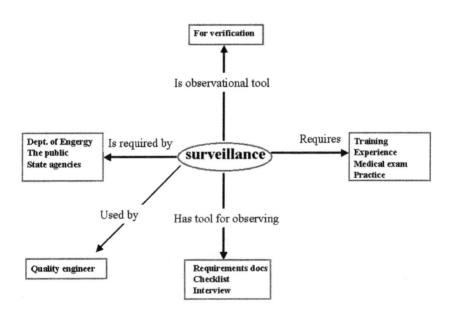

FIG. 6.2.   Part of a semantic network of a propagate transaction.

We were also able to automate the development of instruction from these transactional shells at a fairly primitive level using a program that would convert the semantic network into a standalone HyperCard stack (thanks to Brock Allen). It was clear that these tools were not robust enough to support commercial production of courseware; however, these tools functioned as cognitive tools (Jonassen, 2000) for modeling the principles of ID2 and therefore generated a better understanding of the theory, which was rich in concepts but short on explanation. What was important about transaction theory was its effort to contextualize micro-level design.

Limitations of Micro-Level Design Models

The assumption of micro-level instructional designs is that individual, component skills are required to perform larger, more complex tasks. Gagne's and Merrill's models are premised on a prerequisites approach to learning, where simpler, prerequisite skills must be mastered prior to developing more complex skills. In the context of contemporary research on situated learning, that assumption is questionable. It is unlikely that learning individual chunks of content or lower level cognitive skills in isolation will result in meaningful learning without a clear purpose for doing so and without some integrative task as well as intentional agency on the part of the learners. Learning component content and skills without a purpose does not engender intentionality on the part of learners. The acquisition of component content and skills while pursuing a meaningful, relevant, and authentic goal engenders intentionality, an essential requirement for engaged, meaningful learning (Jonassen, Hernandez-Serrano, & Choi, 2000). In an effort to provide integrative frameworks for the acquisition of component content and skills, a number of theorists, including Merrill, developed macro-level instructional design models. These are described next.

MACRO-LEVEL DESIGN MODELS

Researchers and designers have developed a number of design frameworks for combining and accommodating individual, component (micro-level) lesson from a variety of intellectual perspectives. These frameworks function as structures for organizing and sequencing micro-level lessons.

Elaboration Theory

Elaboration theory (see footnote 1) is a model for selecting, organizing, and sequencing instructional content at the macro level (Reigeluth, 1979, 1983a, 1987; Reigeluth & Stein, 1983). Elaboration theory is based on subsumption theory (Ausubel, 1968), which asserts that because knowledge is arranged hierarchically in memory, instruction should recapitulate that arrangement by presenting information in a general-to-detailed sequence. The most general or subsumptive ideas are presented first to provide a structure for interrelating detailed ideas that are related back to the broader ideas, the ideas that comprise micro-level lessons. Elaboration theory also assumes, as do Gagné (1977) and Scandura (1973), that learners need to learn simpler, prerequisite knowledge before more complex knowledge.

Elaboration theory contends that there are three ways of hierarchically structuring content: conceptual organizations, procedural organizations, and theoretical (or rule-based) organizations. These organizing structures are among the most systematic and rational for organizing subject matter content. Elaboration-based designs initially present these structural relationships at an application level, using epitomes, then use analogies to relate new information to existing knowledge structures in the learners. Content is progressively elaborated in more detail around the chosen structure using summarizers and synthesizers. Elaboration theory uses the analogy of the zoom lens on a camera, starting the lesson with a wide-angle view, allowing learners to see the whole picture, then successively zooming in to reveal more information, and then zooming back out to the wide-angle view to review and integrate the subparts.

Elaboration theory is one of the best instructional design models for structuring and sequencing content information. What elaboration theory lacks, according to more contemporary learning theories, is meaningfulness and authenticity. Models for teaching content or skills outside of the context of some meaningful human activity requiring some level of human agency are not authentic, according to situated and constructivist learning theories.

Enterprises

In order "to identify learning goals that require an integration of multiple objectives," Gagné and Merrill (1990, p. 23) selected the term *enterprise*. They insisted on the integration of objectives into some rational form, rather than presenting micro-level lessons in a serial format. According to their conversation, learning to perform an enterprise activity requires the development of an enterprise schema, consisting of the individual objectives (remembering, using, or discovering facts, concepts, rules, and principles) as well as some integrative understanding of their common purpose.

Enterprises can be of three types: denoting, manifesting, and discovering (although four more kinds were identified by Merrill and colleagues, 1990). Denoting enterprises describe things, places, or events (their parts, kinds, etc.), manifesting enterprises describe processes, and discovery enterprises focus on discovering how things work. Discovering enterprises could function as support systems of some kinds of problem solving, but the relationships were never designated. It seems reasonable to predict that ill-structured problems would entail more discovery enterprises than well-structured problems.

Enterprises never fulfilled the need for macro-level integrating structures for the micro-level lesson strategies suggested by CDT and transaction theory. They were not comprehensive or integrative enough to describe the range of human activity. Enterprises were content-oriented organizing structures; no methods for organizing these macro-level structures were ever provided, nor were any prescriptions for how to aggregate enterprises into more complex and meaningful activities—they were still relatively micro-level descriptions. Even though they were described as activities, because of their content orientation, enterprises were not comprehended as authentic activities.

4C/ID

Van Merriënboer (1997) borrowed some from elaboration theory in order to provide an organizing structure for micro-level instructional components in his 4C/ID (four-component instructional design) model for designing instruction for complex cognitive tasks, that is, well-structured problems. Van Merriënboer used prerequisites analysis to decompose complex tasks in terms of their prerequisite skills and knowledge. These consist primarily of micro-level instructional units based on component display theory as component skills practice and just-in-time instructional support. Those constituent knowledge and skills are integrated into whole-task practice and elaboration and reflection exercises to promote transfer. The 4C/ID model provides a very rational and coherent objectivist model for organizing micro-level instructional components. Because of their focus on reliable prescriptions, objectivist approaches to instruction do not accommodate uncertainty and complexity very well. They assume that all-important skills can be known and reliably decomposed, and they cannot conceive of enough permutations of instructional components to represent the complexity of real-world problems, especially those ill-structured problems that demand multi-disciplinary solutions. Nonetheless, the 4C/ID model was a major step forward in providing macro-level prescriptions.

Situated Learning Models

The situated learning movement in instructional design that began in the early 1990s sought to replace objectivist models for organizing and teaching content, claiming that authentic activity, rather than subject matter content, should be the unit of analysis when constructing instruction or learning environments. Those environments would better accommodate the uncertainty and complexity inaccessible to objectivist models. I briefly describe a number of conceptual models for situated learning environments.

Rich environments for active learning (REALs) are instructional systems that engage learners in realistic, authentic, complex, and information-rich learning contexts, support intentional, self-regulated learning, support cooperative efforts in learning, and engage learners in complex problem solving (Grabinger, 1996). REALs emphasize authentic learning contexts for anchoring the meaning-making processes. They are student centered and learner controlled, emphasizing student responsibility and initiative in determining learning goals and regulating their performance toward those goals, not just determining the path through a prescribed set of learning activities.

Open-ended learning environments (OELEs) stress the use of manipulable objects to support experiential learning and student model building (Hannafin, Hall, Land, & Hill, 1994; Land & Hannafin, 1996). OELEs provide rich contexts, friendly interfaces, manipulation tools, supporting resources, and guidance to facilitate learner understanding. They support identifying, questioning, and testing personal models of phenomena as learners develop theories-in-action.

In goal-based scenarios (GBSs), students become active participants in complex systems. They employ a "learning-by-doing" architecture (Schank, Fano, Bell, & Jona, 1993/1994) in which learners are immersed in a focused, goal-oriented situation and are required to perform authentic, real-world activities. They are supported with advice in the form of stories that are indexed and accessed using case-based reasoning. Skills are acquired through practice in an authentic environment. Learning is driven by acceptance of a meaningful goal beyond the requirements of a particular task.

These are useful models for theoretically describing meaningful learning activities, but they are very short on instructional design prescriptions (see footnote 2). For example, a few REALs and OELEs have been identified, but none (to my knowledge) has ever been built. Many GBSs have been built for millions of dollars, but no one knows for sure how to do it, except for Roger Schank. In addition to contending that GBSs are the only form of instruction necessary anywhere, Schank provided few useful prescriptions for how to represent missions or create case libraries, let alone how to use the nearest neighbor algorithm to access relevant cases on demand. However, we have found that it is indeed very practical to construct a case-based retrieval engine and use it to access relevant stories in support of learning (Jonassen, Wang, Strobel, & Cernusca, 2003). Also, we believe that GBSs represent only a single approach to meaningful learning. We embellish our learning environments with many other characteristics.

Summary

In different ways, the macro-level design models just described provide structures for sequencing individual, component, micro-level lessons. Elaboration theory provides, I believe, the best integrative structures for organizing content lessons among all of the subject-matter structures.[4] Enterprises were never implemented, so their efficacy is unknown. Both elaboration theory and enterprises provide subject matter structures for organizing component content lessons. Contemporary situated and constructivist epistemologies recommend embedding content in au-

---

[4]It is a regular requirement in the subject-matter part of my task analysis course.

thentic activity, which is what 4C/ID attempts to do. However, 4C/ID limits its pre-scriptions to very prescriptive, well-structured tasks that are engaged only in educational and limited everyday contexts. Although the situated and constructivist design models, including OELEs, REALs, and GBSs, focus on au-thentic tasks, they provide inadequate prescriptions for how to develop instruction to support them. They are useful descriptions for existing environments; however, they are, I believe, inadequate frameworks for designing instruction. What is needed is meaningful, prescriptive task-based frameworks for integrating compo-nent content and skill lessons. Some of those frameworks, I believe, should specify different kinds of problem solving as their outcome (see footnote 2).

PROBLEM SOLVING AS THE KEY ENTERPRISE

In this section of the chapter, I first argue that problem solving is among the most consistently complex and authentic forms of human cognitive activity and that mod-els for supporting how to learn to solve different kinds of problems are among the most effective structures for organizing and sequencing micro-level instruction (see footnote 3). Even Merrill (2000) recently identified problem solving as an organiz-ing focus for micro-level instruction in his first principles of instruction. He claimed that "learning is facilitated when the learner is engaged in solving a real-world prob-lem, solves a progression of problems, [and] is guided to an explicit comparison of problems" (p. 1). Problem solving, according to Merrill's *First Principles*, requires a problem to solve, the tasks that comprise the problem, the operations that comprise the task, and the actions that comprise the operations. Although the differences be-tween tasks, operations, and actions are not clear (they could be construed in many ways), it is clear that they are the micro-level instructional components described in component display theory and ID2. I agree wholeheartedly with Merrill that the most meaningful, purposive, integrative focus for micro-level instruction and learn-ing is problem solving. Why? Human cognitive activity (and a lot of affective and emotional activity as well) is focused on solving problems. In our personal, profes-sional, formal, informal, and social lives, we invest more cognitive effort into solv-ing problems than into any other activity. Unfortunately, Merrill's first principles do not explicate the form, function, or components of problems. They do include con-sistent instructional components of activation, demonstration, application, and inte-gration, which are derivatives of component display theory.

Merrill (2000) went on to claim that comparing and contrasting successive problems is likely to result in more robust mental models required to support trans-fer. Again, I agree. Compare-and-contrast thinking is one of the most basic and im-portant cognitive operation required for higher order tasks.

Next, I briefly describe the nature of problem solving and different kinds of problems. Then, building on my current and previous work (Jonassen, 1997, 1999, 2000, 2004), I describe different problem-solving instructional design models and show how they can subsume micro-level instruction.

PROBLEM SOLVING

Rationale

Content-based approaches to organizing instruction lack authenticity for at least two reasons. First, they lack explicit purpose, which translates to a lack of intentional conceptual engagement on the part of learners (Sinatra & Pintrich, 2003). Telling students about the world in however complex ways and assessing their recall and comprehension is doomed because learners have no reason to learn. Meaningful learning requires a meaningful purpose for learning. The most consistently meaningful purpose for thinking is problem solving. Why? In everyday and professional contexts, memorizing information occurs in the context of more meaningful tasks, not as a goal unto itself. People are expected to solve problems and are rewarded for solving problems. Therefore, an important focus for organizing instruction should be on how to solve problems. This assumes that content is learned most effectively in the process of learning to solve problems.

Second, meaningful knowledge cannot be represented by a single ontology. One of the clearest findings from expert–novice research is that experts constructed multiple knowledge representations about their field. Experts represent what they know in different ways than novices do (Adelson, 1984; Chi, Feltovich, & Glaser, 1981; Reif, 1987), that is, using different ontologies. An ontology is a specification of a conceptualization (Gruber, 1994). Ontologies are formal systems for representing a task or a knowledge domain. As such, they represent theories of what exists in the mind of a knowledgeable agent (Wielenga & Schreiber, 1993). The ontology that underlies most instruction, curricula, and information access systems is hierarchical organization of domain concepts.

Unfortunately, this organizational structure is not how humans understand phenomena best. Rather, humans also naturally use epistemological (task-specific) ontologies, such as situational and strategic knowledge, and phenomenological ontologies, such as tacit, automated, sociocultural, and experiential knowledge, in order to solve problems (Jonassen, in press). The point is that no single taxonomy of learning outcomes, regardless of how coherent it is, can adequately describe all that someone needs to know in order to solve problems.

A Primer on Problem Solving

Problem solving has a few critical attributes, to use a concept from component display theory. First, problem solving requires an unknown, the answer to which is of sufficient value to find. Second, problem solving requires the mental representation of the unknown along with the situation in the world that surrounds the problem. That is, human problem solvers construct a mental representation of the problem, known as the problem space (Newell & Simon, 1972). Third, problem solving requires some active manipulation of the problem space. When we manipulate the problem space, we represent the components and dimensions of the problem, generate hypotheses about how to find the unknown, test those solutions, and draw conclusions. So manipulation of the problem space, be it an internal mental representation or an external physical representation, necessarily engages conscious activity.

Jonassen (1997) distinguished well-structured from ill-structured problems and recommended different design models for each. The most commonly encountered problems, especially in schools and universities, are well-structured problems. Well-structured problems require the application of a finite number of concepts, rules, and principles being studied to a constrained problem situation. Well-structured problems typically present all elements of the problem, engage a limited number of rules and principles that are organized in a predictive and prescriptive arrangement, possess correct, convergent answers, and have a preferred, prescribed solution process. Ill-structured problems, on the other hand, are the kinds of problems that are encountered in everyday practice. Ill-structured problems have many alternative solutions, are vaguely defined or have unclear goals and constraints, have multiple solution paths, and have multiple criteria for evaluating solutions—they are, therefore, more difficult to solve.

Just as ill-structured problems are more difficult to solve than well-structured problems, complex problems are more difficult to solve than simple ones. Complexity of a problem is a function of the number of issues, functions, or variables involved in the problem, the number of interactions among those issues, functions, or variables, and the predictability of the behavior of those issues, functions, or variables (Jonassen, 2003b).

Dynamicity is another dimension of complexity. In dynamic problems, the relationships among variables or factors change over time. Why? Changes in one factor may cause variable changes in other factors. The more intricate these interactions, the more difficult it is to find any solution.

A final dimension of problems and problem solving that is somewhat orthogonal to the other dimensions is domain specificity. In contemporary psychology, there is a common belief that problems within a domain rely on cognitive strategies that are specific to that domain (Mayer, 1982; Smith, 1991). Traditional conceptions of problem solving have been domain independent. That is, problem solving was conceived of as a mental skill that could be generalized across domains.

Jonassen (2000) described a typology of problems. This typology assumes that there are similarities in the cognitive processing engaged within these classes of problems and differences between classes. This range of problem types describes a continuum of problems primarily from well-structured to ill-structured. Within each category of problems that are described, problems can vary with regard to abstractness, complexity, and dynamicity. Kinds of problem solving include logic problems, algorithmic problems, story problems, rule-using problems, decision-making problems, troubleshooting problems, diagnosis–solution problems, strategic performance problems, case/system analysis problems, design problems, and dilemmas. In the next section, I elaborate on a few of these problem types and show how micro-level instructional components could be subsumed by problem-solving instruction.

MICRO-LEVEL SUPPORT FOR PROBLEM SOLVING

In this section, I briefly describe instructional design architectures for three different kinds of problems: story problems, troubleshooting problems, and case analysis problems. I also show how micro-level instructional components can be used to support these problem-solving enterprises.

Story Problems

Jonassen (2003b) described an architecture for building learning environments to help students to learn how to solve story problems (Fig. 6.3). The architecture emphasizes the qualitative representation of the problem prior to the quantitative (Jonassen, 2003; Ploetzner & Spada,1998).

The student first views the verbal and visual representations of the problem. Contrasting the problem as presented from other types they have solved before, students must first select the problem type they believe describes the problem, supported by prior or just-in-time instruction. This would require a series of use-concept lessons assembled in a part–whole sequence. Alternatively, a sequence of classify transactions could be used to support this activity. Using the Problem Classifier on physics problems, for instance, students might select increasingly specific classes of problems, including kinematics, then constant velocity, and then two-dimensional to describe a specific problem. The ability to compare and contrast problem types is essential to conceptual understanding of the problems

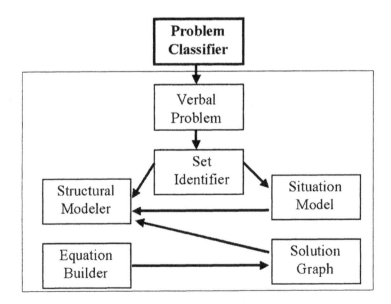

FIG. 6.3.   Architecture for designing story problem instruction.

and transfer of problem solving. Comparing and contrasting problem classes supports the construction of an integrated mental model of the physics domain. Next, parsing any story problem requires that learners identify the sets (numbers representing physical quantities) that are important to the solution and assign values to them. Completing and assigning values to these propositions supports the construction of distinct models for each type of problem (Mayer, 1982).

The student highlights the entities and their quantities in the verbal problem space and drags each value from the problem into the Set Identifier. The student must identify the object, the quantity, and the units describing the object. This task requires identify and interpret transactions or use-procedure lessons.

Working on any kind of story problem requires that learners recognize the underlying structures of the problems. The underlying principles of all domains are predicated on causal relationships among concepts. Each problem type in physics has a different structural model depicting a different combination of entities interrelated in unique ways. Having selected the problem type and identified the sets, the student drags and drops the sets from the Set Identifier onto the Structural Modeler. The model describes the structural and causal components of the problem. These models focus on describing the causal relationships between problem components. Why is that important? Ploetzner, Fehse, Kneser, and Spada (1999) showed that when solving physics problems, qualitative problem representations are necessary prerequisites to learning quantitative representations. Thus, students should map problem values onto a qualitative (causal) representation of the problem before mapping the values onto a formula. Using such a model requires a number of use-principle lessons or interpret transactions.

From the Structural Modeler, students assign values from the structural model onto an equation using the Equation Builder. In order to use the Equation Builder, the student drags values from the Structural Modeler into the equation space, and cancels out and then reorganizes the variables. Once the student has completed the formula, he or she clicks a calculate button. In order to test the accuracy of the values and the formula, an animated vector map will plot the results in the Run Solution window. These processes consist of use-principle and use-rule lessons or generalize, transfer, and substitute transactions.

Students view the situational model throughout the process because students make constructive inferences based on situational models. Situational content is also valuable because it affects access to internal, mental problem schemas. The situational model for each story problem lesson should consist of classify, generalize, and transfer transactions.

Instruction in the architecture that I have described is provided primarily through worked examples. Worked examples of problem solutions that precede practice improve practice-based problem solving by reducing the cognitive load and helping learners to construct problem-solving schemas (Cooper & Sweller, 1987; Sweller & Cooper, 1985). In my architecture, an animated, life-like pedagogical agent works through at least two examples of each problem type. Naturally, practice opportunities with increasingly differentiated examples are provided to students with feedback. These might consist of execute and transfer transactions. Because each problem integrates numerous rules, principles, and procedures, the combination of components required to provide practice are too great.

Troubleshooting Problems

Effective troubleshooting requires system knowledge, procedural knowledge, and strategic knowledge, indexed by experiential knowledge. Unfortunately, experiential knowledge is exactly what novices lack. Experienced technicians index their knowledge around troubleshooting experiences. Thus, teaching novices to troubleshoot requires that they troubleshoot as many problems as possible in order to gain the experiential knowledge that will integrate the conceptual, procedural, and strategic knowledge that is required to troubleshoot.

Figure 6.4 illustrates an architecture for building troubleshooting learning environments. The architecture assumes that the most effective way to learn to troubleshoot is by troubleshooting problems. Learning to troubleshoot problems requires presenting learners with the symptoms of novel problems and requiring learners to solve problems. The major components of troubleshooting instruction are a case library of previously solved problems, a troubleshooter that enables the learner to practice troubleshooting, and a rich conceptual model of the system being troubleshot. The conceptual model supports the construction of systems knowledge; the troubleshooter supports the construction of procedural and strategic

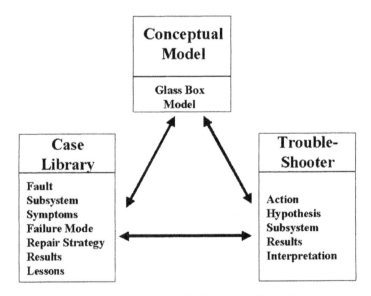

FIG. 6.4.   Architecture for designing troubleshooting learning environments.

knowledge; and the case library supports the construction of the experiential knowledge that integrates all of the other kinds of knowledge.

Troubleshooting is oriented by a conceptual model of the system being troubleshot. The Conceptual Model illustrates the interconnectedness of systems components. When troubleshooting a car that will not start, the mechanics will not resort to trial and error, serial elimination, or other weak troubleshooting strategies if they have a well-developed conceptual model of how the system works. The novice may access conceptually oriented information about the system just in time or prior to attempting to troubleshoot. The information specified in any conceptual model would require a host of use-concept, use-rule, and use-principle lessons that could be organized using elaboration theory structures (preferably theoretical, given the causal nature of systems).

The heart of troubleshooting instruction is the Troubleshooter, where the learner acts like an experienced troubleshooter by troubleshooting new cases. After listening to a story describing the symptoms of the problem, the learner (like an experienced troubleshooter) first selects an action to be taken, such as ordering a test, checking a connection, or trying a repair strategy. The novice may be coached about what action to take first based on the problem symptomology. Each action taken by the troubleshooter shows up in the systems model. For each action the learner takes, the Troubleshooter next requires the learner to state or select a fault hypothesis that he or she is testing. This is an implicit form of argumentation that requires the learner to justify the action taken. If the hypothesis is inconsistent with the action, then feedback can be immediately provided about the rationale for taking such an action. Next, the learner must also identify the subsystem in which the fault occurs. If the subsystem is inconsistent with the action, the learner is immediately sent to the Conceptual Model to better understand the workings of the subsystem that leads to the action or hypothesis. The learner then receives the result of action (e.g., test results, system information, etc.) and must interpret those results using a pull-down menu in the Troubleshooter. If the interpretation is inconsistent with the action, hypothesis, or subsystem, then an error message is triggered. The error checking uses a very simple evaluation system. The Troubleshooter requires the learner to think and act like an experienced troubleshooter. The Troubleshooter would be difficult to represent or support using micro-level interactions. It would require a complex combination of use-concept, use-rule, use-procedure, and use-principle instruction. Alternatively, it would require a very complex combination of execute, interpret, judge, and propagate transactions.

The environment integrates the troubleshooting actions, knowledge types (conceptual, strategic, and procedural), and conceptual systems model with a database of faults that have occurred with the system that the learner and others have solved. Initial instruction in how to use the system is provided by worked examples. As learners solve troubleshooting problems, the results of their practice cases can be added to the learner's case library of fault situations, so that the learner can learn from his or her own personal experience.

If the Troubleshooter is the heart of instruction, the Case Library is the head (memory). In troubleshooting situations in everyday contexts, the primary medium of negotiation is stories. That is, when a troubleshooter experiences a problem, he or she most often describes the problem to someone else, who recalls from memory a similar problem, telling the troubleshooter about the recalled experience. These stories provided contextual information, work as a format for diagnosis, and express an identity among participants in any kind of community. Stories about how experienced troubleshooters have solved similar troubleshooting problems are contained in, indexed by, and made available to learners in a Case Library (also known as a Fault Database).

The Case Library or Fault Database contains stories of as many troubleshooting experiences as possible. Each case represents a story of a domain-specific troubleshooting instance. Case libraries, based on principles of case-based reasoning, represent the most powerful form of instructional support for ill-structured problems such as troubleshooting (Jonassen & Hernandez-Serrano, 2002). The Case Library indexes each case or story according to its system fault, the system or subsystem in which the fault occurred, and the symptoms of the fault, similar to the way a troubleshooter would. The failure mode, hypotheses, or strategies that were tested, the results of those tests, and the lessons learned from the experience are also contained in the Case Library. The Case Library represents the experiential knowledge of potentially hundreds of experienced troubleshooters. That experiential knowledge is precisely what learners do not possess. So when a learner encounters any difficulty or is uncertain about how to proceed, the learner may access the Case Library to learn about similar cases, what was done, and what the results were. The environment can automatically access a relevant story when a learner commits an error, orders an inappropriate test, or takes some other action that indicates a lack of understanding. Stories are easily collected from experienced troubleshooters by presenting them with a problem and asking them if they are reminded of a similar problem that they have solved. Hernandez-Serrano and Jonassen (2003) showed that access to a case library during learning how to solve problems improved complex problem-solving performance on an examination. Learning to use the Case Library would require a host of identify, classify, generalize, and analogize transactions.

Similar to learning how to solve story problems, learners will be introduced to the Troubleshooter, Case Library, and Conceptual Model through worked examples that not only illustrate how to use the environment but also model different troubleshooting strategies (e.g., space-splitting), in order to isolate the faulty subsystem before conducting any tests.

Practice consists of using the Troubleshooter to troubleshoot new problems. During practice, new problems are presented to the learner, who uses the Troubleshooter to isolate the case of the problem. It is worth noting that most of these actions that learners take during their practice (actions in the Troubleshooter, accessing information in the Conceptual Model, or accessing cases from the Case Library) can be used to assess the learners' understanding and troubleshooting skills.

Case/Systems Analysis Problems

These ill-structured problems are often solved in professional contexts (Fig. 6.5). Systems analysis problems require the solver to articulate the nature of the problem and the different perspectives that impact the problem before suggesting solutions (Jonassen, 1997). They are more contextually bound than either story problems or troubleshooting problems. That is, their solutions rely on an analysis of contextual factors. Business problems, including planning production, are common systems analysis problems. Deciding production levels, for instance, requires balancing human resources, technologies, inventory, and sales. Classical situated systems analysis problems also exist in international relations, such as, "Given low crop productivity in the Soviet Union, how would the solver go about improving crop productivity if he or she served as Director of the Ministry of Agriculture in the Soviet Union?" (Voss & Post, 1988, p. 273).

Supporting case analysis problems with micro-level lessons is problematic. Most case analysis problems would require hundreds of use-concept, use-rule, and use-principle lessons that would have to be accessed just in time. It is more likely that ID2 transactions, accessed just in time, would be more productive. The particular combination of transactions would depend on the nature of the system being analyzed while solving a problem related to it.

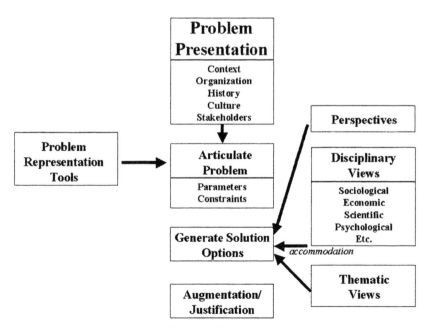

FIG. 6.5.   Architecture for case/system analysis problem-solving environment.

CONCLUSION

Few models or theories for organizing micro-level lessons for individual objectives exist in the instructional design literature, and most of those are content oriented, rather than activity oriented. Current situated learning models and theories, while activity oriented, ignore the need for micro-level lessons. The basic premise of this chapter is that problem-solving outcomes are the most meaningful and authentic learning outcomes and can provide effective organizing structures (enterprises) for arranging and sequencing micro-level, component lessons. I have shown how well-structured problem-solving outcomes, among the most pandemic of all problem solving in schools, can comprise enterprises for integrating lessons for multiple objectives.

I agree with van Merriënboer (1997) that the most appropriate application of these micro-level lessons is just-in-time support of more complex and authentic activities such as problem solving. However, as problems become more complex and ill-structured (e.g., strategic performance, case analysis, or design problems), the macro-level, problem-oriented designs cannot be as prescriptive, especially regarding instructional sequences. No strategies for integrating micro-level lessons into complex, problem-solving organizing structures exist. We simply do not know what level of complexity and uncertainty in problems (ill-structuredness) can accommodate micro-level lessons or how those lessons should be accessed. More research and development work on problem-solving design models is needed. That is a goal that I shall pursue for the remainder of my career.

REFERENCES

Adelson, B. (1984). When novices surpass experts: The difficulty of a task may increase with expertise. *Journal of Experimental Psychology, 10*(3), 483–496.

Ausubel, D. P. (1963). *Educational psychology: A cognitive view.* New York: Holt, Rinehart, & Winston.

Chi, M. T. H., Feltovich, P. J., & Glaser, R. (1981). Categorization and representation of physics problems by experts and novices. *Cognitive Science, 5,* 121–152.

Cooper, G., & Sweller, J. (1987). Effects of schema acquisition and rule automation on mathematical problem solving. *Journal of Educational Psychology, 79,* 347–362.

Courseware, Inc. (1978). *Author training course.* Pensacola, FL: Naval Education & Training Command.

Ellis, J. A., & Wulfeck, W. H. (1978). *Instructional quality inventory; Job performance aid.* San Diego, CA: Navy Personnel Research and Development Center (ED 169287).

Fisher, K. M. (1991). SemNet: A tool for personal knowledge construction. In D. H. Jonassen & P. Kommers (Eds.), *Mindtools* (pp. 63–77). Berlin: Springer-Verlag.

Gagné, R. M. (1977). *The conditions of learning* (3rd ed.). New York: Holt, Rinehart & Winston.

Gagné, R. M., & Merrill, M. D. (1990). Integrative goals for instructional design. *Educational Technology Research and Development, 38*(1), 23–30.

Grabinger, R. S. (1996). Rich environments for active learning. In D. H. Jonassen (Ed.), *Handbook of research for educational communications and technology* (pp. 665–692). New York: Macmillan.

Gruber, T. (1994). Toward principles for the design of ontologies used for knowledge sharing. *International Journal of Human-Computer Systems, 43*(5/6), 199–220.

Hannafin, M. J., Hall, C., Land, S., & Hill, J. (1994). Learning in open-ended environments: Assumptions, methods, and implications. *Educational Technology, 34*(5), 48–55.

Hernandez-Serrano, J., & Jonassen, D. H. (2003). The effects of case libraries on problem solving. *Journal of Computer-Assisted Learning, 19*, 103–114.

Jonassen, D. H. (1997). Instructional design model for well-structured and ill-structured problem-solving learning outcomes. *Educational Technology Research and Development, 45*(1), 65–95.

Jonassen, D. H. (1999). Designing constructivist learning environments. In C. M. Reigeluth (Ed.), *Instructional design theories and models: Their current state of the art* (2nd ed., pp. 215–240). Mahwah, NJ: Lawrence Erlbaum Associates.

Jonassen, D. H. (2003). Using cognitive tools to represent problems. *Journal of Research in Technology in Education, 35* (3), 362–381.

Jonassen, D. H. (2004). *Learning to solve problems: An instructional design guide.* San Francisco: Jossey-Bass.

Jonassen, D. H. (in press). Knowledge is complex: Accommodating human ways of knowing. *Knowledge Organization.*

Jonassen, D. H. (2003b). Designing instruction for story problems. *Educational Psychology Review, 15*(3), 267–296.

Jonassen, D. H., & Hernandez-Serrano, J. (2002). Case-based reasoning and instructional design: Using stories to support problem solving. *Educational Technology Research and Development, 50*(2), 65–77.

Jonassen, D. H., Hernandez-Serrano, J., & Choi, I. (2000). Integrating constructivism and learning technologies. In J. M. Spector & T. M. Anderson (Eds.), *Integrated and holistic perspectives on learning, instruction, and technology* (pp. 103–128). Amsterdam: Kluwer Academic.

Jonassen, D. H., Wang, F. K., Strobel, J., & Cernusca, D. (2003). Application of a case library of technology integration stories for teachers. *Journal of Technology and Teacher Education, 11*(4), 547–566.

Jones, M. K., Li, Z., & Merrill, M. D. (1990). Domain knowledge representation for instructional analysis. *Educational Technology, 30*(9), 7–31.

Land, S. M., & Hannafin, M. J. (1996). A conceptual framework for the development of theories-in-action with open-ended learning environments. *Educational Technology Research & Development, 44*(3), 37–53.

Mayer, R. E. (1982). Memory for algebra story problems. *Journal of Educational Psychology, 74*(2), 199–216.

Merrill, M. D. (1973). Content and instructional analysis for cognitive transfer task. *AV Communication Review, 21*, 109–126.

Merrill, M. D. (1983). Component display theory. In C. M. Reigeluth (Ed.), *Instructional design theories and models: An overview of their current status* (pp. 279–333). Hillsdale, NJ: Lawrence Erlbaum Associates.

Merrill, M. D. (1987). The new component design theory: Instructional design for courseware authoring. *Instructional Science, 16*, 19–34.

Merrill, M. D. (2000, October). *First principles of instruction.* Paper presented at the annual meeting of the Association for Educational Communications and Technology, Denver, CO.

Merrill, M. D., Jones, M. K., & Li, Z. (1992). Instructional transaction theory: Classes of transactions. *Educational Technology, 32*(9), 12–26.

Merrill, M. D., Li, Z., & Jones, M. K. (1990). Second generation instructional design (ID2). *Educational Technology, 30*(2), 7–14.

Merrill, M. D., Li, Z., & Jones, M. K. (1991). Instructional transaction theory: An introduction. *Educational Technology, 31*(6), 7–12.

Merrill, M. D., Li, Z., & Jones, M. K. (1992). Instructional transaction shells: Responsibilities, methods, and parameters. *Educational Technology, 32*(2), 5–26.

Merrill, M. D., Reigeluth, C. M., & Faust, G. W. (1979). The instructional quality profile: Curriculum evaluation and design. In H. F. O'Neal (Ed.), *Procedures for instructional systems development* (pp. 165–204). New York: Academic Press.

Merrill, M. D., Richards, R. E., Schmidt, R., & Wood, N. D. (1977). *The instructional strategy diagnostic profile training manual.* Provo, UT: Brigham Young University, David O. McKay Institute.

Montague, W. E. (1983). Instructional quality inventory. *Performance and Instruction, 22*(5), 11–14.

Montague, W. E., & Wulfeck, W. H. (1982). *Improving the quality of Navy training: The role of R&D in support of instructional systems design, final report.* San Diego, CA: Navy Personnel Research and Development Center. (ERIC Document Reproduction Service No. ED243472)

Newell, A., & Simon, H. A. (1972). *Human problem solving.* Englewood Cliffs, NJ: Prentice Hall.

Ploetzner, R., Fehse, E., Kneser, C., & Spada, H. (1999). Learning to relate qualitative and quantitative problem representations in a model-based setting for collaborative problem solving. *Journal of the Learning Sciences, 8*(2), 177–214.

Ploetzner, R., & Spada, H. (1998). Constructing quantitative problem representations on the basis of qualitative reasoning. *Interactive Learning Environments, 5,* 95–107.

Reif, F. (1987). Instructional design, cognition, and technology: Application to the teaching of science concepts. *Journal of Research in Science Teaching, 24*(4), 309–324.

Reigeluth, C. M. (1979). In search of a better way of organizing instruction: The elaboration theory. *Journal of Instructional Development, 2*(1), 8–15.

Reigeluth, C. M. (1983a). Meaningfulness and instruction: Relating what is being learned to what a student knows. *Instructional Science, 12,* 197–218.

Reigeluth, C. M. (1983b). Instructional design: What it is and why it is. In C. M. Reigeluth (Ed.), *Instructional design theories and models: An overview of their current status* (pp. 3–36). Hillsdale, NJ: Lawrence Erlbaum Associates.

Reigeluth, C. M. (1987). Lesson blueprints based on the elaboration theory of instruction. In C. M. Reigeluth (Ed.), *Instructional theories in action: Lessons, illustrations, theories and models* (pp. 245–288). Hillsdale, NJ: Lawrence Erlbaum Associates.

Reigeluth, C. M., Merrill, M. D., & Bundeson, C. V. (1978). The structure of subject matter content and its implications for instructional design. *Instructional Science, 7,* 107–126.

Reigeluth, C. M., & Stein, F. S. (1983). The elaboration theory of instruction. In C. M. Reigeluth (Ed.), *Instructional theories and models: An overview of their current status* (pp. 335–382). Hillsdale, NJ: Lawrence Erlbaum Associates.

Scandura, J. M. (1973). *Structural learning: Theory and research.* New York: Gordon & Breach.

Schank, R. C., Fano, A., Bell, B., & Jona, M. (1993/1994). The design of goal-based scenarios. *Journal of the Learning Sciences, 3*(4), 305–345.

Sinatra, G. M., & Pintrich, P. R. (Eds.), (2003). *Intentional conceptual change.* Mahwah, NJ: Lawrence Erlbaum Associates.

Smith, M. U. (1991). *Toward a unified theory of problem solving.* Hillsdale, NJ: Lawrence Erlbaum Associates.

Sweller, J., & Cooper, G. A. (1985). The use of worked examples as a substitute for problem solving in learning algebra. *Cognition and Instruction, 2*(1), 59–89.

van Merriënboer, J. J. G. (1997). *Training complex cognitive skills: A four component instructional design model for technical training.* Englewood Cliffs, NJ: Educational Technology.

Voss, J. F., & Post, T. A. (1988). On the solving of ill-structured problems. In M. T. H. Chi, R. Glaser, & M. J. Farr (Eds.), *The nature of expertise* (pp. 261–285). Hillsdale, NJ: Lawrence Erlbaum Associates.

Wielenga, B. J., & Schreiber, A. T. (1993). Usable and sharable knowledge bases: A European perspective. In *Proceedings of the First International Conference on Building and Sharing of Very Large-Scaled Knowledge Bases* (pp. 000–000). Tokyo: Japan Information Processing Development Center.

Chapter
7

Elementary Principles of Design Languages and Design Notation Systems for Instructional Design

Andrew S. Gibbons
Brigham Young University

Erin K. Brewer
Utah State University

Design languages, formal or intuitive, lie at the heart of all design and development processes and tools. Instructional designers tend to be unaware of the multiplicity of design languages they use. This is not surprising because in most fields the use of design languages to improve precision and productivity is relatively new. However, the identification and use of design languages in many design and manufacturing fields has greatly benefited growth and maturation over a very short span of years. Instructional design will also benefit from this trend as designers and theorists become aware of the existence and use of design languages and their related notation systems.

This chapter encourages the study and principled use of languages of instructional design. It does so not only for the benefits of precision and improved productivity that are possible, but also because design languages are a part of the larger issues of design architecture and design theory. Gibbons (2003a, 2003b) described a theory of design layering in which design languages supply the structures and structuring rules needed to complete designs within each layer. Multiple languages within each layer provide the opportunity for variations within each layer and define the design building blocks designers are likely to use as they design. This places great importance on the study of the many languages and their relationship to each other.

The scope of this chapter is limited to design languages and their corresponding systems for notation. An extended discussion of notation systems, their characteristics, and their relation to design is available in Waters and Gibbons (2004). First, we describe design languages in general: what they are, what purpose they serve, how they originate, and how their notation systems make possible the sharing of design plans. We then describe examples from fields whose design technologies have advanced due to the exploitation of design languages and their principled application. After a review of the impact of design languages on other design fields, we propose the value of design language study to instructional technology. We feel that the exploration of the many languages of instructional design will open new avenues of progress in design theory and design practice. Finally, we recommend directions for the study and application of design languages for instructional technology that may be fruitful.

A Design Language Example

Rheinfrank and Evenson (1996) described the subtle but powerful effects of a design language on the design of physical workspaces. Offices were once designed as fully partitioned spaces, enclosed by costly and permanent wall barriers. The terms used by the designers of these workspaces caused them to create very specific kinds of places: "Closed offices and broken up spaces … required extensive (and expensive) remodeling to accommodate the natural variety of uses" (p. 75).

Over time, as the nature of the work in offices changed, a new design language for office spaces emerged:

> In the mid-fifties, modular office systems were developed. They introduced an entirely new language for the production of offices. Along with that language came assumptions about openness and flexibility, and radically new building economies. A new industry formed around this primary innovation and the attached set of assumptions. (p. 75)

Continuing changes in work patterns may be expected to lead to yet another shift:

> The office-building industry today faces the challenge of readdressing its assumption base. The original design language was deeply grounded in the productivity of single individuals during a time when the prevailing work tools were calculators and typewriters. Current work practices seem to be evolving toward conditions that call for collaboration, communication, geographically distributed work teams, and orga-

nizations with fluid structure. None of these conditions can be addressed effectively with the current office design language. (p. 75)

In other words, before a new generation of offices is designed to accommodate this changing need, we might expect design languages to evolve containing new terms representing structures and structuring processes aligned with new requirements. As Cole, Engestrom, and Vasquez (1997) pointed out, the languages used "to a great extent shapes what can and cannot be thought and said, or in this case remembered" (p. 231).

WHAT IS A DESIGN LANGUAGE?

Winograd (1996) described design languages as:

visual and functional languages of communication with the people who use an artifact. A design language is like a natural language, both in its communicative function and in its structure as an evolving system of elements and relationships among those elements. (p. 64)

If language is what people use for communicating information and ideas to each other, then a design language is what designers use to communicate designs, plans, and intentions to each other and to the producers of their artifacts. We tend to be unaware of our use of design languages to generate and express designs. Rheinfrank and Evenson (1996) explained:

Design languages consist of design elements and principles of composition. Like natural languages, design languages are used for generation (creating things) and interpretation (reading things). Natural languages are used to generate expressions that communicate ideas; design languages are used to design objects that express what the objects are, what they do, and how they are to be used, and how they contribute to experience. (p. 68)

As writers, we school ourselves in the use of natural languages in order to communicate ideas more effectively. As designers, we should become more conscious of our use of instructional design languages to better express and share design ideas.

The Variety of Design Languages

Some of our design languages, such as computer programming languages, are formal, and when we use them it is a conscious, deliberate design activity. Many of our design languages, however, are so subtle that we do not recognize them and realize that we use them to structure designs. Rheinfrank and Evenson (1996) said that "we do not just use our language: we *live* with it" (p. 65).

Design languages are used to express designs, intentions, and plans. Familiar design languages are those used in architecture, music composition, writing, choreography, mathematics, and computer programming. However, myriad less familiar, personal design languages make up the very essence of our personal style and underlie how we design and create our interactions with others.

Design languages take many forms and yet can be seen as the order-giving principle at the heart of many of our technologies—even something as unexpected as a fountain. For example, for the 2002 Winter Olympics, Salt Lake City created a public fountain consisting of a flat, open plaza with water pipes embedded in a radiating pattern beneath the concrete, showing at the surface as open nozzles pointing upward. Water columns spurt upward in planned synchrony as the fountain executes one of its designed cycles of operation. Beautiful and dynamic structures of water appear and disappear in synchrony with the ebb and flow of music, creating a pleasing effect. The emotional impact on an observer watching and listening to the fountain can be very agreeable.

The fountain does not usually promote analytic thoughts, and a performance does not usually remind the observer of the structures used to create its effects. However, a designer can see the fountain's creations in the terms of a language of individual water jets. By watching just one pipe for a few minutes, it becomes apparent that there are roughly 16 different jet types that an individual pipe can produce. Each type can be characterized in terms of the duration of the spurt (long–short), the height of the water column produced (tall–short), and the manner in which the jet is initiated (rapid–slow) and ended (rapid–slow). Modifiers applied to all of these basic terms (very rapid, very tall, etc.) create a larger range of nuanced expressions. The complicated and beautiful transient structures of the fountain as a whole are an emergent phenomenon produced by the actions of individual valves and their programming, and the program is written in the terms of a simple design language.

The fountain is capable of a seemingly infinite variety of combined expressions, but all of them are generated from the same 16 basic spurts (as modified), shot from different individual pipes, across time. In effect, there are 16 words in the fountain's dictionary. The variety of effects arises from various synchronous patterns of the individual pipes "speaking" one of the 16 language terms and its modifiers at a precise moment. When we see the fountain, we do not see the individual jets of water; we see the larger patterns: walls, pinnacles, cascades, and valleys made of columns and voids of water moving in graceful coordination. These are water sentences created using 16 words of a jet design language. A random pattern of jets is less likely to produce a pleasing effect, although some random patterns may be interesting. We are more likely to enjoy the production of larger structures in a sequence that produces pleasing contrasts: the gradual rise and fall of a wall, the sudden eruption of a pinnacle, a retreating curtain, and so on. This realization reveals the existence of a set of rules governing the formation of expressions in this design language. We may not assume that there is but one set of correct rules, and we can see the possibility that favoring different rules creates divergent styles that program designers can choose or create.

Our discussion of design languages will help us explore how small sets of simple constituent terms have been combined to form designs of fascinating variety in many different design fields. It will also help us explore how design and development processes create language expressions and how design and development tools—also founded on their own design languages—can then help reify abstract ideas as artifacts that can be experienced.

The Dimensions of Design Languages

One way to bring the concept of design languages into sharper focus is to look at the many dimensions along which design languages vary.

Complexity. Design languages emerge as sets of terms we use in our thinking and planning. As we abstract these as patterns from experience, we can name them and use them in our designs. At some point, the terms *arch, musical measure,* and *program loop* occurred to someone's mind as useful elements of a design. The simplest design language posits these primitive building blocks from which designs can be composed. A nuanced design language describes more complex combinations of building blocks as well.

Somewhat more complex design languages use terms that are formed into useful categories. Usually these categories will be related in such a way that if something does not represent one category then it will represent another. Thus, a landscape designer might classify plants in a way that simplifies planning a flower garden that will remain colorful throughout the season: "early-blooming, low-height, white, spreading" plants will be differentiated from "mid-blooming, mid-height, yellow, vertical," plants and "late-blooming, tall, green, shrubs." Category systems allow us to organize our terms into more or less independent, more or less exclusive categories.

The most sophisticated and complex design languages possess many, clearly defined, independent and exclusive categories. In addition, they possess clear and unambiguous rules for forming design expressions that include these terms—in other words, a grammar. Programming languages fall into this type; natural language does not. Both the categories and the rules of the natural language are full of irregularities, overlaps, fuzziness, and conflicting rules. Although the grammatical rules of a language are meant to govern acceptable expression, the rules and categories of human languages are not unambiguous. Thus, a properly formed expression in natural language can have two competing interpretations, but a properly formed C++ expression cannot. Programming languages meet the criterion of unambiguous categories and clear rules. They are created with those properties in mind: Every written symbol representing a language term has either a single meaning or multiple meanings that cannot become confused.

Precision. Natural languages have some fuzzy and conflicted categories and rules for two reasons: (a) The languages grow by an unstructured process over time and continue to change according to common usage, and (b) some degree of looseness and language definition is tolerable and actually helpful. A fuzzy, imprecise language can get the job done for most people. "Whoa! Dude!" carries enough meaning to be useful in some situations, although it can mean different things. In fact, requiring too much precision in natural language expressions can create cognitive overload and stifle pleasant emotional experiences that may result from double meanings—taking from us, for instance, the enjoyment of Shakespeare.

On the other hand, mathematical expressions and computer programs cannot tolerate ambiguity. Mathematical expressions must be unambiguous; there can only be one meaning, even when the expression is defining an area, such as "greater than" or "less than." The typical computer program cannot execute properly if there is ambiguity, because the computer is not given enough information to resolve the ambiguity. At any time when the computer confronts an ambiguity such as in conditional statements, there must be enough information available to resolve the ambiguity (e.g., data to determine whether a condition exists). Precision in the design language is created through the measurability and exactness of its terms and relationships. It must be possible to determine the meaning of a term unambiguously. The degree of precision of a language varies as a result of how reliant it is on context. Speakers of natural language use a wide variety of contextual cues, such as intonation, gestures, and surroundings, to imbue the words they speak with added meaning. Computer languages, on the other hand do not benefit from a rich field of contextual cues. Because of this, languages that rely on context can be more flexible. Precision and flexibility differ correspondingly between a general language that can be used for a variety of needs being adapted for multiple tasks and a specific language that has a single use and purpose (Cole, 1971).

Formality and Standardization.   Terms in a precise design language should mean the same thing for all users. It is agreement among users of the meaning of terms within a precise language that allows these kinds of languages to work. This is possible when design languages become public (through a process described later) and rules within the domain of the language are generally accepted by a large number of language users. This describes the formality and standardization of design languages. Some languages are so formalized, and the categories and rules so explicit, that expressions incorrectly made (poorly formed according to the rules) turn the entire expression into nonsense. This is true especially of the highly formal languages used in computer programming and mathematics. Of course, nonsense can occur in less formal languages as well.

Personal Versus Shared.   Design languages originate with individuals and emerge more or less automatically from the design process (Rheinfrank & Evenson, 1996). A design language is possessed by an individual. Design languages only become public or shared through negotiation and interaction between individuals. As agreement on terms and rules of expression emerges from interactive practice, the language becomes public and can be shared by many users. Making a language public for a broad audience requires that some form of symbolic notation system be devised for writing down expressions in the language (Waters & Gibbons, 2004). Symbolic notation systems are not the same as design languages themselves, as we describe later.

Implicit versus explicit.   Many design languages are personal and idiosyncratic, belonging to us alone. Some of these personal languages exist in our minds at levels that we cannot verbalize but that we can use to make decisions. We may not be aware of many of the languages we possess. We can call these *implicit* design languages. We use them to design our conversations, much of our written communication, our strategies for action, our personal plans, our relationships with other people, and our daily routines. At the opposite end of the spectrum, we also use design languages whose terms and rules are completely specified. We can call these *explicit* design languages. We often learn these languages through study or by shared practice with others. In shared languages, as disagreements or anomalies reveal an area not explicitly addressed by the language, negotiations can begin to deal with the uncertainty, usually resulting in additional language specification or modification of someone's understanding of the language.

Standardized Versus Nonstandardized.   Some design languages are of sufficient economic importance that users form standards organizations to work out detailed formal terminology and rules of usage. Once a standard is set, those who conform to the standard in their designs expect their products to function smoothly within a context that includes other products. Those who differ from the agreed standard either risk their product being nonfunctional in some contexts or expect competitive advantage from setting their own standard.

Design languages for which standards have evolved are especially common in the fields of engineering, manufacturing, electronics, computers, and computer software. Instructional designers are influenced by the programming standards their design and development tools adhere to, but standards for instructional designers are not confined to software. Designs for computer-based instruction for some clients may have to conform to instructional or product packaging standards such as those set by the Aviation Industry CBT Consortium (AICC, n.d.). The IMS Global Learning Consortium (IMS, n.d.), Sharable Content Object Reference Model (SCORM, n.d.), Advanced Distributed Learning initiative (ADL, n.d.), and IEEE Learning Technology Standards Committee (IEEE/LTSC, n.d.) are parts of a large movement to create design language standards for reusable design objects. The object types constitute some of the terms of an object design language. However, even with languages that have very clear standards, dialects may occur, and this is one way that languages evolve and improve.

Computability.   Some design languages are so formalized and precise that computer programs are written to test major portions of the designs they create without having to build an actual product. For instance, this is true of the languages used to design computer chips. Chip design has become such a complex design problem that large areas of the design are automated. That is, part of a computer's design is carried out by a computer. In order for this to happen and for the complex designs to be tested before chips are built, the design language must be computable. Terms in the language must be turned into computer program terms and then executed. In such automated design (and design testing) systems, the design itself consists of expressions in the design language resulting from computations by the design program.

Design languages of this sort are often generated from a set of core principles, rather than evolving haphazardly from general patterns of usage. It is frequently this core of formulated principles that gives the language its computability. The large majority of design languages, however, are not formal, computable, or standard.

DESIGN LANGUAGES AND NOTATION SYSTEMS

An important quality of a design language is whether or not it has been coupled with a sharable, public, consistent notation system. A notation system is the set of symbolic, graphic, gestural, artifactual, auditory, textual or other conventions for expressing outwardly designs created using a particular design language. For a more detailed discussion of notation systems, see Waters and Gibbons (2004).

A design language is a set of categories or terms and a set of rules for making design expressions in those terms that represent plans and intentions. A design language has no outward expression, however, unless some system of markings, symbols, motions, or verbalizations is invented in which there is some degree of correspondence between design language terms and elements of the markings. Often a temporal or spatial convention exists for showing relations among various elements. An artifact is a reified expression of the language used to design it. Often, as in the case of the Olympic fountain, some of the languages used by the designer can be discerned in the final product.

Design language is abstract; it has no outward form that can be sensed until we give it expression in drawings, in words, in sounds, in symbols, in physical objects, or in gestures. We can compose sonnets in our head, but until they are expressed in writing or through speech, there is no public, shareable form, and the sonnet exists only for us personally. No one else can see the sonnet; no one else can memorize it, modify it, repeat it, print it, or in any way share it effectively with others without some tangible form of the design being created. But once it is expressed in some way, it can be translated into other forms of notation; for example, a spoken sonnet can be written down or translated into Braille. Similarly, we can conceive the details of a building's design in our mind, but until we have a system for graphical and textual notation, the design cannot be shared. Moreover, if notations are in a notational system not known to another person, then many of the details of the plan will not be communicated.

A design can be shared in two ways: (a) by a description that relies on natural language, or (b) through a specialized notation system that uses figures, drawings, models or other standard symbolic representations of any kind (which may include words) to express the elements and relationships of a design. A notational system must be considered separately from the design language it externalizes and whose designs it makes public, because there are multiple ways that a design can be communicated.

The Emergence of Notation Systems

Most of the personal design languages that we use have no explicit system for external representation. Instead, an individual translates their design language into some language that is already shared. In the process of translating from the design language used to a common natural language, the fidelity of the design can be jeopardized.

A design language begins with an individual who thinks and solves design problems using whatever familiar, comfortable, and useful terms the person possesses (keeping in mind that in this usage, *term* can be an unnamed category that is felt or sensed but not easy to express). The personal terms and their possible relations form a personal design language. The terms identify elements of a solution that the individual has found useful in the past or even elements the individual has just conceived and thinks might provide a key to the solution. Personal design languages come about either as we hear them from others, or as we invent them.

As people interact with us in solving design problems, they may see the value of our personal, idiosyncratic design language or some of its terms and begin to share use of the language. Also at some point, in order to communicate ideas or structures using fewer words, we may begin to write or sketch or in some way capture in externalized form the structures of the design, using some combination of words, graphics, symbols, gestures, models, or sounds to represent specific terms of the language and relationships that link terms into higher-order design expressions. This is the beginning of a notation system, and to the extent that more users can agree on notation conventions and their relation to design language terms, the use of the notation can become widespread.

The Development of a Musical Notation System

This process took place in the historical development of musical notation, which really consists of an agreed-on notation system for capturing abstract musical designs in graphical, textual, and symbolic representation. Many different systems of musical notation have been proposed and used over many years. Originally, in the Western or European musical tradition, there was music, but there was no consistent notation system for capturing and making public musical designs. But from 900 A.D. to about 1300 A.D., musical ideas and structures found symbolic expression through a series of notation system innovations and their cultural acceptance.

At the beginning of the period, church music had to be sung from memory because there was no standard system for writing down melodies, harmonies, and rhythms. The words to be sung were written, but the musical content (the tune) had to be memorized. The amount of music that could accumulate was therefore limited by the collective memory those who had to remember it. Training took years of apprenticeship, and the complexity of the music was limited to simple melody lines. The earliest form of musical notation simply added accent marks to the written words to indicate rising or falling pitch, but these marks indicated only relative pitch change (upward or downward), not specific levels or note values. Adding that information to a notational system required new symbology. A major step forward in this direction was to give notes individual identity within a spatial representation matrix. In the early 1000s, Guido d'Arezzo labeled the joints and tips of his fingers with specific musical tones. This placed the notes in a fixed relationship with each other and provided a shared reference notation for individual tones. To remind singers which note to sing, Guido simply pointed to the appropriate joint or fingertip on his marked hand.

It was a short jump from lines formed by finger joints to lines on paper that represented a fixed relationship between notes. Many systems emerged for drawing calibration lines—the number of them varied—and placing markings on or between the lines to indicate notes at specific pitches. Variations on this basic notation scheme included experimenting with color, more or fewer lines, different-shaped markings to indicate note values, and other mechanisms that communicated additional terms and structures from abstractions in the mind of the writer to the visible representation. When a music writer could conceive of a quality in the music for which there was no notational convention, then the writer might invent a notational mark for that purpose. Experimentation with notation systems continues today as composers and theorists continue to search for the best way to express their musical ideas.

The general form of the music notation system became structurally complete when notation of timing was introduced with the addition of the *musical measure* structure to both the music design language and the notation system. This completed the conversion of musical notation from being marks added to words; in the process it freed the expression of music from words altogether and gave music a rich new set of design language terms related to the time dimension: time signature, rhythm, measure, and so forth.

The Interplay Between Design Languages and Notation Systems

Written musical notation is not music design language. It is simply a visible representation—a notation—of the terms and relations that exist in the musical design language that exists in the mind of the composer. We may speculate that some of the differences in composer excellence are the result of a more expressive set of (personal) design language terms or a better set of (personal) rules for synthesizing expressions from the terms.

After about 1300 A.D., with a growing notation system, music ideas and expressions could also grow in precision and complexity. Systems of harmony could be sung, recorded, and studied; their principles were extracted and applied to new compositions in a cycle of musical sophistication that is still being explored by composers and jazz musicians. When composers have had musical ideas that could not be expressed using existing notation conventions, they have invented notational terms that corresponded with the new terms of the music design language they were adding. The noted composers of Western-tradition music used notation as a tool for invention. In this way, both the design language and the notation system evolved together and took on new detail, formal rules, standards, and variations. According to Crosby (1997):

> Between the sixth and the fourteenth centuries something unique happened in Western Europe: the writer of music achieved control over the fine detail of sound, a physical phenomenon, moving through time. The composer learned how to extract music from actual time, put it on parchment paper, and make of it something that was satisfying as symbol as well as sound and vice versa. Deaf Beethoven writing his last quartets became a possibility. (p. 157)

Any design language that exists in a designer's mind or in the minds of a group of designers may give rise to one or more systems of notation. Notation systems give imperfect but public expression to design structures and grow with—and help to grow—the design language itself. Written and spoken languages are but the visible representation of a mental language in which we design thoughts, and their interaction with thought has been a major tool for human cultural and intellectual development.

This reciprocal, mutually supportive relationship between the abstract design language as it exists in the designer's mind and the notational system used to express designs publicly is a very important one: A notation system becomes the first necessity for a design language to grow and mature beyond its often vague and fuzzy personal rudiments. Until there is a system of notation (even a primitive and completely personal and idiosyncratic one), the precision of designs and the expression of increasingly complex and nuanced designs are not possible, and designers become captured by the lack of a notation system. In this condition, they are at the mercy of whatever their tools make easy.

Once a consistent notation system is established, if it is used with discipline, it can become (a) a tool for remembering designs, (b) a structured problem-solving work space in which designs can take form and be shared, and (c) a kind of laboratory tool for sharpening and multiplying abstract design language categories. It permits ever more complicated and interesting structures to be built and new dimensions of the design language, such as musical harmony, to be considered and explored in detail. Moreover, as these experiments yield new insights into the design language, they find expression through corresponding growth of the notation system. Thus, through a continuing cycle of refinement, both design language and notation system grow together in parallel, and more sophisticated technological ideas can result.

The qualities of a notation system, of course, have major impact on the rate of growth of the related design language. Prove this to yourself by first multiplying two roman numerals and then by multiplying the same quantities using Arabic numerals (Simon, 1999). It is not hard to see the great facilitation to numeracy that comes from the numerical and place value notation systems we now use.

Architectural Notation

Over the years, architects have evolved standards for graphical representation of a structure's design. Drawings of a building are seen from different vantage points, and different drawings have the function of relating certain elements of the design to each other while ignoring others. One drawing may relate the floor plan to electrical circuits; another may relate the floor plan to air conditioning and heating components. Different types of drawings allow the design to be seen from different vantage points: the floor plan, the elevation, the perspective, the axonometric drawing, and so on. Additional details of the plan are added through textual annotations added to the graphic and through tables of data that give detail properties of elements represented in the drawings. This system of notation has matured to the point where it has been standardized for a community of professional practitioners. The standardized notation system shows us that in order to capture enough aspects of a design, sometimes multiple notational views of the design may be necessary, to allow it to be inspected for soundness, conflicts among elements, sensory impact, articulation and integration of parts, functionality, and many other properties. The variety of drawing types allows the architect (and an engineering and construction team) to inspect the design from the viewpoint of many different team members.

The computerization of many parts of designing has been accomplished by finding areas of alignment between the architect's design languages and those of the computer programmer and by using existing notation system standards and inventing new ones. Today, most building drawings, which used to be made by hand, are made by computers. The most current versions of computer-assisted design (CAD) systems go beyond simply recording notations of designs; they create a complete three-dimensional computer model of the object being designed (building, aircraft, automobile, etc.). These systems allow the designer to manipulate the design's notation (the public, externally visible form) on display terminals. Such manipulations change a separate model of the object that is kept internal to the computer and that is expressed in a model design language. When representations or views of different aspects of the invisible model are needed, they can be generated by special notation-generation software. In addition to being designed by this system, the model can be subjected to many kinds of automatic tests, before anything is built, to determine the design's strength, function, failure modes, manufacturability, and even production cost. The Boeing 777 aircraft was designed using a system of this type. The same system that supported the design of the aircraft supported the design of machinery used in the manufacture of the aircraft. The design of both the aircraft and the manufacturing machinery was so precise and well coordinated by the language-based CAD system that the first wing assembled using the automated manufacturing system was fully usable (Sabbagh, 1996). Overall, this design and manufacturing system, which was based on the knowledge and calculated use of several design languages and associated notation systems, saved millions of dollars and person-years of design team work in addition to improving the quality of the design.

Software Design Using the Notation System as a Tool

A multiperspective notation system has also been found useful as a tool in the creation of computer programs. The Unified Modeling Language (UML) (Booch, Jacobsen, & Rumbaugh, 1998) specifies a graphical language (notation system) for making symbolic notations that represent the functions and organization of a computer program. The symbolic notations are organized into several views of the program that the designer constructs. In these views, designers describe in symbols the program's function, its structure, how it stores and uses data, and many other details. Because programs have no outward physical dimensions, the multiple views are just symbolic notations of abstract functionalities of the program.

A computerized version of UML's notation system is capable of turning this set of diagrams directly into computer code using special translation programs (Quatrani, 1999). *Translation* is the best term to describe this process, as one language—a symbolic language—becomes translated into another language—a precise, computable programming language. In this way the design language facilitates the transformation of the design directly into a manufactured product in a manner analogous to computer chip design systems and the architectural design system used on the Boeing 777. UML is also amenable over time to constructing its own programs from fewer and fewer specifications, bypassing, at some point, the multiperspective drawings altogether, except as inspection and review tools for the designer. Recent developments include a set of proposals for improving UML to expand these functions and to add other design-supporting features (Miller, 2002).

APPLICATION OF DESIGN LANGUAGES WITHIN INSTRUCTIONAL DESIGN

Up to this point, this chapter has concentrated on examining the use of design languages and notation systems in many design fields to show through examples how they have improved design practice and contributed to design tools and processes. Rheinfrank and Evenson (1996) described how pervasive their influence has been:

Design languages have been used to design things as diverse as products, buildings, cities, services, and organizations. They are often used unconsciously, arising out of the natural activity of creation and interaction with created things. Yet, when consciously understood, developed, and applied, design languages can build on and improve this natural activity and can result in dramatically better interactions, environments, and all kinds of things.

The power of using design languages consciously has been recognized and described by other design theorists, such as Christopher Alexander (1979) for architecture and urban design, William J. Mitchell (1992) for architecture and media, Edward Tufte (1990) for visualization, and Terry Winograd (Alder & Winograd, 1992) for software design. (p. 65)

This chapter has been written out of a conviction that instructional design theory and practice will benefit from the study of the languages of instructional design. What benefits might we expect in the long term from research on this topic? If we can take the experience of other fields as a guide, we should anticipate the ability to make designs that are:

- More adaptable to individual needs and circumstances.
- Generated more rapidly and flexibly.
- Manufacturable in quantity at high quality without proportional cost increase.
- More easily and fully communicated between designers.
- Less costly.

Within the community of instructional design practitioners, increased interest in design languages will cause the design process itself to be reexamined. A view of the activities of instructional design might emerge that incorporated the best of what is known about design in other fields. This will lead to a better understanding of what design means in the field of instructional design, and discussion will be focused to a greater extent on design architecture and the many layers of design structure. This will result in better, more easily adapted guidelines and standards for designers and design teams and the ability to specify more clearly the characteristics of good designs. Discussions of design will be better grounded, and comparisons of designs and design approaches will be more detailed. This will also lead to a clearer definition of needed design support tools that encourage a greater variety of designs.

Suggestions for a Program of Design Language Study

How might instructional designers and design theorists pursue the study of instructional design languages and notation systems? Some suggestions are given in what follows.

Identification, Documentation, and Study of Existing Design Languages.
Well-delineated public design languages will emerge as we open discussion on what are now private and idiosyncratic languages. The discipline of clear and critical discourse can be applied to considering the origins, use, and growth of our

commonly held design languages in some of the following ways. The current literature can be examined in terms of the use of both implicit and explicit languages built into our thinking and discourse. Design languages can be recognized as a legitimate subject of academic study, especially studies of how groups of designers evolve shared design languages (see Seo & Gibbons, 2003). Classical standards for making definitions can be reviewed and applied. Terms from many languages can be collected, compared, and catalogued in dictionary-like repositories that draw on the wording and intent of original sources (see Reigeluth & Keller, 2002). Families and types of languages can be identified. Exemplary cases of language creation or application can be studied and reported—not from the point of view of judging the correctness of the language itself, but as a case study of the manner of use of languages. Histories of key terms in languages can be researched and traced to their roots, providing new, correct perspectives on their origins and the problems they were invented to solve.

Extraction of Principles in Existing Languages and Their Deliberate Application.   Increased study and discussion of design languages will improve our understanding of design languages in general. It will reveal ways in which we can improve the deliberate application of the languages to designing. Lessons from the use of design languages in other fields can be considered for transfer into the practices of instructional designers. This will give designers a better idea of the many purposes design languages serve in other fields such as: automating parts of design, testing designs before building, anticipating manufacture, automating manufacture, reducing design and development costs, increasing the sophistication of designs, improving design and development tools, reducing modification and maintenance costs, evolving new design processes, and many other uses. Not only will our proficiency with languages improve, but so will our insight into the process of translating between languages, which can give our designs increased portability with respect to today's specific technologies.

Better Language Grounding Through Attachment to Theory.   The design languages that exist in most designers' minds represent a mixture of theoretical concepts, prior examples, personal ideals, and idiosyncratic—sometimes superstitious—opinions. Awareness of languages and deliberate use of language principles can make the function of instructional theory in relation to languages more evident. The origins of theoretical categories can become plainer in the light of language studies, and the manner of relating practice to theory can become clearer. Personal design languages can enrich and be disciplined by theoretical connections with languages, and it can become more obvious how to bridge the gap between theory and its application.

Identification of the Generative Principles of Language That Lead to New Languages.   Questions regarding design languages can lead to larger questions about the framework within which languages are used and within which design takes place: questions about nature of designs themselves. The recent and rapid advances in other design fields described in this chapter not only have involved recognition of the important role of design languages in improving and speeding designs but also have involved the willingness to *see* new languages. Computer-aided design (CAD) systems that initially adopted the language of two-dimensional drawings now operate using the language of three-dimensional (3-D) solid models. The result is that these systems are now able to produce drawings as before, but also they are able to produce 3-D drawings from any perspective, detect space conflicts, simulate artifact performance, predict production costs, perform production breakdowns, and feed production data into numerically controlled manufacturing equipment. These are benefits attributable to numerous new design languages and notation systems and programs capable of translating expressions in one language to expressions in another.

Improvement of Design Languages and Grammars.   Reigeluth and Keller (2002) described a "tower of babble," referring to the lack of clear and unambiguous definitions of terms that designate instructional constructs, methods, techniques, and types. Overcoming this problem of long standing will require a concerted and prolonged effort and will depend on the evolution of a standard for defining design language terms. That standard will probably call for definitions to be expressed using more explicit and technical properties than designers are now accustomed to. Usefulness of a language, however, requires more precise definition of design language terms. Moreover, this will have to be accompanied by the development of what Stolurow (1969) called *grammars of instruction*: rules describing how the terms of a given language can be combined to form meaningful expressions. Such rules can form the basis for the development of generative grammars for instruction.

Stolurow's use of the term *generative* implies that the languages and their rules will not only classify surface forms of expression but will have deep structures to expressions that allow design expressions to be transformed through the application of transformational rules that preserve meaning, even when surface structure is altered.

Evolution of Tools That Emphasize the Designer's Languages Rather than the Computer's.   Tools used by instructional designers have been shaped by economic and market factors, rather than being designed for and by instructional designers. Instructional designers use tools created by computer programmers to meet the needs of a larger non-instructional software market. This has created "a subtle but important semantic gap ... between the conceptual structures used by the [programming] languages and those used in instruction" (Gibbons & Fairweather, 2000, p. 419). Both designs and design tools are based on design languages. Understanding design languages is essential to the creation of tools for design support and to understanding the translation process by which abstract designs expressed in one set of design languages are produced using tools built by programmers around a different set of languages. Attention to design languages can improve design support tools, and attention to design languages that are *computable* allows us to create design tools capable of translating designs more directly into products.

Use of Design Languages as a Basis for Defining Design Processes.
Process models that specify some sequence of design activities dominate current design practice. However, solutions to design problems are seldom as straightforward as these process models would lead us to believe. The order and type of decisions made during designs are largely dependent on the constraints, criteria, and resources that come with the problem. Set process models seldom anticipate the needs of individual projects and are difficult to adjust to their details.

An alternative to breaking design problems into process steps is to break them into subproblems corresponding to instructional functions—product qualities rather than process steps. When this is done, it creates a layered view of the design process in which design languages are nested within layers (see Gibbons, 2003a, 2003b). Design languages for capturing and defining instructional content reside within the content layer; all of the languages for expressing the various aspects of instructional strategy reside within the strategy layer. Respectively, languages for expressing control structures, message structures, representation structures, media-logic structures, and data management structures reside within their corresponding layers. In this view, the designer chooses among languages within each of the layers, selecting the ones most capable of producing the desired qualities in the product being designed and articulating with the languages chosen for use in the designs of the other layers.

This way of decomposing the design problem offers the designer flexibility in planning the order of design decisions and includes in the design process only those decisions that pertain to the constraints, criteria, and resources of the specific design problem. Problem constraints (such as the requirement that the product use video) may automatically include certain layers (and languages) into the design while excluding others; they may also favor the choice of certain languages within each layer and suggest the order in which design decisions for this particular project might unfold. Although this is just one framing of the design problem, it is one that illustrates the value of deliberately using design languages.

CONCLUSION

We have attempted in this chapter to introduce into the foreground of discussion the concept of design languages that has been a powerful tool contributing to the rapid maturation of other design fields when used deliberately. We have tried to show design languages and their accompanying notation systems as a natural phenomenon that can be harnessed for a multiplicity of purposes but for the main purpose of improving design productivity, sophistication, and cost. Many design fields have found that the deliberate use of design languages improves the rate of progress, influences designer conceptions, improves design processes, improves design and development tools, and brings design and manufacture closer together. We are confident that increased dialogue related to design languages for instructional design can provide a level of discipline to design practice to bring these benefits to us as well. Most importantly, it will open us up to new ways of thinking about designs and designing.

REFERENCES

ADL. (n.d.). Advanced distributed learning. Retrieved April 9, 2004, from http://www.adlnet.org AICC. (n.d.). Aviation Industry CBT Committee. Http://www.aicc.org
Alder, P., & Winograd, T. (1992). *Usability: Turning technologies into tools.* New York: Oxford University Press.
Alexander, C. (1979). *The timeless way of building.* New York: Oxford University Press.
Booch, G., Jacobsen, I., & Rumbaugh, J. (1998). *The Unified Modeling Language user guide.* Reading MA: Addison-Wesley.
Cole, M. (1971). *The cultural context of learning and thinking.* Basic Books; New York.
Cole, M., Engestrom, Y., & Vasquez, O. (1997). *Mind, culture, activity: The seminal papers from the Laboratory of Comparative Human Cognition.* Cambridge, UK: Cambridge University Press.
Crosby, A. W. (1997). *The measure of reality: Quantification and Western society, 1250–1600.* Cambridge, UK: Cambridge University Press.
Gibbons, A. S. (2003a). What and how do designers design? A theory of design structure. *Tech Trends, 47*(5), 22–27.
Gibbons, A. S. (2003). Where from here? *Technology, Instruction, Cognition and Learning, 1*(3), 226–233.
Gibbons, A. S., & Fairweather, P. G. (2000). Computer-based instruction. In S. Tobias & J. D. Fletcher (Eds.), *Training and retraining: Handbook for business, industry, government, and military* (pp. 410–441). New York: Macmillan.
IEEE/LTSC. (n.d.). *Learning Technology Standards Committee.* Retrieved April 9, 2004, from http://ltsc.ieee.org
IMS. (n.d.). *IMS Global Learning Consortium.* http://www.imsglobal.org
Miller, J. (2002). What UML should be. *Communications of the ACM, 45*(11), 67–85.
Mitchell, W. J. (1992). *The reconfigured eye: Visual truth in the post-photographic era.* Cambridge, MA: MIT Press.
Quatrani, T. (1999). *Visual modeling with Rational Rose 2000 and UML.* Reading, MA: Addison-Wesley.
Reigeluth, C., & Keller, J. M. (2002, October). *Deconstructing a tower of babble: Clarifying terms and concepts in instructional theory.* Paper presented at the Annual Conference of the Association for Educational Communications and Technology, Dallas, TX.
Rheinfrank, J., & Evenson, S. (1996). Design languages. In T. Winograd (Ed.), *Bringing design to software* (pp. 63–80). Reading, MA: Addison-Wesley.
Sabbagh, K. (1996). *21st Century jet: The making and marketing of the Boeing 777.* New York: Charles Scribner's Sons.
SCORM. (n.d.). *The Sharable Content Object Reference Model.* Retrieved April 9, 2004, from http://www.adlnet.org
Seo, K. K., & Gibbons, A. S. (2003). Design languages: A powerful medium for communicating designs. *Educational Technology, 43*(6), 43–46.
Simon, H. A. (1999). *Sciences of the artificial* (3rd ed.). Cambridge, MA: MIT Press.

Stolurow, L. M. (1969). Some factors in the design of systems for computer-assisted instruction. In R. C. Atkinson & H. A. Wilson, *Computer-assisted instruction: A book of readings* (pp. 65–93). New York: Academic Press.

Tufte, E. (1990). *Envisioning information.* Cheshire, CT: Graphics Press.

Waters, S., & Gibbons, A. S. (2004). Design languages, notation systems, and instructional technology. *Educational Technology Research and Development, 52*(2), 57–68.

Winograd, T. (1996). *Bringing design to software.* Reading, MA: Addison-Wesley.

Chapter
8

Teamwork Skills: Assessment and Instruction

Lori Marshall
Harold F. O'Neil
Ashley Chen
Marcia Kuehl
I-Lin Hsieh
University of Southern California

Jamal Abedi
University of California, Los Angeles

This chapter discusses the application of Merrill's (2002a, 2002b) pebble-in-the-pond model and principles of instruction to teach teamwork skills that are measured by our Teamwork Skills Questionnaire. David Merrill's work predominantly focused on the teaching of various types of knowledge and skills, whereas our work has predominantly focused on the measurement of various types of knowledge and skills, particularly what could be considered metacognitive and cognitive strategies. This chapter focuses on both the teaching and the assessment of team skills that could be considered a type of cognitive strategies. We first present a linkage between Merrill's (1997, 2002a, 2002b) work and the teaching of teamwork skills. Next we discuss definitions and perspectives from the literature, followed by some psychometric background on the teamwork questionnaire. Finally, we provide implications for using Merrill's (1997, 2001, 2002a, 2002b, in press) model and principles when providing teamwork training specifically when using the Teamwork Skills Questionnaire (O'Neil, Lee, Wang, & Mulkey, 1999).

MERRILL'S INSTRUCTIONAL PRINCIPLES AND TEAMWORK SKILLS

An Overview of Merrill's Instructional Principles

When performing organizational assessments for training, providing a comprehensive set of assessment measures increases the ability to accurately measure how to proceed with team development for the target population (Salas & Cannon-Bowers, 2000). Training teamwork based on Merrill's (2001) instructional models begins with the pebble-in-the-pond model. The model was described by Merrill (2002b) as a content-based model and uses the metaphor of casting a pebble, thus creating a rippling effect of subsequent circles of activity. The initiating activity is the task or problem the learners need to address. For our discussion, improving teamwork represents the task or problem. The second ripple is a progression of subtasks that must be learned and which comprise the whole task. According to O'Neil et al. (1999), teamwork skills are composed of six subskills that could be considered subtasks. The third ripple is task knowledge. Teamwork skills task knowledge is represented through specific tasks that are part of a subskill. The fourth ripple is how teamwork will be taught—the instructional strategy. A fifth implicit ripple is how to assess learning.

Instructional strategies for teamwork skills training include the use of multiple strategies (Merrill, 1997). An instructional strategy to support teamwork might include concepts or a kind of strategy where the learner is able to recognize unfamiliar examples of procedures or actions belonging to a particular group or category of knowledge (Merrill, 1997). The procedure strategy is important in teamwork skills training, whereby the learner can perform a sequence of actions leading to a desired outcome. Finally, the process, principle, or how-does-it-work strategy is also key in teamwork skills training. This strategy aims to enable the learner to be able to predict an outcome or consequence of an event, given a set of conditions (expected or unexpected). An important task is the blending of the content and instructional strategies. A final task is to assess the result of training via the teamwork skills questionnaire.

According to Merrill (1997), effective instruction is problem based and is promoted when: (a) A learner solves real-world problems; (b) previous knowledge is activated to provide a basis for what is to be learned; (c) new knowledge is demonstrated for the learner to promote learning; (d) the learner has opportunities to apply the new knowledge; and (e) the learner can integrate the new knowledge (Merrill, 2002a). Additionally, an instructional strategy should consist of relevant discussion or rehearsal strategies as well as learner support, including feedback, in order to ensure that the strategy will be effective.

The following subsection is intended to assist the reader with the link between Merrill's work and our work on the Teamwork Skills Questionnaire. We describe the background, definitions and reliability validity information for our team training assessment tool: the Teamwork Skills Questionnaire.

The Teamwork Skills Questionnaire

For the purpose of this chapter, a team can be characterized as a group of people who are adaptive to change and have shared goals, interdependent functioning, and special knowledge, skills, and designated roles/responsibilities (Paris, Salas, & Cannon-Bowers, 2000). Teamwork activities are coordinated among the group with focused communication. Additionally, teamwork involves processing information from multiple sources (Paris et al., 2000). Based on the work of Morgan, Salas, and Glickman (1993), O'Neil, Chung, and Brown (1997) suggested that

> teamwork track or team skills influence how effective an individual member will be as part of a team and are domain-independent team skills. Team skills encompass skills such as adaptability, coordination, cooperation, and communication. (p. 412)

A review of the literature on measurement of teams and teamwork in industry (Marshall, 2003) showed some similarities across industries. Measurement often focused on team functioning (team type, communication, cohesion, and group dynamics), team outcomes (cost, quality, and models), team training and development (teaching teams, and work skills assessment), and team characteristics (innovation and general styles of team behavior). Additionally, the literature showed variation in the measurement of teams and teamwork (e.g., multiple methods) and a variety of team and teamwork variables and models (i.e., communication, care delivery, problem solving, and social identity).

For example, Greenbaum, Kaplan, and Damiano (1991) performed an analysis on group and team measurement tools used from 1950 through 1990. An important finding from their study was that psychometric information on reliability and validity was available for only a few teamwork skills inventories. They found that most of the existing team measurement tools have poor or no reliability information. For instance, out of 200 instruments, 40 provided reliability information, and of those 40, only 19 had undergone confirmatory factor analysis.

The Teamwork Skills Questionnaire (O'Neil et al., 1999) is intended to measure teamwork skills and focuses on the skills a person needs to have in order to be able to work as part of a team. It is a self-report indirect teamwork measurement tool. The best way to measure teamwork skills is to use an existing team to provide a context to directly measure these skills (e.g., Hsieh & O'Neil, 2002; O'Neil, Wang, Chung, & Herl, 2000). But in many cases, this direct approach is not feasible. Thus, we also focused on measuring teamwork skills indirectly (i.e., by using a questionnaire methodology). The Teamwork Skills Questionnaire has six scales:

(a) adaptability; (b) communication; (c) coordination; (d) decision making; (e) interpersonal skills; and, (f) leadership (O'Neil et al., 1997, p. 413).

To date, the questionnaire has been used with participants in several settings (O'Neil, Wang, Lee, Mulkey, & Baker, 2003): (a) an electronics firm in the United States (O'Neil et al., 2003); (b) an air conditioning and refrigeration union in the United States (O'Neil et al., 2003); (c) a temporary workers' agency (O'Neil et al., 2003); (d) a Canadian union (O'Neil et al., 2003); (e) a U.S. Marine Corps Aviation Logistics Squadron (Kuehl, 2001); (f) Asian American junior high school and high school students (Hsieh, 2001); (g) nurses in Australia (Marshall, 2003); and (h) engineers and assembly workers in an electronics firm in Taiwan (Chen, 2002). With the exception of the Taiwanese group (tested in Mandarin), all of the participants were tested in English. Cronbach's alpha reliability coefficient measurements for the total questionnaire ranged from .84 to .97 (Chen, 2002; Hsieh, 2001; Kuehl, 2001; Marshall, 2003; O'Neil et al., 2003; Weng, 1999). In this chapter, we report on the test of a predicted six-factor model (e.g., adaptability, communication, and leadership) using multigroup confirmatory factor analysis.

METHODS

Teamwork Skills Questionnaire

The Teamwork Skills Questionnaire (Kuehl, 2001; O'Neil et al., 2003; Weng, 1999) was used to measure individual trait teamwork skills of team members. The version used by Kuehl (2001) was selected for use with this study. Kuehl added items to the version used by Weng (1999) for the purpose of better defining a predicted six-dimension factor structure instead of the two-factor structure found by Weng (1999) and O'Neil et al. (2003). All questionnaire items used a 4-point Likert scale (1 = *almost never,* 2 = *sometimes,* 3 = *often,* and 4 = *almost always*). The revised version (Kuehl, 2001) contained 52 items to measure the predicted six dimensions. However, Kuehl's study only supported a two-factor model and not the proposed six-factor model. She conducted an exploratory factor analysis followed by a confirmatory factor analysis rather than the more powerful approach used in the current study (i.e., a multigroup confirmatory factor analysis for cross-validation purposes).

In this chapter, construct validity for the six dimensions of the Teamwork Skills Questionnaire was determined using confirmatory factor analysis. Previous studies have demonstrated that these six dimensions loaded on two factors, one cognitive and the other affective (Hsieh, 2001; Kuehl, 2001; O'Neil et al., 1999; Weng, 1999).

The predicted dimensions of the Teamwork Skills Questionnaire were the participant's perceptions of his or her (a) adaptability, (b) communications, (c) coordination, (d) decision making, (e) interpersonal skills, and (f) leadership. Definitions of these constructs and a sample item for each scale are provided here.

- Adaptability—recognizing problems and responding appropriately. A sample item is: "When I work as part of a team, I willingly contribute solutions to resolve problems" (Kuehl, 2001).
- Communication—the overall exchange of clear and accurate information. A sample item is: "When I work as part of a team, I listen attentively" (Kuehl, 2001).
- Coordination—organizing team activities to complete a task on time. A sample item is: "When I work as part of a team, I track other team members' progress" (Kuehl, 2001).
- Decision making—using available information to make team decisions. A sample item is: "When I work as part of a team, I know the process of making a decision" (Kuehl, 2001).
- Interpersonal skills—interacting cooperatively with other team members. A sample item is: "When I work as part of a team, I respect the thoughts and opinions of others in the team" (Kuehl, 2001).
- Leadership—providing direction for the team. A sample item is: "When I work as part of a team, I exercise leadership" (Kuehl, 2001).

Participants

The reliability of the Teamwork Skills Questionnaire was investigated using participants from four settings: 269 participants from an aviation logistics squadron at a U.S. Marine Corps base in southern California, 273 participants from an electronics company in Taiwan, 120 participants from a sample of Asian American junior high and high school students, and 149 participants from a sample of nurses in Australia.

U.S. Marine Corps Aviation Logistics Squadron.   Most participants were males (only 19 of the 271 participants were female). This sample was taken from an environment where teamwork is inherent in daily activities. In terms of specific job functions, there were 90 avionics workers, 37 ordnance workers, 76 power-plant workers, 24 air-frame workers, 41 support equipment workers, and 3 quality assurance workers. Participants' mean age was in the early 20s.

Taiwanese Electronics Company.   This study was conducted in Chinese, using samples from two different departments in the same company in Taipei, Taiwan: engineers from the research and development department and a group of employees from the assembly line. Of the 152 engineers, 124 (81.6%) were male, with a mean age of 33 years. Of the 121 assembly workers, 110 (90.9%) were female, with a mean age of 36 years.

Asian American Junior High and High School Students.   This sample of 120 students was from southern California and ranged in age from 12 through 18 years.

Australia Nurses.   The Australia nurses sample was mostly female. Participants were from a children's hospital in southern Australia.

PROCEDURE

For the U.S. Marine Corps sample, the Teamwork Skills Questionnaire was administered to participants by the investigator with help from Marine Corps quality assurance representatives. The participants took about 15 minutes to complete the questionnaire. For the Taiwanese electronics company sample, the questionnaire was administered in Chinese (Mandarin) by the workers' supervisors or the manager. Participants took approximately 20 minutes to complete the questionnaire. For the Asian American junior high and high school student sample, the questionnaire was administered by the investigator. Participants took approximately 20 minutes to complete the questionnaire. For the Australia nurses sample, during a change-of-shift report, participants were asked to take 20 minutes to complete the questionnaire.

For all samples, human subjects procedures of both the University of Southern California and the target organization were followed. Prior approval of all procedures was gained by this approach.

RESULTS

Descriptive Statistics

Means and standard deviations for the item level for each study are presented in Tables 8.1 through 8.4. The findings indicate that the interpersonal skills scale had the highest mean scores across the four groups of participants, with the exception of the U.S. Marine Corps sample, for which the decision-making scale had the highest mean score. The leadership scale had the lowest mean score across the groups. These findings are consistent with the previous multigroup analysis of the Teamwork Skills Questionnaire performed by O'Neil et al. (2003), who found that the interpersonal skills scale had the highest mean score of all the scales and leadership the lowest mean score. In addition, when comparing total mean scores (i.e., for all six dimensions), the Australia nurses sample had the highest total mean scores, followed by the U.S. Marine Corps sample, the Asian American junior high and high school students sample, and the Taiwanese engineers and assembly workers, who had the lowest mean scores.

TABLE 8.1
Item Means and Standard Deviations for the U.S. Marine Corps Sample, Teamwork Skills Scales (N = 269; Kuehl, 2001)

Scale	Number of Items	Item Mean	Item SD
Adaptability	8	3.22	.49
Communication	8	3.21	.52
Coordination	8	3.22	.48
Decision making	9	3.23	.47
Interpersonal skills	11	3.16	.53
Leadership	8	3.20	.56

TABLE 8.2
Item Means and Standard Deviations for the Taiwanese Electronics Company Sample, Teamwork Skills Scales (N = 273; Chen, 2002)

Scale	Number of Items	Item Mean	Item SD
Adaptability	8	2.91	.51
Communication	8	3.09	.46
Coordination	8	3.06	.49
Decision making	9	2.96	.53
Interpersonal skills	11	3.11	.46
Leadership	8	2.64	.63

TABLE 8.3
Item Means and Standard Deviations for the Asian American Junior High and High School Students Sample, Teamwork Skills Scales (N = 120; Hsieh, 2001)

Scale	Number of Items	Item Mean	Item SD
Adaptability	8	2.91	.45
Communication	8	3.13	.43
Coordination	8	2.97	.46
Decision making	9	2.87	.47
Interpersonal skills	11	3.18	.43
Leadership	8	2.77	.63

TABLE 8.4

Item Means and Standard Deviations for the Australia Nurses Sample,
Teamwork Skills Scales (N = 149; Marshall et al., 2003)

Scale	Number of Items	Item Mean	Item SD
Adaptability	8	3.34	.46
Communication	8	3.56	.42
Coordination	8	3.32	.48
Decision making	9	3.33	.46
Interpersonal skills	11	3.58	.38
Leadership	8	3.18	.64

Reliability of the Teamwork Skills Questionnaire

As shown in Table 8.5, Cronbach's alpha reliability coefficients for the Teamwork Skills Questionnaire were acceptable for all four samples, as all reliability coefficients were greater than .70; adaptability ranged from .78 to .86; communication, from .73 to .86; coordination, from .70 to .81; decision making, from .81 to .86; interpersonal skills, from .78 to .86; and leadership, from

TABLE 8.5

Cronbach's Alpha Coefficients for the Teamwork Skills Scales
for the Four Samples

Scale	U.S. Marine Corps (Kuehl, 2001)	Taiwanese Electronics Company (Chen, 2002)	Asian American Junior High and High School Students (Hsieh, 2001)	Australia Nurses (Marshall et al., 2003)
Adaptability	.81	.85	.78	.86
Communication	.84	.81	.73	.86
Coordination	.76	.79	.70	.81
Decision making	.82	.85	.81	.86
Interpersonal skills	.85	.86	.78	.86
Leadership	.86	.88	.88	.92

.86 to .92. All of the reliability coefficients indicate a high degree of internal consistency. The reliabilities for the total questionnaire by sample were .95 (Kuehl, 2001), .97 (Chen, 2002), .93 (Hsieh, 2001), and .97 (Marshall et al., 2003). These findings indicate excellent internal consistency reliability for the Teamwork Skills Questionnaire.

Confirmatory Factor Analysis

EQS 6 (Bentler, 2002) was used to investigate the predicted six-factor model. Current practice for reporting goodness of fit (GFI) addresses the use of multiple parameters for decision making without relying on one type of fit index or absolute values (Bentler & Yuen, 1999; Boomsma, 2000; Cheung & Rensvold, 2002; McDonald & Ho, 2002). Thus, several fit indices were used with various decision-making criteria. First is the chi-square (c^2), including the number of degrees of freedom (df), the p value (which ideally is not significant), and the c^2/df ratio (c^2 divided by the number of degree of freedom, which should be < 3.0) (Boomsma, 2000). Second is the root mean square error of approximation (RMSEA), which should be < .05 for a good fit and < .08 for an acceptable fit (McDonald & Ho, 2002). It should also be reported with a 90% confidence interval (Boomsma, 2000). Finally, the EQS fit indices should be used and are considered a good fit if they are higher that .90; a perfect fit is 1.0. Thus, the closer to 1.0 the better the model fit. The EQS fit indices include the Normed Fit Index (NFI), the Non-Normed Fit Index (NNFI), and the Comparative Fit Index (CFI; Bentler, 2002). In addition, maximum likelihood estimation (MLE) was used as recommended for smaller sample sizes (Bentler & Yuen, 1999).

The model was tested using the previously reported two-factor structure (cognitive and affective dimensions) and with the predicted six-factor structure (e.g., adaptability, leadership, etc.). For this chapter, only the two-factor and six-factor correlated models were run, based on findings from Marshall et al. (2003). The revised six-factor correlated model presented in Marshall et al. was also tested for all groups. We first tested each sample separately (a single-group analysis) and then all samples collectively (a multigroup analysis). The same approach was used by O'Neil et al. (1999, 2003).

Single-Group Analysis

Each group was tested independently for model fit. The results are presented in Tables 8.6 through 8.9. All p values are < .0001. For all samples, results indicated that model fit was improved by using the six-factor structure. When the revised six-factor structure was tested for each group, fit indices improved even more. The c^2 ratio and RMSEA fit our decision criteria; the other fit indices did not.

Using the revised six-factor model, factor loadings for the Australia nurses sample ranged from .638 to .852. Loadings for the U.S. Marine Corps sample ranged from .443 to .792. The Taiwanese electronics company sample had only one loading

TABLE 8.6
Two-, Six-, and Six-Factor Revised Correlated CFA Model, U.S. Marine Corps Sample, Teamwork Skills Scales (Kuehl, 2001)

Model	χ^2	df	χ^2/df	NFI	NNFI	CFI	RMSEA	90% Confidence Interval
Two-factor	1766.38	901	1.96	0.7	0.816	0.825	0.06	.056, .064
Six-factor	2379.14	1259	1.89	0.683	0.809	0.819	0.058	.054, .061
Six-factor revised	1128.67	614	1.84	0.778	0.874	0.884	0.056	.051, .061

Note. NFI = Normed Fit Index; NNFI = Non-Normed Fit Index; CFI = Comparative Fit Index; RMSEA = root mean square error of approximation.

TABLE 8.7
Two-, Six-, and Six-Factor Revised Correlated CFA Model, Taiwanese Electronics Company Sample, Teamwork Skills Scales (Chen, 2002)

Model	χ^2	df	χ^2/df	NFI	NNFI	CFI	RMSEA	90% Confidence Interval
Two-factor	2771.9	901	3.08	0.663	0.702	0.717	0.087	.084, .091
Six-factor	3663.98	1259	2.91	0.613	0.689	0.704	0.084	.080, .087
Six-factor revised	1727.56	614	2.81	0.709	0.771	0.789	0.082	.977, .086

Note. NFI = Normed Fit Index; NNFI = Non-Normed Fit Index; CFI = Comparative Fit Index; RMSEA = root mean square error of approximation.

< .40 (for item 26 = .362). Factor loadings for the remaining items ranged from .401 to .734. The Asian American junior high and high school students sample had three items loading < .40. The range for the remaining items was .429 to .835.

Multigroup Analysis

A multigroup analysis was performed using all four samples. The data were tested using composite mean scores for the teamwork dimensions. The composite scores were used as a latent factor (teamwork skills) where each composite score became a parcel. Using this approach, the data revealed the following: chi-square = 310.67,

TABLE 8.8

Two-, Six-, and Six-Factor Revised Correlated CFA Model, Asian American Junior High and High School Students Sample, Teamwork Skills Scales (Hsieh, 2001)

Model	χ^2	df	χ^2/df	NFI	NNFI	CFI	RMSEA	90% Confidence Interval
Two-factor	1637.37	901	1.82	0.411	0.579	0.599	0.084	.077, .090
Six-factor	2042.1	1259	1.62	0.441	0.646	0.664	0.073	.067, .079
Six-factor revised	963.0	614	1.57	0.56	0.751	0.77	0.07	.061, .078

Note. NFI = Normed Fit Index; NNFI = Non-Normed Fit Index; CFI = Comparative Fit Index; RMSEA = Root mean square error of approximation.

TABLE 8.9

Two-, Six-, and Six-Factor Revised Correlated CFA Model, Australia Nurses Sample, Teamwork Skills Scales (Marshall et al., 2003)

Model	χ^2	df	χ^2/df	NFI	NNFI	CFI	RMSEA	90% Confidence Interval
Two-factor	1810.82	901	2.01	0.622	0.751	0.763	0.083	.077, .088
Six-factor	2366.62	1259	1.88	0.612	0.756	0.768	0.077	.072, .082
Six-factor revised	1146.39	614	1.87	0.724	0.834	0.847	0.077	.069, .083

Note. NFI = Normed Fit Index; NNFI = Non-Normed Fit Index; CFI = Comparative Fit Index; RMSEA = Root mean square error of approximation.

$df = 51$, $c^2/df = 6.09$, NFI = .918, NNFI = .918, CFI = .931, and RMSEA = .08 with a 90% confidence interval between .071 and .088. All variables loaded on their assigned factor and were above .565. In addition, the communication, coordination, decision making, interpersonal skills, and leadership scales loaded significantly on their respective factors across all groups.

Although the c^2/df ratio was above 3.0, the remaining fit indices indicate the teamwork skills model was a good fit using six dimensions. The chi-square ratio above 3.0 (6.09) can be partially explained by the large sample size ($n = 811$) used in this analysis. These findings are consistent with the previous multigroup analysis performed on the Teamwork Skills Questionnaire by O'Neil et al. (1999, 2003), who found that the NNFI (.97), CFI (.98), and RMSEA (.50, with a 90% confidence interval between .021 and .08) indicated a good fit. The c^2 ratio, however, was 18.93.

SUMMARY

The multigroup analysis supports the use of the Teamwork Skills Questionnaire as a reliable and valid teamwork assessment tool. The reliability information consisted of excellent internal consistency estimations, and the validity consisted of excellent confirmatory factor analyses results. For the purpose of conducting research it is an acceptable measure. For high-stakes personnel decisions, additional validity data would be needed (e.g., relationship with job proficiency and salary).

Regarding the Teamwork Skills Questionnaire, reliability for the instrument ranged from .93 to .97. Item scale reliabilities for all six dimensions were between .70 and .92. The revised six-factor model demonstrated a good fit using when using the NNFI (.918), CFI (.931), and RMSEA (.08), even though the chi-square ratio was > 3.0. Thus, the original concept of a six-factor correlated teamwork skills model was supported.

Krohne, Schmukle, Spaderna, and Spielberger (2002) addressed the issue of model fit when the c^2 ratio is > 3.0 for an international multiple-group CFA for state-trait depression scales. Because chi-square is sensitive to larger sample sizes and the probability of rejecting the model increases as the n increases, Krohne et al. (2002) used the CFI value and RMSEA < .09 as the decision criteria. Using this decision-making value of < .09, our RMSEA of .08 would be acceptable. The use of multiple criteria reinforces the finding that the six-factor revised model described in this chapter does indeed provide a good model fit.

In all of our studies, teamwork was measured as a trait. As previously discussed, few other instruments in the literature have undergone such extensive psychometric testing. (We assume that if such data were available they would have been reported.) The short administration time (approximately 20 min) supports an ease of administration for the Teamwork Skills Questionnaire. The instrument is simple to administer and provides an indirect measure of teamwork skills in which each dimension can be viewed as a focus for development or used as part of a composite score in conjunction with other factors if desired (e.g., efficacy or effort).

IMPLICATIONS FOR TEAM WORK INSTRUCTION BASED ON MERRILL'S FIRST PRINCIPLES

There are several implications for using this teamwork skills assessment linked with instruction using Merrill's first principles. Given what is known about the need to develop teamwork skills for service providers, it is important to understand the factors that may influence team training and development. Weak or poorly functioning teams are a liability to an organization and society. Any tools that may help target deficiencies in team functioning might serve as a useful resource for early intervention and team development. One of the initial model steps mentioned by Merrill (2002a, 200b) is the identification of the problem. Our Teamwork Skills assessment provides an empirical measurement for problem identification. This is equivalent to the casting of the pebble in the pond for the purpose of specifying the problem that corresponds to the whole task that the learner will be able to do following the training (Merrill, 2002b).

Merrill's (2002a, 2002b) model promotes the concept that effective learning environments are problem centered. The Teamwork Skills Questionnaire is a problem-based measurement tool that helps to identify real-world problems that teams may have within six task-specific teamwork skills dimensions. Finally, a key issue when using Merrill's (2002a) principles of instruction is that the degree to which each of the five principles is implemented impacts the learning from a given program. Integrating Merrill's (2002a, 2002b) model of principles and the teamwork skills questionnaire not only sets the stage to apply Merrill's principles for designing training but also helps to determine the likelihood of success of the training in relation to the number of principles being implemented. When the training is completed, the teamwork skills assessment also provides an empirically based measurement of effectiveness of the teamwork skills training based on Merrill's (1997, 2001, in press) models and principles.

ACKNOWLEDGMENTS

The work reported herein was supported in part under the Educational Research and Development Centers Program, PR/award number R305B960002, as administered by the Office of Educational Research and Improvement, U.S. Department of Education. The findings and opinions expressed in this report do not reflect the positions or policies of the National Institute on Student Achievement, Curriculum, and Assessment, the Office of Educational Research and Improvement, or the U.S. Department of Education.

REFERENCES

Bentler, P. M. (2002). *EQS 6: Structural equations program manual.* Encino, CA: Multivariate Software, Inc.

Bentler, P. M., & Yeun, K. (1999). Structural equation modeling with small samples: Test statistics. *Multivariate Behavioral Research, 34,* 181–197.

Boomsma, A. (2000). Reporting analysis of covariance structures. *Structural Equation Modeling, 7,* 461–483.

Chen, H.-I. (2002). *Relationships of teamwork skills with performance appraisals and salary information in a Taiwanese high performance work organization.* Unpublished doctoral dissertation, University of Southern California, Los Angeles.

Cheung, G., & Rensvold, R. (2002). Evaluating goodness of fit indices for testing measurement invariance. *Structural Equation Modeling, 9,* 233–255.

Greenbaum, H., Kaplan, I., & Damiano, R. (1991). Organizational group measurement instruments: An integrated survey. *Management Communication Quarterly, 5,* 126–148.

Hsieh, G. (2001). *Types of feedback in a computer-based collaborative problem solving group task.* Unpublished doctoral dissertation, University of Southern California, Los Angeles.

Hsieh, I.-L., & O'Neil, H. F., Jr. (2002). Types of feedback in a computer-based collaborative problem-solving group task. *Computers in Human Behavior, 18,* 699–715.

Krohne, W., Schmukle, S., Spaderna, H., & Spielberger, C. (2002). The state-trait depression scales: An international comparison. *Anxiety, Stress and Coping, 15,* 105–122.

Kuehl, M. A. (2001). *Teamwork skills and their impact upon the United States Marine Corps aviation community.* Unpublished doctoral dissertation, University of Southern California, Los Angeles.

Marshall, L. C. (2003). *The relationship between efficacy, teamwork skills, effort and patient satisfaction.* Unpublished doctoral dissertation, University of Southern California, Los Angeles.

Marshall, L. C., O'Neil, H. F., Abedi, J., Johnston, L., Visocnik, F., & Kainey, G. (2003, April). *Reliability and validity of the Healthcare Teams Questionnaire (HTQ).* Poster presented at the 2003 annual meeting of the American Educational Research Association, Chicago.

McDonald, R., & Ho, M. (2002). Principles and practice in reporting structural equation analyses. *Psychological Methods, 7,* 64–68.

Merrill, M. D. (1997, November/December). Instructional strategies that teach. *CBT Solutions,* pp. 1–11.

Merrill, M. D. (2001). *5 Star instructional design rating.* Retrieved April 9, 2004, from http://id2.usu.edu/5Star/FiveStarRating.PDF

Merrill, M. D. (2002a). First principles of instruction. *Educational Technology, Research and Development, 50,* 43–59.

Merrill, M. D. (2002b). A pebble-in-the-pond model for instructional design. *Performance Improvement, 41,* 39–44.

Merrill, M. D. (in press). *Components of instruction: Toward a theoretical tool for instructional design.* Instructional Science. Retrieved October 14, 2004, from http://www.id2.usu.edu/Papers/Components.pdf

Morgan, B. B., Jr., Salas, E., & Glickman, A. S. (1993). An analysis of team evolution and maturation. *Journal of General Psychology, 120,* 277–291.

O'Neil, H., Chung, G., & Brown, R. (1997). Use of networked simulations as a context to measure team competencies. In H. F. O'Neil, Jr. (Ed.), *Workforce readiness: Competencies and assessments* (pp. 411–452). Mahwah, NJ: Lawrence Erlbaum Associates.

O'Neil, H. F., Jr., Lee, C, Wang, S., & Mulkey, J. (1999, March). *Final report for analysis of teamwork skills questionnaire* (Deliverable to Statistics Canada). Sherman Oaks, CA: Advanced Design Information.

O'Neil, H. F., Jr., Wang, S., Chung, G. K. W. K., & Herl, H. E. (2000). Assessment of teamwork skills using computer-based teamwork simulations. In H. F. O'Neil, Jr., & D. Andrews (Eds.), *Aircrew training and assessment* (pp. 245–276). Mahwah, NJ: Lawrence Erlbaum Associates.

O'Neil, H. F., Jr., Wang, S., Lee, C., Mulkey, J., & Baker, E. L. (2003). Assessment of teamwork skills via a teamwork questionnaire. In H. F. O'Neil, Jr., & R. Perez (Eds.), *Technology applications in education: A learning view* (pp. 283–303). Mahwah, NJ: Lawrence Erlbaum Associates.

Paris, C., Salas, E., & Cannon-Bowers, J. (2000). Teamwork in multi-person systems: A review and analysis. *Ergonomics, 43,* 1052–1075.

Salas, E., & Cannon-Bowers, J. A. (2000). The science of training: A decade of progress. *Annual Review of Psychology, 52,* 471–499.

Weng, A. L.-B. (1999). *A teamwork skills questionnaire: A reliability and validity study of the Chinese version.* Unpublished doctoral dissertation, University of Southern California, Los Angeles.

APPENDIX : REVISED TEAMWORK SKILLS QUESTIONNAIRE SCORING KEY AND REVISED TEAMWORK SKILLS QUESTIONNAIRE

Scoring Key

Scales	Items
Coordination (n = 5)	6, 11, 17, 23, 32
Decision Making (n = 6)	3, 7, 12, 18, 24, 28
Leadership (n = 7)	1, 4, 8, 13, 19, 25, 29
Interpersonal Skills (n = 6)	5, 9, 14, 20, 33, 36
Adaptability (n =5)	15, 21, 26, 30, 34
Communication (n = 7)	2, 10, 16, 22, 27, 31, 35

COORDINATION—Organizing team activities to complete a task on time

6. When I work as part of a team, I allocate the tasks according to each team member's abilities.
11. When I work as part of a team, I help ensure the proper balancing of the workload.
17. When I work as part of a team, I do my part of the organization in a timely manner.
23. When I work as part of a team, I track other team members' progress.
32. When I work as part of a team, I emphasize the meeting of deadlines.

DECISION MAKING—Using available information to make decisions

3. When I work as part of a team, I understand and contribute to the organizational goals.
7. When I work as part of a team, I know the process of making a decision.
12. When I work as part of a team, I know how to weigh the relative importance among different issues.
18. When I work as part of a team, I prepare sufficiently to make a decision.
24. When I work as part of a team, I solicit input for decision making from my team members.
28. When I work as part of a team, I am able to change decisions based upon new information.

LEADERSHIP—Providing direction for the team

1. When I work as part of a team, I exercise leadership.
4. When I work as part of a team, I teach other team members.
8. When I work as part of a team, I serve as a role model in formal and informal interactions.
13. When I work as part of a team, I lead when appropriate, mobilizing the group for high performance.
19. When I work as part of a team, I lead the team effectively.
25. When I work as part of a team, I demonstrate leadership and ensure team results.
29. When I work as part of a team, I try to bring out the best in others.

INTERPERSONAL SKILLS—Interacting cooperatively with other team members

5. When I work as part of a team, I interact cooperatively with other team members.
9. When I work as part of a team, I conduct myself with courtesy.
14. When I work as part of a team, I respect the thoughts and opinions of others in the team.
20. When I work as part of a team, I treat others with courtesy.
33. When I work as part of a team, I accept individual differences among members.
36. When I work as part of a team, I treat all my team members as equals.

ADAPTABILITY—Recognizing problems and responding appropriately

15. When I work as part of a team, I can identify potential problems readily.
21. When I work as part of a team, I willingly contribute solutions to resolve problems.
26. When I work as part of a team, I adapt readily to varying conditions and demands.
30. When I work as part of a team, I recognize conflict.
34. When I work as part of a team, I identify needs or requirements and develop quality/timely solutions.

COMMUNICATION—Clear and accurate exchange of information

2. When I work as part of a team, I ensure the instructions are understood by all team members prior to starting the task.
10. When I work as part of a team, I ask for the instructions to be clarified when it appears not all the team members understand the task.
16. When I work as part of a team, I communicate in a manner to ensure mutual understanding.
22. When I work as part of a team, I seek and respond to feedback.
27. When I work as part of a team, I listen attentively.
31. When I work as part of a team, I clearly and accurately exchange information.
35. When I work as part of a team, I pay attention to what others are saying.

Revised Teamwork Questionnaire

Directions: This set of questions is to help us understand the way you think and feel about working with others. We know that different parts of your life, such as your job, recreational activities, or service to your community, may involve working with others and have different requirements, and that you may react differently in each kind of activity. Nonetheless, read each statement below and indicate how you generally think or feel. There are no right or wrong answers. Do not spend too much time on any one statement. Remember, give the answer that seems to describe how you *generally* think or feel.

	Almost never	Sometimes	Often	Almost always
1. When I work as part of a team, I exercise leadership	1	2	3	4
2. When I work as part of a team, I ensure the instructions are understood by all team members prior to starting the task.	1	2	3	4
3. When I work as part of a team, I understand and contribute to the organizational goals.	1	2	3	4
4. When I work as part of a team, I teach other team members.	1	2	3	4
5. When I work as part of a team, I interact cooperatively with other team members.	1	2	3	4
6. When I work as part of a team, I allocate the tasks according to each team member's abilities.	1	2	3	4
7. When I work as part of a team, I know the process of making a decision.	1	2	3	4
8. When I work as part of a team, I serve as a role model in formal and informal interactions.	1	2	3	4
9. When I work as part of a team, I conduct myself with courtesy.	1	2	3	4
10. When I work as part of a team, I ask for the instructions to be clarified when it appears not all the team members understand the task.	1	2	3	4
11. When I work as part of a team, I help ensure the proper balancing of the workload.	1	2	3	4
12. When I work as part of a team, I know how to weigh the relative importance among different issues.	1	2	3	4
13. When I work as part of a team, I lead when appropriate, mobilizing the group for high performance.	1	2	3	4

	Almost never	Sometimes	Often	Almost always
14. When I work as part of a team, I respect the thoughts and opinions of others in the team.	1	2	3	4
15. When I work as part of a team, I can identify potential problems readily.	1	2	3	4
16. When I work as part of a team, I communicate in a manner to ensure mutual understanding.	1	2	3	4
17. When I work as part of a team, I do my part of the organization in a timely manner.	1	2	3	4
18. When I work as part of a team, I prepare sufficiently to make a decision.	1	2	3	4
19. When I work as part of a team, I lead the team effectively.	1	2	3	4
20. When I work as part of a team, I treat others with courtesy.	1	2	3	4
21. When I work as part of a team, I willingly contribute solutions to resolve problems.	1	2	3	4
22. When I work as part of a team, I seek and respond to feedback.	1	2	3	4
23. When I work as part of a team, I track other team members' progress.	1	2	3	4
24. When I work as part of a team, I solicit input for decision making from my team members.	1	2	3	4
25. When I work as part of a team, I demonstrate leadership and ensure team results.	1	2	3	4
26. When I work as part of a team, I adapt readily to varying conditions and demands.	1	2	3	4
27. When I work as part of a team, I listen attentively.	1	2	3	4
28. When I work as part of a team, I am able to change decisions based upon new information.	1	2	3	4
29. When I work as part of a team, I try to bring out the best in others.	1	2	3	4
30. When I work as part of a team, I recognize conflict.	1	2	3	4
31. When I work as part of a team, I clearly and accurately exchange information.	1	2	3	4
32. When I work as part of a team, I emphasize the meeting of deadlines	1	2	3	4

	Almost never	Sometimes	Often	Almost always
33. When I work as part of a team, I accept individual differences among members.	1	2	3	4
34. When I work as part of a team, I identify needs or requirements and develop quality/ timely solutions.	1	2	3	4
35. When I work as part of a team, I pay attention to what others are saying.	1	2	3	4
36. When I work as part of a team, I treat all my team members as equals.	1	2	3	4

Chapter
9

Design Science as a Frame for Evaluation of Technology in Education and Training

Wellesley R. Foshay
PLATO Learning, Inc.

D. William Quinn
Quinn Evaluation

The current educational policy rhetoric in the United States promotes the experimental paradigm as the "gold standard" of inquiry for educational evaluation research. Experimental methods are viewed as the most appropriate strategies for examining causal relationships between variables. However, in educational technology research there are many important questions that do not involve causal relationships. Experimental methods are inappropriate for evaluating the use of educational technology when noncausal questions are being addressed, when assumptions required for experimental methods are not met, or when implementing experimental methods is infeasible in a given context (this point is discussed by Wilson in his chapter). The inevitable conclusion is that experimental methods provide an incomplete framework for evaluation of educational technology.

A better framework for evaluation comes from David Merrill's work on design science (Collins, 1990; Merrill, 1980). Design science establishes the principle that technology is as much an engineering discipline as a scientific one. This work anticipated the current interest in design experiments (Collins, 1990; Design-Based Research Collective, 2003) and the use of evaluation to validate design strategies as part of development, in preference to summative evaluation of technology products (Baker & O'Neil, 2003). In this chapter, we first examine the question of what effects of technology to evaluate, relating this question to the design science perspective. We then show how different inquiry strategies can be applied to evaluating the effects. Examples involving the PLATO Learning System will be used to illustrate key points.

DESIGN SCIENCE AND TECHNOLOGY EVALUATION

In the last 50 years educational technology evaluation has matured from the "gee whiz!" stage (focused on what we can make the technology do) through the "does it work?" phase (focused on proving that it is possible to learn from technology), and now to the "what's it good for?" phase (focused on each technology's relative strengths and weaknesses). It seems only reasonable that because the intent of educational technologists is to improve learning, the best way to evaluate technology's impact is by a comparison of posttest scores in classes that do and do not use technology. Unfortunately, this kind of comparison is usually done under conditions that make it impossible to attribute results, whether desirable or undesirable, to the specific use of the technology as such (computers, as an example).[1] Furthermore, there are substantial reasons to conclude that this is really the wrong question. In most circumstances, there probably are no effects of computer use, as such. More generally, an evaluation based on a simple comparison of posttest scores (whether comparing two groups or making a "before-and-after" or time-series comparison) usually will fail to reveal many important effects of technology, or will grossly underestimate them (Berliner, 2002).

This is a matter of no small consequence. National policy initiatives to support computer technology are under way in many countries, and many of the policies wisely include a requirement for research-based evidence of effectiveness. However, in the United States, as an example, the criteria for acceptable research-based evidence according to policymakers appear to emerge from the belief that only experimental or quasi-experimental comparison studies should be considered rigorous. This is a posture educational technology policymakers would do well to avoid. Limiting legitimate research to experimental methods will obscure many important effects and cause policymakers to fail to recognize many important technological effects. It is also inconsistent with current thinking on evaluation methodology, especially when applied to technology (Heinecke, Blasi, Milman, & Washington, 1999). Furthermore, restricting the range of inquiry in this way will lead to the erroneous conclusion that there is little evidence of the effectiveness of technology. Many causal relationships in education are not easily detected by the experimental paradigm (Berliner, 2002).

---

[1]When the design strategy is a mixed model of computer-based and non-computer activities, isolating the effects of computers makes even less sense.

Understanding the effects of technology requires a clear understanding of the distinction between the science of learning, the science of instruction, and the technology of instruction. Merrill (Merrill, Drake, Lacy, Pratt, & ID$_2$ Research Group, 1996) made the point clearly: Instructional science involves identifying variables to consider (a form of descriptive theory), identifying potential relationships among these variables (a form of prescriptive theory), and then empirically testing these relationships in both laboratory and field settings. Merrill and colleagues (1996) further distinguished between instructional science and the technology of instructional design, which is defined as "the technology of creating learning experiences and learning environments which promote these instructional activities" (p. 6).

The distinction is critical to understanding the appropriate application of the experimental paradigm and the development of questions appropriate for the evaluation of technology. Instructional science is based on a *combination* of descriptive and prescriptive theory; only the prescriptive theories are testable using the experimental paradigm. Instructional design is a technology of design, and cannot be tested experimentally. The *products* of instructional design, such as particular computer-based learning environments, can be studied for their effects and their effectiveness in relation to defined criteria of success. However, these studies must often be *descriptive* in nature; at most, quasi-experimental designs can compare effectiveness of two or more products of different design technologies, because experimental designs are rarely feasible in real-world implementations of products. Furthermore, any design technology carries with it assumptions about context of application and implementation. Therefore, to the extent that the products' designs are executions of the particular instructional design technology, with our assumptions about its context and implementation, then conclusions about the products can be used to draw inferences about the success of the instructional design technology. However, these inferences will necessarily be fairly weak and always subject to contextual constraints (Bannan-Ritland, 2003)

An illustration might help. Consider the case of a bridge collapse. The collapse does not call into question the principles of physics (the science), which were established through a combination of observation and experimentation. The collapse may call into question the methodology used to design the bridge (design technology), but it is possible that some error in the execution of the design technology led to construction of a weak bridge. Or, it may be that an otherwise sound design technology was misapplied to the context, and the result was the right bridge in the wrong location. Or, it may be that poor workmanship or incorrect materials weakened the bridge—in effect, a sound design was not implemented properly. Only investigation (descriptive research of a nonexperimental kind) can determine the cause of the collapse. The experimental paradigm may have a role to play in resolving underlying questions of science, if any arise. Some research activities, such as materials testing, are descriptive in nature, but they need not involve experimental methods with random assignment to control groups. Thus, although the experimental paradigm is of great use in establishing the science of instruction, it is of limited use in studying the design science—whether of bridges or of instruction.

In evaluation, there is often a requirement to draw conclusions about particular products. It is perhaps more common, especially in policy discussions, to seek conclusions about the effects of entire classes of products. These conclusions are implicitly about design technologies. Therefore, we believe that the primary focus of technology evaluation should be on design technology. By examining the effects of particular products (implementations of design technologies), the most important goal is to validate the design technologies themselves (including issues of context and implementation), although by relatively indirect inference. This argument is particularly important, given the relatively short life cycle of specific products and platforms, and the corresponding difficulty of completing strong summative evaluations on them early enough in their life cycles to be of use to decision makers.

WHAT ARE THE EFFECTS OF TECHNOLOGY?

We are now ready to consider the effects of technology. Instructional design technologies often are created with the intent of defining a way to make products with a variety of effects. Improvement of learning outcomes is only one of the reasons to use educational technology. We believe the five basic reasons to use technology are to improve:

- Learning outcomes.
- Instructional processes.
- Access.
- Cost.
- Organizational capability.

It is usually important to examine learning outcomes regardless of the reason for implementing technology, but only for the first reason is such an evaluation sufficient. To formulate an appropriate evaluation question, it is important to understand which of the five basic reasons, separately or in combination, are providing the motivation for a given project. We examine each of them, and describe the effects to be measured in an evaluation.

Effects on Learning Outcomes

Educational technology researchers have been comparing the effects of various media to classroom instruction and to each other for a generation. The results of such studies are, however, almost invariably weak. Reviews of research (see Clark, 2000) commonly discard more than half of the studies reported because methodological limitations make the comparison uninterpretable. Attention to the sound studies, however, has led Clark and others to conclude that the apparent effects of technology are really attributable to superior instructional design. Clark (1994) concluded that expecting technology to improve learning is like expecting a bakery delivery truck to improve the quality of the bread it carries.

Reviewing the research on technology in schools, Honey, Culp, and Carrigg (1999) came to a similar conclusion: "Technologies by themselves have little scaleable or sustained impact on learning in schools" (p. 2). We concur that there are probably few effects on learning from media technology as such, and simply introducing computers, networks, or any other hardware into the classroom is likely to lead to few coherent and worthwhile effects.

Whatever differences are observed are likely to be due to subtle changes in instruction, such as the quality and frequency of presentations, responses and feedback, or more sophisticated analysis facilitated through use of better tools. This means that the conclusions of an evaluation study usually must be limited to the particular software and hardware involved and the particular way in which they are used; it is not possible to make general conclusions about the use of computers in classrooms because of the lack of an underlying design technology and its consistent application. By analogy, we know that some teachers are better than others, and teachers do not all do the same thing in their classrooms. Thus, it makes no sense to draw conclusions about all teachers simply by looking at the results obtained by a few. It makes little sense to attempt a similar generalization when evaluating technology's effects. We can, however, evaluate specific uses of technology, as defined by their instructional design, which in turn is shaped to some degree by the physical characteristics of the media in use. This is consistent with the premise of the design science approach.

A Typology of Educational Software

There is a wide variety of types of software intended to affect learning outcomes. The effects observed vary according to the type of software and the way in which it is intended to influence learning, so it is important for technology evaluators to understand the intended role of the software in the teaching/learning process, and, thus, learning outcomes which might reasonably be observed.

A recent internal concept paper by the Software and Information Industries Association (SIIA, 2003) addresses the task of relating software type to intended use and expected learning outcomes. It begins with a distinction between instructional and management software, and includes these classes within each type:

Management.

1. Student Information Systems.
2. Instructional Management Systems.

3. Standards Alignment Tools/Systems.
4. Professional Development Programs.
5. Parent and Home Connections Tools/Systems.
6. Higher Education and Workplace Articulation Programs.

Instruction.

1. Content/Curriculum.
2. Documentary/Dramatization.
3. Problem Solving.
4. Simulation.
5. Skill Building/Drill and Practice.
6. Tutorial.
7. Learning Tools.
    a. Productivity tool.
    b. Reference.
    c. Subject-specific tool.
8. Assessment Applications.
    a. Observational assessments.
    b. Quiz makers.
    c. Standardized testing applications.

The paper further expands the typology by adding details on the variations of each type that may be found within each of the major school content domains.

Because the varying types of software carry with them different assumptions about their intended use, their expected effect on learning outcomes is likely to vary. For example, tutorial software usually includes clear objectives and a fairly complete direct instructional experience within the software, and is intended for self-study. In contrast, a data analysis tool typically seeks only to structure and represent patterns in data. It is designed for a very wide range of purposes, access methods, and uses, so its objectives and expected learning outcomes are much more broadly defined. As a result, it is often easier to show the impact of tutorial software on a test score than is the case for tools. An evaluation design that examines only test scores is likely to miss some of the impact on learning outcomes of tools. Analogous issues are common with assessment applications and with the various classes of management software.

Effects on Process

Contrary to some statements and actions by policy and legislative groups, neither education's nor training's worth is defined by a single test. In a learning environment, certain processes are valued particularly because they are believed to be closely associated with important curriculum objectives. The processes may suggest both cognitive and other learning outcomes. They are often best measured by indicators other than tests, such as observations, self-reports of behavior, and various work products and artifacts.

A simple example may help to illustrate the point. Many educators believe that it is important to teach their students to be self-sufficient learners (McCombs, 2000). Educators seek to construct learning environments that empower their students to question, seek information, initiate their own learning tasks, and judge the results obtained. Technology advocates often claim that computers give learners the tools to be much more self-sufficient in their learning. Many of the types of software described in the previous section are often designed to support this goal. In this case, the technology evaluation should examine evidence of self-sufficient learning by the participating students. This evidence would be independent of any cognitive learning measures. For example, McCombs (2000, p. 8) argued that this type of evaluation should focus on:

- The learner and each learner's perceptions, needs, and motivation
- Learning opportunities and the types of teaching and learning experiences that can meet learner needs for success, belonging, and autonomy.
- Learning outcomes that include affective, cognitive, social, and performance domains.
- The learning context or climate for learning, including expectations, teacher and technology support, time structures, and adaptability to student needs.

Even when examining cognitive learning, effects on process may be important. No matter how well constructed, no conventional test provides acceptably valid and reliable measures of all the cognitive learning outcomes, which are an important part of a curriculum. Consequently, most well-planned education and training curricula use a portfolio of assessment techniques, which may include work products, observations of task performance, tests, oral performance, and other data. Because many of these data are often the most important measures of problem solving, thinking skills, and other higher order learning outcomes that are the intended outcomes of many uses of technology, it is important to give them appropriate weight in the technology evaluation. They will support conclusions about learning outcomes such as problem-solving processes and other indicators of thinking skills.

The values of an education or training environment often define learning outcomes that encompass lessons, which relate to goals such as initiative, persistence, citizenship, teamwork, and character. Foshay (2000) defined the emotional (affective), social, aesthetic, physical (psychomotor), and spiritual domains, in addition to the intellectual (cognitive). He argued that a fully defined curriculum includes goals in all six of these domains, and that many of the characteristics of excellent teachers address all of these domains. Defining a curriculum solely in terms of the cognitive domain may impoverish that curriculum.

Excellent teachers know this intuitively. They do many things in a classroom that are intended to convey lessons in all six domains. For example, a mathematician or scientist who praises an "elegant" solution is making an aesthetic judgment. A teacher who shows enthusiasm for the subject may be teaching important social and emotional lessons. When learners work together on a learning task, many important lessons about teamwork and the value of collaboration become part of the curriculum. Many of the design features of software are intended to convey lessons in domains beyond the cognitive, and users of educational technology often comment on effects that seem to correspond to these domains. For example, teachers often comment that learners who show little motivation for conventional classroom activities are so motivated by their technology use that their efforts far exceed the minimum assignments. In PLATO evaluations, one of the most common observations is that learners feel successful in learning, whether or not they have a history of success in conventional school learning: another example of an outcome in the emotional domain. In another example, teachers and learners both react very strongly to the aesthetic design of software; such reactions often serve as a "gatekeeper"—only if the reaction is positive will the teachers and learners engage the intended learning task. Process indicators such as these often can reveal much about the attractiveness, acceptability, and user-friendliness of educational software. Peer teaching and collaborative work on problem solving are an important part of PLATO's design, and can be observed in the classroom. Even if there are no measured changes in cognitive learning, it is often the case that process indicators such as these can play an important role in assessing the impact of technology.

Taken to its logical extension, effects on process can lead to an argument that the goal of technology is to produce a different *kind* of learning experience, with different goals, than those that are feasible by conventional classroom methods. In this case, the argument is that technology's goal is *not* to improve, or even to improve on, the conventional classroom learning environment. Nor is equivalence with the conventional classroom's learning outcomes a goal. Instead, the goal is to provide an alternative learning environment, capable of addressing important learning outcomes, which may or may not be attainable through conventional classroom methods. Evaluating a technology implementation of this type might well require considerable data gathering on process well beyond the effects measured by achievement tests. Comparative study designs could be quite informative, but they probably will require qualitative methods.

Effects on Access

Many educational technology implementations have as their primary goal improved access to learning for some defined population of learners. This goal is quite independent of learning outcomes. Technologies may improve access but produce learning outcomes that are no different than, or perhaps even inferior to, those of conventional classroom methods. Such an implementation might be judged successful when improved access to learning was a primary goal. Examples of such implementations include distance learning initiatives designed to reach rural or home-bound students, continuing education programs, e-learning on demand in work settings, and programs designed for countries that face a shortage of qualified teachers. In addition, some applications of technology are designed to improve access of learners and instructors to each other by creating online communities, whether or not the context of the classroom is maintained. Finally, some technology applications (particularly in corporate settings) seek to embed learning and knowledge management technologies directly in the work environment and its tools, thus bypassing much formal classroom training.

In these cases, it is important to recognize that equivalence of technology-based learning experiences with conventional classroom learning is not a relevant goal. The effectiveness of the technology should be judged on the basis of its ability to reach the intended learners and to meet their needs.

We can examine three general approaches to improving access to see how this argument applies: distance education, online learning communities, and technologies for just-in-time learning.

Distance Education.   In secondary and postsecondary education, it is often tacitly assumed that the goal of distance education methods is to recreate the classroom experience in an online environment. This assumption even underlies the online offerings of some corporate universities. Moller and colleagues (Moller, Prestera, Douglas, Downs-Keller, & McCausland, 2002) pointed out, however, that this goal is scarcely relevant to the distance education enterprise. Distance learning often is intended to reach learners for whom campus-based learning is an undesirable option. They differ from the typical campus learner in a number of characteristics, such as age, time available, work and family commitments, and learning needs. It is often the case that not only is the campus-based classroom not a good fit for them, neither is the conventional academic curriculum and its practices.

A further complexity surrounds the structure of distance education solutions. Some distance solutions are purely online, but some have recognized that online and classroom methods are complementary, and various mixed models of instruction are in use. This renders the technology-versus-classroom comparison strategy even less applicable. We conclude that evaluations of distance education programs should evaluate the entire program, whether purely online or using a mixed model, rather than attempt to isolate the effects of particular portions of such programs in comparison with classroom counterparts.

A distance education program evaluation that recognizes the preceding argument should examine carefully the learning needs and characteristics of its learners. Then the evaluation should examine how well the program meets the needs of the learners. Then, in the context of these needs, it is reasonable to assess the program's effectiveness in meeting them. Comparisons between distance education modalities, rather than with classrooms, could be quite informative.

Learning Communities.   Another way computers are used to improve access is by creation of online communities, which may include any combination of learners, teachers, practitioners, and experts. Such communities have the goal of providing access to participants with a common interest (and usually a common frame of reference), even when the participants are dispersed. Often the intent is to recreate the collegiality of classroom or small group interaction, while "breaking down the walls of the classroom" by making it possible for collaborative groups to operate over separations of space and time.

The most basic criterion for evaluating learning communities is to examine participation, to see if the goal of access has been realized. Beyond this basic measure, it may make sense to evaluate the quality of interaction in the online community. This is especially the case if particularly desirable processes can be identified. For example, it may make sense to code interactions according to their relevance to course procedures, technical help with tools, or substantive questions on course content. Or, it might make sense to code responses by their level according to Bloom's (1974) *Taxonomy of the Cognitive Domain* or a published coding scheme of interest.

Just-in-Time Learning, Performance Support, and Knowledge Management.

Another popular application of technology to improve access is to embed directly into the work environment activities and tools that facilitate learning, work, and the capture and dissemination of new knowledge (Rosenberg, 2001). The goal with these strategies is to make new knowledge instantly available to all who need it, without the costs and delays of conventional training and education. These methods have a major influence in corporate environments, but in principle they could find application in education.

As with other access-oriented technology strategies, the most basic evaluation question for just-in-time learning, performance support, and knowledge management is whether the goal of access has been achieved. For this purpose, simple utilization statistics are of use. More sophisticated measures can examine impact on productivity (Hale, 2002). Subjective self-reports of value or ease of use have many limitations, but may be useful in judging an implementation.

A brief example may illustrate the suggested strategy. A corporate e-learning strategy for its field sales and service force might include an integrated mix of self-instructional and instructor-facilitated distance learning, a variety of templates and tools for sales and service, a database of knowledge related to products, service, best practices, clients, and competition, and a number of online communities for each key role, with participants drawn from the field and headquarters. Evaluation of this technology might first focus on utilization patterns, to determine if the goal of improved access to knowledge and skill has been met. Process measures might focus on analysis of interactions in a range of case problems. Performance measures might include sales figures, customer satisfaction, and perhaps additional key process measures such as time to develop proposals, competitive loss analysis, and the like.

Effects on Cost

Especially in the private sector, a common motive for technology use is cost reduction. Technology implementations with this goal often seek no particular improvement in learning outcomes; instead, their purpose is to reduce the costs associated with education and training development and delivery. This goal is common in corporate training; it is perhaps the most common motive behind e-learning in corporate contexts. It is less common in education because most educational organizations have no way to offset the fixed costs of conventional instruction by use of technology-based delivery, and often don't even have detailed cost models of their service delivery. However, educational examples of cost reduction are found in special cases, such as advanced placement courses, home schooling and special needs, after-school programs, alternative schools, and charter schools.

However, cost analysis should be part of almost any major program evaluation, especially when technology is involved. Worthwhile accomplishments typically involve a cost. Unfortunately, it is all too easy to get *nothing* for *something* if a program is ill-conceived, poorly implemented, or misdirected. The goal of cost analysis is to help to design programs that give greater value for the investment.

The True Meaning of ROI.   An important issue in evaluating technology in the public or private sector is to determine whether using technology to solve an education or performance problem provides enough benefits to justify the investment of money and effort to implement the program. Decision makers and other constituents are asking: "What is the return on the investment (ROI) made in technology-based systems?" Answering this question means considering the issue of money as well as program effects (Lloyd, 1989).

Decision makers and evaluators of technology often assume by default that cost-benefit comparisons must be made in terms of impact on the organization's balance sheet. However, it is often the case that this approach is needlessly restrictive and uninformative. Characterizing the costs and benefits of an alternative action solely in terms of expenses and revenues can be highly misleading.

Gauging monetary effects of technology-based training beyond savings in delivery cost is often difficult. Effects of training or education on organizational effectiveness are often very indirect and complex, unless the organization has a detailed model of value added for their products.[2] However, it may be possible to define the benefits of technology in terms of attainment of improved organizational capability (described later) to achieve strategic objectives. The strategic objectives, in turn, often have considerable value to the organization in whatever terms it uses to define its critical goals. For example, any of the examples of improved organizational capability given earlier could be critical to a strategic objective for an education or training organization. By using them, it would be possible to demonstrate how technology is facilitating attainment of the organization's mission and vision. This approach, called *cost-effectiveness* analysis, is described later in this chapter. Obviously, this

---

[2]An exception is organizations that have implemented a total quality management system, often in compliance with a standard such as ISO-9000. These systems typically include intermediate measures of quality and process that are fine-grained enough to detect the effects of training and education. In the absence of such a system, however, creating the measures solely to gauge the ROI of training is rarely worth the effort.

approach depends on availability of careful strategic planning, and alignment of technology applications to the strategic plan. Organizations that have weak or incomplete strategic plans, or that have implemented technology plans without relating them to the strategic plan, will be unable to use this strategy.

An example can illustrate the point. In PLATO Learning, Inc., the majority of new revenue comes from repeat business. Client satisfaction has a direct relationship to revenue, and thus to our profitability. Impact on client satisfaction from changes in product features or services may be critical to the long-term health of the business. Measures of client satisfaction are repeated from time to time, and their relative improvements are viewed operationally as a benefit. This makes it possible to array the costs of various alternatives to improve client satisfaction against their impact on the satisfaction measures. In this case, the cost-benefit comparison includes a financial measure on the "cost" side, but nonfinancial measures of client satisfaction on the "benefit" side.

This example brings to the surface another issue in any cost study: the need to get the time frame right. It is often the case that actions taken to improve outcomes have most of their effects in the long term. To continue with our example, changes in products or services by PLATO Learning typically show their impact on client satisfaction only after considerable delay. For example, an effort to eliminate hardware compatibility issues has costs that appear in the short term, but it may be years before any benefit in client satisfaction or reduced support cost is detectable. Thus, a time frame that is too short will capture only the costs of improving compatibility and not the benefits.

Intellectual Capital.   An important variation of the ROI argument concerns management of intellectual capital (Stewart, 1997). Valuation of intellectual capital is based on the principle that the basic asset of an organization is its knowledge: its procedural "know-how," and its knowledge of its clients, competitors, and the environment in which it operates. In many, perhaps most, organizations, such knowledge remains locked in the brains of its employees, and there is little or no systematic attempt to capture and manage it. Thus, the principal asset of the organization does not show on its balance sheet, but the costs of that asset, such as salaries, do. In an important sense, therefore, the corporate balance sheet provides a distorted view of the wealth of an organization. E-learning technologies (including training technologies, electronic performance support systems [EPSS] and knowledge management systems [KM]) play a key role in many strategies for maximizing intellectual capital (Rosenberg, 2001). Taken together, these technologies provide powerful ways to capture the knowledge of an organization, and to disseminate it efficiently on a just-in-time basis. Strategies for capturing, managing, and valuing the knowledge assets of an organization are gaining recognition in the accounting community. The interested reader is referred to Sullivan (2000). The intellectual capital approach provides a way to provide meaningful cost-benefit analyses for technologies which resist more traditional means of analysis.

Effects on Organizational Capability

Many applications of technology have important goals that go well beyond improved learning. Four examples of the potential impact of educational technology on organizational capability are sketched in order to establish the need to take a broad and long-term view of the return on investments made in educational technology.

Example 1: Personalized Decision Making and Real-Time Reporting.
Technology can be used to improve the timeliness, completeness, and usability of data for the purpose of decision making. In academic and training contexts, it is often the case that instructors and administrators have only incomplete, indirect, and delayed information on the effects of their efforts. Furthermore, such data is often obtained only at great cost, by manually marking tests and assignments and by manually recording and reporting results. The effort involved displaces higher value activities (such as efforts to improve instruction). The effect is that in a real sense, instructors and administrators are making decisions without adequate information; they find out if their efforts are effective only when it is too late to do anything, and the information they have lacks sufficient detail to be useful for many purposes. Desirable goals such as individualization of instruction are impractical and collapse under the weight of paperwork. On the other hand, it is quite feasible to develop a near-real-time picture of each individual learner's progress using software to automate testing, marking, record keeping, and reporting. Such a strategy makes it possible for the organization to automate and personalize instruction in a way it could not before.

Example 2: Improved Consistency and Responsiveness to Change. One of the big problems any education or training organization faces is that what happens in the classroom is unknown except by the participants. Instructors teaching the same content are often isolated from each other. This makes it extremely difficult to ensure quality of instruction, to change the practices of the organization, and to ensure consistency and currency in what is taught. Given the importance of curriculum standards and accountability in many areas of education and training, this problem is particularly acute. Technology can be used to address this problem by providing instructors with databases of instructional resources, tools, and plans that are aligned precisely to clearly defined curriculum standards. With networked systems it becomes easy to quickly push information on new curriculum standards and new resources into daily classroom practice. At the same time, it is likely that irrelevant classroom activities can be discouraged, because they won't be included in alignments. The overall effect on organizational capability is improved consistency and responsiveness to change.

Example 3: Individualization and Mastery Learning. Conventional large-group classroom methods teach the same content to each learner in a uniform way. Despite the well-understood limitations of this approach, it remains prevalent in classrooms of all types. One reason may be that true individualization and self-paced, mastery-model learning often is prohibitively difficult to administer in conventional classrooms. Technology can help, by directly providing some instruction, and by performing the frequent assessment and prescription tasks that mastery learning requires, thus relieving the instructor of a number of "low-level" tasks and creating time for more high-value tasks. The overall effect for the organization's capability is the ability to provide individualized instruction with consistent learning outcomes.

Example 4: Improved Time on Task and Higher Value Activity.   PLATO evaluations often show that self-instructional use of technology increases time on task by learners when compared to conventional classroom methods. Furthermore, if the software is well designed, rate of responding by individual learners goes up, and quality of responding (thoughtfulness of response) may rise. The net effect is that technology can be used to change the role of the instructor, from "sage on the stage" to "guide on the side," by freeing time for the teacher to engage in individual and small-group interaction. In this way, technology can enable the organization to change its basic instructional model.

These examples are not exhaustive in terms of indicating how technology can be used to make organizations more nimble, responsive, and resource-flexible, but they do suggest how educational technology can help organizations achieve strategic objectives. Technology applications driven by intents such as these are common in business and industry e-learning settings (Rosenberg, 2001), but they are still fairly rare in academic settings. In evaluating them, attention should focus on the change in organizational capability, such as successful implementation of change objectives. Direct measurement of learning outcomes may be needed, but the entire data collection effort should also include indicators of implementation such as classroom observations, analysis of work products, and the like.

It should be clear from this overview that the effects of technology can be varied, even within a single application. It is likely, therefore, that a carefully defined evaluation plan should examine a number of effects. Basing the evaluation on a single measure (such as test scores or cost) is likely to fail to capture important technology effects, and may miss the primary goal of the technology's application entirely.

Two additional considerations are important in deciding what to evaluate: whether to attempt to isolate the effects of technology, and whether to evaluate the processes of technology use. These considerations affect both the goals of the evaluation and its methods: They often drive decisions on the use of experimental and quasi-experimental (comparative) evaluation designs. We discuss each of these next.

ARE EFFECTS DUE TO TECHNOLOGY—SHOULD WE CARE?

Decision makers and prospective evaluators of technology often assume that they should isolate the effects of technology from other effects of the training or education program under study. In many cases, however, we recommend against such attempts, and recommend in favor of studying entire programs, using comparative designs where feasible. The reasons are based on a basic principle of technology and a methodological issue.

A basic principle of educational technology is that it always is used within a context (framework) that extends beyond the technology and creates the purpose for its use. Often, learners depend on the instructor to create this framework by relating the technology use to a specific task that supports a larger goal. Stated differently, technology is almost always integrated into a learning environment that includes many nontechnology elements, such as a purpose and learning goal, motivation, frame of reference and prior knowledge, a work product, feedback on performance, and in all likelihood, the social structure of the work group or class, as well as other nontechnology resources for information, learning, and work. Of course, there is a wide range of learner characteristics that determine what the learner brings to the learning experience and to the technology.

It is thus an oversimplification to portray any learning outcome as solely the product of the technology component(s) of the learning environment. Learning outcomes are always a result of the interaction of the learning environment and the learner, and the technology is just one part of the learning environment. Effects due solely to the media are likely to be relatively insignificant; effects due to instructional design are likely to be larger; both will be necessary, but not sufficient, causes. Interaction effects with various environmental and learner factors are likely to be critically important to the success of the learning experience and the technology. A comparative design that isolates the effects of technology will show this if the within-treatment effects are larger than the between-treatment effects—a common observation (Berliner, 2002). Practitioners know this is true: No technology is teacher-proof. If the teachers and learners do not understand the technology and support its appropriate use, the technology will fail. Thus, it is critically important to understand *technology in context.* The goal of evaluation should be to understand the results that occur when technology is used in a particular way in a particular context. Comparative designs that isolate the effects of technology are typically of much less interest to the practitioner, although it may be a valid research objective (see footnote 1). If comparative designs are to be used (as current U.S. government guidelines suggest), it may be of greater interest to compare intact programs rather than components.

The methodological reason to study intact programs concerns the cost, intrusiveness, and complexity of the study required. Typically, studying technology in context can be done using *case study* and *qualitative* research techniques (see next section). These techniques are very labor-intensive, and require detailed observation and description of the inputs, processes, and outputs of the whole learning environment as the evaluator finds it in the school or training organization. In contrast, isolating the effects of technology from the interactions with the rest of the learning environment usually requires an experimental or quasi-experimental study, in which the strategy is to compare the users of technology with a similar group of users who did not use technology.

Another common concern is over the desired length of the study. Again, the recommendation is to study an entire program, where possible, whether the program spans a few days, weeks, or months of use. The reason is that it is usually desirable for the study to avoid "novelty effects" having to do with the initial wave of interest and confusion often associated with introduction of a new technology. The best way to be sure that the effects observed are stable and replicable is to view the evaluation of the first iteration of a new program as purely formative (note that this conflicts with the evaluation requirements of many technology grant programs). Any summative evaluation of the program's worth should be attempted only in the second or later iteration of the program; repeated studies in subsequent years are even more preferable. Thus, for example, a school implementing new technology used all year long should only evaluate the success of its implementation in the first year; examination of learning outcomes in the first year may be helpful for formative purposes, but will not be indicative of stable results. The program is not likely to produce typical learning outcomes until the second year or later.

HOW IS THE TECHNOLOGY USED?

In addition to evaluating the effects of technology, it is often important to examine how the technology is used. There are two reasons: first (as discussed earlier), the effects of a technology are a complex result of the interaction of the technology with the learner and with other elements of the learning environment. Thus, the same technology is likely to be used differently in every environment in which it is employed. To understand the effects of technology, therefore, it is important to understand how it has been used in a particular environment.

Second, technology is rarely used in the way the designers intended, especially during the first iteration of the program. Especially with computers, various startup and initial learning issues usually affect the way in which a technology is used at first. Various technology problems often affect availability and reliability. In addition, both instructors and learners need to learn what the product does, and how best to use it. Thus, it is likely that the technology will not be used in the way the designers intended until the second or later iterations of the education or training program, if ever. In particular, evaluators should consider examining these utilization effects.

Consistency in Delivery

Check to see if the hardware and software were in fact available and working reliably throughout the intended period of use. Computer and network problems often preclude ready access to the technology.

Total Quality Management Effects

Check to see if all users, both instructors and learners, know how to use the product, and are using it in the way(s) intended in the program design. It is common for instructors to use high-powered technologies for low-powered purposes, or for the product to "hijack the curriculum" by becoming the center of attention, serving as a distraction from the main goals of the training or education curriculum.

Scalability Effects

Often technologies are intended for innovative applications that will not scale well. Limitations to scalability often include insufficient availability of computers or network capacity, an unsustainable requirement for technical or educational support or professional development, or apathy or disincentives to adoption by the larger community of practice. Technologies often seem to yield products designed for use by the enthusiastic "early adopters," but they do not have the support, structure, and robustness needed to be useful to "middle adopters" who may be interested in the product for what it can do for them but have no patience with the technology as such. It is important to consider these scalability issues in the evaluation, both during small-scale pilot projects and during large-scale implementations.

Time of Delivery Effects

Often, especially when using experimental or quasi-experimental designs, it is desirable in terms of organizational culture to position technology as an additional activity intended to enhance learning but not to displace any current practice. However, this technology strategy often is a two-edged sword: This makes the technology "nonthreatening" to practitioners, but it also relegates the technology in their minds to a "nice-to-have" rather than a "need-to-have" posture. This, in turn, may cause the instructors to limit the use of technology to short periods that will not disrupt normal activity, or to weaken unintentionally the motivational structure supporting the implementation. Furthermore, if there are limitations on resource availability or delivery, then the technology-based learning experiences may occur out of synchronization with other activities for a given topic, thus precluding any synergies between technology-based and other learning experiences, and perhaps even causing confusion. To detect these effects, it is important to examine detailed records of when and how much the technology was used, and to compare this pattern of use with the timing of other related learning activities.

Instructional Management Effects

Instructional management includes all the decisions instructors and administrators make about what to do when with their learners, in what groups, using what resources, where, for how long, and with what incentives and feedback to the learners. In conventional classroom environments, these decisions are often so tradition bound that instructors don't even realize they may not be optimum, and that they can be changed. As discussed earlier, one major class of potential benefits of computer technology concerns instructional management. However, it is common for instructors without training to fail to exploit these benefits and to instead force the technology into the traditional instructional management structure. To see if this is happening, it is important to examine how technology use was scheduled and how it actually occurred, who used the technology for what, how the instructors positioned the technology with their learners, and whether the instructional management practices observed correspond to the intended use of the technology.

Although it is certainly possible to use experimental or quasi-experimental designs to isolate these implementation effects, it is more common to examine them using descriptive methods, either in an independent study, or as part of a larger experimental or quasi-experimental study.

CONCLUSION

There is greater need, and greater demand, for evaluation of technology than at any time in the past generation. However, although thousands of studies have been published over the 40-year life of computer-based learning, only a few hundred are sound enough to be interpretable and useful. Furthermore, far too many expensive programs have yielded little in the way of results. If the promise of computers is to be realized in the everyday practice of education and training, practitioners must invest more effort in evaluation of their programs, and must be more willing to study their programs, than has often been the case historically. The studies we need must be more sophisticated than is usually the case now, and more sophisticated than policymakers often know to request. As professionals, we must steer the policy agenda for research and evaluation of technology away from simplistic studies that are too flawed to tell us anything useful, and toward studies that show a sophisticated awareness of the history of technology evaluation and research, the methodological tradeoffs involved, and the real issues which determine the effectiveness and scalability of technology. Only if we do so will the potential of technology to restructure education and training be realized.

We believe Merrill's distinctions between learning science, design science and technology, and the products of the technology are essential to appropriate application of the methods of evaluation research to educational technology in general, and computer-based educational technologies in particular. We must use Merrill's distinction to achieve a useful degree of generality in our findings, and to develop really useful evaluation questions and designs. Because of the complexities of technology implementation that we have described, and because of the many purposes and effects of technology, it is likely that an adequate evaluation plan will include a mix of quantitative and qualitative, experimental or quasi-experimental and descriptive methods.

REFERENCES

Baker, E., & O'Neil, H. (2003). Evaluation and research for technology; Not just playing around. *Evaluation and Program Planning, 26*(2), 169–176.

Bannan-Ritland, B. (2003). The role of design in research: The integrative learning design framework. *Educational Researcher, 32*(1), 21–24.

Berliner, D. (2002). Educational research: The hardest science of all. *Educational Researcher, 31*(8), 18–20.

Bloom, B. S. (1974). *Taxonomy of educational objectives; The classification of educational goals.* New York: D. McKay.

Clark, R. E. (1994). Media will never influence learning. *Educational Technology, Research and Development, 42*(2), 21–29.

Clark, R. E. (2000). Evaluating distance education: Strategies and cautions. *Quarterly Review of Education, 1*(1), 5–18.

Collins, A. (1990). *Toward a design science of education.* Technical Report 1. Cambridge, MA: B. Bolt and Newman, Center For Technology in Education.

Design-Based Research Collective. (2003). Design-based research: An emerging paradigm for educational inquiry. *Educational Researcher, 32*(1), 5–8.

Foshay, A. W. (2000). *The curriculum: Purpose, substance, practice.* New York: Teachers College Press.

Hale, J. (2002). *Performance based evaluation: Tools and techniques to measure the impact of training.* San Francisco: Jossey-Bass/Pfeiffer.

Heinecke, W. F., Blasi, L., Milman, N., & Washington, L. (1999). New directions in the evaluation of the effectiveness of educational technology. *Prepared for the secretary's conference on educational technology, 1999: Evaluating the effectiveness of technology.* Washington, DC. Retrieved April 9, 2004, from http://www.edgov/technology/techconf/1999

Honey, M., Culp, K. M., & Carrigg, F. (1999). *Perspectives on technology and education research: Lessons from the past and the present.* Presented at The Secretary's Conference on Educational Technology, 1999, Evaluating the Effectiveness of Technology, Washington, DC, July 12–13, 1999. Retrieved April 9, 2004, from http://www.ed/gov/Technology/TechConf/1999

Lloyd, T. (1989, May). Winning the budget battle. *Training,* pp. 57–62.

McCombs, B. (2000). *Assessing the role of educational technology in the teaching and learning process: A learner-centered perspective.* Presented at The Secretary's Conference on Educational Technology, 2000. Retrieved April 9, 2004, from http://www.ed.gov/Technology/TechConf/2000

Merrill, M. D. (1980). Can the adjective instructional modify the noun science? *Educational Technology, 20*(2), 37–44.

Merrill, M. D., Drake, L., Lacy, M. J., Pratt, J. A., & ID2 Research Group. (1996). Reclaiming instructional design. *Educational Technology, 36*(5), 5–7.

Moller, L., Prestera, G., Douglas, H., Downs-Keller, M., & McCausland, J. (2002). Creating an organic knowledge-building environment within an asynchronous distributed learning context. *Quarterly Review of Distance Education, 31*(1), 47–58.

Rosenberg, M. J. (2001). *E-Learning: Strategies for delivering knowledge in the digital age.* New York: McGraw-Hill.

Software and Information Industries Association. (2003). *Study of the effectiveness of educational technology: Selecting technologies & identifying schools.* Washington, DC: Software & Information Industries Association.

Stewart, T. (1997). *The new wealth of organizations.* New York: Doubleday.

Sullivan, P. (2000). *Value-driven intellectual capital: How to convert intangible corporate assets into market value.* New York: Wiley.

Chapter
10

Validating Instructional Design and Development Models

Rita C. Richey

Wayne State University

Throughout his career, David Merrill has viewed instructional design as being "built upon the rock of instructional science" (Merrill, Drake, Lacy, Pratt, & ID2 Research Group, 1996, p. 7). He viewed instructional design not as a philosophy nor as a set of procedures arrived at by happenstance or discussion, but rather he advocates using scientific evidence as the foundation of design principles. This chapter is an extension of this position. It speaks, however, not of design principles but of design models. It speaks specifically of the need for empirically validating the many models of instructional design and development that exist in the literature and in practice, and it describes processes for doing so.

Many recognize that instructional design and development (ID) models should be substantiated by systematic validation rather than relying primarily on user testimonials as evidence of their effectiveness (Gustafson & Branch, 2002). Model validation projects, however, seldom become a priority. The paucity of such efforts may be more a reflection of time constraints and ill-defined model validation procedures, rather than a lack of appreciation of the fundamental need for validation. This chapter describes the general nature of ID models and ID model validation, and then explores five alternative approaches to the validation process.

THE NATURE OF ID MODELS

Models, by definition, are simplified representations, and they are often idealized. Nonetheless, models provide structure and order to complex real life events that on the surface can seem chaotic. ID models are no different. However, as Andrews and Goodson (1980) noted, "The fidelity of the model to the actual processes it represents will diminish as the specificity of the model diminishes" (p. 3). In most cases, the use of an ID model calls for considerable interpretation and amplification to provide the detail required for specific applications.

ID models can be used in a variety of ways. For the most part, they create standards for good design, but there are other common functions. Frequently, they are used as communication tools so that one can visualize and explain an intended plan. They can serve as marketing devices and as project management tools. They also can play a part in theory development and in translating theory into practice.

There are two major types of ID models, both of which are candidates for validation. One identifies variables that impact the design process and shows their interrelationships. The second represents the recommended steps to follow in a design process (Seels & Glasgow, 1997). Richey (1986) called these two configurations conceptual models and procedural models, respectively.

Procedural Models

Most ID models are visual diagrams and are procedural in nature. Notable examples are the generic flowchart models of Dick, Carey, and Carey (2001) and Smith and Ragan (2005). Other visual formats are also used, such as the embedded circle design of the Morrison, Ross, and Kemp (2003) model. The majority of these procedural models pertain to comprehensive design projects. They are, for the most part, derived from applications of general systems theory. Gustafson and Branch (2002) described these models as beginning with various forms of analysis, and progressing through the design of a set of specifications for the learning environment and the development of learning materials. Evaluation activities permeate the entire process, even through the management of the ongoing implementation of the products. There are many variations of this general ID process often represented by more specific models intended to relate to the idiosyncrasies of specific groups of learners, learning environments, types of delivery systems, or even specific design philosophies.

Other ID procedural models address more specific aspects of the design, development, and evaluation processes. For example, there are models that speak to the selection and sequencing of specific learning activities, such as Gagné's Events of Instruction Model (Gagné, Briggs, & Wager, 1992) or Rothwell and Kazanas's (1998) models for writing and sequencing performance objectives. There are media selection models, such as Reiser and Gagné's (1983) flowchart model. There are motivation design models such as Keller's (1987) ARCS Model.

Conceptual Models

Conceptual design models have less consistent formats than procedural models, but there is one large segment of conceptual models that use the taxonomy format. Seels (1997) has explored a range of taxonomic models in our field. These models began with Dale's (1946) Cone of Experience, an early media selection model that classified media on a concrete-to-abstract continuum. Seels also cites the various taxonomies of learning outcomes, including Bloom's (1956) taxonomy of cognitive objectives, Gagné's (1972) domains of learning, and the Martin and Briggs (1986) taxonomy of the affective domain.

Other conceptual models in the literature are more varied in format. Some path diagrams can also be viewed as conceptual ID models. These are graphical displays of the patterns of direct and indirect relationships between variables. One such example is Richey's (1992) model of factors predicting employee training outcomes. This model was constructed on the basis of research that identified pertinent variables and hypothesized the predictive relationships among them. Another type of conceptual model is Hannafin and Rieber's (1989) ROPES+ metamodel for designing computer-based instruction. This is a clustering of design elements into a framework that provides direction for strategy selection.

Model Orientations

Models can vary in terms of their philosophical or theoretical orientation. For example, models may have a constructivist perspective such as the R2D2 (recursive, reflective design and development) model described by Willis (1995). There are also a large number of behaviorally oriented ID models. Gropper (1983) describes one such model for designing instructional treatments. Barrett (2002) identifies others, from the early task-analytic approach of Gagné to Morningside generative instruction. Such theoretical distinctions are evident in both procedural and conceptual ID models.

There are also ID models that are organization specific, and they are oriented to the particular processes and language adopted in that work environment. They reflect the feelings of many that instruction should have a local quality (Logan, as cited in Andrews & Goodson, 1980). Most of these models are not readily available in the professional literature.

All of these ID models are based on an assumption that they are both authoritative and sound. In other words, they are based on an assumption that they are valid.

THE GENERAL NATURE OF ID MODEL VALIDATION

Practically speaking, most designers seem to view models as "valid" if they address the needs and constraints of their workplaces, are easily used, and if their use tends to result in products and programs that are well received by one's clients. One's own experiences or the recollections of others serve as the supporting data. Theorists and model developers, on the other hand, are likely to assume the validity of a model if it is a logical, coherent entity with literature support. They are also influenced by the practical results of its use and user satisfaction. Certainly the prominent models in the ID literature have been used successfully for many years. However, even with these models, the data supporting validity tends to be rare or nonexistent.

In this chapter and context, ID model validation is viewed as a carefully planned process of collecting and analyzing empirical data to demonstrate the effectiveness of a model's use in the workplace or to provide support for the various components of the model itself. Akin to the use of the term *validation* in relation to measurement and research design, this is a process that concerns the extent to which inferences are appropriate and meaningful.

Internal and External Validation of ID Models

ID model validation is viewed here in two ways—as either internal validation, that is, a validation of the components and processes of an ID model, or external validation, that is, a validation of the impact of the products of model use. The findings of all model validation studies form critically needed parts of the instructional design knowledge base.

Internal Model Validation

Internal validation focuses on the integrity of the model and its use. Such studies are typically conducted during model construction or in the early stages of use. They provide data to support each component of the model, as well as the relationship between the components and the processes involved. In many respects, internal validation studies can be seen as a type of formative evaluation of the model. These investigations answer questions such as the following:

Model Components.

1. Are all steps included in the model necessary? Are there any steps missing in the model? Are there any that need to be clarified?
2. Is the sequence of steps appropriate? Are the steps manageable in the prescribed sequence?
3. To what extent does the model address those factors in the instructional, preinstructional, and work environments that contribute to learning?
4. To what extent does the model address those factors in the instructional, preinstructional, and work environments that contribute to transfer or performance improvement?

Model Use.

1. To what extent is the model usable for a wide range of design projects? Does it easily accommodate many types of content, instructional products, delivery systems, and instructional strategies?
2. To what extent is the model usable in a wide range of work environments given varying organizational cultures and learner populations, as well as varying resources and constraints?
3. Can the steps be reasonably implemented by both novice and expert designers? Can the model be used without assistance by a trained designer?
4. Can the steps be completed efficiently under most working conditions?
5. Is the level of client involvement in the design and development process appropriate for most work settings? To what extent are the clients satisfied with the design and development process?
6. Is the use of this model cost-effective?

It would be unlikely that a particular validation study would address each of these concerns, or give equal emphasis to each factor. Nor is this list presumed to be complete; other issues may be pertinent to particular models or particular users.

External Model Validation

External model validation addresses the effects of using the model—the instructional products themselves, and impact of these products on learners, clients and organizations. In many respects, these studies can be seen as summative or confirmative evaluations of the model. They address questions such as the following:

Product Characteristics.

1. To what extent does the resulting instruction meet learner needs, client needs, and client requirements?
2. To what extent is the resulting instruction motivating and interesting to the target audience? Were the learners engaged in the instructional activities?
3. To what extent do learners accept the resulting instruction, its delivery system, and its navigation techniques (if applicable)?

Impact of Instruction.

1. To what extent do changes occur in learners' knowledge, attitudes, and/or behaviors after instruction?
2. To what extent are these changes retained over time?
3. To what extent does the instruction result in efficient learning?
4. To what extent do resulting behavior changes impact the organization's performance?

5. To what extent are the clients satisfied with the instruction and its impact?

External validations can be complex research undertakings due to the large number of extraneous factors that can influence the findings. Such findings may be impacted by factors such as instructor characteristics, learner distractions, past history and organizational priorities to name just a few. Nonetheless, external validations address those factors that many consider to be the central focus of design efforts.

KEY FACTORS IMPACTING ID MODEL VALIDATION

ID model use, and its subsequent validation, are affected by a large number of factors. Some of these factors tend to lead to variations in the model's use, and at times they even lead to variations in the models themselves. An important part of any validation effort is to identify those factors that may be influencing the use of an ID model in the target environment. It is one function of the validation research design to control for these variables. In a typical work setting this is not always easy. Nonetheless, there are two factors that are especially critical to address: the context in which the model is used and the expertise of the designer.

Design Context Effects

There is an implicit (if not an explicit) assumption that most of the widely published and taught models can be used in all design contexts, and there is a long history of many ID models being successfully used in a variety of settings— corporate, educational, health care, and military, for example. Most assume the universal applicability of instructional systems design (ISD) procedures, and traditionally this has been viewed as a major advantage of the methodology.

Edmonds, Branch and Mukherjee (1994) posited that the success of an ID model is dependent on the extent to which a match between the application context and the context for which the model was originally intended. The contextual elements they stress are not only setting, but also differences in type of content and the type of product being produced. The complexities that are suggested by the questions I have posed for both internal and external validation studies can also lead one to consider the possibility that ID models may be valid for one design setting and not for another. Design contexts vary not only in terms of available resources and facilities, but also in terms of the climate and emphases imposed by factors such as the organization's mission and leadership style. They also vary in terms of the characteristics of the learning and performance environments in which the subsequent instruction is implemented. The many aspects of context that impact the design process have been identified and discussed in Tessmer and Richey (1997). Some of the updated ID models (e.g., Dick et al., 2001) specifically recognize these factors and include procedures for dealing with them. More often than not, however, designers modify the generic models to accommodate their unique work environments. For example, they may eliminate or curtail the analysis phase and use previously collected data or the input of supervisors. Thus, detailed design procedures can vary depending on context even when the same model is being used ostensibly.

Designer Expertise Effects

Design models are also typically interpreted differently by expert designers and novice designers. This has been well established by researchers such as Rowland (1993), Perez and Emery (1995), Saroyan (1993), and others. Although the key tasks are still completed by experts, experts tend to treat all design problems as ill-defined. They consider a wide variety of situational factors in combination, as well as both instructional and non-instructional solutions, but delay making design decisions as long as possible. Perez and Emery (1995) noted that experts "*interpreted* the design problem—novices *identified* the problem" (p. 92).

Some approaches to design demand more experienced designers than others. This is true, for example, of rapid prototyping procedures (Jones & Richey, 2000). Expert designers basically use a general ISD model, but the design process tends to be more iterative, and the sequencing of design steps varies to meet the demands of an individual design project. Design tasks are performed concurrently. This procedure is common in larger organizations where projects are typically completed by design teams, with members each having expertise in a unique area required by the project at hand.

Edmonds et al. (1994) saw that ID models themselves are often oriented toward either expert or novice designers. Experts use intuitive judgment stemming from their past experiences to provide design guidance. The design experience of experts, they further contend, is necessary to use the Layers of Necessity approach to design (Tessmer & Wedman, 1990), as well as the rapid prototyping model proposed by Tripp and Bichelmeyer (1990). Another explanation of expert design behavior is that they modify standard models to meet the demands of a given situation. In either case, designer expertise and design context interact to shape the design task, and these interactions have important implications for the systematic validation of an ID model.

ID MODEL VALIDATION PROCEDURES

There are various ways of conducting both internal and external validations. In this section five different validation procedures are discussed. These alternative approaches can be viewed as types of instructional design and development research (see Richey, Klein, & Nelson, 2004). These validation processes are not mutually exclusive; the various approaches can be combined to reinforce the data base and, in turn, to strengthen the conclusions. Table 10.1 compares each of these valida-

TABLE 10.1
A Comparison of Five Approaches to ID Model Validation

Validation Process	Types of ID Models Addressed	Typical Focus	Research Techniques Employed	Time of Completion
Internal validation:				
Expert review	Conceptual Procedural	Model components; model use	Survey Delphi	During model development
Usability documentation	Procedural	Model use	Case study	During model try-out or use
Component investigation	Conceptual Procedural	Model components	Survey Experimental or Quasi-Experimental Path analysis, LISREL analysis	Prior to model development; During model use
External validation:				
Field evaluation	Procedural	Product characteristics; Instructional impact	Case study evaluation survey	During model try-out or use
Controlled testing	Procedural	Instructional impact	Experimental or quasi-experimental	During model use

tion processes in terms of the typical types of ID models addressed, the focus, the research techniques employed, and when the validations are typically undertaken.

Internal Validation Procedures

Expert Review.   One of the most commonly used approaches to internal validation is expert review. Expert review is a process whereby ID experts critique a given model in terms of its components, overall structure, and future use. It is the most expeditious of the internal validation methods. Essentially, this is a cyclical process of model review and critiquing based on prespecified criteria, and subsequent model revision based on the data. Often Delphi techniques are employed as a framework for achieving consensus among the participants. Participants need not physically meet; instead, data are typically collected via mail, e-mail, telephone, or Web-based instruments. The process continues until there is a consensus among the panel of experts as to the completeness and the utility of the model.

Some of the best examples of expert review validations are in doctoral dissertations. For example, Sleezer (1991) developed and validated a Performance Analysis for Training (PAT) model using expert review methods. She used experts in training needs assessment to evaluate the content and face validity of the PAT model. Adamski (1998) and Tracey (2002) also used expert review in part to validate their newly developed, specialized design models. The Adamski model pertained to the development of job performance aids for high-risk situations, whereas the Tracey model provided a way to incorporate a consideration of multiple intelligences into a standard ISD orientation.

In this approach, the soundness of the validation is dependent to a great extent upon the number of reviewers and the authority of the reviewers. This validation relies on the experiences and knowledge of the reviewers. Often, reviewers represent both design practitioners and design theorists, but persons are also selected so that a variety of theoretical orientations and work settings are represented. It is increasingly important to include experts with geographical diversity, taking special care to reflect design practice in countries other than the United States. Participants may be suggested by peer experts, or they may be identified by using detailed selection criteria.

One can typically expect expert reviews to be most credible with respect to verifying model components. Unless the participating experts have used the target model themselves or have extensive work experience in a given environment, their predictions of model use may be open to question. More robust data on model use are usually gathered from documentation of the actual design and development process as it occurs.

Usability Documentation.   The second approach to internal validation involves the systematic documentation of designers using a particular model. This involves keeping records of actual implementation procedures, time taken, resources used, problems and difficulties encountered using the model, and resolutions of these problems. It involves systematically describing the background and abilities of those involved and of the work environment. Although in the past this process has typically been an added task for designers, such documentation is more common today as organizations strive to establish quality standards and gain recognition of their standards through avenues such as ISO certification.

The integrity of usability documentation data is dependent on its authenticity and objectivity. Care must be taken to insure objectivity through consistent, systematic data collection techniques and the collection of corroborating data. Often structured logs and diaries completed by several project participants according to a regularly established schedule create a structure that facilitates the generation of reliable data. Recall data should be avoided when possible.

It is possible that usability documentation research is being done within large corporations to examine their own model use. If so, it is unlikely that these studies would be published and available to the larger ID community. The examples of usability documentation vary considerably. For example, Forsyth's (1998) usability data describe the specific steps completed when following her model for designing community-based train-the-trainer programs, the time allocated to each phase of the model, and the lessons learned throughout. The researcher and the designer in this case were one in the same. Data were obtained from logs and designer reflection.

Carr-Chellman, Cuyar, and Breman (1998) documented the implementation of the user-design model in a health care training setting. Their research is structured as a case study. Each step is carefully described as it occurred, and strengths and weaknesses of the process are discussed. This particular study not only explicates the lessons learned in terms of the situation at hand, but generalizes these lessons for designers in other situations as well.

Both expert review and user documentation validation schemes depend primarily upon reaction data. A key difference between them is that the latter demands actual use of the model, whereas expert review data requires reflection and analysis. Component investigation, on the other hand, typically involves research with a fairly rigorous statistical verification of the factors addressed in a given design model.

Component Investigation.   ID models have many parts. In general, procedural models consist of separate steps, and conceptual models consist of factors critical to the instructional design process. Each of these elements can be initially identified or confirmed through research. This is the essence of component investigation.

The research directed toward procedural model validation seeks to provide evidence of the effectiveness of the various steps in the process. For example, very early in the use of ISD procedures, Kibler, Cegala, Barker, and Miles (1974) sought to establish an empirical base for the use of behavioral objectives. However, they could make no conclusive conclusions based upon the literature available at that time. Of the 33 studies that compared student learning with and without instructional objectives, only 11 reported that they enhanced learning. They did suggest much of the research was lacking methodological rigor, however.

The research directed toward conceptual model validation, on the other hand, typically seeks to identify variables that predict key outcomes of instruction—either knowledge acquisition, attitude change, or performance change. These predictive variables then become factors that should be addressed in the design of instruction. For example, various studies have validated the ARCS model of motivation design by studying the impact of the various model components (i.e., attention, relevance, confidence, and satisfaction) on achievement (Brolin, Milheim & Viechnicki, 1993–1994; Means, 1997; Small & Gluck, 1994).

Other studies have tested an array of variables that are hypothesized to predict successful learning. For example, Quinones, Sego, Ford, and Smith (1995/1996) in their investigation of transfer of training used LISREL analysis techniques to support a model of factors that predict the opportunity to perform in a work environment after training. These factors included supervisor attitudes, work-group support, career motivation, learning, and locus of control. Noe and Schmitt (1986) used path analysis techniques to develop models of training effectiveness. They looked specifically at the role a variety of trainee attitudes play in shaping successful training. The strength of these findings as validation tools is naturally dependent on the integrity of the foundational research.

These first three approaches to ID model validation are internal, speaking only to the worth of the model itself without examining the results of using the model on learners or on the organizations in which they are used. Approaches that address these latter issues are external in nature.

External Validation Procedures

Field Evaluation.   Field evaluation is the most commonly used external validation process. As with usability documentation, it involves actually using the model to produce instruction. However, here the instructional product is also implemented in the setting for which it was designed. Data are collected to facilitate a study of the nature of the resulting product and the impact of the instruction on learners and organizations. The impact of the entire process on clients is also documented in some situations.

Sullivan, Ice, and Niedermeyer (2000) systematically field tested a comprehensive K–12 energy education curriculum that tested a long-term instructional development and implementation project. The project has been ongoing for 20 years. The field evaluation report includes first a description of the program design and the products that were developed. Implementation and revision procedures were then documented and impact data were collected using student and teacher attitude surveys and student achievement tests. Conclusions were drawn that could be generalized to other long-term projects.

McKenney (2002) validated her design and development model through an extensive field evaluation. She studied the development of a computer program to support curriculum materials development in the context of secondary science and mathematics education in southern Africa. She not only documented the ISD phases employed, but used the field evaluation data as a basis for her assertions of the validity, practicality, and potential impact of the computer-based performance support program. This was a data-rich project, using 108 data-collection instruments. Finally, McKenney reexamined the design principles and the ID model she followed.

Superior field evaluations draw upon the methodologies of any product or program evaluation effort. However, when used for ID model validation the results need to be examined in terms of their implications for confirming or altering the basic design model that guided the project.

Controlled Testing.   Design models can also be validated by establishing experiments that isolate the effects of the given ID model as compared to the use of another model or approach. This is the object of controlled testing validation. This type of research provides data that supports the validity of a given procedural model under controlled conditions.

There are examples of controlled model testing available. Higgins and Reiser (1985) did this, as well as Tracey (2002). There are similarities between each of these validation efforts. Higgins and Reiser compared the use of the Reiser–Gagné media selection model and an intuitive model. Tracey compared the use of the Dick and Carey model with an ISD model enhanced with a consideration of multiple intelligences. Both experiments were controlled in terms of task, time, and designer expertise. In the Higgins–Reiser study, students served as subjects and designers using the models. Their design task had correct and incorrect solutions, and the number of correct media solutions served as the dependent variable—the measure of model effectiveness. In the Tracey study there were two design teams, each with two novice designers. Each team worked with a different model. Both groups designed a two-hour instructor-led workshop. The resulting programs were actually implemented and evaluated. Her verification of model effectiveness was based on measures of learning and participant reactions to the instruction.

Research such as this is more likely to be undertaken by academics than practitioners, but when it can take place in natural work environments the results are apt to be seen as more trustworthy among practicing designers. There is a dilemma then with respect to actual workplace settings. Their very richness can make it more difficult to prevent unrelated factors from impacting the results.

Comprehensive Model Validation

Given the contextual nature of ID model use, there is the question whether model validation findings can be generalized to other settings. This concern speaks to the need for comprehensive validation efforts. All of the examples discussed have been situation specific. This reflects the nature of the vast majority of validation efforts. Comprehensive validations, on the other hand, would examine ID model use under a variety of conditions. To meet these goals, the validation research requires systematic replication.

Systematic replication of ID model validation research would allow the field to determine the impact of factors such as

- Alternative settings.
- Alternative types of learners.
- Designer expertise.
- Alternative content areas.
- A variety of delivery strategies.

It seems to make the most sense for comprehensive research to be conducted during model use (e.g., usability documentation studies, field evaluations, and controlled testing) rather than model development.

When the time comes that a large number of validation studies appear in the ID literature (especially those of a controlled testing variety), it will be possible to employ meta-analytic or other integrative research procedures using these findings. Meta-analysis is a technique for quantitatively "comparing and combining the results of a series of studies" (Rosenthal, 1984, p.19). It would allow one to summarize the findings pertaining to the effectiveness of a particular ID model that has been employed in a variety of situations. Replication of model effectiveness under a variety of conditions and integration of the various findings not only would increase the credibility of that particular model, but also would provide data to support (or refute) the field's assumption that ISD processes are generic.

CONCLUSIONS

The underlying theme of this chapter is that as a field we should be validating our many ID models as well as developing them, and that validation should become a natural part of the model development process. This message stems from a belief that instructional design itself is a science, but one that is practiced by blending creative and rule-bound activities. This deviates somewhat from Merrill's position that ID is a technology-based science and that ID is essentially invention (Merrill et al., 1996). In viewing design itself as a science rather than an extension of science, it follows that its overarching theories and models should be grounded not only in research on instruction, but in research on instructional design and development.

Merrill et al. (1996) asserted that "instructional science is concerned with the discovery of the natural principles involved in instructional strategies; instructional design is the use of these scientific principles to invent instructional design procedures and tools" (p. 5). I believe that this is true, but insufficient. Instructional design procedures encompass far more than strategy selection—a micro-design activity. Instructional design can also be viewed in a macro fashion, which is the design orientation typically assumed in the ISD models. This is the part of ID that has a woefully deficient research foundation, in spite of the fact that it has a clear theoretical point of reference (i.e., general systems theory). ID model validation is one way to start filling this vacuum.

ACKNOWLEDGMENTS

I thank Janice Forsyth, Marguerite Foxon, and James Klein for their thoughtful input and suggestions, which have greatly improved this chapter.

REFERENCES

Adamski, A. J. (1998). *The development of a systems design model for job performance aids: A qualitative developmental study.* Doctoral dissertation, Wayne State University. *Dissertation Abstracts International-A, 59*(03), 789.
Andrews, D. H., & Goodson, L. A. (1980). A comparative analysis of models of instructional design. *Journal of Instructional Development, 3*(4), 2–16.
Barrett, B. H. (2002). *The technology of teaching revisited: A reader's companion to B. F. Skinner's book.* Concord, MA: Cambridge Center for Behavioral Studies.

Bloom, B. S. (Ed.). (1956). *Taxonomy of educational objectives: The classification of educational goals. Handbook I: Cognitive domain.* New York: Longman.

Brolin, R. M., Milheim, W. D., & Viechnicki, K. J. (1993–1994). The development of a model for the design of motivational adult instruction in higher education. *Journal of Educational Technology Systems, 22*(1), 3–17.

Carr-Chellman, A., Cuyar, C., & Breman, J. (1998). User-design: A case application in health care training. *Educational Technology Research and Development, 46*(4), 97–114.

Dale, E. (1946). *Audio-visual methods in teaching.* New York: Dryden Press.

Dick, W., Carey, L., & Carey, J. O. (2001). *The systematic design of instruction* (5th ed.). New York: Addison-Wesley Longman.

Edmonds, G. S., Branch, R. C., & Mukherjee, P. (1994). A conceptual framework for comparing instructional design models. *Educational Technology Research and Development, 42*(4), 55–72.

Forsyth, J. E. (1998). *The construction and validation of a model for the design of community-based train-the-trainer instruction.* Doctoral dissertation, Wayne State University. *Dissertation Abstracts International-A, 58*(11), 4242.

Gagné, R. M. (1972). Domains of learning. *Interchange, 3,* 1–8. Reprinted in R. M. Gagné (1989), *Studies of learning* (pp. 485–496). Tallahassee, FL: Learning Systems Institute.

Gagné, R. M., Briggs, L. J., & Wager, W. W. (1992). *Principles of instructional design* (4th ed.). Fort Worth, TX: Harcourt Brace Jovanovich.

Gropper, G. L. (1983). A behavioral approach to instructional prescription. In C. M. Reigeluth (Ed.), *Instructional-design theories and models: An overview of their current status* (pp. 101–161). Hillsdale, NJ: Lawrence Erlbaum Associates.

Gustafson, K. L., & Branch, R. M. (2002). *Survey of instructional development models* (4th ed.). Syracuse, NY: ERIC Clearinghouse on Information & Technology.

Hannafin, M. J., & Rieber, L. P. (1989). Psychological foundations of instructional design for emerging computer-based instructional technologies: Part 2. *Educational Technology Research and Development, 37*(2), 102–114.

Higgins, N., & Reiser, R. (1985). Selecting media for instruction: An exploratory study. *Journal of Instructional Development, 8*(2), 6–10.

Jones, T. S., & Richey, R. C. (2000). Rapid prototyping in action: A developmental study. *Educational Technology Research and Development, 48*(2), 63–80.

Keller, J. M. (1987). The systematic process of motivational design. *Performance and Instruction, 26*(10), 1–8.

Kibler, R. J., Cegala, D. J., Barker, L. L., & Miles, D. T. (1974). *Objectives for instruction and evaluation.* Boston: Allyn & Bacon.

McKenney, S. (2002). *Computer-based support for science education materials development in Africa: Exploring potentials.* Doctoral dissertation, Universiteit Twente, the Netherlands. *Dissertation Abstracts International-C, 63*(03), 355.

Martin, B. L., & Briggs, L. J. (1986). *The affective and cognitive domains: Integration for instruction and research.* Englewood Cliffs, NJ: Educational Technology Publications.

Means, T. B. (1997). Enhancing relevance: Embedded ARCS strategies vs. purpose. *Educational Technology Research and Development, 45*(1), 5–171.

Merrill, M. D., Drake, L., Lacy, M. J., Pratt, J. A., & the ID2 Research Group. (1996). Reclaiming instructional design. *Educational Technology, 36*(5), 5–7.

Morrison, G. R., Ross, S. M., & Kemp, J. E. (2003). *Designing effective instruction* (4th ed.). New York: Jossey-Bass/Wiley.

Noe, R., & Schmitt, N. (1986). The influence of trainee attitudes on training effectiveness: Test of a model. *Personnel Psychology, 44,* 51–65.

Perez, R. S., & Emery, C. D. (1995). Designer thinking: How novices and experts think about instructional design. *Performance Improvement Quarterly, 8*(3), 80–95.

Quinones, M. A., Sego, D. J., Ford, J. K., & Smith, E. M. (1995/1996). The effects of individual and transfer environment characteristics on the opportunity to perform trained tasks. *Training Research Journal, 1*(1), 29–49.

Reiser, R. A., & Gagné, R. M. (1983). *Selecting media for instruction.* Englewood Cliffs, NJ: Educational Technology Publications.

Richey, R. C. (1986). *The theoretical and conceptual bases of instructional design.* London: Kogan Page.

Richey, R. C. (1992). *Designing instruction for the adult learner: Systemic theory and practice for employee training.* London: Kogan Page.

Richey, R. C., Klein, J. D., & Nelson, W. A. (2004) Developmental research: Studies of instructional design and development. In D. H. Jonassen (Ed.), *Handbook of research for educational communications and technology* (2nd ed., pp. 1099–1130). Mahwah, NJ: Lawrence Erlbaum Associates.

Rosenthal, R. (1984). *Meta-analytic procedures for social research.* Beverly Hills, CA: Sage.

Rothwell, W. J., & Kazanas, H. C. (1998). *Mastering the instructional design process: A systematic approach* (2nd ed.) San Francisco: Jossey-Bass.

Rowland, G. (1993). Designing and instructional design. *Educational Technology Research and Development, 41*(1), 79–91.

Saroyan, A. (1993). Differences in expert practice: A case from formative evaluation. *Instructional Science, 21*, 451–472.

Seels, B. (1997). Taxonomic issues and the development of theory in instructional technology. *Educational Technology, 37*(1), 12–21.

Seels, B., & Glasgow, Z. (1997). *Making instructional design decisions* (2nd ed.). Columbus, OH: Merrill.

Sleezer, C. M. (1991). *The development and validation of a performance analysis for training model* (Vol. I–III). Doctoral dissertation, University of Minnesota, 1990. *Dissertation Abstracts International-A, 52*(01), 144.

Small, R. V., & Gluck, M. (1994). The relationship of motivational conditions to effective instructional attributes: A magnitude scaling approach. *Educational Technology, 34*(8), 33–40.

Smith, P. L., & Ragan, T. J. (2005). *Instructional design* (3rd ed.). Hoboken, NJ: John Wiley.

Sullivan, H., Ice, K., & Niedermeyer, F. (2000). Long-term instructional development: A 20-year ID and implementation project. *Educational Technology Research and Development, 48*(4), 87–99.

Tessmer, M., & Richey, R. C. (1997). The role of context in learning and instructional design. *Educational Technology Research and Development, 45*(2), 85–115.

Tessmer, M., & Wedman, J. F. (1990). A layers of necessity instructional development model. *Educational Technology Research and Development, 38*(2), 77–85.

Tracey, M. W. (2002). *The construction and validation of an instructional design model for incorporating multiple intelligences.* Doctoral dissertation, Wayne State University, 2001. *Dissertation Abstracts International-A, 62*(12), 4135.

Tripp, S., & Bichelmeyer, B. (1990). Rapid Prototyping: An alternative instructional design strategy. *Educational Technology Research and Development, 38*(1), 31–44.

Willis, J. (1995). A recursive, reflective instructional design model based on constructivist-interpretivist theory. *Educational Technology, 35*(6), 5–23.

Chapter

11

Cognition
and Instructional Design
for Problem-Based Learning

Sanne Dijkstra
University of Twente

DEVELOPMENTS IN INSTRUCTIONAL
DESIGN THEORIES AND MODELS

The past 50 years showed many changes in instructional design theories and models. Three influences accounted for these changes. The first influences were the results of research on cognition and learning, starting in about the 1950s, the importance of which for the design of instruction was soon recognized. Although a clear breakthrough in cognitive psychology and instruction came in the 1970s, Gagné (1962) and Bruner (1966) did pioneering work earlier. The second was the rediscovery of epistemology and the renewed interest in the nature and acquisition of knowledge (Lakoff, 1987; Von Glasersfeld, 1996). The third was the invention of the computer and the development of information and communication technology. This last development has been of tremendous importance for the whole field of education. Technology has influenced the administration of education; it caused the introduction of new subjects into the curriculum; it became integrated into the subjects, and technology made computer-based coaching and learning possible. Computers stimulated instructional designers to design and develop learning environments that required instructional messages and problem-solving activities designed for specific media. How to sequence instructional messages and problems became increasingly complicated. Moreover, the computer provided an excellent form of experimental control, which made research on the design and effects of instruction possible.

Two of these influences are discussed in this chapter. Most attention is paid to the relation between the knowledge of cognition and learning on the one hand and the design of instruction on the other. Some attention will be paid to the use of information and communication technology in so far as this is related to the first issue. See Dijkstra (2000) for a discussion of the importance of epistemology for the description of knowledge acquisition.

INSTRUCTION, COGNITION, AND LEARNING

The Context

The idea that instruction and learning are related has been with us for at least two millennia. The research on learning and the use of the results of this research for the design of instruction (teaching methods or didactics) came much later, roughly in the last three centuries. Seel and Dijkstra (2004) provided an overview of what has been accomplished in Europe and in the United States of America. Many results of the research on learning are being used for the design of instruction. It may be expected that the scientific foundation of instructional design should lead to clear rules for the design of learning environments and to clear models and rules for the design of instruction. Many applied sciences have productive technologies, and the same can reasonably be expected for instructional technology. Though much has been achieved, especially during the past 50 years, there is still uncertainty among designers about which design models and rules should be used for specific instructional needs. The many adjectives that are used to characterize instruction (e.g., anchored, didactic, direct, problem-based, programmed, thematic, etc.) illustrate the proliferation of instructional models.

In spite of the progress made in the psychology of cognition and learning, the development of a general instructional technology or general instructional design theory has been slow to emerge for a number of reasons. First, it is well known that for some students the goals of education are not achieved. Irrespective of the cause in individual cases for nonattainment of goals, there is an assumption by the public and by policymakers that the quality of education and especially the quality of instruction are responsible for these failures; the foregone conclusion is that "education has to be improved." When a new design model or a new learning environment is proposed, the burden is then to demonstrate that the proposed changes will lead to improved outcomes. The claim that a changed design or new learning environment is responsible for improved outcomes should be supported by design research. However, many variables influence cognition and learning. As a consequence, the research on instruction often is unable to show convincing support for such a causal link between design and outcomes. In such a situation, it may happen that an instructional-design model is simply declared to yield better outcomes than another model. This predisposition to adopt a particular model without adequate justification or sufficient knowledge of its limitations does not foster progress of the scientific enterprise and may cause confusion among instructors and students who are the intended beneficiaries of a new model or approach.

A second reason for the slow development of a general instructional design theory is found in the enormous amount of information and methods on the different domains. In most cases the design models of instruction are directly related to the content of the domain or subject matter, such as in science education, chemistry education, mathematics education, second-language education, and so on. Only a relatively small number of studies are available to understand learning and instruction across various subject domains, because only a very few researchers have both expertise in different domains and relevant instructional expertise. The integration of the psychology of cognition and learning and the design of instruction for learning the highly specialized domain content requires at least domain and instructional expertise. A proposed cooperation in such a case between a subject-matter expert and an instructional technologist can easily lead to misunderstanding and doubts about the value of the technology. Regardless, linking the design itself to improved learning outcomes is especially important when the implementation of the design is so closely linked to and dependent on the instructor or subject matter specialist.

A third challenge for instructional design research is the differing developmental situations of learners, which may create a need for specific instructional designs and complicate the process of attributing differences in outcomes to a design or to changes in a design. For example, learning to read is possible when children are about 6 years of age. The instructional design rules for learning to read are fairly specific and reasonably well established. However, there is no basis on which to say that an instructional design that works well for teaching reading to 6-year-olds will also work for teaching a high school curriculum. Thus, the development of cognition has to be taken into account if the knowledge of cognition and learning is used for the development of instructional technology.

Instructional Technology

Broadly conceived, a technology can be regarded as the whole of the science (theory and research methods) that is valid for a domain, including the rules for solving a design problem in that domain in order to realize a public or an individual goal (Dijkstra, 2004a). For example, chemical technology comprises the theory and research methods that are valid for molecules and substances (their structure and how they change) and the rules to construct devices and installations for producing substances and other chemically based objects that can be used for a public or an individual goal. Examples are the design of refineries for producing gas for transport and heating and the design (and development) of kilns to heat clay and produce earthenware (see also Seel & Dijkstra,

2004). The use of the label *technology* emphasizes what actions are taken within a domain, while taking into account the theory and laws of that domain. Thus, knowledge of a domain and rules for starting and controlling processes of change are included in the connotation of the label. The actions and decisions cannot be separated from the domain knowledge. The use of labels such as *chemical technology* and *biotechnology* illustrates the tight connection between domain knowledge and the use and application of that knowledge as comprising a technology.

To describe instructional technology, it is appropriate to indicate the domain. Quite often the label *learning* is used to indicate the domain of instructional technology, but this label is not adequate. Actually, the domain of instructional technology includes the whole (human, not animal, in this chapter) organism, both the mind (psyche) and the body. Research on learning showed that cognitive activity is correlated with muscular, chemical, and electrical activity of the organism (e.g., Razran, 1971). Motor activity (including verbal activity), secretion of glands, transfer of blood to different parts of the brain, and patterns of electrical activity are the dependent variables to find evidence for cognitive activity of which learning is a part. The domain comprises many subdomains, such as personality as well as the physiological, neurological, and muscular systems. The acquisition of knowledge and skills is described as processes of change in these domains and subdomains, for which labels such as *insight, thinking,* and *learning* are used. The results of these processes can be inferred from the organism's actions. The author supposes that the personality directs and controls cognition and learning. Personality features and functions, such as intelligence and motivation, strongly influence metacognitive processes and learning. The student's intelligence and motivation are basic for learning and for the enrichment of the cognitive constructs.

Thus the domain of instructional technology is complex and encompasses subdomains. The processes that originate in these subdomains cooperate in the acquisition of knowledge and skills. The label *learning* is used to refer to the complex acquisition process. Although the label *learning technology* shows more similarity with labels such as *biotechnology* and *chemical technology,* the label *instructional technology* has become more familiar. Instructional technology comprises models and rules pertaining to the design of instruction for different categories of learning. If the models and rules are correctly applied, it is supposed that desired outcomes will be realized effectively and efficiently. The use of models and rules, however, does not guarantee that students always will acquire knowledge and skills, which are the general objectives of an educational program. The complexity of the organism, the personality features and functions, and the processes that are initiated within the subdomains may interact in such a way that the student may become confused or quit the scene. In general, however, the use of models and rules leads to instruction that helps students to effectively and efficiently acquire the desired knowledge and skills. If knowledge of cognition and of cognitive processes is part of instructional technology, then this critical question arises: Which part of that knowledge is especially relevant for the design of instruction? An answer to this critical question is discussed next.

COGNITION, PROBLEM SOLVING, AND LEARNING

Although cognition and learning have general relevance for the design of instruction, the following aspects are directly relevant to instructional design: knowledge representation, conceptual knowledge, schemata and scripts, problem solving, and the development of expertise. A short overview starts with problem solving.

"Human cognition is always purposeful, directed to achieving goals and to removing obstacles to those goals" (Anderson, 2000, p. 240). This is the "basic argument" that "all cognitive activities are supposed to be fundamentally problem solving in nature" (Anderson, 2000, p. 240). Problem solving is a purposeful cognitive activity. A problem is a question without an immediate answer but with some apparently possible solution. Behind the problem is the need or motive to find a suitable answer and realize the solution to the problem. If the solution is realized, then the goal is reached. Before an answer can be given to a question, one or more steps or operations have to be taken to reach or approach the goal. The steps make up the procedure or method to reach the answer (or reach the goal or solve the problem). A goal can often be decomposed into subgoals, which have the general form of "what do I have to do now?" The execution of a step or operation realizes a subgoal and is a condition for the execution of the next operation. People who know which steps to execute have procedural knowledge at their disposal.

The execution of a sequence of steps over and over again usually results in the automation of the procedure (Anderson, 1982). If the procedure is trained in this way, it becomes automated and the person involved becomes skilled in performing that procedure. Learning to use a procedure is learning by doing. Sometimes the objection is made that problem solving means to develop the procedure or method once the answer to a question cannot be given and that the skilled application of the procedure should not be considered problem solving. In the author's conception, the application of a procedure to reach a goal basically means problem solving, whether the procedure is automated or not. The reason behind this view is that knowing when and where to apply a procedure, even one that is automated, requires certain problem-solving skills. If the circumstances change and the goal can no longer be reached, the question is reformulated and the procedure will be adapted to the new circumstances or a new procedure developed.

The development of the content of the sciences, both information (knowledge) and methods (procedures) are results of problem solving. For different domains the methods for the development of new knowledge are detailed. Systematic observation, exploration and discovery, imagination, brainstorming, research, and development are mentioned as phases in or parts of problem solving in earlier publications (Dijkstra, 1997; Dijkstra & van Merriënboer, 1997).

Some of these are common in special categories of problem solving, which are discussed in a later section.

For solving problems, a sequence of operations has to be selected and applied to reach the goal. This includes both the action (operator) and that to which the act is applied. The way this is done is called means–ends analysis. This is the reduction of the distance or difference between the goal state and the current state of the problem. Problem solving and means–ends analysis comprise the repeated creation of a "new goal (end) to enable an operator to apply" (Anderson, 2000). Take the following problem. You need to store a fluid that can be purchased in plastic containers of 5 liters. You have a big container made of steel, in which you wish to store the fluid, but the volume is not imprinted on the container and you have to calculate the volume. The container is half a meter in width, half a meter in depth, and half a meter in height. How many liters can you pour in such a container? To solve this problem, the number of liters that the container can contain has to be calculated. There are many ways to solve this problem. A laborious method is to pour fluid into the container from a 5-liter can and count the number of cans required to fill the container.

The creation of subgoals that are based on knowledge will help to select more efficient ways to solve the problem. Such a subgoal can be to calculate the volume in cubic meters (m^3) using the measures that are given in meters. If the student knows that 1 m^3 equals 1,000 liters, the problem can easily be solved by calculating cubic meters ($\frac{1}{2} \times \frac{1}{2} \times \frac{1}{2} = 0.125$). A more efficient subgoal may be to initially change meters to decimeters and then calculate the volume, which immediately results in the amount of liters. Both of these solutions assume that the problem solver knows that 1 liter equals one dm^3 or that 1,000 liters equal 1 m^3. In means–end analysis, subgoals are created that help solve the problem in both an effective and efficient way.

Those who wish to solve this problem try to represent it, either mentally or on paper, and then they try to retrieve knowledge that is relevant to solve the problem. The subjects to whom I presented this problem sometimes reported that they tried to construct a mental image of a container or cube of one cubic meter in volume. This often resulted in creating an incorrect solution, because the subjects took half the amount of a thousand liters. The representations that are shown in Fig. 11.1 and Fig. 11.2 can help the problem solver avoid this incorrect solution. When only a container of .5 × .5 × .5 m and the cans are shown it will probably not help to solve the problem. Figure 11.1 represents a more helpful diagram.

Figure 11.2 may provide even more support for solving the problem, because the student can imagine that eight such cubes fit into the larger cube (dashed line). The right-hand container will help to calculate the correct solution to the problem.

The representation of a problem state influences problem solving. Human beings try to represent problem states mentally; sometimes they make sketches of the problem state that may help in finding a solution. If a representation is given, it should be done in such a way that it helps to find a correct solution. A mental image of a spatial structure is an instance of perception-based knowledge representation.

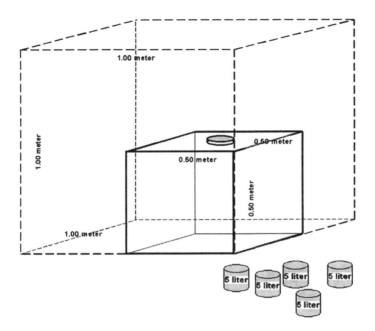

FIG. 11.1.   Initial illustration for calculating the volume of a container.

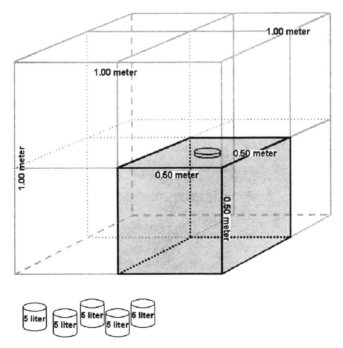

FIG. 11.2.   Refined illustration to calculate the volume of a container.

Such representations can lead to insight—the perception of new and unobvious relevant relationships between parts of the representation or between parts and the whole. Insight in the problem representation will help in finding a solution. The representation can help to find an operator that will reduce the difference between the final goal and the initial problem state. In the aforementioned problem, the representation of the container inside a bigger cube allows the problem solver to make an estimate of the volume of the smaller container and use the volume of the bigger cube to directly calculate the volume of the given container (Figs. 11.1 and 11.2). For the purpose of instruction, the choice of representation of one of the problem states should be done in such a way that it always helps the students to find a solution and prevent them from making mistakes.

It is beyond the scope of this chapter to elaborate all the ways that the meaning of objects, including their changes and associated events, might be represented, such as propositions, propositional and semantic networks, part–whole structures, and others. An exception is made for the concept of a schema to represent conceptual knowledge. The meaningful representation of many individual objects is handled by concepts that assign individual objects to categories. Such knowledge of categories can be represented in two ways: (a) semantic networks and (b) schemata. Schemata consist of the generalities of properties, both perceptual and functional, in dimensions and values. Thus, a value associated with a dimension specifies a feature of an object. A possible schema representation of a car is presented in Table 11.1.

A schema is able to represent functional properties and perceptual properties of a category of objects in a general, abstract way. It can comprise both perceptual and propositional representations, such as the shape of a car as well as the function of a car. A schema comprises the dimensions and the possible range of default values. Not all values are contained in the schema. The concept "racing car" is not included if all the dimensions given are checked, but a racing car can

TABLE 11.1

Schema Representation of a Car

Property	Dimensions/Values
Is_a	vehicle
Parts_of	Body, engine, shafts, wheels, and seats
Materials_used	Steel, copper, synthetic materials, leather, glass
Function_of	Means of transport of persons and freight
Shape_of:	Related to function—private car, bus, pickup truck, truck
Weight_of	From about 900 kg
Color_of	Any

easily be recognized as a car from that part of the schema that comprises the typical features. Based on these schemata of categorical knowledge, individual objects can be easily recognized and categorized even if they depart from the typical ones. A possible disadvantage is that categorization errors can be made if a general schema is erroneously applied.

Schemata develop after considerable training or practice. In some cases involving specialized categorizing—for example, with regard to diagnosing a disease—training of the relevant identification algorithms may take years before they are automated or sufficiently expertlike in their deployment in order to pass a medical exam. Experts in categorizing or diagnosing special categories or subcategories of objects, such as mushrooms, types of grasses, phytopathologies, illnesses, groups of insects, and so on, often have fully automated identification algorithms. Such algorithms comprise the defining features and their logical connectives and the typical features of the objects together with the correlations among the typical features.

Categorizing is a type of problem solving, and the development of expertise in applying the method, in this case an identification algorithm, typically involves three stages. First, there is a cognitive stage in which the subjects develop relevant declarative encoding (Anderson, 1982, 2000). This includes the recognition of relevant features for determining what the object is. The learner tries to store each feature in memory as a mental image with an associated label. When all of the features that are relevant for categorizing are observed and stored, the learner assigns a label to that category, which can then be retrieved and used to identify objects.

In the second stage, the associative stage, these encodings are strengthened. More attention is paid to defining features and combinations of features, or feature clusters are recognized and stored.

In the third stage, the autonomous stage, the application of the algorithm becomes autonomous and rapid. The problem solver immediately recognizes a pattern of features and categorizes the object. In some cases in which a wrong categorization has harmful consequences, one or more features will be carefully observed before the categorization decision is made.

Nearly all objects change, so a categorization is made that is relevant to some stage of the object. A feature that is used for categorizing may indicate the course of a process—for example, a feature of a plant when it starts growing may predict the quality of the vegetable at the end of the growth. A patient's feature (symptom) may indicate a phase in the course of a disease process. Those features will be observed carefully, because they are used for treatment.

Anderson (2000) provided examples that show the process of the development of expertise and training that is needed to reach an expert level of skill. In reaching expertise, the problem solver switches from explicit use of declarative knowledge to direct use of procedural knowledge. The procedure that can be used is related to the level of declarative knowledge. The knowledge, both declarative and procedural, of the empirical and formal sciences is hierarchically organized. Problem solvers who have a rich basis of declarative knowledge, including hypotheses, hierarchies of relationship (e.g., in describing conceptions of physics such as velocity, acceleration, and force), and theories, can use this declarative knowledge to select an appropriate method to solve the problem.

What do these conceptions of cognition and learning mean for the design of instruction? This question is addressed in the next section.

INSTRUCTION AND INSTRUCTIONAL DESIGN

The acquisition of knowledge and skills is a goal-directed process. The process of acquiring knowledge and skills is a cognitive process and presupposes cognitive activities and abilities, which is also true for training motor skills. Because these activities are purposeful and directed to achieving goals and removing obstacles, they involve problem solving in essential ways.

It is nearly impossible to independently acquire all of the knowledge and skills that are the goal of education. The acquisition is realized in a social situation, at home or at school. Schools and specialized training institutes are organized for the acquisition of knowledge and skills. The social situation in these settings is of paramount importance for learning.

For initiating and maintaining the acquisition of knowledge and skills, instruction is required. Instruction is an activity intended to promote the purposeful cognitive activities that lead to learning, that is, the modification or extension of existing knowledge and skills. Learning environments and instruction are needed to help students to structure and understand information and practice methods. Instruction should help students to develop conceptions about the world by observation and manipulation and by constantly asking questions about the features and change of objects. Instruction involves communication between a student (usually a novice in the subject domain) and a teacher (typically an expert in the subject domain). Models and rules pertaining to the design and development of such communication are labeled *instructional design*. Instructional design includes verbal and written communication between students and teachers and takes on special forms, such as explaining information and tasks and using illustrations to communicate information and methods. Instructional design further comprises the formulation of questions (problems) that students should solve and tasks that they should execute, individually and in teams, in order to develop knowledge.

A problem-solving procedure that is used to solve a category of problems is labeled a *task,* and practice of a task leads to skilled performance. All this is realized in a special setting labeled a *learning environment,* in which the many and varied tasks are assigned to participants. Because instruction should initiate and maintain purposeful cognitive activities, leading to the acquisition of knowledge and skills, the students need to solve problems. And the associated instructional-design model is labeled an *instructional design model for problem-based learning.* This does not mean that all instruction should present only new problems from which the students can construct new knowledge and methods. Instruction is successful when it is able to initiate the required purposeful cognitive activities that lead students to successful task performance. Direct instruction, in which a teacher explains to students the questions and experiments that lead to the knowledge content of a domain and then illustrates the steps of a problem-solving procedure, is often sufficient to initiate purposeful cognitive activities that lead to understanding. Moreover such instruction can be motivating as well.

The earlier description of instructional technology demonstrated that the features and functions of personality influence the acquisition of knowledge and skills. The design of instruction should take into account intelligence and motivation and be embedded in the knowledge of the domain of cognition and learning (see Dijkstra, 2004a). The many labels that are used to characterize instruction mostly emphasize only one feature of this domain, or one feature of how to operate on it. One feature of a subdomain of psychology, or one feature of a representational medium, or one epistemological point of view may be useful in characterizing a design, but no one of these features can cover all the components of an instructional design.

Instruction requires a representation of a reality to which the goals of education are directed. This can be any existing or imagined domain or subdomain of a reality. For example, the domain of astronomy is the universe, the domain of physics is matter, the domain of biology consists of living organisms, and the domain of history is comprised of nations.

Information about a domain and methods to solve categories of problems within a domain make up the content of a curriculum and are acquired as new knowledge and skills. In order to initiate and facilitate learning, an instructional design often selects and depicts only a part of a domain or a category of elements. These parts are labeled *objects,* a label borrowed from Piaget (1937). The label *object* can mean any entity that is perceived or imagined. Instructions are about objects and what to do with them. These include: (a) real objects such as plants, birds, houses, cars, the earth; (b) inferred objects, such as atoms, the psyche, a group, a nation; and (c) systems of objects, such as the solar system.

For instruction, the object is often depicted in a way that represents a problem state. The depiction has to support the acquisition process by: (a) showing the features that are relevant to explain the problem state and make these features salient; (b) helping to develop insight how to reach a solution to a problem; and (c) supporting the development of a useful mental image that represents the meaning of the instructional message.

This framework for instructional design is extended for different categories of problems, discussed in the next section with emphasis on the features of the objects involved and the related choice of code-related media (Seel & Winn, 1997).

AN INSTRUCTIONAL DESIGN MODEL
FOR PROBLEM-BASED LEARNING

Many different instructional-design theories and models have been proposed and published (see Tennyson, Schott, Seel, & Dijkstra, 1997). An instructional-design theory, also labeled *instructional theory*, is a set of statements that interpret why an instructional program leads to the acquisition of knowledge, skills, and attitudes. A model is a heuristic or plan that prescribes the general phases and steps of the design before the development of the actual instructions starts. All theories and models of instructional design were founded in theories and models of learning. The author supposes that the theory of cognition and learning as outlined in the previous section provides sufficient conditions for the design model of instruction. A special instructional design theory separate from theories of cognition and learning is not promoted. The integration of theories of cognition and learning, cognitive development, and the theories and concepts of a domain (e.g., mathematics), however, may be characterized as an instructional design theory and lead to some advantage of such a theory for the instantiation of an instructional design model. Nevertheless, labels such as the *psychology of mathematics learning and instruction* cover the same thing.

Based on different points of departure, such as conditions of learning or the analysis of subject matter into behavioral and content dimensions, several design models have been proposed (e.g., Gagné & Briggs, 1974; Merrill, 1983). These models were and are used by many practitioners in the field of education and training. The models provided support in the design of the instructional plan or outline of instruction. The support was based on (a) the integration of categories of learning outcomes with categories of subject matter and (b) the sequence of the components of instruction that need to be elaborated for the different categories. Further support was given for the design of the communication (presenting information and asking questions) and for the evaluation of results. The field has learned much from those pioneers. For the problem-based instructional design model, the idea that different contents require different instructional design models was borrowed from these authors.

The problem-based instructional design model (see Dijkstra, 2000) is based on the following basic tenets:

- Human beings construct interpretations of the world and develop a conception of things as substantial and permanent objects with constant dimensions (Piaget, 1937).
- In the process of cognitive development (with help in a social situation), the concept of an object is extended to the whole universe.
- Objects are perceived, imagined, and/or manipulated (both physically and mentally), and, as language develops, problems pertaining to these objects are formulated.
- The result of a problem-solving activity or a cognitive activity is the development of knowledge and the use of procedures. If the procedures or methods are trained, this will lead to the development of skills.

- Three basic categories of problems lead to three different kinds of knowledge and skills that require different instructional designs.
- The three basic kinds of questions (problems) that human beings try to answer are: (a) What is this object? (b) Why does it change the way it appears to change? (c) What objects can be made or modified and then used to satisfy human needs and desires? The three categories of problems are labeled: (a) problems of categorization, (b) problems of interpretation, and (c) problems of design (Dijkstra, 1997; Dijkstra & van Merriënboer, 1997).

The result of solving a categorization problem is the assignment of objects to classes. The cognitive activity leads to the development of concepts (both class and relational concepts) and of identification algorithms (see the previous section). A concept categorizes objects into classes. For the design of instruction for the acquisition of concepts the reader is referred to Merrill, Tennyson, and Posey (1992).

The result of solving an interpretation problem is the development of a hypothesis or theory about a process that interprets changes in objects. If a change can be measured exactly or at least quantified probabilistically, it can be recorded in formulas (laws) that can be used to predict future events. The representation of change can be accomplished with a network of propositions (see Dijkstra, 2000). Mostly, the declarative knowledge is developed into hierarchies. Students should understand this knowledge at each level. This means that they have to represent the objects and what happens to them by answering questions and practicing procedures. For example, to understand the law of force, the concepts of distance, time, velocity, and acceleration have to be understood and the methods to calculate outcomes have to be practiced.

The result of solving a design problem is the sketch of a new object, often followed by the development of the object. Problem solvers (students) should develop a mental image of an artifact; then, a first sketch, outline, or plan should be created. In a brainstorming session, students can discuss the object to be designed based on the program of requirements; this may result in an unorthodox solution. When the first sketch is ready, the process can be repeated. Concepts and interpretations form the knowledge that is used to solve design problems. The cognitive constructs are the perceptual images of the artifact and the rules and criteria that have to be met in order to achieve a good design. If those who requested the new object accept the design, then it can be realized. This means that it can be produced (a car), constructed (a house, a bridge), interpreted (a composition by an orchestra), developed (an instructional program), or implemented (an organizational structure). A design problem has different subproblems, which are dependent on the life cycle of the artifact: (a) the design; (b) the realization; (c) the use and maintenance; and (d) archiving, restoring, discarding, or recycling. Objects to be designed, realized, used, and maintained should meet different sets of conditions and criteria. For an elaborate description the reader is referred to Dijkstra (2000). Often, design problems and their subproblems are complex, especially in the case of machines, for example, power plants, airplanes, and so on. The cognitive constructs that are needed to solve such a problem are a mental representation of a system and the theory about the process of its functioning.

Rationale and Design

The solution of the categories of basic problems resulted in the huge amount of information and problem-solving procedures found in the various domains of the empirical and formal sciences. The categories of problems may help to understand the design of instruction across these domains. The structure and the analysis of these problems may help the instructional designer to isolate and structure the cognitive activities that are needed for learning and to describe the procedures that the students have to execute. Without student engagement in *doing* various problem-solving activities, learning is unlikely or impossible. The idea of basic problems further helps the designer to represent the objects involved and to structure the subject matter content into hierarchies. Moreover the idea helps in distinguishing subcategories of problems that are useful to understand the task in a framework of a superordinate category of problems. Figure 11.3 shows that the categories of problems are related. They mostly appear in combination.

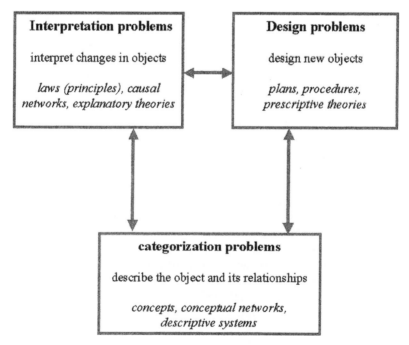

FIG. 11.3.   Three types of problems and their relationships.

Once the global structure or outline of a curriculum is designed, the objectives the students should reach are described. This is done as a description of knowledge that should be acquired and skills that should be practiced (see Dijkstra, 2004b). Then the design of instruction starts and consists of the following main components:

- The design of the learning environment (see the next section for details).
- The choice of whether to use real or represented objects for categorization of objects and for the interpretation of changes of objects. In the case of design and development problems, the instructional designer illustrates how a program of requirements can lead to different designs of new objects and how these are created.
- The global design of communication about conceptions and application of methods and the ways this will be accomplished (verbal, text on paper, images on a screen, etc.). This part of the design includes the explanation of the domain content, why human beings developed the knowledge, what question they had, how it can be used in daily practice (contexts), what is the possible quality of a solution, and so on.
- The design of problems for the acquisition (development) of the conceptions of the domain and for practicing relevant procedures.
- The criterion for all this design activity is that each component should promote cognitive and motor activities that lead to the intended goal in the most effective, efficient and motivating way. For the choice of represented objects, the content of the next section may help the designer.

REALITY AND REPRESENTATIONS OF REALITY

Objects, Representations, and Learning Environments

Problems are formulated about objects and operations on these objects in a specifiable reality. For instruction, these objects are needed for the purpose of perception and observation of their features and the change of these (indicated in problem states) and for practicing the operations. The instructional designer has to solve the problem of whether to use real objects or a representation of those objects or both. The designer has to make a decision on whether to use either the real or the represented objects in a real environment or in a classroom environment. In a virtual environment, all represented objects are virtual. The real environment is used during an internship. The classroom is a traditional environment in which both real objects and representations are used. Virtual environments can be used if a powerful computer with special equipment is available for the students. What are we to choose? The answer to this question simply is that a real or represented environment and those objects that initiate and maintain the cognitive and motor activities that lead to the intended goal in the most effective, efficient, and motivating way are those which should be used.

The argument in favor of using real objects is that students can immediately perceive them with their senses, experience them directly, operate on them to learn how they behave and how they are used, and probably more easily transfer learning outcomes outside the instructional context. It is clear, however, that real objects are not always available or appropriate. Even if the real objects are available, the representations of these are needed to show relevant features and to facilitate thinking and communication about them. There are special reasons to use a representation of a reality, which include the following: (a) The objects are not (easily) perceivable or not available (e.g., bacteria, planets, historic monuments in a foreign country); (b) necessary experiments to determine the structure of reality are inappropriate in an instructional setting; (c) the duration of a process makes it inappropriate for an instructional context (e.g., an evolutionary process might be accelerated using a simulation); and (d) using real objects involves a risk for damage and personal safety. When a representation of real objects is used, the teacher has to answer two questions. The first question is whether and how an object should be represented (picture, drawing, photograph, slide, transparency) or whether the change of an object or change of its position has to be shown (movie, time-lapse photography, animation, simulation). The second question is whether a demonstration model or a simulator has to be used. In the last case, the objects may be used in such a way that the risk of damage is minimized and/or experiments can be conducted artificially that would not otherwise be possible.

The arguments in favor of one of the environments are comparable with those for the choice of objects. In real settings the students develop the required knowledge and knowledge of the context. Practicing in real settings makes the students feel the consequences of actions and decisions. For example, in the vocational training of Dutch sailors, the students spend over 50% of their training at sea; the remainder is spent on shore in classrooms and labs. Virtual environments can be used to immerse the students in worlds that they may never encounter in reality but in which they can interact continuously. These environments are valuable for exploration. Such experiences may be motivating and help to answer internally generated questions (Seel & Winn, 1997).

Medium and Multimedia

Summarizing relevant literature, Seel and Winn (1997) emphasized that the evolution of human culture was strongly dependent on the use of signs. A sign is an artifact that is made by humans on an information carrier, the function of which is to denote objects of the real or of any imagined world and operations that are possible on and with these. The use of pictures and picture language appeared first, the remainders of which can be found in cave paintings. Seel and Winn supposed that "people's thinking consists of the use of and manipulation of signs as media for the representation of ideas as well as objects" (p. 298). Every sign refers to an object or represents it in three ways: index, icon, and symbol. An index refers to the meaning of a feature, such as red means "danger" or "wait." Icons are depictions of an object or an operation. These representations differ in the number of features that correspond with the object or operation, from many to at least one. For example, many features correspond with the object in a detailed photograph of it. The arrow on a traffic sign of a roundabout refers only to the direction to drive. Symbols are arbitrary signs. They are nearly always independent of the designated objects. Students have to acquire the meaning of icons and symbols, both from explanation and from practicing, before they can easily use them in their cognitive activities and in the communication that is needed for the acquisition of new knowledge and skills. Thus, instruction is impossible without a medium. Moreover, the represented objects should stimulate the cognitive and motor activities that lead to the intended goal. The designated object should clearly refer to the problem state involved, which means that the features that are relevant for categorization and for observation of change are made salient and that the use of depictions of a situation can lead to insight (see Figs. 11.1 and 11.2).

The label *medium* has several meanings. Seel and Winn (1997) provided an overview of these meanings. For the design of instruction, the technical conception and the code-related conception are discussed shortly. The technical meaning refers to the technical device (book, projector, video, and computer) that is used for the production and presentation of signs. The computer can replace almost all other technical media. The anticipated instructional communication can be made in different ways: (a) orally supported by a medium, (b) as text with pictures on paper, or (c) as text and pictures on a screen. The change of objects, event concepts, and stories in which the problems are embedded, as in anchored instruction (CTGV, 1992) are shown on screen with the information stored on disks. The way the communication is made depends on the content of the subject and the students' preference. In some cases the type of technical medium is prescribed by the content of the problem. For example, in solving social communication problems relevant to the training of social skills, oral communication and the use of video may be used. Students need practice in communicating and they need feedback about that practice.

Media also refers to the rules through which users denote messages by signs (indices, icons, and symbols) in a communication. This is an important conception of medium in education. It makes the representation of the reality in signs possible. It is the meaning of the signs and how they relate to the reality that is acted upon in problem solving that students should understand. The computer made a new and unique contribution within the framework of this meaning of the concept of medium. This is the possibility to interactively study the change in an object as the change in a representation, and from that change to develop the conception of why it happens and then make predictions.

The label *multimedia* means the combination of stored information that is prepared for different codes (e.g., index, icons, and symbols) and for different sense organs (visual, auditory). The digital storage makes a mix of representations for educational purposes possible. It is assumed that multiple representations will support integration of concepts into more knowledge-rich concepts. Dijkstra (2004b) showed examples of how this enrichment works.

CONCLUDING REMARKS

This chapter discussed the domain of instructional technology and argued that knowledge of the domain of cognition and learning cannot be separated from instructional technology. Because cognitive activity is purposeful and problem-solving in nature, this point of view is used to analyze the way human beings develop their knowledge and methods. All the results of cognitive activity and motor activity that follow naturally from it are arguably a product of three basic categories of problems: (a) problems of categorization, (b) problems of interpretation, and (c) problems of design. Instructional design models are derived from the common features of the problems and the resulting knowledge and the methods that are used for the solution. From these basic categories many subcategories of problems can be derived. The declarative and procedural knowledge of all these categories is used to structure the instruction.

For the design of instruction, the conceptions of cognition and learning are basic. A problem-solving activity includes the perception of features of objects and their changes (phenomena), questions to be answered (goals), means–end analysis to reach goals (cognitive activity, development of conceptions and procedures), and assessments of solutions. In order to support the initiation and maintenance of this process, the instructional designer models the learning environment, communications, and the (representation of) objects and their features.

Communication includes information, examples, tasks and problems. The use of the structure of basic categories of problems does not mean that instructional designers and teachers should only give new problems to students in a way such as they are described by scientists and different groups of designers. The instructional communications include explanations why a problem was formulated and how it was solved. The explanation should be supported with illustrations and devices, giving tasks to the students for reading information, rehearsing (e.g., words in a foreign language), and practicing steps of a task. All this is done in such a way that the cognitive and motor activities that lead to the intended goal are initiated and supported in the most effective, efficient, and motivating way. A serious mistake can occur—namely, presenting the knowledge that is a final result of problem solving to students without making clear why that knowledge was needed and how it was developed. Direct instruction is often criticized for this particular shortcoming.

Although instructional communication has general components, much variation is possible that is supposed to influence the cognitive activity (Dijkstra, 2003). These variations include: (a) how much information is provided to students about the problems and task; (b) different ways of (re)presenting reality in both real objects and/or different categories of signs (pictures, icons, symbols) in order to enrich the students' conceptions; (c) the use of multiple representations in instruction and how this influences the quality of the new conceptions and their use and how and when information technology can be of help; and (d) the integration of new information with existing knowledge in order to solve problems of increasing complexity and the study of cognitive load. Research can be executed with subject-matter content taking into account such variations, all within an ecologically valid situation. The results will inform and shape instructional design models. Over time and in this way, instructional technology will develop in depth.

ACKNOWLEDGMENT

The author thanks J. H. Vermaat for providing Fig. 11.1 and Fig. 11.2.

REFERENCES

Anderson, J. R. (1982). Acquisition of cognitive skill. *Psychological Review, 89,* 369–406.
Anderson, J. R. (2000). *Cognitive psychology and its implications.* New York: Worth.
Bruner, J. S. (1966). *Toward a theory of instruction.* Cambridge, MA: Harvard University Press.
Cognition and Technology Group at Vanderbilt. (1992). The Jasper series as an example of anchored instruction: Theory, program description, and assessment data. *Educational Psychologist, 27,* 291–315.
Dijkstra, S. (1997). The integration of instructional systems design models and constructivistic design principles. *Instructional Science, 25,* 1–13.
Dijkstra, S. (2000). Epistemology, psychology of learning and instructional Design. In M. Spector & T. Anderson (Eds.), *Holistic and integrated perspectives on learning, instruction and technology* (pp. 213–232). Dordrecht: Kluwer Academic.
Dijkstra, S. (2003). *Kennis, vaardigheden en competentie* [Knowledge, skills and competency]. Valedictory lecture. Enschede, the Netherlands: University of Twente.
Dijkstra, S. (2004a). Theoretical foundations of learning and instruction and innovations of instructional design and technology. In N. M. Seel & S. Dijkstra (Eds.), *Curriculum, plans and processes of instructional design: International perspectives* (pp. 17–24). Mahwah, NJ: Lawrence Erlbaum Associates.
Dijkstra, S. (2004b). The integration of curriculum design, instructional design and media choice. In N. M. Seel & S. Dijkstra (Eds.), *Curriculum, plans and processes of instructional design: International perspectives* (pp. 145–170). Mahwah, NJ: Lawrence Erlbaum Associates.
Dijkstra, S., & Van Merriënboer, J. J. G. (1997). Plans, procedures, and theories to solve instructional design problems. In S. Dijkstra, N. Seel, F. Schott & R. D. Tennyson (Eds.), *Instructional design: International perspectives* (Vol. 2, pp. 23–43. Mahwah, NJ: Lawrence Erlbaum Associates.
Gagné, R. M. (1962). The acquisition of knowledge. *Psychological Review, 69,* 355–365.
Gagné, R. M., & Briggs, L. J. (1974). *Principles of instructional design.* New York: Holt, Rinehart & Winston.
Lakoff, G. (1987). *Women, fire and dangerous things.* Chicago: University of Chicago Press.
Merrill, M. D. (1983). Component display theory. In C. M. Reigeluth (Ed.), *Instructional-design theories and models: An overview of their current status* (pp. 279–334). Hillsdale, NJ: Lawrence Erlbaum Associates.
Merrill, M. D., Tennyson, R. D., & Posey, L. O. (1992). *Teaching concepts: An instructional design guide* (2nd ed.). Englewood Cliffs, NJ: Educational Technology Publications.

Piaget, J. (1937). *La construction du réel chez l'enfant* [The child's construction of the reality]. Neuchâtel: Delachaux et Niestlé.

Razran, G. (1971). *Mind in evolution: An East–West synthesis of learned behavior and cognition.* Boston: Houghton Mifflin.

Seel, N. M., & Dijkstra, S. (2004). Instructional design and curriculum development: An introduction. In N. M. Seel & S. Dijkstra (Eds.), *Curriculum, plans and processes of instructional design: International perspectives* (pp. 1–16). Mahwah, NJ: Lawrence Erlbaum Associates.

Seel, N. M., & Winn, W. D. (1997). Research on media and learning: distributed cognition and semiotics. In R. D. Tennyson, F. Schott, N. Seel, & S. Dijkstra (Eds.), *Instructional design: International perspectives* (Vol. 1, pp. 293–326). Mahwah, NJ: Lawrence Erlbaum Associates.

Tennyson, R. D., Schott, F., Seel, N., & Dijkstra, S. (Eds.). (1997). *Instructional design: International perspectives* (Vol. 1). Mahwah, NJ: Lawrence Erlbaum Associates.

von Glasersfeld, E. (1996). *Radical constructivism.* London: Falmer Press.

van Merriënboer, J. J. G. (1997). *Training complex cognitive skills. A four-component instructional design model for technical training.* Englewood Cliffs, NJ: Educational Technology Publications.

Chapter 12

New Instructional Theories and Strategies for a Knowledge-Based Society

Charles M. Reigeluth
Indiana University

Industrial nations are undergoing massive changes as they evolve into post-industrial societies (Bell, 1973; Toffler, 1980). These changes are being brought about by the development of information technology, which has transformed the industrial sector of the economy and has spawned the knowledge-work sector (Duffy, Rogerson, & Blick, 2000). Just as the percentage of the workforce in agriculture dropped dramatically in the early stages of the industrial age, so the percentage in manufacturing has been declining dramatically over the past few decades, while the percentage doing knowledge work has been increasing dramatically. As Reich (1991) pointed out, even in manufacturing companies, a majority of the jobs today entail working with knowledge rather than materials. Just as the industrial age represented a focus on, and extension of, our physical capabilities (mechanical technology), so the knowledge (or information) age represents a focus on, and extension of, our mental capabilities (intellectual technology). Employees need to be able to think about and solve problems, work in teams, communicate, take initiative, and bring diverse perspectives to their work (Reich, 1991; Toffler, 1980). The prevalence of such knowledge work makes effective learning paramount.

However, this massive societal transformation is creating very different learning needs from those which our educational and training systems (herein referred to as "learning systems") were designed to meet. The success of learners in our schools, universities, and corporate training programs depends on our ability to redesign those learning systems to meet the new learning needs of the knowledge age (Reigeluth, 1994). This chapter explores the kinds of changes that are needed in our learning systems, with a particular emphasis on changes in instructional theories and strategies required for effective learning in the knowledge age.

KEY MARKERS FOR CHANGES IN OUR LEARNING SYSTEMS

Because the need for fundamental changes in our learning systems is driven by massive changes in our knowledge-age society, we must look at the ways our society in general—and its learning needs in particular—are changing in order to determine what features our learning systems should have. Table 12.1 shows some of the major differences between the industrial age and the emerging knowledge age. These differences, or "key markers," have important implications for how our learning systems should be structured, what should be taught, and how it should be taught.

TABLE 12.1

Key Markers That Distinguish Industrial-Age and Knowledge-Age Organizations

Industrial Age	Knowledge Age
Standardization	Customization
Bureaucratic organization	Team-based organization
Centralized control	Autonomy with accountability
Adversarial relationships	Cooperative relationships
Autocratic decision making	Shared decision making
Compliance	Initiative
Conformity	Diversity
One-way communications	Networking
Compartmentalization	Holism
Parts-oriented	Process-oriented
Planned obsolescence	Total quality
CEO or boss as "king"	Customer as "king"

Note. From Reigeluth (1999b), with permission.

According to Reigeluth (1999b), as indicated by Table 12.1, students in our current school systems are typically treated as if they are all the same and are all expected to do the same things at the same time (standardization). Consolidated districts are highly bureaucratic and centrally controlled. Students get insufficient preparation for participating in a democratic society. Leadership is vested in individuals according to a hierarchical management structure, and all those lower in the hierarchy are expected to obey their superiors. Our current school systems usually foster adversarial relationships, not only between teachers and administrators, but also between teachers and students, and often between teachers and parents. Students are typically molded (implicitly or explicitly) to be passive learners and passive members of their school community. Learning is highly compartmentalized into subject areas that often have little apparent relevance to students' lives.

These common features of current school systems are also found in higher education and corporate training systems, and they are not unique or specific to the United States. These features of school systems should change (and are indeed beginning to change), for they are counterproductive—harmful to our citizens and our society—in the knowledge age.

The "key markers" shown in Table 12.1 provide us with a general idea of the ways in which learning systems—and the instructional theories and strategies that guide their design—need to change. However, there are other changes that provide a clearer picture of the ways instructional theories need to change: (a) the growing complexity of tasks; (b) the increasing reliance on collaboration in performing tasks; (c) the growth of Web-based learning; (d) the increasing power of performance support systems; and (e) the emergence of personal tutor systems. The remainder of this chapter is devoted to discussing the implications of each of these five changes for instructional theories and strategies.

COMPLEX COGNITIVE TASKS

As our society evolves deeper into the knowledge age, our systems are becoming more complex, and the tasks we are called on to perform are becoming ever more complex (Caine & Caine, 1997). The lower levels of learning—information and procedures—by themselves are inadequate to deal with such complexity. Learners must develop deep understandings, complex causal dynamics, highly conditional heuristics (rules of thumb or guidelines), and powerful metacognitive skills (Merriënboer, 1997). These higher levels of learning require instructional theories and strategies different from those typically used in our learning systems today.

The first challenge in teaching these higher levels of learning is to discover what to teach. This task is made especially difficult by the tacit (unconscious) nature of much of that knowledge. The field of instructional development has done a fine job of generating techniques for analyzing the simpler forms of knowledge: information and procedural (or "routine") tasks. However, we are in dire need of better methods for analyzing complex cognitive (or heuristic) tasks. Reigeluth and colleagues attempted to synthesize and extend the knowledge in this area through the development of the heuristic task analysis (HTA) method (Lee, 2002; Lee & Reigeluth, 2003; Reigeluth, 1999a). HTA includes guidance for eliciting, analyzing, and representing various kinds of knowledge—often tacit—that experts use in performing complex cognitive tasks. However, much work remains to be done to develop more powerful tools in this area.

A second challenge in teaching these higher levels of learning is to not overwhelm learners with the great complexity of real-world tasks. Although it is important for instruction to utilize authentic tasks, it is counterproductive to provide too much complexity to the learner at once (Pollock, Chandler, & Sweller, 2002; Vygotsky, 1978). Reigeluth (1999a) attempted to synthesize and extend the knowledge in this area through the development of the Simplifying Conditions Method. It offers guidance on identifying the simplest real-world version of a complex cognitive task, identifying progressively more complex versions of the task (along with identifying the conditions that make each version more complex), and organizing the versions in a way that ensures both a simple-to-complex sequence and some degree of learner choice as to which dimensions of complexity to elaborate on first (or next).

A third challenge in teaching these higher levels of learning is to use instructional strategies and theories that most powerfully foster each type of learning: deep understanding, complex causal dynamics, heuristics, and metacognitive skills. For deep understanding, the work of David Perkins (Perkins & Unger, 1999), Howard Gardner (Gardner, 1999), and other researchers (Spector & Anderson, 2000; Wiske, 1998) provides some insights as to instructional strategies that may help most to foster such learning. Those strategies include selecting generative or significant topics for study, selecting and publicly stating goals for understanding, using entry points (based on multiple intelligences) to engage students in the topic, portraying the topic in a number of ways, engaging students in performances for understanding, and providing ongoing assessment of understanding.

For highly conditional heuristics and complex causal dynamics, the work of researchers like van Merriënboer (1997) and Spector (2000, 2001) provides some knowledge about what instructional strategies and theories may help most to foster their acquisition. These include a macro-level sequence of whole tasks (skill clusters), meso-level sequencing comprised of simple to complex cases for a single task, and instruction for specific cases (or problems). The latter includes a variety of product-oriented problem formats (e.g., worked-out problems, reverse problems, conventional problems) and process-oriented problem formats (e.g., modeling examples, process worksheets, use of cognitive tools) (van Merriënboer, 1997). Simulations are particularly valuable for fostering the acquisition of complex causal dynamics. In addition to learning from "playing" a simulation, it is sometimes useful to have learners create their own simulations using such tools as Stella, StarLogo, and NetLogo (Milrad, Spector, & Davidsen, 2002; Spector, 2000).

For metacognitive skills, several researchers (Hacker, Dunlosky, & Graesser, 1998; Hartman, 2001; Weinert & Kluwe, 1987) provided some ideas as to what instructional strategies and theories may help most to foster their development. These include promoting students' metacognitive awareness by providing explicit instruction about metacognitive knowledge and metacognitive strategies, providing tasks or problems that require metacognitive skills, providing models of metacognition, engaging students in self-regulated learning activities (e.g., planning, self-questioning, self-monitoring, self- assessment, reflection, revision), engaging students in collaborative thinking (e.g., dialogue or discussion, collaborative decision making, collaborative planning or writing, study group), providing feedback, and using motivational strategies for enhancing students' self-efficacy. Given the two fundamental aspects of metacognition—awareness of and control over one's thinking (Hartman, 2001)—it is critical for instructional designers or teachers to help students to develop skills for planning, monitoring, evaluating, and revising their thinking and learning as well as their metacognitive knowledge (domain-general and/or domain-specific).

COLLABORATIVE TASKS

As our society evolves deeper into the knowledge age, it is becoming increasingly apparent that knowledge work is more effective when done in collaboration with other workers. This places on our learning systems new learning demands that go far beyond a new course in a curriculum or training program—it requires the use of collaborative learning as an instructional strategy that helps learners to improve their collaboration skills as an integral part of learning other skills or knowledge. Several researchers (Bruffee, 1993; Nelson, 1999) provided some ideas as to what instructional strategies and theories may help most to foster effective collaborative learning. There are various kinds of collaboration, as well as approaches to collaborative learning. For example, the use of consensus groups for collaborative learning includes five major steps (Bruffee, 1993):

- Divide a … class into small groups, usually of about 5 learners.
- Provide a task, usually designed ahead of time, for the small groups to work on.
- Reconvene students into a plenary session to hear reports from the small groups and … negotiate a consensus of the class as a whole.
- Lead students to compare the class's plenary consensus with the current consensus of the knowledge community.…
- Evaluate explicitly the quality of students' work. (p. 21)

WEB-BASED LEARNING

The Internet represents a powerful tool for more than information retrieval—it is also a powerful tool for providing interactive, dynamic, multimedia instruction (Khan, 1997). However, such instruction is fundamentally different from classroom instruction for many reasons. Unlike face-to-face instruction, there is less pressure to give all students the same instruction at the same time. Its technological strengths (e.g., asynchronous communication capabilities) and weaknesses (e.g., difficulty of natural, real-time group discussions) require a different mix of instructional methods than classroom instruction. But perhaps most importantly, the remoteness of the learners and the flexibility of the medium put more onus on the learners to direct their own learning. This also creates greater demands for fostering intrinsic motivation.

The net effect of these factors is a greater need for methods of instruction that engage the learners in authentic tasks that are relevant to their personal needs and goals. Such methods include problem-based learning and self-regulated learning. This also creates greater demands for learning from one's peers through such methods as team-based learning and peer review of student work. Many researchers (Barrows, 1985; Hannafin, Land, & Oliver, 1999; Jonassen, 1999; Khan, 1997, 2001; Nelson, 1999; Schank, Berman, & Macpherson, 1999; Schwartz, Lin, Brophy, & Bransford, 1999) provide some ideas as to what instructional strategies and theories may help most to foster these kinds of learning. These include such methods as:

- Clarifying the learning goals.
- Presenting an appropriate problem, mission, or challenge.
- Having students engage in such activities as generating ideas, sharing multiple perspectives, and conducting research.
- Providing such resources as worked examples, information, cognitive tools, and collaboration tools.
- Providing coaching, scaffolding, and feedback or formative assessment.

PERFORMANCE SUPPORT SYSTEMS

Information technology has improved the power and flexibility of electronic performance support systems (EPSSs) as tools to provide just-in-time support for performance on the job (Gery, 1991). Such just-in-time support can work very well for relatively routine tasks that do not require fast performance, but for routine tasks that need to be automatized and for highly complex cognitive tasks, EPSSs need to take on a highly instructional, rather than purely informational, role. For example, some skills require much practice to become sufficiently automatized for an employee to perform well under the time constraints and other constraints of the task (Neves & Anderson, 1981). Neves and Anderson (1981) and Salisbury (1990) provided some ideas as to what additional instructional theories and strategies are needed to help automatize routine tasks. These include such methods as:

- Use lots of practice to automatize routine tasks.
- Provide practice on a small subset of items at a time (e.g., 7 plus or minus 2).
- Determine mastery by speed of response as well as accuracy of response.

- When an item is mastered, a new item should be introduced.
- Practice should be "spaced" at different times rather than concentrated all at once. When practice is resumed, it should resume where the learner left off.
- Systematically review items that have already been learned. Each time a review item is answered correctly, there should be a longer delay before it is reviewed again. Over time, the ratio of review items to new items should increase.
- Use mnemonic devices or memory devices to make the learning more meaningful.

Also, complex cognitive tasks frequently require an expert to have a deep understanding of causal models and systemic interrelationships whose acquisition requires considerable exposure (van Merriënboer, 1997). Compounding this challenge is the difficulty of identifying the frequently tacit heuristic knowledge that experts use to perform complex cognitive tasks (discussed earlier). Once such tacit heuristic knowledge is discovered, instructional theories and strategies should be built into EPSSs to help novices internalize it. Several researchers (van Merriënboer, 1997; Spector, 2000, 2001) provide some ideas as to what instructional strategies and theories may help most to foster learning of complex cognitive tasks. They were discussed earlier, in the section Complex Cognitive Tasks.

PERSONAL TUTOR SYSTEMS

One of the most promising developments of the knowledge age is our growing knowledge about how to create an electronic *personal tutor* for learners. It would be a personal tutor in the sense that the instruction would be customized to the individual learner's needs, interests, and learning style. It would be adaptive in that it would constantly monitor and improve its selection of instructional methods for the learner. But it would also allow the learners to play a major role in designing their own instruction by selecting from a menu of methods or at least a menu of specifications for the methods that the personal tutor system selects. The personal tutor system would, of course, provide advice and feedback about the learner's selections, so the learner would be coached to improve his or her learning strategies.

For this kind of personal tutor system to be feasible, it is important for the system to separate instructional methods from content and then combine them in appropriate ways (Merrill & ID2 Research Group, 1996). For example, there is ample research evidence that to teach a skill, it helps to tell the learner what to do (a generality), show the learner what to do (an example), and have the learner do it (practice) with immediate feedback (Merrill, 1983). The system needs a knowledge base about what to teach (*knowledge components*), it needs a knowledge base about how to teach (*strategy components*), and it needs to maintain current knowledge about what the learner knows and how the learner learns best.

The research of Merrill (1997, 1998, 2001) provides some ideas to guide the design of this kind of personal tutor system:

- Knowledge components that exist universally across all subject areas are identified as "entities (things), actions (procedures that can be performed by a student on, to, or with entities or their parts), processes (events that occur often as a result of some action), and properties (qualitative or quantitative descriptors for entities, actions, or processes)," as well as parts, kinds, and properties (Merrill, 2001).
- Each of these knowledge components has its own types of subcomponents, such as a name, a description, and/or a consequence.
- The primary strategy components include *tell* (to present general information to the student), *show* (to demonstrate specific information), *ask* (for the student to recall information), and *do* (for the student to use knowledge in a specific situation).
- There are other strategy components for sequence and for learner guidance.
- Instruction occurs in the form of *transactions*, which require the appropriate combination of knowledge components with strategy components for a given instructional goal.

Merrill developed ID Expert[1] with *transaction shells,* which provides a proof of concept for creating powerful personal tutor systems that can work efficiently across subject areas (Merrill, 1998).

CONCLUSION

As we evolve deeper into the knowledge age, this massive societal transformation is creating learning needs very different from those that our educational and training systems were designed to meet. For the success and stability of our society, it is essential that we redesign those learning systems. The key markers of our societal transformation provide some guidance as to how our learning systems should be redesigned. Additional guidance can be found in other changes more closely related to learning systems: the growing complexity of tasks, the increasing reliance on collaboration in performing tasks, the growth of Web-based learning, the increasing power of performance support systems, and the emergence of personal tutor systems.

The broader societal transformation we are undergoing places our society in a vulnerable state. That vulnerability requires the development of effective learning systems that can help us meet the new learning needs. It is clear that instructional theorists have begun developing knowledge to guide the transformation of learning systems based on all these changing needs and tools, but much more work remains to be done to develop such knowledge. There is also the formidable task of using that knowledge to redesign our learning systems. We can meet these challenges. We must meet these challenges. But do we, as a society, have the will to meet these challenges? Do you have the will to help?

---

[1]This has become a commercially successful system marketed by Leading Way Technology.

ACKNOWLEDGMENT

I thank Yun-Jo An for her contributions to this chapter.

REFERENCES

Barrows, H. S. (1985). *How to design a problem-based curriculum for the pre-clinical years.* New York: Springer-Verlag.

Bell, D. (1973). *The coming of post-industrial society: A venture in social forecasting.* New York: Basic Books.

Bruffee, K. A. (1993). *Collaborative learning: Higher education, interdependence, and the authority of knowledge.* Baltimore, MD: Johns Hopkins University Press.

Caine, R. N., & Caine, G. (1997). *Education on the edge of possibility.* Alexandria, VA: ASCD.

Duffy, F. M., Rogerson, L. G., & Blick, C. (2000). *Redesigning America's schools: A systems approach to improvement.* Norwood, MA: Christopher-Gordon Publishers.

Gardner, H. E. (1999). Multiple approaches to understanding. In C. M. Reigeluth (Ed.), *Instructional-design theories and models, Vol. II: A new paradigm of instructional theory* (pp. 69–89). Mahwah, NJ: Lawrence Erlbaum Associates.

Gery, G. (1991). *Electronic performance support systems: How and why to remake the workplace through the strategic application of technology.* Tolland, MA: Gery Performance Press.

Hacker, D. J., Dunlosky, J., & Graesser, A. C. (Eds.). (1998). *Metacognition in educational theory and practice.* Mahwah, NJ: Lawrence Erlbaum Associates.

Hannafin, M., Land, S., & Oliver, K. (1999). Open learning environments: Foundations, methods, and models. In C. M. Reigeluth (Ed.), *Instructional-design theories and models, Vol II: A new paradigm of instructional theory* (pp. 115–140). Mahwah, NJ: Lawrence Erlbaum Associates.

Hartman, H. J. (Ed.). (2001). *Metacognition in learning and instruction: Theory, research, and practice.* Boston: Kluwer Academic.

Jonassen, D. H. (1999). Designing constructivist learning environments. In C. M. Reigeluth (Ed.), *Instructional-design theories and models, Vol. II: A new paradigm of instructional theory* (pp. 215–239). Mahwah, NJ: Lawrence Erlbaum Associates.

Khan, B. (Ed.). (1997). *Web-based instruction.* Englewood Cliffs, NJ: Educational Technology Publications.

Khan, B. (Ed.). (2001). *Web-based training.* Englewood Cliffs, NJ: Educational Technology Publications.

Lee, J. Y. (2002). *Heuristic task analysis on expertise in designing web-based instruction (WBI).* Unpublished doctoral dissertation, Indiana University, Bloomington, IN.

Lee, J. Y., & Reigeluth, C. M. (2003). Formative research on the heuristic task analysis process. *Educational Technology research & Development, 51*(4), 5–24.

Merrill, M. D. (1983). Component display theory. In C. M. Reigeluth (Ed.), *Instructional-design theories and models: An overview of their current status* (pp. 279–333). Hillsdale, NJ: Lawrence Erlbaum Associates.

Merrill, M. D. (1997). Learning-oriented instructional development tools. *Performance Improvement, 36*(3), 51–55.

Merrill, M. D. (1998). ID Expert: A second generation instructional development system. *Instructional Science, 26*(3–4), 243–262.

Merrill, M. D. (2001). Components of instruction toward a theoretical tool for instructional design. *Instructional Science, 29*(4–5), 291–310.

Merrill, M. D., & ID2 Research Group. (1996). Instructional transaction theory: Instructional design based on knowledge objects. *Educational Technology, 36*(3), 30–37.

Milrad, M., Spector, J. M., & Davidsen, P. I. (2002). Model facilitated learning. In S. Naidu (Ed.), *Learning and Teaching with Technology: Principles and Practices* (pp. 13–27). London: Kogan Page.

Nelson, L. M. (1999). Collaborative problem solving. In C. M. Reigeluth (Ed.), *Instructional-design theories and models, Vol II: A new paradigm of instructional theory* (pp. 241–267). Mahwah, NJ: Lawrence Erlbaum Associates.

Neves, D. M., & Anderson, J. R. (1981). Knowledge compilation: Mechanisms for the automatization of cognitive skills. In J. R. Anderson (Ed.), *Cognitive skills and their acquisition* (pp. 57–84). Hillsdale, NJ: Lawrence Erlbaum Associates.

Perkins, D. N., & Unger, C. (1999). Teaching and learning for understanding. In C. M. Reigeluth (Ed.), *Instructional-design theories and models, Vol. II: A new paradigm of instructional theory* (pp. 91–114). Mahwah, NJ: Lawrence Erlbaum Associates.

Pollock, E., Chandler, P., & Sweller, J. (2002). Assimilating complex information. *Learning and Instruction, 12*(1), 61–86.

Reich, R. B. (1991). *The work of nations: preparing ourselves for 21st-century capitalism.* New York: A. A. Knopf.

Reigeluth, C. M. (1994). The imperative for systemic change. In R. J. Garfinkle (Ed.), *Systemic change in education* (pp. 3–11). Englewood Cliffs, NJ: Educational Technology Publications.

Reigeluth, C. M. (1999a). The elaboration theory: Guidance for scope and sequence decisions. In C. M. Reigeluth (Ed.), *Instructional-design theories and models, Vol II: A new paradigm of instructional theory* (pp. 425–453). Mahwah, NJ: Lawrence Erlbaum Associates.

Reigeluth, C. M. (1999b). What is instructional-design theory and how is it changing? In C. M. Reigeluth (Ed.), *Instructional-design theories and models, Vol II: A new paradigm of instructional theory* (pp. 5–29). Mahwah, NJ: Lawrence Erlbaum Associates.

Salisbury, D. F. (1990). Cognitive psychology and its implications for designing drill and practice programs for computers. *Journal of Computer-Based Instruction, 17*(1), 23–30.

Schank, R. C., Berman, T. R., & Macpherson, K. A. (1999). Learning by doing. In C. M. Reigeluth (Ed.), *Instructional-design theories and models, Vol. II: A new paradigm of instructional theory* (pp. 161–181). Mahwah, NJ: Lawrence Erlbaum Associates.

Schwartz, D., Lin, X., Brophy, S., & Bransford, J. D. (1999). Toward the development of flexibly adaptive instructional designs. In C. M. Reigeluth (Ed.), *Instructional-design theories and models, Vol. II: A new paradigm of instructional theory* (pp. 183–213). Mahwah, NJ: Lawrence Erlbaum Associates.

Spector, J. M. (2000). Constructing learning environments using system dynamics. *Journal of Courseware Engineering, 1*(1), 5–11.

Spector, J. M. (2001). Tools and principles for the design of collaborative learning environments for complex domains. *Journal of Structural Learning and Intelligent systems, 14*(4), 483–510.

Spector, J. M., & Anderson, T. M. (Eds.). (2000). *Integrated and holistic perspectives on learning, instruction and technology: Understanding complexity.* Dordrecht: Kluwer Academic Press.

Toffler, A. (1980). *The Third Wave.* New York: Bantam Books.

van Merriënboer, J. J. G. (1997). *Training complex cognitive skills: A four-component instructional design model for technical training.* Englewood Cliffs, NJ: Educational Technology Publications.

Vygotsky, L. S. (1978). *Mind in society: The development of higher psychological processes.* Cambridge, MA: Harvard University Press.

Weinert, F. E., & Kluwe, R. H. (Eds.). (1987). *Metacognition, motivation, and understanding.* Hillsdale, NJ: Lawrence Erlbaum Associates.

Wiske, M. S. (Ed.). (1998). *Teaching for understanding: Linking research with practice.* San Francisco, CA: Jossey-Bass.

Chapter
13

Learning Theories and Instructional Design: A Historical Perspective of The Linking Model

Robert D. Tennyson
University of Minnesota

The roots of instructional theory can be traced back to early efforts by learning psychologists to develop a connection between the science of psychology and the practical application of learning theory in educational settings. Two theorists of particular importance at the turn of the century were John Dewey (1910), who envisioned a special *linking science* between learning theory and educational practice, and Edward Thorndike (1913), who investigated principles of learning that could be directly applied to the teaching process (i.e., the laws of effect and exercise). Thorndike developed a body of instructional design principles that included task analysis and teaching methods based on his research findings and student evaluation methods.

Contemporary roots of instructional theory can be traced both to behaviorism and to the general trend in the 1950s toward applying scientific approaches to the social sciences. Attempts to integrate psychology and instructional technology had emerged during and after World War II as educational psychologists became involved with the U.S. military in efforts to research and develop military training materials and instruction. The focus of instructional research programs was two-

219

fold: first, development of instructional systems design (ISD) methodologies for the analysis of content and tasks; and second, testing of variables of design to achieve specific learning outcomes. At that time, the ISD approach to learning was related to theories of automation and the concept of systems as a complex interrelationship of components, flow and control of information, thorough analysis of a task, and careful planning and decision making. Intrinsic to such instructional theories was the embrace of advanced technology and the "automation" of the learning process (Finn, 1957).

Technology and instruction research testing the programmed instruction paradigm (e.g., step-by-step vs. branching) and the development of teaching machines pioneered by Skinner are of particular interest to the historical development of instructional theory. A pivotal article by Skinner (1954) entitled *The Science of Learning and the Art of Teaching* outlines principles of a technology of instruction, which include: (a) small, incremental steps; (b) sequencing from simple to complex; (c) learner participation; (d) reinforcement of correct responses; and (e) individual pacing. It is significant that several of the leading figures in the early development of instructional theory (e.g., Robert Gagné, Leslie Briggs, and Robert Glaser) were also proponents of programmed instruction and later in varying degrees moved away from the behavioral paradigm to cognitive theory.

In the 1950s, two developments outside the fields of education and psychology played an important role in establishing momentum for increased instructional theory research. First, the post-World War II baby boom presented a challenge to the existing educational system. Within a very short period in the early 1950s, schools were forced to absorb a significant increase in students, necessitating rapid changes in instructional methods. Second, in 1957, the Russians launched Sputnik, shattering the comfortable image of American educational and technological superiority and calling into question the adequacy of contemporary methods of instruction. In response to the perceived challenge, the U.S. government increased its interest in and funding of research and development of new curricular and teaching methods.

EARLY DEVELOPMENTS

In the early stages, instructional theory was defined primarily in behaviorist terms as:

> Small, incremental steps sequenced to link information in a logical order; active learner participation in responding to instructional stimuli with immediate feedback as a positive reinforcer. Learner progress based on successful attainment of defined behavioral objectives. (Skinner, 1954, p. 88)

The instructional design field was seen as an attempt to develop a single, ideal instructional theory based in systems theory that would specify teacher characteristics, classification and evaluation procedures, and the means to modify the design systems being tested. The goal from this perspective was the development of instructional programs that would enable the majority of students to achieve levels of performance that were pre-determined in terms of behaviorally defined objectives. Robert Mager's (1962) influential book, *Preparing Instructional Objectives,* helped to popularize the use of measurable behavioral objectives. Much of the early work in the instructional development (ID) field was directed at the establishment of taxonomies for classifying learning objectives and codifying the interactions between the various classifications.

BEHAVIORAL INFLUENCES

Throughout most of the 1960s, instructional research continued to be based on behaviorist learning models and theories. Empirical studies sought to determine the most effective means of implementing a stimulus–response–reinforcement model (i.e., operant model) to insure that the prescribed learning outcomes would be achieved. A major goal of instructional research centered on methods of task analysis and the development of behavioral objectives for learning. The goals of the behavioral task analysis were on (a) identifying small, incremental tasks or subskills that the learner needed to acquire for successful completion of the instruction, (b) preparing specific behavioral objectives that would lead to the acquisition of those subskills, and (c) sequencing subskill acquisition in the order that would most efficiently lead to successful learner outcomes. Also important to researchers' investigations was the search for variables of individual differences in what the learner brings to the learning task. The concept of individual differences in the behavioral paradigm focused on how to manipulate the environment to account for student differences. For example, students with a high aptitude in a given content would receive an instructional strategy that would be different from that for students with a low aptitude. This particular instructional strategy was labeled *aptitude–treatment interaction* (ATI).

As already noted, programmed instruction had been a key element in the design of instruction in the 1960s. Toward the end of that decade, however, the interest in such instruction declined. Research findings revealed that the programmed materials were often no more effective than conventional materials and that students often found the materials to be uninteresting. In addition, many of the principles of learning proposed by Skinner and other behaviorists were found to be untrue, especially for the complex learning tasks required in the classroom. Research in the early 1970s revealed findings that contradicted previous ideas about the role those behavioral principles such as feedback, rewards, sequencing, and definition of objectives played in the learning process.

CONTRIBUTORS TO INSTRUCTIONAL THEORY

A major contributor to instructional theory development in the 1960s was Robert Gagné, who theorized that the acquisition of knowledge is facilitated by the hierarchical sequencing of content from elemental subordinate information to more complex skills (Gagné, 1962). Additional contributors, but in contrast to the behavioral paradigm, were psychologists who proposed cognitive-based paradigms. For example, David Ausubel's theory of progressive differentiation proposed the use of advance organizers (i.e., broad, general ideas) followed by a sequence of more concrete and detailed ones (Ausubel, 1969). Jerome Bruner proposed that ideas should be reintroduced in increasingly complex ways as the learner matures (Bruner, 1964). Other significant instructional theory contributions during this period were made by Susan Markle and J. William Moore in their development of instructional design theories to improve concept acquisition (see, Markle, 1969; Smith & Moore, 1962).

TRANSITION TO COGNITIVE LEARNING THEORY

In the late 1960s and throughout the 1970s, the behavioral paradigm gradually gave way to the cognitive approach to learning. Beginning with Bruner (1964), instructional researchers began to move away from the stimulus–response–reinforcement model of instruction and to develop instructional theories based, at least in part, on the mental processes of the learner. The definition of instructional design at this point shifted to considerations of learning theory and to the development of models linking those theories to the design of instruction. The result was rapid proliferation of instructional systems development (ISD) models and instructional design (ID) theories covering a wide range of perspectives, as psychologists and educators pursued their individual ideas in a generally competitive environment.

Instructional design researchers in the 1970s tried to establish a more complete picture of the *conditions of learning*. Theories sought to incorporate individual differences into the instructional design process, leading to the extensive use of pretests and formative evaluation procedures. Sequencing still played a vital role, but its direction was somewhat altered as instructional theorists sought to develop sequences that corresponded most closely with the learner's individual cognitive growth (Snow, 1997). Research was centered on identifying those aspects of cognitive psychology that were central to the design of instruction. An example of this trend was the work of Joseph Scandura, which lead directly to his theory of structured learning. Scandura (1970) focused his theory in large part on rule acquisition and structure of the knowledge base. Shifting in the late 1980s to ISD methodology, Scandura continued to contribute to the instructional design field by developing automated systems of instructional design (Scandura, 2001).

INFORMATION ANALYSIS

Throughout the 1970s, information analysis procedures (including task and content) shifted away from behavioral objectives toward an understanding of stages of competent performance in various domains of knowledge and skills relevant to education. Cognitive researchers used information analysis to identify the levels of learning that distinguish a novice from an expert in a subject-matter domain. Much of the research work was on describing the complex structure and sequencing of cognitive processes such as attention and memory, and recognized the importance of perception in the performance of individuals who are highly skilled in specific domains.

Content and Task Analysis

This trend toward methods of information analysis continued, with advancements coming first from cognitive psychology and more recently from constructivist theory. Thus, an important component of instructional design theory is the analysis of the information to be learned. Two basic types of information analyses are: (a) content analysis, which focuses on defining the critical attributes of the given subject matter and the relationship of those attributes according to superordinate and subordinate organizations; and (b) task analysis, which focuses on a hierarchical organization of human performances. Both of these analyses identify the external structure of the information but do so independent of how it might actually be stored in human memory. However, research in cognitive psychology on human memory suggests that the internal organization of information in a knowledge base is formed more on employment needs rather than by attribute or hierarchical associations (Carroll, 1993). That is, the utility of the knowledge base is attributed to its situational organization, not the amount of information. The implication of a knowledge base organization is the need for a further analysis of the information to better understand the possible internal organization and representation of the knowledge.

Merrill, Li, and Jones (1990) stated that a content analysis focuses on components, rather than on integrated wholes, in the context of describing the limitations of first generation instructional design (ID_1). The components that result from a content analysis are individual items, such as facts, concepts, principles, and procedures. Instruction derived from this form of content analysis may allow students to pass tests, but is not effective in helping students integrate information into meaningful wholes. These integrated wholes are essential for understanding complex and dynamic phenomena and for using knowledge in complex problem-solving situations. That is, a well-developed cognitive structure (schema) is necessary for new information to be learned meaningfully and for accurate recall later. Merrill suggested that this cognitive structure consists of mental models, but that no ID_1 content analysis procedure takes this notion of mental models (cognitive structure) into account. Most of these task and content analysis procedures were developed before interactive media was widely available and result in passive, rather than interactive, instruction. It follows that these task and content analysis procedures are not well suited to highly interactive instructional situations, such as computer-based simulations (Breuer & Kummer, 1990).

Problem-Solving Analysis

Better organization in memory may also imply better accessibility within the knowledge base for such higher order cognitive activities such as problem solving and creativity. To understand the nature of the knowledge base organization, cognitive psychologists analyze problem complexity and the way individuals try to solve given problems. By analyzing problems, it is possible to identify the concepts used; by analyzing the solutions, it is possible to identify the associations of those concepts within given problem situations. The implication for instructional theory is that the sequence of information for instruction should be based in part on internal situational associations, as well as external structures. The assumption is that because external structures are independent of employment needs, an analysis of possible internal associations would improve the initial organization of the new information, resulting in better employment (Tennyson & Elmore, 1997).

Situation and Context Analysis

In addition to the analysis of problems and solutions is the issue of problem situation and/or context. For example, expert systems reside within the constraints of a specific context; that is, they can solve problems only associated with that given context. Similarly, research in cognitive psychology shows that individuals can solve complex problems only if they possess the necessary contextual knowledge. For example, the objective in learning to play chess is the learning of problem-solving strategies within the context of both the given game and the current move, not just how the various chess pieces move (i.e., procedural knowledge). Thus, the key to both effective acquisition and employment of knowledge is the organization of the knowledge according to contextual applications. That is, contextual knowledge includes not only content/task information, but also the cultural and situational aspects directly associated with that information (Brown, Collins, & Duguid, 1989). Cultural aspects imply the selection criteria, values, feelings, and appropriateness associated with the information of given contextual situations.

TRANSITION TO COGNITIVE INSTRUCTIONAL THEORY

Gagné and Briggs (1979) early on incorporated cognitive theory into their instructional theory for conceptualizing instructional development. They defined a set of requirements for instructional systems development, including:

- The system must be designed for the individual.
- It should include immediate and long-range phases.
- It should substantially affect individual development.
- It must be based on knowledge of how people learn.

Their instructional theory was based on a set of capabilities, or learning outcomes, that students would acquire through instruction. These outcomes were classified into five categories: (a) verbal information, (b) intellectual skills, (c) cognitive strategies, (d) motor skills, and (e) attitudes. Instead of emphasizing generalized factors such as practice and reinforcement in the learning process, their theory required that the conditions of external events and internal processes must be specified separately for each learning outcome. Also important to their instructional design theory was the interaction of instruction with the student's previously acquired learning.

The component display theory developed by Merrill was a prescriptive instructional design theory rooted in Gagné's theories and directed toward improving instructional quality. Merrill and his collaborators worked to develop a taxonomy of instructional presentation types for conveying information and asking questions. Separating performance level from the content type extends the system of outcome classification (Merrill, 1997).

Another concept developed in the field of cognitive psychology that was relevant to instructional theory was learner production of knowledge. Investigations in cognitive strategies that guide internal learning and thinking processes resulted in specific strategies for such processes as problem solving, organizing information, reducing anxiety, developing self-monitoring skills, and enhancing positive attitudes. Researchers also investigated metacognition (a process of being aware of specific cognition skills) and the executive strategies experienced learners use to develop awareness and control of their own acquisition and employment of knowledge. Researchers paid renewed attention to the role of automaticity and the necessity of practicing subskills as a prerequisite foundation for more advanced learning (Winn, 1993).

INTEGRATED INSTRUCTIONAL DESIGN THEORIES

By the early 1990s, the trend in instructional design moved toward a synthesis of elements of the various instructional theories and advancements from cognitive science and educational technology. The notion of developing a single, most effective approach for all instructional situations was replaced by attempts to find the best approaches to achieve specific, well-defined performance outcomes in terms of knowledge and cognitive processes. The emphasis was on instructional variables and conditions based on individual learner progress and need. That is, by assessing the learner's progress, the learning need could be established from which appropriate instructional strategies, sequences, and media could be determined. The role of the instructor continued to change to reflect more flexibility in the learning environment. The role of technology changed as well, as instructional design researchers worked with computer software specialists to develop interactive instructional systems.

INTERACTIVE MEDIA AND LEARNING

Interaction of learners with media and learning environments became important in the 1990s and continues to be an area of increasing focus. For example, the constructivist view of learning positions is that an active, self-regulated, goal-directed, and reflective learner constructs personal knowledge through discovery and exploration in a responsive learning environment (Schott & Driscoll, 1997). Interactive technologies that can adaptively and intelligently respond to at-the-moment learning needs and progress can activate that environment.

SELECTING INSTRUCTIONAL STRATEGIES

Although many instructional design experts continued to revise their theories (e.g., Dick, 1997; Merrill, 1997) in an attempt to arrive at a theory of instruction that could be applied to all learning situations, a number of theorists changed directions in the late 1990s. These researchers sought to analyze the theories already in existence to determine their relative strengths and weaknesses for dealing with specific instructional situations. Rather than trying to synthesize elements of the existing theories into a new hybrid theory, these researchers tried to assemble the strongest theories into a large-scale, diverse system that encompassed many possible strategies. Strategies were combined in new ways to determine which combinations and sequences were most effective for well-defined instructional settings. Instructional designers could then select the specific segments of the larger, integrated instructional theories that were directly applicable to the learning outcomes they desired, introducing greater flexibility into instructional design.

DOMAIN-SPECIFIC COMPETENCY:
STRUCTURED VERSUS SELF-REGULATION

Structured Approach

Researchers continue to investigate the processes and structures of competent performance in specific domains and to develop instructional programs to produce such competence. Two often-dichotomous stances toward instruction are reflected in such programs. One stance is that of a mastery approach, which emphasizes learning proceduralized knowledge through extensive practice with problem solving. In this paradigm, the teacher controls the direction of learning, with learners following a specific path of carefully structured subgoals leading toward the efficient performance of a well-defined cognitive skill. Practice with successful performance is thought to lead to subsequent metacognitive abilities.

Self-Regulated Approach

A second stance toward instruction emphasizes self-regulated control of instructional strategies by the learner in accomplishing a complete, non-decomposed task. The teacher provides modeling of the metacognitive strategies necessary for beginning the task, and when problems are encountered, assistance is provided by the teacher or group. One learning procedure reflecting this stance, *reciprocal teaching*, structures collaborative group works in sharing a complex problem-solving task. This approach is based on learning theories about the social genesis of learning, in which the learner is characterized as being motivated to seek explanations through exploration.

The structured approach and the self-regulated approach share several underlying premises. One is that learning should be contextual and a process of active application of knowledge toward specific problem-solving goals. Second is the general agreement regarding the importance of modeling problem-solving strategies, as well as the role of conflict or failure in providing an impetus toward new learning. In contrast to the behaviorist view of the learner as shaped by the environment, instructional design researchers in the 21st century are investigating ways that the learner can actively shape the environment to facilitate learning.

TRANSITION FROM INSTRUCTIONAL THEORY TO INSTRUCTIONAL DEVELOPMENT MODEL

In this section, two examples of instructional theories are presented to illustrate the transition from learning theory to instructional design models. The two theories presented are the elaboration theory and the linking theory. These two instructional theories offer direct transitions between learning theory, instructional theory, and instructional development process and methodology. They are in fact cumulative theories that can be applied directly in the ID process.

Elaboration Theory

Elaboration theory (Reigeluth & Stein, 1983) is a theory of instructional design aimed at telling people how to teach rather than focusing on why and how people learn. It is concerned with the structure and organization of instructional material (stimuli) rather than the material itself. Elaboration theory is based on cognitive psychology and seeks to be consistent with cognitive theories of learning.

Two primary components of elaboration theory are: (a) that instruction should proceed from the general to the specific, referred to as *sequencing*; and (b) that each part should be related to the general context and to the other parts, referred to as *synthesizing*. The method for implementing the theory is to start with a general overview of the material, then divide it into parts and elaborate on each part. Each part is then further subdivided into smaller parts, which are elaborated, and those parts divided again, until the desired level of detail has been reached.

In the sequencing procedure, the concept of an *epitome* is used. An epitome is much like an advance organizer; that is, an epitome is a general and brief summary of the material to be learned, intended to provide a general context for the new information. The synthesizing procedure is intended to facilitate the integration of new information with existing knowledge and to form meaningful relationships in cognitive structure.

Linking Theory

The second example of an instructional theory that illustrates the transition from instructional theory to instructional development models is the *linking theory* first proposed by Tennyson and Rasch (1988). This theory directly links learning theory to educational goals, learning objectives, and instructional prescriptions. Additionally, it goes beyond any other instructional theory by attaching specific allocations of academic learning time to desired educational goals and objectives (Table 13.1). Tennyson and Rasch prescribed an instructional design theory that includes behavioral, cognitive, and contextual learning theories with appropriate instructional prescriptions. By allocating academic learning time across a range of learning objectives, they blend the structured and self-regulated philosophical approaches to learning. In the acquisition of knowledge, both structured and self-regulated strategies are employed. Although the goal is improving employment of knowledge, the authors specified both group and individual situations to help learners elaborate and extend their individual knowledge bases and cognitive processes.

In the following sections, two instructional design components are added to the Tennyson and Rasch linking model. These two additions are mode of instruction and learner assessment. The revised model is presented in Table 13.1. The six instructional design components of the linking theory form a matrix, crossing

TABLE 13.1
Linking Theory Educational Goals

Instructional Design Components	Educational Goals				
	Acquisition of Knowledge and Skills			Employment, Elaboration, and Construction of Knowledge, Skills, and Strategies	
Cognitive subsystem	Declarative knowledge	Procedural knowledge	Contextual knowledge	Differentiation/ integration	Construction
Learning objectives	Verbal/visual information	Intellectual skills	Contextual skills	Creativity skills/strategies	Creativity
Academic learning time	10%	20%	25%	30%	15%
Instructional prescriptions	Expository strategies	Practice strategies	Problem-oriented	Complex–dynamic strategies	Self-directed experiences strategies
Mode of instruction	Didactic	Tutorial	Artificial reality	Virtual reality	Experimental
Learner assessment	Objective	Performance	Authentic/ artificial	Authentic/ virtual	Portfolio

the educational goals of knowledge and skill acquisition with employment, elaboration, and construction of knowledge, skills, and strategies. The learning philosophy of the linking theory is embedded in these two educational goals, which emphasize the roles of the teacher, peer, and self in the learning process. Thus, this makes use of four basic concepts of a philosophy of learning (Tennyson, 2002). Nurture is highlighted by the design of the learning environment provided by the instructional designer. Planning is essential to the application of the linking theory. On the other hand, the self is primarily responsible for a large part of the learning process and management. This also includes the concept of nature as having a major effect on self-regulation aspects of learning. Society is an integral mode of instruction in those objections reflecting higher order cognitive activities in problem solving, decision making, and troubleshooting. Finally, learner assessment methods are directly linked to the other five instructional design components. Too often, learner assessment is reduced to only one or two forms, followed by attempting to generalize to other educational goals. The assumption in the revised linking theory is that assessment methods should reflect the type of learning that is occurring.

The linking theory emphasizes that learning involves three types of knowledge: (a) declarative, (b) procedural, and (c) contextual. Each type of knowledge requires a different instructional prescription. Selection of a given instructional prescription is based on an analysis of the content and learner need. The information analysis focuses on the context of the learning situation rather than a behavioral or features analysis. The instructional prescriptions are:

- *Expository* (context statement, label/definition, best example, matched/divergent examples, and worked examples).
- *Practice* (problem examples, feature elaboration, and feedback strategies).
- *Problem-oriented* (contextual modules—simulations, case studies, role playing—with cooperative learning).
- *Complex–dynamic* (situational units—complex simulations, case studies, role playing—with cooperative learning).
- *Self-directed experiences* (manipulative software, lab/field experiments, projects).

A key factor in implementing the educational goals of knowledge acquisition and employment in the Tennyson and Rasch instructional design theory is the allocation of academic learning time by defined learning objectives. For example, Tennyson and Rasch suggested that if improvements in problem solving and creativity are to occur, there needs to be a significant change in how instructional time is allocated. They recommended that the conventional instructional time allocation for learning be altered so that instead of 70% of instruction being aimed at the declarative and procedural knowledge levels of learning, 70% would be devoted to learning and thinking situations that involve acquisition of contextual knowledge and development of cognitive abilities of differentiation, integration, and construction.

Tennyson and Rasch (1988) recommended allocation of instructional prescriptions and academic learning time (ALT) according to the following learning objectives:

- Verbal/visual information. The learner is aware of meaning and understanding of declarative knowledge (e.g., facts, propositions, rules, principles, and concepts).
- Intellectual skills. The student is able to employ procedural knowledge with newly encountered situations and problems).
- Contextual skills. The learner is able to employ declarative and procedural knowledge in complex situations and problems.
- Cognitive skills/strategies. The learner is able to employ the cognitive complexity strategies of differentiation and integration in the service of dynamic situations and problems.
- Creativity. The learner is able to construct necessary knowledge in both predefined and self-defined situations and problems.

For the educational goal of knowledge acquisition (see Table 13.1), ALT is allocated among the three cognitive subsystems making up a knowledge base as follows: declarative knowledge 10%, procedure knowledge 20%, and contextual knowledge 25%. Tennyson and Rasch recommended that contextual knowledge ALT be about equal to the other two knowledge forms because of the necessity to both organize a knowledge base and develop cognitive skills necessary to access appropriate knowledge (i.e., the *why* as well as the *when* and *where*). They maintained that the value of a knowledge base is primarily in the functionality of its organization and accessibility. Without a sufficient base of contextual knowledge, the opportunity for employment, future elaboration, and extensions of the knowledge base is limited.

For the goal of knowledge and skill acquisition, the focus of ALT allocation is on contextual knowledge. This is in contrast to the usual practice in education of heavy emphasis on amount of knowledge acquired. As such, Tennyson and Rasch emphasized a context learning theory base that assumes that declarative and procedural knowledge acquisition is an interactive process that is improved when employing the knowledge base in the service of higher order thinking situations (i.e., problem solving and creativity). In their instructional design theory, time allocated for declarative and procedural knowledge focuses on establishing an initial base of necessary knowledge that can be used within a context of a problem situation. That is, learning time should include the opportunity for the learner to gain experience in employing, elaborating, and constructing knowledge, skills, and strategies.

The learning times presented in Table 13.1 do not imply a step-by-step sequence of knowledge acquisition going from declarative to contextual. Rather, they represent curricular times in an iterative learning environment where learners are continuously acquiring each form of knowledge. For example, students may engage in contextual knowledge acquisition prior to declarative knowledge acquisition if they currently have sufficient background knowledge (i.e., a problem-oriented strategy of instruction as contrasted to a structured method).

Teaching methods form the core of the mode of instruction instructional design component. In this application, the linking theory favors methods of instruction that are directly related to the desired learning objectives. Modes of instruction include a range of learning theories from behavioral to constructivism as follows:

- *Didactic* (structured form of delivery, e.g., lecture, books, print, video, etc.).
- *Tutorial* (structured form of delivery with high interactivity between learner and medium of instruction).
- *Artificial reality* (self-regulated forms of contextual situations).
- *Virtual reality* (self-regulation of the decision rules as in complex/dynamic simulations).
- *Experimental* (self-regulation of the learning tools and management of environment).

Learner assessment is an area of educational and psychological foundations that has seen much growth in the two last decades of the 20th Century. Research work in testing and measurement is tied to the range of developments in learning theory. Classical measurement theory is based in the behavioral tradition of observable behaviors and rigorous quantitative statistical methods. Cognitive psychology has led the search for more process related methods of assessment through item response theory and adaptive testing methods. More recently, the need to evaluate learner higher order cognitive activities that do not lend themselves to right or wrong answers, and that exhibit growth rather than just end of instruction performances, has seen developments in portfolio types of learning evidence. The linking theory includes the following types of learner assessments:

- *Objective* (standardized testing format with correct and incorrect answers).
- *Performance* (standardized format with range of outcomes from high to low).
- *Authentic/artificial* (standardized format in a contextual environment with a range of outcomes from known criteria).
- *Authentic/virtual* (open-ended format with criteria determined by the learner from normed validity).
- *Portfolio* (a collection of works, exhibitions, and experiences constructed by the learner; evaluation from learner defined validity).

SUMMARY OF DEVELOPMENTS AND TRENDS

Although building on earlier theories of learning, researchers working toward interactive technologies perceived limitations in earlier methods. By developing instructional theories that emphasize synthesis and integration of sets of knowledge and skills, researchers hope to address such limitations as:

- An emphasis on components instead of integrated wholes.

- A closed instructional system that makes incorporation of new knowledge difficult and that results in essentially passive instruction.
- The labor-intensive practice in design and development of instruction.

Future Trends in Instructional Theory

Human relations and resources will likely be a center of much instructional design progress in the coming years. Learner variables, for example, have already begun to play an important role in instructional theory, and the area of motivation promises to be of particular significance in the near future. The role of the instructor has again emerged as a topic of interest. Instructional design researchers are concluding that a major contributing factor inhibiting the acceptance of instructional design principles in the K–12 school system is the resistance of teachers. It will be necessary for instructional design advocates to address the issues of teacher involvement if they hope to implement their systems models in the K–12 educational domain. I look for future instructional systems development models to take into account the unique situation of teachers. For the most part, ISD models assume development of new materials, whereas teachers rarely if ever develop new materials. Rather, teachers with good foundation knowledge will adapt or adopt existing instructional materials. The employment of instructional theory for teachers would focus on how to evaluate the foundations of existing materials within a maintenance program.

Learner-Centered Approaches

I also expect that instructional designers will concentrate increasingly on developing instructional theories that are learner centered rather than technology centered. The shift of emphasis may, in the long run, improve the effectiveness of computer delivery systems (e.g., Internet applications in education) by allowing software to catch up with hardware and thereby improve application coordination. This trend does not, however, discount the importance of technological advances to the future of instructional design. Some areas of particular interest include increased development of automated ISD expert systems with extensive authoring capabilities to aid inexperienced developers; design of simulations that create low-risk environments for learners trying to acquire complex skills (Tennyson & Breuer, 1997); and emphasis on the level of interactivity between computers and learners (Seel & Winn, 1997).

Quantitative and Qualitative Research

It is likely that disciplined, quantitative and qualitative research methods will both play greatly increased roles in the future of instructional theory. Quantitative research, long linked with the behaviorist tradition, has been largely displaced by the more intuitive approach of the cognitive movement. Instructional designers are beginning to recognize that many aspects of the ISD methodology could profit by more rigorous research methods, whether they be quantitative or qualitative.

Metatheories

In general, I predict that the instructional design field will finally abandon the pursuit of a single, all-encompassing instructional theory and concentrate on establishing an interactive network of metatheories. Instructional designers, I believe, will increasingly choose to apply a particular learning and/or instructional theory only to those narrow learner outcomes toward which it works most effectively. The acquisition of a complex mental skill might, for example, include learning various subskills on the basis of several different learning theories. The result would be enhanced flexibility and increased efficiency. Instructional designers could then take the process a step further and alter each of the original models used on the basis of formative evaluation at the subskill level. These refinements hold great promise for fluid, complex instructional designs, but can only emerge from a spirit of balance and increased cooperation among instructional designers in both academic and applied environments.

Recommendations

I conclude this section on developments and trends in learning theories and instructional design by offering several recommendations for preparation of a personal (i.e., individual instructional designer or organization) instructional theory that would compliment a written educational learning philosophy and theory statements. These recommendations include the following:

- Instructional theory should be usable. It should be stated with enough clarity to allow successful implementation.
- Instructional theory should be valid. It should have evidence of empirical testing and practical evaluation.
- Instructional theory should be theoretical. It needs to explain theoretically how a particular instructional procedure works.
- Instructional theory should be linked to learning theory. It must use the wealth of research in learning and cognition.

CONCLUSION

A fundamental improvement offered by learning theory is the explicit placement of educational foundations into the methodology of instructional systems development. There are two reasons for this overt action. First, ISD was founded during a period in which American behaviorist philosophy and learning theory was the dominant foundational force in education. Most educational practices and methods were by default thought to be founded in behaviorism. That is, practices and methods of classroom teaching and instruction assumed to have an underlying behavioral nature whether or not they did or not. What developed in the absence of a strong commitment to defining a philosophy for educational practice was the growing acceptance of fads as the solutions to learning problems in American schools. Tracing a new method or practice to a well-defined philosophy or even learning theory was dropped as part of the educational process. Much of the blame for ills in American education continue to be placed ironically on the last (and perhaps only) large-scale educational philosophy defined in this country. That philosophy was developed in the 1930s at the prestigious schools of education at Teachers College, Columbia University and at the University of Chicago. What was known as the *progressive movement* profoundly changed both American curricula and classroom instructional methods. The paradox is that most schools today do not resemble in any way the progressive philosophy. However, the scientific method of linking learning theory with instructional design, which is in turn confirmed by research before employment, continues to be ignored in educational practice.

Instructional design models continued the usual educational practice of adopting methods of doing without concern for learning foundations. It is not surprising that early instructional design theory assumed the prevalent learning theory at their time of conception. Later, instructional designers, in piecemeal fashion, adopted the new fads associated with cognitive psychology. Likewise, the fads currently circulating with constructivism seem to suggest that a systemic change in the process of education is needed. The fad nature of constructivism is to view instructional design as only capable of performing behavioral actions. However, the problem with instructional development continues to be the lack of a means of defining a philosophy and learning theory by which the instructional design methodology can be driven.

REFERENCES

Ausubel, D. P. (1969). A cognitive theory of school learning. *Psychology in the Schools, 6,* 331–335.
Breuer, K., & Kummer, R. (1990). Cognitive effects from process learning with computer-based simulations. *Computers in Human Behavior, 6,* 69–81.
Brown, J. S., Collins, A., & Duguid, P. (1989). Situated cognition and the culture of learning. *Educational Researcher, 18,* 32–42.
Bruner, J. S. (1964). *Study of thinking.* New York: Wiley.
Carroll, J. B. (1993). *Human cognitive abilities.* New York: Cambridge University Press.
Dewey, J. (1910). *How we think.* Boston: D. C. Heath.
Dick, W. (1997). A model for the systematic design of instruction. In R. D. Tennyson, F. Schott, N. Seel, & S. Dijkstra (Eds.), *Instructional design: International perspectives, Vol. I: Theory and research* (pp. 361–370). Mahwah, NJ: Lawrence Erlbaum Associates.
Finn, J. D. (1957). Automation and education: General aspects. *AV Communications Review, 5,* 343–360.
Gagné, R. M. (1962). Military training and principles of learning. *American Psychologist, 17,* 83–91.

Gagné, R. M., & Briggs, L. J. (1979). *Principles of instructional design* (2nd ed.). New York: Holt, Rinehart, & Winston.

Mager, R. (1962). *Instructional behavioral objectives.* San Francisco: Fearon Press.

Markle, S. M. (1969). *Good frames and bad: A grammar of frame writing* (2nd ed.). New York: John Wiley and Sons.

Merrill, M. D. (1997). Instructional transaction theory: An instructional design model based on knowledge objects. In R. D. Tennyson, F. Schott, N. Seel, & S. Dijkstra (Eds.), *Instructional design: International perspectives, Vol. I: Theory and research* (pp. 215–241). Mahwah, NJ: Lawrence Erlbaum Associates.

Merrill, M. D., Li, Z., & Jones, M. K. (1990). Limitations of first generation instructional design. *Educational Technology, 30*(1), 7–11.

Reigeluth, C. M., & Stein, F. S. (1983). The elaboration theory of instruction. In C. M. Reigeluth (Ed.), *Instructional-design theories and models: An overview of their current status* (pp. 335–381). Hillsdale, NJ: Lawrence Erlbaum Associates.

Scandura, J. M. (1970). The role of rules in behavior: Toward an operational definition of what (rule) is learned. *Psychological Review, 77,* 516–533.

Scandura, J. M. (2001). Structural learning theory: Current status and recent developments. *Instructional Science, 29*(4), 311–336.

Schott, F., & Driscoll, M. P. (1997). On the architechtonics of instructional theory. In R. D. Tennyson, F. Schott, N. Seel, & S. Dijkstra (Eds.), *Instructional design: International perspectives, Vol. I: Theory and research* (pp. 135–173). Mahwah, NJ: Lawrence Erlbaum Associates.

Seel, N., & Winn, W. D. (1997). Research on media and learning: Distributed cognition and semiotics. In R. D. Tennyson, F. Schott, N. Seel, & S. Dijkstra (Eds.), *Instructional design: International perspectives, Vol. I: Theory and research* (pp. 293–326). Mahwah, NJ: Lawrence Erlbaum Associates.

Skinner, B. F. (1954). The science of learning and the art of teaching. *Harvard Educational Review, 24,* 86–97.

Smith, W. I., & Moore, J. W. (Eds.). (1962). *Programmed learning.* Princeton, NJ: Van Nostrand.

Snow, R. E. (1997). Individual differences. In R. D. Tennyson, F. Schott, N. Seel, & S. Dijkstra (Eds.), *Instructional design: International perspectives, Vol. I: Theory and research* (pp. 215–241). Mahwah, NJ: Lawrence Erlbaum Associates.

Tennyson, R. D. (2002). Linking learning theories to instructional design, *Educational Technology, 42*(3), 51–55.

Tennyson, R. D., & Breuer, K. (1997). Psychological foundations for instructional design theory. In R. D. Tennyson, F. Schott, N. Seel, & S. Dijkstra (Eds.), *Instructional design: International perspectives, Vol. I: Theory and research* (pp. 113–133). Hillsdale, NJ: Lawrence Erlbaum Associates.

Tennyson, R. D., &. Elmore, R. L. (1997). Learning theory foundations for instructional design. In R. D. Tennyson, F. Schott, N. Seel, & S. Dijkstra (Eds.), *Instructional design: International perspectives, Vol. I: Theory and research* (pp. 55–78). Mahwah, NJ: Lawrence Erlbaum Associates.

Tennyson, R. D., & Rasch, M. (1988). Linking cognitive learning theory to instructional prescriptions. *Instructional Science, 17,* 369–385.

Thorndike, E. (1913). *The psychology of learning: Educational psychology* (Vol. 2). New York: Teachers College Press.

Winn, W. D. (1993). A constructivist critique of the assumptions of instructional design. In T. M. Duffy, J. Lowyck, & D. H. Jonassen (Eds.), *Designing environments for constructive learning* (pp. 213–234). Berlin: Springer.

Chapter
14

Foundations for Instructional Design: Reclaiming the Conversation

Brent G. Wilson
University of Colorado at Denver

Three or four years ago, David Merrill told me he wrote his now-classic manifesto *Reclaiming Instructional Design* (Merrill, Drake, Lacy, Pratt, & the ID_2 Research Group, 1996) in direct response to a lunchtime conversation we had enjoyed together at an American Educational Research Association (AERA) meeting. By his report, I had been looking for another name to call myself—perhaps the *instructional* part of instructional design felt too limiting at the time. Merrill and colleagues described a science of instruction and a technology of instructional design (ID).

> Many persons associated with educational technology today are engaged in a flight from science. Instruction is a scientific field and instructional design is a technology founded in this science. Instructional design is not merely philosophy; it is not a set of procedures arrived at by collaboration; it is a set of scientific principles and a technology for implementing these principles in the development of instructional experiences and environments.... Those persons who claim that knowledge is founded on collaboration rather than empirical science, or who claim that all truth is relative, are not instructional designers. (Merrill et al., 1996, p. 5)

Although I had earlier written a paper partly in response (Wilson, 1997), I had no idea that Merrill's spirited charge had been largely targeted, at least originally, at me. I do not consider myself anti-science, but I believe ID need not be narrowly framed in strictly scientific terms. In this chapter, I continue the conversation about ID's foundations by exploring some ways to think more liberally about its practice. This contribution is not a point-by-point response to Merrill's paper, but covers much of the same ground from a different perspective. My hope is to work toward a conception of ID practice that is inclusive of different perspectives while preserving a coherent identity through shared concerns and purposes.

ID AS PRACTICE

The practice of instructional design has been defined as a science, a technology, a craft, and even an art (e.g., Davies, 1991; Glaser, 1965; Lumsdaine, 1964; Melton, 1959; Merrill et al., 1996; Reigeluth, Bunderson, & Merrill, 1978; Skinner, 1954; for additional definitions see Ryder, 2003a). What instructional designers *do*, in essence, is design instruction and related resources that meet learning needs for defined audiences and settings. This includes tasks of management, implementation, and evaluation—all in the service of designing and delivering good instruction.[1]

From the earliest days of Thorndike (1913) and Skinner (1954) to Gagné (1962) and Glaser (1964), instructional design has been offered in direct response to challenging problems of practice facing the education and training professions. Thus, instructional design can be best understood within a context of reform, that is, working to improve how instruction gets designed and delivered, applying the best available principles of learning and instruction so that learners do not have to suffer through the excruciatingly bad practices that define the period. Although to some extent ID theories reflect that period and its practices, they are also intended to be a stimulus to reform and improved practice.

Instructional design's origins, even present practices, relate closely to the fields of instructional technology and educational psychology (Dick, 1978, 1987; Reiser, 1987, 2001). ID has grown up, however, without a single enduring professional home. The only professional organization I am aware of that includes the specific words "instructional design" is Professors of Instructional Design and Technology (PIDT), a group of about 100 professors who have met annually with their doctoral students for nearly two decades. Other American-based organizations for instructional designers include the Association for Educational Communications and Technology (AECT) and the International Society for Performance Improvement (ISPI). In 1977, AECT and ISPI formed a joint task force to establish

---

[1] I use the term *good* intentionally. Good instruction goes beyond effective, which I take to mean accomplishing one's goals, because technologies inevitably entail unintended consequences. It goes beyond efficiency or productivity, although these are important considerations. The goodness of instruction should be judged by considering the total systemic impact, short-term and long-term, including moral and ethical impacts, as I suggest further in the chapter.

professional competencies for instructional designers, leading in 1984 to the independent incorporation of the International Board of Standards for Training, Performance and Instruction (IBSTPI; see Richey, Fields, & Foxon, 2001, for current ID competencies). Both AECT and ISPI have played important roles in the historical development of instructional design (Reiser & Ely, 1997; Rosenberg, 1982; Rosenberg, Coscarelli, & Hutchison, 1992; see also Dean & Ripley, 1998).

How ID Gets Done

Through professional organizations, conferences, journals, books, Web sites, and various other tools, the current ID community helps designers be more effective in their work by:

- Promoting practice that meets a professional standard, including the education of new designers in graduate programs.
- Developing promising and useful models, theories, and procedures, based on experience, direct research, or often derived from related disciplines.
- Advancing usable knowledge through the sharing of professional experience, codified into stories, cases, listserv exchanges, and conference presentations.
- Further advancing knowledge by refereed reports of systematic inquiry around models, theories, procedures, and practices, to test their validity, effectiveness, and range of use.

Although most instructional designers can substantially agree on the general aims of practice, the *how* question is more controversial. In some ways, ID practice can be seen as a *technology*—applying known techniques and procedures to yield defined outcomes (Gibbons, 2003). Like engineers, architects, or computer programmers, designers develop systems that meet objectives within the constraints of a given situation. Also in common with these design professionals, instructional designers rely on more than just established technique to solve problems. Outstanding practitioners of ID must demonstrate high levels of creativity, general knowledge, wisdom from past experience, and ability to adapt to location conditions. I tend to think of ID expertise as a *craft* (cf. Osguthorpe, Osguthorpe, Jacob, & Davies, 2003). Craft knowledge is practical knowledge owned and transmitted within a community about how to design and make things. That knowledge is partially encoded in published models, theories, techniques, and rules, but another part remains tacit within the community's culture, transmitted by shared work experience, stories, mentoring, and apprenticeships (Hung, 1999; Polanyi, 1958).

Two core ideas permeate thinking and theorizing in instructional design: conditions-of-learning theories of instruction, and a systems approach to instruction and instructional development. These central ideas affect how ID gets done in real life. Each is discussed in the following subsections.

Conditions-of-Learning Theories

In the days of programmed instruction, researchers held to a few general principles of learning, based on behavioral psychology, which were thought to apply universally to all settings and organisms. Results of programmed-instruction research, however, showed that some strategies worked better than others, depending on conditions. This led Lumsdaine (1964) and others to articulate a vision for an emerging science of instruction: Through factorial experiments, instructional scientists would develop a sophisticated series of rules, subrules, and metarules for employing instructional strategies to teach different kinds of content in different settings. This idea of a rule set that links conditions, instructional methods, and learning outcomes was promoted and refined by other theorists such as Gagné (1965), Bruner (1966), and Reigeluth (1983) as a defining feature of instructional theories. These prescriptive theories could be considered technologies in their function as tools for designers of lessons and courses.

The publication in 1965 of Robert Gagné's *Conditions of Learning* was a seminal event in the history of instructional design. Since then, ID theorists have taken for granted the conditional nature of design prescriptions offered for various kinds of learning outcomes. The conditions-of-learning framework continues to guide theory development and professional practice (Ragan & Smith, 1996). However, a few questions, presented next, still remain concerning the nature of prescriptive theories of instruction.

What Is Their Ontological Status?   Typically, scientific theories include principles describing how the world is—the way things are. These are formulated in a particular way to allow explanations or precise understandings about mechanisms, dynamics, processes, and so on. Theories of instruction contain a similar descriptive element. For example, Gagné (1965) presented a typology of different learning outcomes, ordered from simple to complex. Attainment of these learning outcomes may be observed in the world. However, the heart of instructional theory is not in the description of outcomes, but rather in the *prescriptive* linking between outcomes and related conditions. Here the ontological status of the rules becomes less clear. We are moving beyond descriptions to guidelines, or rules for action. The link to traditional science is often quite indirect (Simon, 1996), but the link to observed practices is equally obscure (Wedman & Tessmer, 1993). In other words, prescriptive theories of instruction lie in a space between descriptions of the world and direct guidelines for practitioners.

How Are They Validated?   Descriptive claims about the world can be tested by systematic observation. Prescriptive rules of design are not so easily or directly validated. Design prescriptions may be grounded directly in a scientific theory, as is the case with Ausubel's (1963) strategy of advance organizers and its link to his theory of meaningful learning; or the design rules may be tested themselves (providing advance organizers and experimentally observing their effects). Challenges occur when testing prescriptions due to the many forms and contexts of practice. If an advance organizer fails to teach, it may be that the particular organizer was poorly written or that it was not appropriate for the particular situation in which it was used. Maybe it was not a proper advance organizer after all. Many contingencies exist in practice, making direct empirical validation of general instructional design prescriptions very difficult.

Because of this fuzzy link between the idealized design prescription and what really happens in practice, we may need to look beyond the traditional method–conditions–outcomes model (Reigeluth, 1983) to account for learning outcomes. That is to say, it is *what happens* during instruction that mediates learning, not what theory was applied or what design heuristic was supposedly followed. The details of interaction and activity—the *experienced* instruction rather than the *designed* instruction—are so often what make the difference between good and bad instruction (see Feyerabend, 1975; Palmer, 1997; Ryder, 2003b).

Are They for People or Machines?   People routinely look for guides to action in the form of conceptual models, rules of thumb, mnemonics, recipes, and so on. Often, guidelines for action can be directly designed into a tool or automated machine, as in the affordances of a saw or hammer, a tax form, or an online interactive program. Some instructional prescriptions seem clearly intended for designers to keep in mind as they approach design problems, such as using the rule–example–practice model for tutorial design or following Gagné's (1985) nine events of instruction in lesson design. The prescription is simple enough to hold in working memory and serves as a heuristic or template for developing a lesson. Other formulations of instructional theory, however, are so technically defined and presented that intentions for use are unclear. Diagrams can be overburdened with hard-to-read detail; jargon can be far removed from normal discourse. Although such technical models may serve as blueprints or specifications that could be programmed into automated instruction, their use by practicing designers on everyday projects is problematic.

In spite of these concerns, heuristics, or guidelines for design, are essential. The challenge is how to formulate them in a way that is useful in practice. This requires that design prescriptions be sensitive to the complexity of real-life conditions of use.

Systems Thinking

The second core idea, thinking systemically about instruction—seeing learners, teachers, content, and so on as components in a larger system—has a surprisingly long history in education (Banathy, 1968; Finn, 1956; Lumsdaine, 1960; Merrill, 1968). By combining behavioral principles of learning, information-processing principles of message and content, and systems principles of interactivity and interdependence, early instructional theorists established a frame for viewing instruction as a system that could be designed, measured, and optimized. Instruction was seen as more than what the teacher did, but rather as the complex interaction between participants within a larger systemic context. The discourse could also be quite progressive, with advocacy for learner control, conversation, and open systems (e.g., Merrill, 1975; Pask, 1975; Silber, 1972; Winn, 1975). In the last decade, systems theory has enjoyed a resurgence due largely to advances in complexity theory and self-organizing systems (Kelly, 1994; Senge, 1990), with continuing implications for instructional design (e.g., Carr, 1997; Land, 2000; Milrad, Spector, & Davidsen, 2002; Spector, 2000; Spector & Anderson, 2000; Wilson & Ryder, 1996).

A systems model of instructional development (ISD) has been used and taught for more than forty years among instructional designers (Gustafson & Branch, 1997). Many think of ISD as being a core model defining the field. However, I am not aware of a solid body of research empirically demonstrating its advantage over other curriculum-development models (see Hannafin, 1983a, 1983b, and Sullivan, Ice, & Niedermeyer, 2000, as examples of work in this direction). Of course, scientific testing of comprehensive procedures is very difficult, but I also take the lack of research as a sign of the model's axiomatic status within the field. ISD's enduring value lies, I believe, in its embodiment of rational-planning principles and in its cohering role in defining the instructional technology community. The ISD model provides practical value partly by providing management controls, such as decomposing a complex process into parts with deadlines, reviews, and signoffs. Another major strength is that ISD models ensure a logical consistency between learning goals, activities, and assessments. This is hard to argue with, unless somehow in the process an intangible part of instruction—a valued goal, experience, or outcome—is lost as things are documented and codified (Bunderson, Gibbons, Olsen, & Kearsley, 1981). This problem seems avoidable if designers are careful to leave room for unanalyzed or unidentified elements in holistic learning experiences. Instruction that is highly compartmentalized and controlled may be more vulnerable to reductive loss because it relies more on analyzed and predefined content.

ALTERNATIVES TO ISD

After many years of relying almost exclusively on ISD models, more theorists are acknowledging alternatives to the objectives-based efficiency model of curriculum (cf. Kliebard, 1987, for alternatives to Tyler's 1949 objectives-driven curriculum model). One team of theorists (Nieveen & Gustafson, 1999; van den Akker, Branch, Gustafson, Nieveen, & Plomp, 1999; Visscher-Voerman, Gustafson, & Plomp, 1999) called attention to four different *paradigms* (or perhaps aspects) of instructional development:

- Instrumental—linear procedures based on needs and objectives established at the outset; proceeding rationally through development and implementation.

- Pragmatic—continual evaluation and feedback mechanisms within the process, ensuring useful and effective instructional outcomes.
- Communicative—including stakeholders in establishing needs and goals; consensus building and inclusion of diverse perspectives throughout the development process.
- Artistic—such as Eisner's (1979) connoisseurship model of curriculum, relying on the judgment of professionals (teachers) through a process of criticism and reflection.

In Table 14.1, I have collapsed these four approaches into two, while trying to maintain the gist of the original work.

Of course, the two paradigms need not be positions in strict opposition to one another. Most practicing instructional designers identify professionally with the ISD paradigm just described, but I would guess many also employ consen-

TABLE 14.1
Contrasting Paradigms for the Practice of Instructional Design

	A product is good if ...	A design process is good if ...
ISD paradigm: objectives-based design with empirical validation	• It meets a prespecified standard, for example, adheres to an established instructional theory.	• It starts with analysis of needs and goals, and builds systematically and rationally toward a proven instructional solution.
	• It has been proven through cycles of empirical tryout to be useful and effective for users.	• Evaluation activities are fully integrated, including regular prototype testing for usefulness and effectiveness.
Consensual paradigm: reaching consensus through inclusion and critical sharing	• It satisfies the expectations and requirements of the design team and other stakeholders and withstands scrutiny by critical voices from diverse perspectives.	• It results from activities aimed at full participation of stakeholders, leading to consensus about the learning need and the solution; based on democratic values and full inclusion of diverse perspectives.
	• It meets the professional quality criteria of developers and implementers.	

Note.   Information gathered from Visscher-Voerman, Gustafson, and Plomp (1999).

sus-building strategies in much of their work. Curriculum developers outside the ID community often start from consensus-building assumptions, then apply ISD principles to really get the work done once a level of consensus has been achieved.

The emphasis of ISD is focused on efficient and reliable development of products. Consensual approaches do a better job acknowledging the multiple interests, values, and goals in establishing curriculum and on their inclusion in the process. It seems understandable, then, that an ISD emphasis would tend to flourish in training environments where learning goals are often defined in technical terms, whereas a consensual emphasis may work better in nontechnical forms of education, including management education and much K–12 education, where experts and constituencies often disagree. As public education adopts a more technology-centered stance toward curriculum and assessment, with high-stakes testing aligned with standards-based instruction, ISD might be expected to gain in influence (Wilson, 2002).

When seen juxtaposed with other paradigms, the implicit values attending ISD become more apparent. Drawing on earlier work of Nunan (1983), Rose (2002) challenged ISD's pretense as an objective, value-neutral process:

> Instructional design's ideology ... is that it has no ideology.... Allying itself with [a] scientific worldview, instructional design has purported from the beginning to be a value-free mode of instructional development which transcends in effectiveness and efficiency—the only standards it acknowledges—other, more "primitive" approaches to education.... Claiming neutrality is thus a way of asserting superiority. (p. 16)

Unannounced values often accompanying ID practice are carried through an array of questionable assumptions, including:

- Experts if they really are experts—should agree with each other.
- Getting content out of subject experts is an unproblematic extraction procedure.
- Designers can design excellent instruction in content areas they really don't know well.
- Knowledge can be explicitly documented, codified, and transferred through explicit lessons and materials, in the form of clearly defined rules, concepts, and procedures.
- People process information similarly across situations and content areas.
- Novices need high levels of structure and guidance; more experienced learners can be trusted with self-directed activities.
- People of all skill levels benefit from essentially the same well-designed instruction.
- Learners' special needs and cultural backgrounds are nice to know but not essential in designing instruction that works.
- Instructional materials mean what they say; there is no hidden curriculum.
- Instruction not developed systematically is not to be trusted.

• Teachers and instructors are not to be trusted to adapt or modify lessons and strategies.

These implicit values and assumptions are expressed in stark terms that thoughtful ISD followers would disavow. Even so, I believe that daily practice often proceeds with some combination of these values operational—all the more reason to adopt a more critical stance, to avoid negative values and assumptions that might accrue to the process.

Of course, rather than choosing paradigms, designers may choose to keep in mind the values and concerns of both technical and consensual approaches, and even modify procedures to include both. I participate in a research team that has developed a four-level scheme for doing instructional design that combines ideas from social science and the humanities, whose approaches to design can be very different (IDEAL Lab, 2003; see Table 14.2). The four-level scheme outlined next could fit within either ISD or consensual approaches to instructional development.

TABLE 14.2

Levels of Instructional Design, Including Concepts from Learning Theory, Social Learning, Critical Theory, and Aesthetic Design Principles

	Brief Description	Example Terms and Strategies	Sample References
Individual cognition and behavior	Information-processing and behavioral learning theories	Tutorial strategies Practice with feedback Worked examples Cognitive load	Reigeluth (1983) Sweller (1989) Mayer (1997)
Social and cultural learning	Social and group dynamics; situated learning; participation and identity; mediation of culture and language	Learning communities Constructivist learning environments Cognitive apprenticeship	Lave and Wenger (1991) Collins, Brown, and Newman (1989) Wertsch (1998)
Values	Critical and reflective approaches to social justice, morality, equity, and social change	Privilege Voice Power Diversity	Flood and Romm (1996) Bromley and Apple (1998)
Aesthetics	Principles of aesthetic form and structure; aesthetic considerations in design	Narrative Dramatic Tension Balance Beauty	Laurel (1991) Davies (1991) Johnston (1999)

Individual Cognition and Behavior.   The first level of concern is the individual learner's thinking and acquisition of knowledge and skill. The designer considers how lessons and strategies fit with existing theories of learning and cognition. Questions for design include: Do learning activities help the learner acquire new conceptual understanding and procedural skills in an efficient and effective way? Is the cognitive load kept manageable?

Social and Cultural Learning.   The next level turns to issues of cultural context and social support, including peer-to-peer interactions; group identity and motivation; and participation within communities of learning and practice. Questions for design include: Are learners given opportunities for social interaction, collegial support, and inclusion in meaningful practices? Are learners supported as they come to see themselves (and relate to others) in new ways?

Values.   Critical theorists focus on questions of justice, asking questions of instruction like: In addition to the stated objectives, what is this lesson really saying? What is *not* said that reveals something about the values of the people involved? Where is the power? Who is the lesson designed for, and who is left out? How, and on whom, is status granted? What kinds of practices does the lesson encourage or perpetuate? What alignment is there between stated institutional values and observed instructional materials? Questions like these are not usually built into ISD models, although they should come up in consensual development processes.

Aesthetics.   Finally, through an aesthetic layer of analysis, designers ask questions about the shape and form of the learning experience, as well as the design of messages within the experience. Aesthetic considerations might lead to offering learners an adventure by adopting a dramatic journey metaphor to a curriculum, or to a certain pattern of introducing, heightening, and resolving tensions within a lesson. Questions for design include: Is the learning experience satisfying? Is it cathartic? Is there sufficient tension and movement to hold learners' interest? Are the timing and pacing designed to help learners identify with and participate in the experience?

The first two levels come from the social sciences—psychology and anthropology in particular. Indeed, most research in instructional design and technology relies heavily on this social science disciplinary base. The latter two levels are less common; in critical-theory terms, they are less privileged. Like so many other fields, ID places more value on science than on other perspectives, even though, ironically, science is not in a position to define value. Our research team believes the issues raised in the bottom two levels should be integrated into established design practices; in other words, we believe the technical ISD procedures can be revised to include a broader range of concerns when establishing needs, standards, and criteria for success. The four levels reflect more than an expanded view of learning outcomes (e.g., Anderson & Krathwohl, 2001). We are suggesting an expanded view of design processes themselves and criteria for evaluating designed products.

ACHIEVING COHERENCE AMID FORCES OF FRAGMENTATION

Today most academic programs in instructional technology rely, at least implicitly, on a common knowledge base of instructional theories as a curriculum foundation, along with a systems metaphor for instruction and a systems model for developing instructional materials. True to these general models, most departments serve multiple settings; that is, graduates may work in school settings, higher education, business, industry, government, and so on. They may apply ID principles in the classroom, workplace, or online. Regardless of medium or setting, the principles of instructional design are still thought to be generally applicable.

The forces pulling against this general approach to ID practice are formidable, however. For a generation, instructional design has been more positively received in training settings than K–12 schools, leading to higher status for adult-learning settings such as universities and business workplaces.[2] Many academic programs divide students into different tracks according to work setting—for example, K–12 schools versus adult learning settings. Although a challenge to coherence, this seems more consistent with theories of situated learning, which would favor setting-specific practices over general theories.

The changing landscape of ideas is another threat to coherence. The number of competing educational paradigms continues to grow. Most of these paradigms claim to be scientific, yet their notions of science differ dramatically. Designers must choose now from among an increasing array of theories of learning and instruction. Foundations of ID practice, conditions-of-learning and systems thinking, have been examined, critiqued, and deconstructed. Although these foundations have proven impressively resilient, the coherence afforded to an earlier generation seems unavailable to current practitioners and theorists.

Current theorists tend to think about professional knowledge in new ways. Rather than a vast rule base of contingent generalizations, professional knowledge is now seen as more pluralistic: Explicit textbook knowledge complements the tacit knowledge held by practitioners, comprised of skills and understand-

---

[2] Trainers in corporate and military settings have long valued ISD's practical qualities. Recently, the surging interest in educational standards and data-driven assessment signals a shift in American schools that may lead to renewed interest in instructional-design concepts. Schools in many other countries have a centralized curriculum that makes instructional-design models much more relevant and meaningful.

ings developed in the context of everyday practice and shared informally within workgroups and professional meetings. Moreover, the clear emergence of competing paradigms, coexisting together in time, argues for an eclectic, opportunistic stance toward the various theories and models available in the literature. Instead of a single huge rule set, researchers and practitioners alike prefer to think of a somewhat messy toolbox from which a particular model or theory or technique may be chosen, according to the demands of the situation. As Rorty (2000) observed, academic discourse is often a matter of redescription rather than logical argument from shared premises of fixed meanings. Designers can try out lenses of different models or paradigms, and redescribe a given situation many times. This ability to see things through multiple perspectives can serve designers well as they try to fit a number of elements together into a working system, but it comes at a cost to coherence.

We observe, then, some contradiction in our professional identities. Hopes for an integrative foundation—in learning theories, systems theories, learning technologies, and prescriptive principles of instruction—seem at odds with the proliferation of competing perspectives, each carrying a different set of tools, terms, and models. Each perspective serves a somewhat distinct professional subcommunity, discernible by the cliquish clustering of reference lists at the ends of articles. We want to identify with a coherent professional community, but finding the ties that bind can be an elusive task.

As a response to the threat of fragmentation, I return to the enduring aims of instructional design presented at the outset. The field of instructional design is largely defined by the challenges we choose to tackle, which at the most general level are how to design and deliver good learning experiences for learners in a variety of contexts and, secondarily, how to best use various technologies in the service of that learning. The practical problem is the mediocre quality of instruction. The response is instructional design. As Richey (1998) noted, agreeing on the details of formulating a problem requires some degree of shared ideology, but that is precisely where we agree—on the general nature and importance of these problems. Then from that base, competing theories and perspectives enter the dialogue. As researchers and practitioners grapple with problems of practice, they are led to countering explanations and theories, leading to redescriptions of problems and proposed solutions. As so many have argued, the interplay between theory and practice is a dialogue, which is the healthiest possible condition for a field, even in the face of proliferating perspectives. Cutting short that dialogue would be a mistake. Keeping our eye on the end goal, improving instruction, should be enough to hold us together as a community of professionals.

REFERENCES

Anderson, L. W., & Krathwohl, D. R. (Eds.). (2001). *A taxonomy for learning, teaching, and assessing: A revision of Bloom's Taxonomy of Educational Objectives.* New York: Longman.

Ausubel, D. (1963). *The psychology of meaningful verbal learning*. New York: Grune & Stratton.

Banathy, B. H. (1968). *Instructional systems*. Belmont CA: Fearon.

Bromley, H., & Apple, M. W. (1998). *Education/technology/power: Educational computing as a social practice*. Albany: SUNY Press.

Bruner, J. S. (1966). *Toward a theory of instruction*. New York: Norton.

Bunderson, C. V., Gibbons, A. S., Olsen, J. B., & Kearsley, G. P. (1981). Work models: Beyond instructional objectives. *Instructional Science, 10*, 205–215.

Carr, A. A. (1997). User-design in the creation of human learning systems. *Educational Technology Research & Development, 45*(3), 5–22.

Collins, A., Brown, J. S., & Newman, S. E. (1989). Cognitive apprenticeship: Teaching the crafts of reading, writing, and mathematics. In L. B. Resnick (Ed.), *Knowing, learning, and instruction: Essays in honor of Robert Glaser* (pp. 453–494). Hillsdale, NJ: Lawrence Erlbaum Associates.

Davies, I. K. (1991). Instructional development as an art: One of the three faces of ID. In D. Hlynka & J. C. Belland (Eds.), *Paradigms regained: The uses of illuminative, semiotic and post-modern criticism as modes of inquiry in education technology* (pp. 93–105). Englewood Cliffs, NJ: Educational Technology Publications.

Dean, P., & Ripley, D. (1998). *Performance improvement interventions: Instructional design and training. Vol. 2*. Washington, DC: International Society for Performance Improvement.

Dick, W. (1978). The educational psychologist as instructional designer. *Contemporary Educational Psychology, 3*, 265–271.

Dick, W. (1987). A history of instructional design and its impact on educational psychology. In J. A. Glover & R. R. Ronning (Eds.), *Historical foundations of educational psychology* (pp. 183–200). New York: Plenum Press.

Eisner, E. W. (1979). *The educational imagination: On the design and evaluation of school programs*. New York: Macmillan.

Feyerabend, P. (1975). *Against method: The outline of an anarchistic theory of knowledge*. London: NLB.

Finn, J. D. (1956). AV development and the concept of systems. *Teaching Tools, 3*(1), 63–64. [Cited in Dick (1987)].

Flood, R. L., & Romm, N. R. (1996). *Critical systems thinking: Current research and practice*. New York: Plenum Press.

Gagné, R. (1962). Military training and principles of learning. *American Psychologist, 17*, 263–276.

Gagné, R. M. (1965). *The conditions of learning*. New York: Holt, Rinehart & Winston.

Gagné, R. M. (1985). *The conditions of learning* (4th ed.). New York: Holt, Rinehart & Winston .

Gibbons, A. S. (2003). The practice of instructional technology: Science and technology. *Educational Technology, 43*(5), 11–16.

Glaser, R. (1964). Implications of training research for education. In E. R. Hilgard (Ed.), *Theories of learning and instruction* (pp. 153–181). Sixty-third Yearbook of the National Society for the Study of Education, Part I. Chicago: University of Chicago Press.

Glaser, R. (1965). Toward a behavioral science base for instructional design. In R. Glaser (Ed.), *Teaching machines and programmed learning, II* (pp. 000–000). Washington, DC: National Education Association.

Gustafson, K. L., & Branch, R. M. (1997). *Survey of instructional development models* (3rd ed.). Syracuse NY: ERIC Clearinghouse on Information and Technology.

Hannafin, M. J. (1983a). Immediate, sustained, and cumulative effects of an instructional system on mathematics achievement. *Journal of Educational Research, 77*, 89–93.

Hannafin, M. J. (1983b). Fruits and fallacies of instructional systems: Effects of an instructional systems approach on the concept attainment of Anglo and Hispanic students. *American Educational Research Journal, 20*, 237–250.

Hung, D. W. L. (1999). Activity, apprenticeship, and epistemological appropriation: Implications from the writings of Michel Polanyi. *Educational Psychologist, 34*(4), 193–205.

IDEAL Lab. (2003). *IDEAL Lab website*. Retrieved October 15, 2003, from http://www.cudenver.edu/ilt/IDEAL

Johnston, V. S. (1999). *Why we feel*. Cambridge, MA: Perseus Books.

Kelly, K. (1994). *Out of control: The new biology of machines, social systems, and the economic world*. Reading MA: Addison-Wesley.

Kliebard, H. M. (1987). *The struggle for the American curriculum 1893–1958*. New York: Routledge.

Land, S. M. (2000). Cognitive requirements for learning with open-ended learning environments. *Educational Technology Research and Development, 48*(3), 61–78.

Laurel, B. (1991). *Computers as theatre*. Reading MA: Addison-Wesley.

Lave, J., & Wenger, E. (1991). *Situated learning: Legitimate peripheral participation*. New York: Cambridge University Press.

Lumsdaine, A. A. (1960). Design of training aids and devices. In *Human factors methods for system design* (pp. 217–290). Pittsburgh: American Institute for Research.

Lumsdaine, A. A. (1964). Educational technology, programmed learning, and instructional science. In E. R. Hilgard (Ed.), *Theories of learning and instruction: The sixty-third yearbook of the National Society for the Study of Education, Part 1* (pp. 371–401). Chicago: University of Chicago Press.

Mayer, R. E. (1997). Multimedia learning: Are we asking the right questions? *Educational Psychologist, 32*(1), 1–19.

Melton, A. W. (1959). The science of learning and the technology of educational methods. *Harvard Educational Review, 29*, 96–106.

Merrill, M. D. (1968, April). Components of a cybernetic instructional system. *Educational Technology*, pp. 5–10.

Merrill, M. D. (1975). Leaner control: Beyond aptitude-treatment interactions. *AV Communication Review, 23*, 217–226.

Merrill, M. D., Drake, L., Lacy, M. J., Pratt, J. A., & ID2 Research Group at Utah State University. (1996). Reclaiming instructional design. *Educational Technology, 36*(5), 5–7. Retrieved October 15, 2003, from http://www.ittheory.com/reclaim.htm

Milrad, M., Spector, J. M., & Davidsen, P. I. (2002). Model facilitated learning. In S. Naidu (Ed.), *Learning and teaching with technology: Principles and practices* (pp. 13–27). London: Kogan Page.

Nieveen, N., & Gustafson, K. (1999). Characteristics of computer-based tools for education and training development: An introduction. In J. van den Akker, R. M. Branch, K. Gustafson, M. Nieveen, & T. Plomp (Eds.), *Design approaches and tools in education and training* (pp. 155–174). Dordrecht, the Netherlands: Kluwer.

Nunan, T. (1983). *Countering educational design*. New York: Nichols.

Osguthorpe, R. T., Osguthorpe, R. D., Jacob, W. J., & Davies, R. (2003). The moral dimensions of instructional design. *Educational Technology, 43*(2), 19–23.

Palmer, P. J. (1997, November/December). The heart of a teacher: Identity and integrity in teaching. *Change*, pp. 15–21.

Pask, G. (1975). *Conversation, cognition, and learning*. Amsterdam: Elsevier.

Polanyi, M. (1958). *Personal knowledge: Towards a post-critical philosophy*. Chicago: University of Chicago Press.

Ragan, T. J., & Smith, P. L. (1996). Conditions-based models for designing instruction. In D. H. Jonassen (Ed.), *Handbook of research for educational communications and technology* (pp. 541–569). New York: Macmillan Reference USA.

Reigeluth, C. M. (1983). Instructional design: What is it and why is it? In C. M. Reigeluth (Ed.), *Instructional-design theories and models* (pp. 3–36). Hillsdale, NJ: Lawrence Erlbaum Associates.

Reigeluth, C. M., Bunderson, C. V., & Merrill, M. D. (1978). Is there a design science of instruction? *Journal of Instructional Development, 1*(2), 11–16.

Reiser, R. A. (1987). Instructional technology: A history. In R. M. Gagné (Ed.), *Instructional technology: Foundations* (pp. 11–48). Hillsdale NJ: Lawrence Erlbaum Associates.

Reiser, R. A. (2001). A history of instructional design and technology. Part 2: A history of instructional design. *Educational Technology Research & Development, 49*(2), 57–67.

Reiser, R. A., & Ely, D. P. (1997). The field of educational technology as reflected through its definitions. *Educational Technology Research & Development, 45*(3), 63–72.

Richey, R. C. (1998). The pursuit of reusable knowledge in instructional technology. *Educational Technology Research and Development, 46*(4), 7–22.

Richey, R. C., Fields, D. C., & Foxon, M. (2001). *Instructional design competencies: The standards* (3rd ed.). Syracuse NY: ERIC Clearinghouse on Information and Technology.

Rorty, R. (2000). Private irony and liberal hope. In W. Brogan & J Risser (Eds.), *American continental philosophy: A reader* (pp. 45–65). Bloomington: Indiana University Press.

Rose, E. (2002). Boundary talk: A cultural study of the relationship between instructional design and education. *Educational Technology, 42*(6), 14–22.

Rosenberg, M. J. (1982). Our instructional media roots. *Performance & Instruction, 21*(3), 12–15, 33.

Rosenberg, M. J., Coscarelli, W. C., & Hutchison, C. S. (1992). The origins and evolution of the field. In H. D. Stolovich & E. J. Keeps (Eds.), *Handbook of human performance technology* (pp. 14–31). San Francisco: Jossey-Bass.

Ryder, M. (2003a, June). *Instructional design models*. Retrieved June 10, 2003, from http://carbon.cudenver.edu/~mryder/itc_data/idmodels.html

Ryder, M. (2003b, October). *Activity theory*. Retrieved 15 October 2003, from http://carbon.cudenver.edu/~mryder/itc_data/activity.html

Senge, P. M. (1990). *The fifth discipline: The art and practice of the learning organization*. New York: Currency/Doubleday.

Silber, K. H. (1972, September). The learning system: A new approach to facilitating learning based on freedom, the future, and educational technology. *Audiovisual Instruction*, pp. 10–27.

Simon, H. A. (1996). *The sciences of the artificial* (3rd ed.). Cambridge, MA: MIT Press.

Skinner, B. F. (1954). The science of learning and the art of teaching. *Harvard Educational Review, 24*(2), 86–97.

Spector, J. M. (2000). System dynamics and interactive learning environments: Lessons learned and implications for the future. *Simulation and Gaming 31*(3), 457–464.

Spector, J. M., & Anderson, T. M. (Eds.). (2000). *Integrated and holistic perspectives on learning, instruction and technology: Understanding complexity*. Dordrecht: Kluwer Academic Press.

Sullivan, H., Ice, K., & Niedermeyer, F. (2000). Long-term instructional development: A 20-year ID and implementation project. *Educational Technology Research and Development, 48*(4), 87–99.

Sweller, J. (1989). Cognitive technology: Some procedures for facilitating learning and problem solving in mathematics and science. *Journal of Educational Psychology, 81*(4), 457–466.

Thorndike, E. (1913). Educational psychology: The Psychology of learning. New York: Teachers College Press.

Tyler, R. W. (1949). *Basic principles of curriculum and instruction*. Chicago: University of Chicago Press.

van den Akker, J., Branch, R. M., Gustafson, K., Nieveen, M., & Plomp, T. (1999). *Design approaches and tools in education and training*. Dordrecht, the Netherlands: Kluwer.

Visscher-Voerman, I., Gustafson, K., & Plomp, T. (1999). Educational design and development: An overview of paradigms. In J. van den Akker, R. M. Branch, K. Gustafson, M. Nieveen, & T. Plomp (Eds.), *Design approaches and tools in education and training* (pp. 15–28). Dordrecht, the Netherlands: Kluwer.

Wedman, J., & Tessmer, M. (1993). Instructional designers' decisions and priorities: A survey of design practice. *Performance Improvement Quarterly, 6*(2), 43–57.

Wertsch, J. V. (1998). *Mind as action*. New York: Oxford University Press.

Wilson, B. G. (1997). Thoughts on theory in educational technology. *Educational Technology, 37*(1), 2–26.

Wilson, B. G. (2002). Trends and futures of education: Implications for distance education. *Quarterly Review of Distance Education, 3*(1), 65–77.

Wilson, B., & Ryder, M. (1996). Dynamic learning communities: An alternative to designed instruction. In M. Simonson (Ed.), *Proceedings of selected research and development presentations* (pp. 800–809). Washington, DC: Association for Educational Communications and Technology. Retrieved 23 September 2003, from http://carbon.cudenver.edu/~bwilson/dlc.html

Winn, W. D. (1975). An open system model of learning. *AV Communication Review, 23*, 5–33.

Chapter

15

Instructional Design Is Not Peanuts

Allison Rossett
San Diego State University

Dawn Papaila
Tata Interactive Systems

An instructional designer was confronted by a colleague who proclaimed that he was certain that even a monkey could write training. That colleague raised important questions about the profession.

This monkey thing is not new. Many believe it, including some executives, engineers, and even professors from fields other than our own. What matters, in their view, is subject-matter expertise, not knowledge about learning, learners, strategies, or technology. Unlike law or medicine or architecture, just about everyone has had intense exposure to education, years and years of it. What's to know? What's so complicated? When an expert is provided with a few templates and a short briefing, or even nothing at all, instruction happens. That's why monkeys can write training. It's as simple as that.

Enter the monkey. In the 1960s, according to the web site, *Famous Monkeys Through History,* monkeys served as Ape-O-Nauts in space. The gorilla Binti-Jua rescued a boy who fell into an exhibit at the Chicago zoo. Kanzi enjoyed an upbringing similar to human infants and acquired dozens of words, even responding to requests like, "Take off Sue's shoe." Nim Chimpsky, named after linguist Noam Chomsky, learned sign language, watched television, and put on hats and shoes.

253

However, even in light of this string of accomplishments, no pilot, surgeon, or architect would benefit from comparison with a monkey. Neither do we.

NOT JUST MONKEYING AROUND

As training professionals are not just monkeying around, what are they doing?

- Professionals are devoted to achieving strategic *purposes*. Most professionals, in particular those influenced by David Merrill, are dedicated to discerning and expressing meaningful instructional outcomes, and then defining their efforts based on those ends.
- Professionals have *reasons* for doing what they do. Professional decisions are based on the literature and best practices regarding learning, communications, technology, and culture. When deciding how to present, how much to present, the nature of an example, when to include a practice, and how to structure feedback, professionals possess a rationale for their choices. If circumstances change, so would their thinking and execution.
- Professionals seek *understanding of the situation* from many sources, including clients, job incumbents, experts, published literature, strategic statements, work products, and exit interviews. When a client says, "Write training to reduce errors when they operate this equipment," professionals would look to comprehend the problem by turning to data, such as error rates, help-desk logs, accidents, and the opinions of star performers, operators, and their supervisors. Where are the problems? Where are they not? Why do they occur?
- Professionals then *customize solutions*. Causes and drivers matter to professionals, as they attempt to tailor their efforts to the context and learners. When the equipment is working well, they want to know why. When it isn't, why not? Do operators know how? About what are they uncomfortable? Do they care? Is the system clunky? The solution is matched to what is discovered about the circumstances
- Professionals are concerned with developing *programs that grip and hold users*. Professionals must attend to preferences and perceptions, because ongoing participation, particularly online, relies on recognition that the material is worthy and appropriate for challenges and skill levels. Could a monkey create the exhibits at the Holocaust Museum in Washington, DC? Could a monkey build characters for an online scenario about medical ethics? Could a monkey understand what teaches *and* touches people?
- Professionals *turn on a dime*, when the system changes or a crisis occurs. Could a monkey build programs to educate health professionals about SARS or bird flu with no time to spare?
- Professionals honor instruction, while at the same time recognizing that instruction is but one component in a system that might include executive

sponsorship, coaching, clarity about expectations, online communities, reengineered processes, and incentives. They know the challenge of creating instruction and situating it in larger, aligned *systems*.

If the challenge is small and familiar, the context is fixed, and control over the learner is dependable, monkeyish developers might get the job done. But when is that the case? Not often. Most contemporary training programs teach murky or complex and changing content, in volatile contexts, to employees who are often less inclined to learn than their executives.

The field most often associated with writing training is instructional design. Dave Merrill has devoted his career to it, commencing when, as a graduate student, he noticed ample attention to how people acquire and store knowledge, but little guidance on how to construct efficient learning experiences and products. Walter Dick said it succinctly: Instructional design is applied educational psychology (for additional elaboration see Merrill, 1973; Merrill & Twitchell, 1994).

Some see instructional design as procedural and defined. Characterized by one box each for analysis, design, development, implementation, and evaluation, arrows link these boxes and direct what to do and in what order. Others, however, see instructional design as an heuristic. They perceive the field as a good example of knowledge work, with mental guidelines that influence, but do not force, instructional design decisions. Procedural approaches have depicted instructional design as recipes (Gordon & Zemke, 2000; Rossett, 2003; Rossett & Sheldon, 2001; Zemke & Rossett, 2002). A more appealing alternative is continuous tasting of sample efforts, guided by a mental model derived from the literature, data, and past successes.

An example of such a mental model was developed by M. David Merrill in 2002. His "pebble in the pond" metaphor for the instructional design process modifies the procedural ISD construct without abandoning basic tenets. In this model, Merrill promotes a content-centered design approach in place of the process-driven ADDIE model. The whole task is thought of as a pebble that has been cast into a pond. The ensuing ripples, with their allegiance to content and performance, guide the instructional designer to strategy, design and production.

Although we don't know anybody who *really* thinks that monkeys would excel as either an algorithmic or heuristically inspired instructional designer, we do run into those who wish it were true and think it's only a near miss. Why? Why are the efforts of professional designers and developers often dismissed?

We turned to experienced professionals for their opinions. Eight volunteer colleagues were interviewed. The group, despite its small size, represented diverse industries and cultures. Everyone was an old hand at the business, with many years worked in jobs with titles such as consultant, trainer, manager and instructional designer. Joseph Baiocco, Sheila Bobbenhouse, and Jeanne Willoughby now work in high-technology companies; Ivan Cortes and Courtney Bolin are in banking and retail; Susan Phares consults with faculty in higher education; and Kraig Robson heads up an e-learning design company. Seven were scattered across the United States. The eighth participant, Martyn Sloman, works in the United Kingdom as an adviser of learning, training and development at the Chartered Institute of Personnel and Development (CIPD).

WHY THE LACK OF RESPECT?

Respondents pointed to four reasons for halting deference for the profession.

Ignorance

Three respondents said that clients and customers are ignorant about what is involved in creating the right training for the challenge. They don't know what we do for them. Why the ignorance? Why widespread applause for Jack Welch but not Dave Merrill? Our respondents placed blame close to home. People don't understand what we do because we haven't been effective at explaining and promoting the discipline. Our clients are enlightened as they experience the consultative services of a skilled professional, and only when professionals elect to share what was involved in the effort. The story of instructional design has not been told in the *Harvard Business Review*. Until we tell it, others can't know any better.

Invisibility

Recently, tennis great Pete Sampras retired. Although he was ranked number one for 6 years, an astonishing achievement, he has never enjoyed the popularity and recognition of John McEnroe, Venus Williams, Jimmy Connor, or even contemporary Andre Agassi. Tennis commentators suggested that the public never appreciated all that went into Sampras's game, because he didn't rant, rave, preen, or sweat all that much. He made it look effortless. Three respondents, without pointing to Sampras, lamented that their good works and decisions were invisible to customers and clients. SAIC's Sheila Bobenhouse reminded us that a premier performance always looks simple, especially to those who are observing, not doing. By the performers failing to explain and elaborate, deliverables are perceived as no more complicated than clicking a button to convert to HTML. The analysis and design work is embedded, undetectable, and thus goes without kudos.

Lack of Differentiation

Of increasing importance is technology-based learning and performance support. Executives admire these approaches because they are scalable, readily distributed, consistent, and timely. What's missing from that list, typically, is anything about quality. E-learning, for example, is so new that, unlike instructor-led training, there is no vivid and shared definition for what is good and what is not. What was it that made the e-learning experience work? How will the successes be repeated? How will we learn from failures? How will supervisors be involved? What does knowledge management have to do with it? Effective examples of e-learning have not reached critical mass, and the open nature of the Internet allows anyone, yes, even a monkey, to put a page on the Web and dub it e-learning. As Kraig Robson of IsoDynamic pointed out, "There are bucket loads of bad e-learning out in the market today that are nothing more than books on a stick."

Lack of Resources

Our colleagues highlighted the expense involved in hiring a professional to do a job, any job. Training professionals do not work for peanuts. Perhaps the post-bubble economy has kept the monkey metaphor alive. Organizations scrambling to make do with smaller budgets have incentive to believe that instructional design skills evolved from primate cousins, and lie dormant in every subject matter expert. All it takes is a checklist, template, or Flash, and quality training emerges.

GROOMING THE PROFESSION

What's to be done? Our respondents gamely identified strategies for elevating the profession in the eyes of others.

Study the Customer's Business

Six of eight colleagues urged a focus on understanding the organization's goals and objectives and contributing directly to these outcomes. Call it analysis, planning, needs assessment, or whatever. They were keen on knowing the nature of the organization and context. Joseph Baiocco, from Qualcomm, put it this way: "To establish credibility, you must understand the business and the technical aspects of the project to maintain credibility. You must understand the big picture and be a part of the project from inception to implementation. Just as finance is a function that is involved throughout the project's life cycle, so should training."

Courtney Bolin, now at Hotel del Coronado, seconded Joseph. She shared an example from a retailer about to install customer kiosks in stores.

> The customers would use the kiosks to learn about high-end products and to order items on line. The training department heard about this, and got involved right away. Initially, they were told that training would be contacted down the road. But we made a point to stay involved so that the interface design and functionality could support after-hours employee training at that later date.

Document Value

Five of eight practitioners pointed to the importance of evaluating and measuring efforts. Is a measurement strategy in place? Does it extend to capturing results in the workplace? Do the data inform subsequent design and development efforts? Do the data inform supervisors and line leaders?

Ivan Cortes, an Internal Performance Consultant for Citibank, Latin America, produced Table 15.1 to compare an e-learning course designed by a content expert with the same course after an instructional design professional got involved in its redesign. Cortes put it like this: "We cite the learning objectives, chunk the content, establish the appropriate sequence, add examples and non-examples, and build practice opportunities with appropriate feedback."

Susan Phares, formerly of Collegis and now at UCLA, relies on qualitative and quantitative data to evaluate the use of Blackboard at Loyola Marymount University. In addition to counting the number of student log-ins and help-desk tickets generated by faculty and students, she and her colleagues also surveyed faculty and students to understand their experiences with the new technology.

Seek Sweet Spots for Participation

Two professionals qualified customers and challenges. There are no perfect clients, employers, or challenges, of course, but some opportunities are more fertile than others. Seek chances to do what we do well. Find places to do substantive analyses, targeted strategies, vivid learning experiences, blends of learning and performance support, guidance systems, prototyping, measurement, ongoing improvement based on data, and cross-functional systems. Measure results. And then share what happened. Model efforts breed model programs and outcomes; they are more compelling to customers than exhortations and promises.

Rivet Efforts to the Learners

Kraig Robson and Martyn Sloman emphasized the importance of learner-centered design. Sloman noted that early catalogs of e-learning were over-hyped, "lacked humility," and "developed with little regard to learners and the business challenges

TABLE 15.1
Comparison of Design Attributes

Original Design	Professional Design
1 html page—built to scroll and scroll	42 nonscrolling html pages
836 Words—only content	2900 Words—content, examples, and feedback
No practices or progress checks	12 Practices/progress checks
3 Photographs	35 Graphical images
No site map or advance organizer	1 Map/advance organizer
132 Words per "view"	69 Words per html page

they faced." He remarked that "one of those advantages [of e-learning] is discretionary learning. What is exciting about e-learning is the ability to increase discretionary learning; therefore, e-learning is viewed as a very significant change management process."

Robson reported that his company, IsoDynamic, ensures that marketing expertise is added to every eLearning team to assure the "stickiness" of the site. Marketing, he believes, has a knack for addressing the emotional needs of the learner, whereas many instructional designers, in his view, tend toward a more intellectual approach. Robson noted that such dynamic teams are helpful to avoid "snoozeware."

The Congo Gorilla Forest Virtual Field Trip won't make students sleepy. It lures them into meaningful action. A project for the Bronx Zoo and Wildlife Conservation Society, hosted by bigchalk.com, this online experience presses students to learn, ponder, decide, and imagine, all within a vivid environment (Fig. 15.1).

Massage the Request

Although professionals appreciate being asked for assistance, that appreciation does not always extend to the quality of the "ask." Sometimes the request is murky.

FIG. 15.1.   Congo Gorilla Forest Virtual Field Trip—http://www.isodynamic.com

Sometimes overblown. Sometimes just plain weird. And, as four interviewees reminded us, it is not unusual for clients to request X, when Y and Z would be more appropriate. In these cases, we use the request as an opportunity to do the right thing. Any request opens the door for customer education, analysis, and services tailored to the situation.

The professionals we interviewed stressed that it is important to honor the client's original recommendation by seeking details about the problem or opportunity. Ask questions. Ask why. Ask why now. Ask about additional sources. By demonstrating respect for their views, you create a more fertile context for alternatives.

Spread the Message

Ivan Cortes shared an observation made by his new boss after returning from his first International Society for Performance Improvement (ISPI) conference. This executive was impressed by what he'd learned at ISPI about planning, customization, and solution systems. What the executive didn't understand was why he had not heard about these concepts before from his vantage point as a professional in the quality field. He asked Ivan why our community appeared to be so closed, why our discipline was not gaining the attention of major business publications, and why it remains so United States-centric. After all, total quality management (TQM), business process improvement (BPI), and the International Organization for Standardization ISO9000 are known to most business executives, no matter the industry or country.

The professionals we interviewed were devoted to educating clients. Sheila Bobenhouse suggested taking one client at a time and making their experience the best it can be. Ivan Cortes described himself as an evangelist for instructional design. He uses every opportunity he can to show the value of a systematic design process, to help people succeed, and to identify people he can mentor. He said, "Subject matter experts and good will are necessary but not sufficient conditions for an effective learning experience; instructional design is essential."

Qualcomm's Baiocco reported that most people find systematic approaches to instructional design easy to understand, once you take time to explain the process. He said that we haven't done enough to educate our clients, and that we should probably spend as much time educating them as we do our students. Courtney Bolin uses a doctor analogy with her clients: "If you go to the doctor, you don't want him or her to simply write a prescription, you want to know what he's treating, how he came to that conclusion, and what it will feel like when you are healthy."

MONKEY SEE—INSTRUCTIONAL DESIGNER DO

Academics and degreed professionals line up against anybody or thing that trivializes the enterprise. The monkey comparison does just that. Of course it sets teeth on edge. But there are lessons to be learned from monkeys. They are active and nimble. They beguile young and old. What they do commands attention. The way they do it results in smiles.

Are we sufficiently committed to those attributes as we work to elevate our practice and reputation? Do we deliver in concrete and vivid ways? Do our efforts reflect the context and people? Are we consistently active, willing to alter our efforts to shifting realities? Do we worry the response of customers, supervisors, and clients? Are we delivering high-quality programs and simultaneously executing a substantive charm offensive?

Global reach, competition, and tasty technology options create expanding opportunities for instructional design professionals, but only if the outside world is keen on the value we add. Let's learn from the monkeys, and then swing on beyond them.

REFERENCES

Famous Monkeys Through History. (2004). Http://www.ape-o-naut.org/famous/famous/reallife.html. Retrieved February 6, 2004.
Gordon. J., & Zemke, R. (2000, April). The attack on ISD. *Training, 37*(4), 42–45.
Merrill, M. D. (1973). Cognitive and instructional analysis for cognitive transfer tasks. *Audio Visual Communications Review 21*(1), 109–125.
Merrill, M. D., & Twitchell, D. G. (Ed.). (1994). *Instructional design theory.* Englewood Cliffs, NJ: Educational Technology Publications.
Merrill, M. D. (2002). A pebble-in-the-pond model for instructional design. *Performance Improvement, 41*(7), 39–44.
Rossett, A., & Sheldon, K. (2001). *Beyond the podium: Delivering training and performance to a digital world.* San Francisco: Jossey-Bass.
Rossett, A. (2003). Revisiting instructional design. In *Instructional systems design revisited* (pp. 1–5). Silver Spring, MD: ISPI Publications.
Zemke, R. E., & Rossett, A. (2002, February). A hard look at ISD. *Training, 39*(2), 26–34.

Chapter
16

Confessions of a Practitioner

James J. L'Allier
Thompson NETg

I received an e-mail from the editors of this book inviting me to contribute a chapter in a *"festschrift"* celebrating the work of M. David Merrill by relating how his research has influenced my work in the field of instructional technology. Not being familiar with the term *festschrift,* and in order to better understand the book's form, I looked up the term. According to the United States Library of Congress, it is defined as:

> A complimentary or memorial publication usually in the form of a collection of essays, addresses, or biographical, bibliographic, scientific, or other contributions. It often embodies the results of research, is issued in honor of a person, an institution, or a society, and on the occasion of an anniversary celebration. (TLC, 2003)

I decided, in keeping with the spirit of a *festschrift,* that my chapter would be informal in tone and combine the elements of a short technology biography, an essay, and comments on research that influenced the products with which I have been involved. Also, I decided that I would take the point of view of a practitioner involved in the commercial production of technology-based learning materials for almost 30 years, pointing out to readers new to the field some lessons learned so that they don't have to repeat history and waste time reinventing wheels. Thus, this chapter is about the practical experience of applying research and theory within a business environment—it is not a scholarly discourse. There are other authors in this book who will better serve that need.

Before relating how Merrill's work and the work of others have shaped me as a professional and influenced many of the products with which I have been privileged to be involved, I feel the need to put these influences in both a personal and a cultural context. In doing so, some light will be shed on the other powerful forces that have shaped and continue to influence the field of instructional technology and those of us in its service.

Being born in 1945 places me at the front end of the demographic "bump" called the postwar baby boom. All who are members of this group, which includes many who have written chapters in this book, would find themselves exposed to a wide variety of new technologies that would mark them for the rest of their professional lives.

As a generation, we saw the impact of the space race, started by the Russians with the launch of Sputnik and the follow-up challenge by John Kennedy of putting a man on the Moon before the close of the decade. We witnessed Neal Armstrong take that famous step and later viewed the first transatlantic satellite TV broadcast. In high school, many of us took developmental reading courses using the Educational Developmental Laboratory (EDL) Tachistoscope, were taught English grammar from a programmed instruction textbook called *English 3200* (Blumenthal, 1994), and increased our sight vocabulary using Bell and Howell's Language Master. Our classrooms were outfitted with 3M overheads, DuKane synchronized-sound filmstrip projectors, and at least once a week we saw an Encyclopaedia Britannica film in 16-mm format. In our science and math classes, we learned about the ENIAC and ILLIAC computers and gaped at pictures of rooms full of heat-generating vacuum tubes and white-coated technicians operating incomprehensibly complicated control panels. We even learned to program a small personal computer called CARDIAC (Cardboard Illustrative Aid to Computation) developed by Bell Laboratories. If you were a member of the college-bound track and took a foreign language, you were exposed to another new technology called the language lab, replete with individual learning stations, headsets, dual-track reel-to-reel tape recorders, and an instructor who could listen in on your practice sessions and correct your pronunciation. It was an educational technology renaissance.

In college, we read Marshall McLuhan's *Understanding Media* (McLuhan, 1964) and learned about the death of the book and the differences between hot and cold media. In the 1968 movie *2001: A Space Odyssey*, we were exposed to the potential of an artificially intelligent talking computer, HAL, the favorite cybernetic son of Urbana, Illinois. We also saw the dark side of atomic technology represented by the Cold War, with its anxieties of mutually assured destruction, and lived through the Vietnam War, punctuated by daily numbness that only television could bring to such an event.

Taking the dark with the light, we were all nevertheless exposed to the unbridled optimistic belief that technology would be the solution to most, if not all, problems of society. Some embraced this idea, and some did not. I did and still do, especially as it relates to learning. This idea has been at the foundation of many important learning products with which I have been privileged to be associated.

The discussion of these products and related theories found in the remainder of this chapter are not in strict chronological order because sometimes theory and application do not follow each other in a logical or timely manner. Leonardo da Vinci's 15th-century designs for flying machines, the parachute, and the armored tank are dramatic scientific examples of this phenomenon. In the field of instructional design, the adaptive models of instruction, dating as early as the 1970s and referred to in this chapter, are still not widely used even though the technology exists to enable these models.

In order to give the reader a loose historical framework as to when many of these influences came into play, see the chronology in Table 16.1. Within the body of this chapter, I have also indicated the year in which each event took place.

My first exposure to the instructional power of the computer started in the early 1970s when I was an English and reading teacher at Stillwater Senior High School in Stillwater, Minnesota, chipping away at a master's in reading at the University of Wisconsin. Part of my research was doing t-tests on pre- and posttest scores, which is a time-consuming task even with the aid of a calculator. In a discussion in the faculty lounge with one of my colleagues from the math department, I was quickly shown how this all could be done more efficiently on the school's time-share computer system. I gave him the formula for the t-test, and he wrote a simple program in Dartmouth Basic that allowed me to enter in two data sets and calculate the t-values. All I had to do was feed in the data in the form of a roll of punched paper and then run the program.

I was amazed at the speed, but I saw something else—something quite unexpected. In the creation of this simple program, my friend had created a line of code that said, "Enter the data for set No. 1." This was followed by: "Enter the data for set No. 2." This was the first time it had ever occurred to me that a computer could deal with language. I then decided to learn the Basic programming language and how to use Boolean logic in conjunction with strings that named things to be calculated.

TABLE 16.1
Chronology of Personal Development

1971–1980	Stillwater Senior High School	First computer-based course "Cybernetic English"
1980	PhD from University of Minnesota	Exposure to key instructional technology researchers
1980–1990	John Wiley/Wilson Learning	Sales and management interactive video products
1990–1993	Competence Assurance Systems	Pharmaceutical multimedia products
1993–	NEC/Harcourt/Thomson NETg	Information technology products, Skill Builder, and Learning Objects

This was a revelation. Not only could one get the computer to express language as an output, but the computer could also be programmed to recognize language as an input and make a logical decision based on that input and associated data. The combination of being an English teacher and the computer's ability to deal with language started me down the path that was to lead to what I now call the "Utah Connection."

At this time, I also had a group of high school students that needed extensive work in their reading and writing skills. Therefore, during the summer of 1976, I took a number of workshops offered by the organization that supplied time-share services to our district—Total Information for Educational Systems (TIES). Later, this organization was to become a part of the Minnesota Educational Computer Consortium (MECC). One of the summer workshops dealt with Hewlett Packard's Instructional Dialogue Facility (IDF). It was my first experience with an authoring system. It was a simple frame-based system that allowed the user to enter text; a question; the correct response; multiple incorrect responses; unexpected responses; replies to each category of responses; and logical branching based on decision criteria. That year, I purchased a damaged Teletype ASR-33, repaired it, wrote a grant for my school district to develop a course for my remedial reading students using IDF, received funding, and called the resulting course "Cybernetic English." Its purpose was to teach students deficient in reading and writing skills the basics of sentence construction along with punctuation rules.

The course was a qualified success. I also discovered that programming in an authoring system like IDF was faster than coding in Basic. I especially enjoyed using the unexpected response and reply to unexpected response because my students were primarily 17-year-olds building their lexicon of shock-value Anglo Saxon words and phrases. I was greatly, if not perversely, amused when the students literally jumped out of their chairs when they received the response: "If you say that again, I will notify your parents." It turned out that this was a strong motivator, as they began to test the limits of my "unexpected response" database. Early on, I learned that some motivators did not necessarily lead to learning outcomes that the designer intended.

The course not only was used in my district but was placed on the TIES system library for use by other Minnesota teachers. Other time-share systems that had affiliations with TIES wanted copies, and Cybernetic English spread to other states. By today's standards, it wasn't very good. It was linear, the inputs and outputs were all in uppercase characters (upper/lowercase terminals were yet to come), response time was slow, and it was all text. Some of these limitations had more to do with the technology, but the main issue was that my design had more in common with *English 3200* than I realized (Tennyson & L'Allier, 1980). I had written a programmed textbook using a computer.

Wanting to push Cybernetic English to a higher level, I enrolled in a 3-day authoring system workshop in the fall of 1977 at the University of Iowa using IBM's Coursewriter II, a giant step up from IDF. During lunch, I had a conversation with the program's director, Bobbie Brown, and related to him the progress I had achieved with Cybernetic English. I told him I was interested in his program at Iowa and in obtaining more knowledge about this new world of CBT. Because I was from Minnesota, he was surprised that I was unaware of the University of Minnesota's instructional technology program. He told me that before I made any decision I should talk to the program's director, Bob Tennyson. Meeting Bob was the next revelation because I had no idea that there was a field, let alone a science, called instructional design. Although I understood the technology and content, Bob filled in the missing details—a research-based design methodology that went beyond programmed instruction and a body of literature to support this methodology. Shortly after that meeting, I enrolled in the PhD program in curriculum and instructional systems in 1977, with Bob as my advisor.

A brief aside about the Utah Connection is now appropriate. On many speaking occasions, Dave Merrill introduced me as his grandson. Puzzled looks from the audience, some gasps, and a pause by Dave while he let the audience do some mental calculations and ponder the mystery regarding the potential genesis of this relationship always followed. Dave would end by delivering the punch line: He really meant I was his intellectual grandson. He then went on to tell the audience that Bob Tennyson was his first PhD advisee at BYU; consequently, because I was Bob's PhD advisee, that made Dave my intellectual grandfather.

My first contact with Dave's work was in my first year at Minnesota. One of my texts was *Teaching concepts: An Instructional Design Guide* (1977), which Merrill coauthored with Bob Tennyson. This book included procedures for articulating and classifying concepts in order to assign them appropriate instructional strategies. There were two ideas in this book that struck me as key. One was the introduction to the idea of critical and variable attributes to deal with characteristics that determine class membership. The other idea was the employment of nonexamples paired with examples in order to deal with concepts easily confused with each other.

My first use of the matched nonexample to example technique occurred while I was with Wilson Learning's Interactive Technology Group in Santa Fe, New Mexico, in 1983. It was used in the development of our first interactive videodisc product, called *The Versatile Organization* (Wilson Learning, 1984). This course taught the concept of social style, which was premised on the assumption that interpersonal behavior falls into two basic categories: assertiveness and responsiveness. The degree to which behavior is assertive (the degree to which behavior is seen as directive or forceful) and responsive (the degree to which behavior is seen as emotionally responsive) determines social style to be one of four types: analytical (low assertiveness and low emotional expressiveness), amiable (high emotional expressiveness and low assertiveness), expressive (high emotional expressiveness and high assertiveness), or driver (high assertiveness and low emotional expressiveness).

The course's goal was not only to teach the concepts of assertiveness and expressiveness but also to teach participants how to identify social styles in others by rating them on a 2 × 2 assertiveness/expressiveness grid. We knew from the seminar version of this course that learners had a difficult time discriminating between assertiveness and responsiveness. When given video examples of different styles and asked to classify them, learners were unable to do so. Our solution was to construct an interactive simulation in which two slider bars were placed on a touch screen. One bar represented the assertiveness scale, and the other represented the responsiveness scale. We then shot video of an actress speaking on a single topic but scripted to display varying degrees of assertiveness and responsiveness. By using the slider bars, the learner could distinguish between the two behaviors by making the actress more or less assertive or responsive; thus, the learner became better able to correctly classify examples of different style types.

When I was at Competence Assurance Systems in Cambridge, Massachusetts, in 1992, developing multimedia medical simulations for pharmaceutical sales representatives, the use of matched nonexample to example technique was employed in a course teaching basic heart anatomy and function. At first, we were going to use a digital image of a sectioned heart to point out key structures that would be linked to hot spots on a touch screen. The problem became obvious when we attempted to separate the critical and variable attributes of the various heart structures. There was just too much blood, fat, and connecting tissue in the depiction of a real heart. Too much noise was present, which interfered with the learner's ability to identify and differentiate key structures. In this environment, it was impossible to determine class membership. In addition, we were not training medical students, but pharmaceutical sales representatives who would be calling on cardiologists. All that these representatives needed was a basic vocabulary and limited understanding related to heart function. We decided to use for our touch screen a simple drawing of a heart, which clearly outlined the basic structures through the use of color. Classification of key structures became clear, and the generation of matched nonexamples became easier. Right and left heart structures, which may be easily confused, were now obvious, and the learner was able to easily identify the right coronary artery from the left, while also being able to distinguish the left's split into the left anterior descending artery and the circumflex. These differences, which are very difficult to distinguish in a real heart because of their close proximity, became simpler and were also perfect candidates for matched nonexamples to example pairings.

Returning to the late 1970s, while at the University of Minnesota, I became interested in Bob Tennyson's 1977 work on algorithmic instruction (Tennyson & Rothen, 1977), which was grounded in the work of Landa (1974). Of additional interest was the Aptitude Treatment Interaction (ATI) of Cronbach and Snow (1976). The possibility of using preinstruction user data (reading level from a standardized instrument) in conjunction with users' on-task responses to build up a history and to predict the best possible path and sequence broadened my horizons and formed the basis for my dissertation research. Early CBT was primarily text based. As a teacher of reading, I was interested in answering the following question: By monitoring on-task learner characteristics (comprehension and time on task), and using these metrics to adjust reading difficulty levels by altering text density (fewer difficult words, simpler syntax, and restaging of content), would the learners of high, medium, and low reading ability improve their comprehension as measured in a posttest?

Tennyson and a number of his graduate students had demonstrated some powerful relationships between response history and performance results, and I wanted to see if their findings could be generalized to reading comprehension. The findings of this study pointed to strong relationships between pretask reading levels, the on-task reading characteristics of time and comprehension, and performance on a comprehension posttest, all of which supported the growing body of research in this area. Ironically, this research has little use with or impact on the products on which I worked at both Wilson and Competence Assurance Systems. This was due to many factors such as existing design methodology and the production costs associated with creating courses that would have alternate treatments for different learner characteristics. It would be 13 years later that portions of this research would find application in the products of Thomson NETg.

Why was Thomson NETg such fertile ground? In 1993, NETg was a unique environment. Over the years, it had followed a publishing model, generating its revenue through reselling information technology and soft-skill training products developed by other companies. NETg was also producing videotapes with contract labor on various information technology topics, using its well-equipped studio in Naperville, Illinois. In addition, a small development group was developing a CBT product called Skill Builder. The margins realized by reselling other companies' products were very low, and the demand for video-based instruction was decreasing at a rate of 15% per year. The fledgling Skill Builder effort was competing with the resellers without having great impact on revenue. This unique situation presented an opportunity that only comes around once in a lifetime.

Ordinarily, companies already have an existing development technology that generates product revenue. Consequently, any change, regardless of need, is slow and fraught with potentially dangerous consequences. It would be like changing the engine of a Boeing 777 with a full load of passengers at 40,000 feet. However, this was not the case at NETg in 1993 because most of its revenue was coming from its business as a reseller, minimally impacted by its decreasing video business. Because revenue was coming from other sources, it was possible to build a completely new development technology without having to worry about placing existing revenue streams in jeopardy—hence, the unusual once-in-a-lifetime opportunity.

The strategy was three-pronged: Build a new product development department and a technology that would feed the growing demand for multimedia delivery; continue the reseller strategy but phase it out as the new development organization came online; and quickly close the capital intensive video studio so that its budget could be reallocated to build the new product development technology on the basis of Skill Builder (see Fig. 16.1).

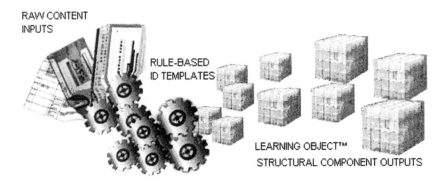

FIG. 16.1.   The Thomson NETg design and development system.

The analogy that was used to describe this new product development technology was similar to a computer-aided design/computer-aided manufacturing (CAD/CAM) model that would automate the instructional design process and guide the actual creation of the code necessary for the final course. This was an important quality because it was related to another part of the strategy: Move to an outsource model, allowing contractors outside the United States to use this unique design and development technology to build Skill Builder products in high volume and at low cost without sacrificing quality. In other words, the technology had to be transferable to development partners. The new development technology and outsource strategy resulted in a product output that went from seven multimedia products in 1993 to 250 in 1997, reducing the time to produce a single title from 18 weeks to an average of 12 weeks.

The qualities of the new Skill Builder development environment were that it had to produce highly modular products against a set of best practices (i.e., practices based in empirical research) of instructional design. It had to allow for a high degree of reuse and customization due to the fast changing nature of the information technology topics. Finally, it had to meet the individual needs of the learner.

In their paper "Reclaiming Instructional Design," Merrill and colleagues (Merrill, Drake, Lacy, & Pratt, 1996) offered the following definition:

> The technology of instructional design is founded on scientific principles verified by empirical data. Like other sciences, instruction is verified by discovery and instructional design is extended by invention. Instructional design is (also) a technology which incorporates known and verified learning strategies into instructional experiences which make the acquisition of knowledge and skill more efficient, effective, and appealing. (pp. 5–6)

These scientific principles, verified through empirical data, form the basis of the best practices that are used by NETg within the Learning Object structural component and its elements.

The main element that would be shaped by these best practices and that would ensure reuse and customizability was the NETg Learning Object, an idea that came from my exposure to the work of Taylor (1991), a pioneer in the area of object-oriented programming. According to Taylor, "The concept of an object is simple yet powerful. Objects make ideal software modules because they can be defined and maintained independently of one another with each object forming a neat, self-contained universe" (p. 8).

The concept of each object being independent and self-contained was key because it allowed a high degree of customization for the individual learner and the client.

The NETg Learning Object, rather than being defined as just a collection of data elements (graphics, audio, animations, code, common instructions, etc.), is defined around three simple parameters grounded more in instructional design pragmatics than in software terms. These parameters are an objective, a learning activity, and an assessment (see Fig. 16.2).

In the production of each Learning object's objective, learning activity, and assessment, a number of instructional design theories come into play in the form of template-based rule sets used by the developer. The rule sets that underlay these templates are extracted from a theory base heavily influenced by the work of Mager, Bloom, Merrill, and Keller (Bloom, 1976; Keller & Kopp, 1987; Merrill, 2000). Not only did NETg use their theories, we also had their direct involvement. During the fine-tuning phase of the development environment, Bob Mager, Dave Merrill, and John Keller were engaged as consultants to review the development process and provide feedback and direction, which helped shape the rule sets used to define the following Learning Object elements.

Objective

Mager's protocols are used to define an objective, which is a statement that describes the intended criterion-based result of instruction. This end result of the ob-

FIG. 16.2.   The elements of the Learning Object.

jective must be specific and measurable in order to determine if the desired criterion has been met. In other words, a well-stated objective must be clear about what the learner is going to be able to do, under what conditions it is to be done, and how well the learner must perform under these conditions, that is, a measurable criterion (Mager, 1997).

At Learning Object level, objectives are seen as *enabling objectives* because they are specific and therefore measurable, and lead to broader unit goals called *terminal objectives.*

Examples of topic-level enabling objectives are:

- Given a bad line of C++ code, the learner will be able to correct its syntax error in three attempts.
- Presented with a sample of unformatted text within Word for Windows, the learner will be able to correctly apply five of the six styles from the Format menu.
- Presented with a sample toolbar of ten buttons within Excel, the learner will be able to correctly identify the functionality of at least nine buttons.

Learning Activity

After following the template-based process to formulate an enabling objective, the developer's next step is to determine the appropriate instructional strategy that will assist the learner in meeting the objective. For example, Objective No. 2 may require a learning activity in which the learner is going to format text. To achieve this objective, the learner will need a direct experience either with the word processing software or with a simulation. On the other hand, Objective No. 3 may require simple identification of an icon. In this case, the learning activity could require the learner match an icon on a toolbar with its functional description.

The template that governs the selection of the appropriate instructional strategy is governed, in part, by Bloom's taxonomy (1976) (see Fig. 16.3). The template assists the developer in determining the level in Bloom's taxonomy by prompting him or her to look at the end goal of the objective and the verbs used to describe it. For example, examine Objective No. 2: "Presented with a sample of unformatted text in Word for Windows, the learner will be able to correctly apply five of the six styles from the Format menu."

The outcome is for the learner to actually complete a formatting task, and the verb used in the instructional objective is *apply.* This combination would indicate level 3 (application). The appropriate way to teach this, within the context of a Skill Builder course, would be to build a simulation of the formatting function and set up a formatting task. Asking the learner to name or list formatting functions (Bloom's level 1, knowledge) or to identify the pull-down menu under which fonts would be found (Bloom's level 2, comprehension) would be inappropriate ways to achieve this objective. This type of error is prevented in NETg's development environment. For example, once the developer has classified the objective at

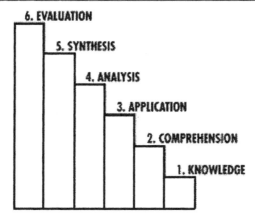

FIG. 16.3.   Bloom's taxonomy.

Bloom's level 3, a rule set disallows inappropriate strategies that would be associated with lower Bloom levels (1 or 2).

Although Bloom is used for classification of objectives and to give the developer a general idea about what instructional strategy to use, it does not provide the specific structure of the learning activity itself. Component display theory (CDT) (Merrill, 1987) was used as the rule set for templates that guide the developer in the creation of the actual elements (problem set[s], examples, nonexamples, sequence, etc.) that make up the instruction.

After the developer assigns a Bloom level to the objective, he or she must make a determination regarding its classification as fact, concept, procedure, or principle. In conjunction with Merrill, NETg broadened these categories into six principles, or recipes: information-about, parts-of, kinds-of, how-to, how-it-works, and guidelines-for. Depending on the classification selected, the developer starts to create the presentation and practice to be used in the learning activity along with the level of performance required of the learner (find, use, remember generality, and remember instance).

For example, if the developer classifies an objective in the how-it-works category, then he or she is presented with the following set of questions that have to be answered by either the developer or the subject matter expert:

1. What is the information the learner needs to know about this process?
2. What goal does the process accomplish? What is the outcome of the process?
3. What is the learner's motivation for learning about this process?
   a. When and why would the learner use/encounter this process?
   b. What work-related tasks are associated with it?
   c. Are there any benefits to the learner (i.e., speed, ease of use, higher quality, etc.)?
4. What are the stages/events of the process?

5. What are the conditions necessary for each event to occur?
6. What are the consequences of each process event/stage (what happens and why)?
7. What are some initial conditions for the process?
8. What are some incorrect conditions for the process?
9. What would be an appropriate way to illustrate this process to the learner?
10. What are four appropriate, business-related examples of this process being carried out in everyday workplace scenarios? These scenarios must be relevant to the course audience and their job role(s).

In should be noted that questions 3 and 10 above relate to affective domain information that is used in the application of the ARCS (Keller & Kopp, 1987) model that will be described shortly. Using the information from these questions, the developer applies the how-it-works recipe.

The application of the various CDT principles, which NETg refers to as recipes, is a critical part of NETg's automated design environment. Figure 16.4 is a screen capture of the portion of the Skill Builder development environment in which the CDT skeletal how-it-works protocol is outlined.

From this skeletal stage, the developer, using a context-sensitive help system, starts to create the specific pages and/or page specifications that will contain an introduction, prerequisite information, a work-related example, an overview of process, and so on. These elements could consist of text, graphics, case studies, simulations, animated screen captures, and practice sessions.

While in the process of creating the instructional components for the learning activity, the development environment also prompts the developer to pay specific attention to the affective domain. In other words, not only must the learning activity be appropriate to the task, it also must engage the learner.

The idea to focus on the affective domain came from a phenomenon observed while at Wilson Learning in the early 1980s. During this time I realized that if relevance was not established in the first 5 minutes of a seminar, learners would lose interest. In other words, if learners could not answer the "What's in it for me?" question, they would not be motivated to continue. Far from being a systematic approach to the affective domain, this simple rule (making sure that learners could answer that question) at least recognized that the learner had a set of expectations that they brought to the instructional experience. I then heard a speech given by John Keller to the design staff at Wilson. This was my first exposure to his research on motivational theory (Keller & Kopp, 1987). What Keller provided in his ARCS (attention, relevance, confidence, and satisfaction) model was a research-based strategy for creating affective effects that could be applied in a systematic way during the design process. However, because of established development practices that employed a motivational model specific to Wilson, it was not possible to use the ARCS model.

A phenomenon that had been present at Wilson was also at NETg. Most multimedia instruction was not addressing the "What's in it for me?" question. Rather,

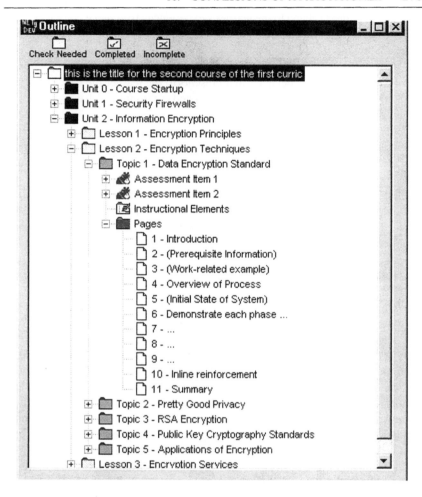

FIG. 16.4.   Component outline for how-it-works.

it focused primarily on cognitive tasks with little or no consideration regarding the motivational aspect of what was to be learned. Creating the new development environment at NETg presented the perfect opportunity to apply Keller's ARCS model in a formal way by incorporating it into the rule-based templates. As the developer creates the instructional components of the learning activity, they are prompted for input with regard to affective considerations by the template.

To gain *attention,* the developer outlines how he or she will gain perceptual arousal through the use of novel situations and/or the use of graphic techniques; inquiry arousal, with the use of posing questions or problems that challenge; and variability, to maintain interest by developing multiple problem sets. To address *relevance,* the developer outlines a plan for creating familiarity through the use of language and ideas related to the learner's experience. To achieve *confidence,* the designer develops strategies that make the learner aware of the performance criteria, allowing for different achievement levels and appropriate feedback that tells the student if he or she has achieved success. Finally, to gain *satisfaction,* a plan is developed by the designer that presents to the learner the benefits of this new knowledge and/or skill in various simulated environments that are similar to what will be found on his or her job.

Keller's model allows a sophisticated and systematic approach to the development of learner motivation. It makes instruction less about "edutainment" (unnecessary graphics and animations) and more about how to keep a continual focus on the audience's needs, goals, and the environments with which they are familiar. In other words, the learner is motivated when the learning is relevant to his or her job and populated with problems/solutions that will make his or her job easier. This grounding in the learner's reality was validated in the recently completed Thomson NETg Job Impact Study described later in this chapter.

Assessment

The final element of the Learning Object structural component is the test that determines whether or not an objective has been met—the assessment. Here, the rule is very simple. Assess in accordance with the learning activity and its objective. Again, consider Objective No. 2: "Presented with a sample of unformatted text in Word for Windows, the learner will be able to correctly apply five of the six styles from the Format menu." The outcome is for the learner to actually complete a formatting task, and the verb used in the instructional objective is "apply." The appropriate way to teach to this Bloom level 3 (application) objective is by creating a simulation. Consequently, to create an appropriate assessment, a Bloom level 3 would also demand that this skill be assessed through the use of a simulation. Conversely, an inappropriate way to assess this objective would be to use a multiple choice, matching, or sequencing item.

Skill Builder has five types of assessments. These are: multiple multiple choice (more than one correct response), multiple choice (one correct response), matching, sequencing, and simulation. Figure 16.5 shows how these assessment types map to Bloom levels.

In order to ensure that we are testing for skills and knowledge and not testing someone's test-taking ability, all assessment items are drawn from a random pool of items, thereby assuring that the learner will not receive the same item twice. In addition, the positions of any correct answer and associated wrong answers are also randomized, thereby ensuring a low probability that the learner will get exactly the same assessment item on each potential retake.

Finally, much of the research in instructional technology has come together in a unique combination that forms the backbone of Skill Builder courses and the Learning Objects with which they are built. All of the courses created in the design and development environment have preassessment and postassessment compo-

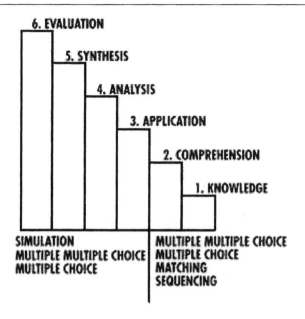

FIG. 16.5.   Bloom's taxonomy applied to assessment types.

nents that draw from an item pool linked to a specific objective for each Learning Object. The preassessment is used to determine prior knowledge and produces a customized learning path made up of assessment items associated with objectives of which the learner did not demonstrate mastery. After the instruction, a postassessment is used to determine mastery of the objectives in the learner's customized learning path. Finally, another process that takes learner characteristics into consideration is that the instruction undergoes readability level checks to make sure that it is commensurate with the target population (L'Allier, 1980).

In review, the foundation for NETg's technology is built primarily on the research of Taylor (1991), Mager (1997), Bloom (1976), Merrill (1977, 1987, 1996, 2000, 2002), and Keller and Kopp (1987), with the additional already noted influences of Tennyson and Schott (1997), Tennyson and Park (1980), Cronbach and Snow (1976), and Landa (1974).

Another NETg technology that was influenced by early research on algorithmic instruction was "Search and Select." Basically it is a performance support system (PSS) that allows the learner to enter a problem via a natural language query. As a result, a specific Learning Object is presented to the learner as a potential solution. Back in 1980, I was intrigued that a Bayesian algorithm could be used "to identify the cause of error thereby lowering the probability that such a mistake will occur" (Tennyson, Tennyson, & Rothen, 1977, p. 9). Essentially, this adaptive strategy relies on the dynamic environment of the computer to maintain records of the distribution of various on-task factors as they relate to error patterns.

In 1999, this concept and advanced forms of it, combined with the Learning Object, came together in Search and Select, which uses a neural network that builds up a history of successful object use against a specific class of problem. For example, if a user needs to know the specific protocol for using Mail Merge in Microsoft Word to print name and address information on an envelope, the user selects the version of Microsoft Word from a pull-down menu and then enters a natural-language query such as, "I would like to know how to merge name and address information." The Search and Select neural net then looks at the various classifications of problems associated with Mail Merge questions and serves up the highest probability of solutions in the form of specific Learning Objects. In other words, if one could read the object's memory (in object programming terms, this is called persistence), we might hear this internal dialogue: "I have seen this classification of problem before. In the majority of cases within this classification, I, along with two other Learning Objects, provided the solution. Based on the number of times that these objects were successfully seen by users as solutions to this classification of problem, I am 85% confident that this solution will work for the currently stated problem." The next step is that the Learning Objects are presented to the user as solutions.

After the user has seen the specific objects, he or she is asked if these objects addressed his or her problem regarding Mail Merge. If the answer is yes, the distribution of the object's memory is incremented by 1; consequently, the next time it sees a similar question, its degree of confidence will be higher that it, in combination with other Learning Objects, is the solution. If the answer is no, the distribution of the Object's memory is decremented by 1 and the confidence level goes down. If the confidence level continues to drop on a specific classification of problem, the neural net determines if the Learning Objects (the solutions) are outdated and if a new classification of problem is needed or both. As this technology develops, the next logical step is to consider how it can be used not just in a PSS mode, but how the neural net can be a part of an adaptive strategy that serves up the appropriate Learning Objects in Skill Builder products.

Considering the research base for NETg's products, what has been their impact on the learner? The opportunity to address this question came up in late 2001 when the training industry was energized about a new concept called *blended learning*. While touring the vendor exhibits at On-Line Learning in October of 2001 in Los Angeles one could see a multitude of banners and literature proclaiming each company's version of blended learning solutions. Simply stated, blended learning was being defined as mixed media. In other words, if the product included e-learning, text references, online mentoring, video, and other media, it was considered a blended solution. Everyone not only had a blend, but they all had the "right" blend. Of course, this was more about marketing than about the effective use of media—effectiveness being defined as learner impact via observed job performance due to the training. NETg decided to ask a simple question: "What blend has the most impact on the learner's job performance, as measured at Kirkpatrick Level 3?" (Kirkpatrick, 1998).

Kirkpatrick's model of evaluation provided additional guidelines that guided NETg's process (see Table 16.2).

In other words, rather than just come up with an arbitrary media blend, NETg research asked the following questions:

1. Does using different instructional components (NETg Learning Objects, text objects, instructor-led training, and online mentoring) alter the job impact of the blended learning solution?
2. Does a blended learning solution using real-world scenarios demonstrate stronger job impact than nonblended training?

In other words, would the impact come from some combination of media and/or a specific instructional design treatment? Merrill was also interested in these questions. As part of a long-standing consulting relationship, Merrill had been working with NETg to apply best practices of instructional design to NETg products. Within this previously established working relationship, this research opportunity not only allowed NETg to see what mix of media and/or treatment would result in maximum impact on on-the-job performance, but it also had the potential to validate Merrill's (2002) *first principles*. Simply stated, various current instructional models suggested that the most effective learning environments are those that are problem based, such as scenario-based exercises,

TABLE 16.2
Kirkpatrick's (1998) Model of Evaluation

Level I Reaction	Reaction assesses participants' initial reactions to a course. This, in turn, offers insights into participants' satisfaction with a course—a perception of value. Trainers usually assess this through a survey, often called a smiley sheet.
Level II Learning	Learning assesses the amount of information that participants learned. Trainers usually assess this with a criterion-referenced test. The criteria are objectives for the course—statements developed before a course is developed that explicitly state the skills that participants should be able to perform after taking a course.
Level III Transfer	Transfer assesses the amount of material that participants actually use in everyday work after taking the course. This assessment is based on the objectives of the course and assessed through tests, observations, surveys, and interviews with coworkers and supervisors.
Level IV Business Results	Business Results assesses the financial impact of the training course on the bottom line of the organization 6 months to 2 years after the course is taken.

and involve the student in four distinct phases of learning: (a) activation of prior experience; (b) demonstration of skills; (c) application of skills; and (d) integration or these skills into real-world activities. One of the treatment variables was called a scenario-based exercise (SBE). Given this dual opportunity to help NETg and validate *first principles* by determining the impact of SBEs, Merrill agreed to act as our external principal investigator.

In keeping with the spirit of a *festschrift,* I stated earlier that my chapter would be informal in tone and would not be a scholarly discourse; consequently, the following description only touches on the highlights of the NETg Thomson Learning Job Impact Study. For those of you who desire more detail as to the methodology, I refer you to the full study (Boyle & Merrill, 2003).

The study involved more than 200 of NETg's clients and consisted of four experimental groups and one control group. The groups received the following treatments:

The Instructor-Led Training (ILT) Blended Group:

- Scenario-based exercises (SBEs) that represented the kind of tasks with Excel that the learner would be given as part of his or her job.
- A live instructor who could facilitate discussion and problem solving.
- Specific text references keyed to specific problems within the SBE.
- NETg Learning Objects (NLOs) keyed to specific problems within the SBE.
- Frequently asked questions (FAQs) keyed to specific problems within the SBE.
- Fully functioning software for practice of concepts given within SBE.
- Real-time, online mentoring related to specific problems within the SBE.
- Authentic assessment: The learner would produce a work product (Excel spreadsheet) based on a specification that would allow the learner to demonstrate mastery of his or her new skills, which would be evaluated with a rubric keyed to the objectives in the instruction.

The Text Blended Group:

- Scenario-based exercises (SBEs) that represented the kind of tasks with Excel that the learner would be given as part of his or her job.
- A live instructor who could facilitate discussion and problem solving.
- Specific text references keyed to specific problems within the SBE.
- NETg Learning Objects (NLOs) keyed to specific problems within the SBE.
- Frequently asked questions (FAQs) keyed to specific problems within the SBE.
- Fully functioning software for practice of concepts given within SBE.
- Real-time, online mentoring related to specific problems within the SBE.
- Authentic assessment: The learner would produce a work product (Excel spreadsheet) based on a specification that would allow the learner to dem-

onstrate mastery of his or her new skills, which would be evaluated with a rubric keyed to the objectives in the instruction.

The SBE Group:

• Scenario-based exercises (SBEs) that represented the kind of tasks with Excel that the learner would be given as part of his or her job.
• A live instructor who could facilitate discussion and problem solving.
• Specific text references keyed to specific problems within the SBE.
• NETg Learning Objects (NLOs) keyed to specific problems within the SBE.
• Frequently asked questions (FAQs) keyed to specific problems within the SBE.
• Fully functioning software for practice of concepts given within SBE.
• Real-time, online mentoring related to specific problems within the SBE.
• Authentic assessment: The learner would produce a work product (Excel spreadsheet) based on a specification that would allow the learner to demonstrate mastery of his or her new skills, which would be evaluated with a rubric keyed to the objectives in the instruction.

The Nonblended Group:

• Scenario-based exercises (SBEs) that represented the kind of tasks with Excel that the learner would be given as part of his or her job.
• A live instructor who could facilitate discussion and problem solving.
• Specific text references keyed to specific problems within the SBE.
• NETg Learning Objects (NLOs) keyed to specific problems within the SBE.
• Frequently asked questions (FAQs) keyed to specific problems within the SBE.
• Fully functioning software for practice of concepts given within SBE.
• Real-time, online mentoring related to specific problems within the SBE.
• Authentic assessment: The learner would produce a work product (Excel spreadsheet) based on a specification that would allow the learner to demonstrate mastery of his or her new skills, which would be evaluated with a rubric keyed to the objectives in the instruction.

The Control Group—No treatment but completed:

• Authentic assessment: The learner would produce a "work product" (Excel spreadsheet) based on a specification that would allow the learner to demonstrate mastery of his or her new skills, which would be evaluated with a rubric keyed to the objectives in the instruction.

Table 16.3 presents the results of the Thomson NETg Job Impact Study. Table 16.3 shows improvement as measured by authentic assessment scores. All of the

TABLE 16.3
Thomson NETg Job Impact Study Results Representing
Improvement as Measured by Authentic Assessment Scores

Comparison	Performance improvement	Decrease in time
ILT Blend vs. Control	163%	
SBE Blend vs. Control	159%	
Text Blend vs. Control	153%	
E-Learning vs. Control	99%	
ILT Blend vs. e-Learning	32%	51%
SBE Blend vs. e-Learning	30%	41%
Text Blend vs. e-Learning	27%	48%
ILT vs. Text Blend	4%	
SBE Blend vs. Text Blend	2%	
ILT vs. SBE Blend	1%	

blended groups did about 158% better on their authentic assessment score than the control group. Even the e-learning group (no SBE) came in at 99% higher than the control. Because these groups are being measured against a group that had no training, you would think that these high performance numbers would not be surprising. However, when these results are presented to Thomson NETg clients, they are always very surprised. Most will say that intuitively they knew that training makes a difference in human performance—they just had never seen hard data to support their observations. Adding to their surprise is the extent of the impact—even for the nonblended e-learning group. Needless to say, Kirkpatrick level 3 studies are very scarce.

Comparing all of the blended groups to the e-learning group (no SBE), the learners in the blended groups did approximately 30% better on their authentic assessment scores. The surprise in these comparisons was that the learners in all of the blended groups completed the authentic assessment in an average of 46% less time. These findings suggest that blended learning not only yielded better results over conventional, nonblended e-learning, but it also produced more efficient learning.

When we look at comparisons within the blends, we get additional data that surprised our research team. One of the main questions was: "Does using different instructional components (NLOs, text objects, ILT, or mentoring) alter the job impact of the blended learning solution?" The research team's original thinking was that there were some mixtures of media that impacted learning outcomes more than other mixtures. However, the data showed us that this was not the case and that the differences between the blended groups were not statistically significant. Therefore, if there were obvious differences between the control group and the blended groups, and/or differences between the e-learning group and the blended groups, and if media mix was not a statistically significant factor, what caused the increases in authentic assessment score and a decrease in time? After eliminating all other factors, we found that it was the use of the SBE that accounted for these positive increases in the learner's effectiveness and efficiency.

This caused NETg to redefine blended learning. It was less about media and more about instructional design. Blended learning occurs when the blend (a) activates prior experience; (b) demonstrates skills; (c) applies the skills; and (d) integrates the skills into real-world activities (Merrill, 2002). These four attributes were the basis for the SBE used in each of the blended groups and represented the key to the success of the learners in all of these groups.

Another example of how research has impacted an area of the NETg product is seen in the learner profile. In 1999, during a usability testing of a beta release of our product, we noticed some interesting learner behaviors. Many of the younger learners, profiled as typical of our client's entry level employees, were not attending to the instructions, not using our note-taking features, and generally just clicking through the various interactions irrespective of the feedback and the help features available. We also observed that many of these users were listening to their portable cassette players during instruction while simultaneously eating their lunches. Although these behaviors made us rightfully look at the design of our interface and overall product, we did see many older users attending to the instruction and using features that their younger counterparts ignored. The behaviors just listed were almost always associated with the 22- to 25-year-olds, which we eventually identified as the *Game Boy* generation. In a set of focus groups, a pattern emerged. Discussion with these participants identified poor time management skills, difficulty setting priorities, self-motivation issues, and the expectation that learning should require little effort on the part of the learner. We had to do more for this group of learners, and it was not enough to optimize the instruction. We had to assist the participants in optimizing themselves as learners. We did this through the development of a learner profile instrument, which not only assessed the learner's study skill behaviors but also suggested strategies for approaching self-paced instruction.

However, we needed a theoretical base and a proof-of-concept for the learner profile instrument. To achieve this, NETg sponsored a doctoral dissertation of one of Merrill's PhD advisees (Hemphill, 2000). Through this research project, the learner profile items were developed, psychometric properties were assessed, and items were refined and finalized. Hemphill tested the prototype instrument at three different colleges to determine if there was a relationship between the use of the suggested learner strategies and the learners' achievement on posttests. She found that there was a statistically significant difference between the achievement score of subjects who followed the learning strategies suggested in their learner profiles and that of those who did not follow prescribed learning strategies. In other words, those who were profiled and informed of their learning styles and preferences scored better on a posttest than those participants who were not aware of their learning styles.

Given Hemphill's findings, NETg decided to offer the NETg learner profile (LP) to our clients. In Phase I, the instrument was used to educate the learners regarding their learning styles and to advise them as to how they may best approach technology-based training (TBT). The learner was provided with necessary information to configure the course to match his or her learning style and preferences. This instrument was available on NETg.com and on NETg's Web-based training site, XtremeLearning, for approximately 30 months. During that time, over 30,000 learner profiles were produced.

In Phase I of the learner profile, we expanded on Snow and Farr's (1987) suggestion that the most realistic way of assessing learner characteristics is to maintain a holistic view that includes cognitive, metacognitive, and affective aspects.

Based on our observations during the usability study regarding learners who listened to music while engaged in learning, we also added a distraction dimension. Research shows that environmental conditions such as noise and movement and external distractions can block learning modalities (Weinstein & Mayer, 1983). Consequently, recommendations that align modality preference to distractibility were also included in Phase I of the NETg LP.

The characteristics assessed in the Phase I LP were:

- Metacognitive characteristics.
- Monitoring.
- Planning.
- Self-evaluation.
- Physical characteristics.
- Learning distracter.
- Affective characteristics.
- Learning confidence (a.k.a. self-efficacy).
- Motivation.

Originally, Phase I of the learner profile was biased to an e-learning environment. In light of the results of the already cited Thomson NETg Job Impact Study and the fact that learners were now experiencing a blend of media, the learner profile was redesigned to account for other learning environments. This became Phase II of the learner profile.

Figure 16.6 is an example of a screen from the learner profile that reports the learner's metacognitive characteristic of planning. Along with the new focus on a blended media environment, this phase of the job impact study focused on the learner's thinking and learning processes and also how his or her knowledge affects these processes—his or her cognitive characteristics. The cognitive characteristics assessed in Phase II LP are learning channel and thinking style.

Cognitive characteristics.

FIG. 16.6.   Sample planning output.

- Learning channel.
- Thinking style.

One of the cognitive characteristics that we included in Phase II is learning channel, also known as modality. Although adults can learn in any modality, learners have a preferred learning orientation of visual, auditory, kinesthetic/tactual, or some combination (Dunn & Dunn, 1993; Eislzer, 1983).

NETg's LP identifies learners as visual, auditory, kinesthetic/hands-on, or some other combination, which could include a primarily auditory learner who also possesses some visual traits or a kinesthetic learner with both visual and auditory learner traits.

An additional cognitive characteristic that was included in Phase II is thinking style or field dependence and field independence. Field dependence and independence describe the ability to analyze and restructure disorganized information. This is a skill essential to problem solving. Field-independent learners impose their own cognitive structure onto information that is presented to them, and consequently, they work well with disorganized information. In contrast, field-dependent learners rely more on the structure that is provided and thus are less able to work with disorganized information. Witkin and Goodenough (1976) found that these traits remain stable across environments.

For the purposes of the NETg LP, field dependents are referred to as detailed thinkers whereas field independents are referred to as big-picture thinkers. It has been found that field independents tend to ignore details that do not support their conceptualization whereas field dependents are more focused on the detail of the problems. When learners are provided with insight into their particular thinking style, it is hoped that they will be better prepared to adapt themselves to whatever learning environment they experience. Figure 16.7 shows a sample thinking style output for a field-dependent or detailed thinker.

The learner profile was undergoing field trials in 2003, which would produce findings that would lead to additional research. As stated earlier, the intent of the learner profile is to balance what we have to do to improve the learning environment with what we also have to do to optimize the learner. We have found that there are many learners who need help in developing appropriate learning strategies. The learner profile is a start in that direction.

CONCLUDING REMARKS

Early in this chapter, I referred to myself as a practitioner. Although I have been heavily influenced by the best practices of instructional design, I have also been driven to create training products that increase my client's competitive edge. Today, when NETg produces an instructional solution, it is intended as a solution that

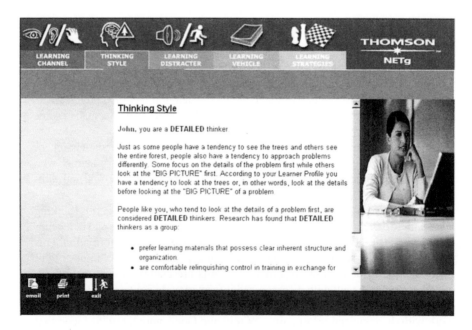

FIG. 16.7.   Sample thinking style output.

directly affects the bottom line of the business. Return on investment (ROI) is not just cost savings, but rather a measurable increase in the value of a business's human capital as demonstrated by increased productivity and profitability for the company. Good instructional design is also good for business. That includes both the training vendor community and their clients.

I have maintained on many occasions and have been quoted as saying, "If our courses do not teach, they have no value." With tight training budgets, training directors and managers are focused on the cost of training. In this environment, it is easy to create inexpensive training that can be sold at an attractive price. However, if you are paying out dollars for solutions, then the focus should be on how effective the training is at producing employees with stronger and better skills. Training is not cost-effective if the learner does not learn, and it is most cost-effective when the learner quickly, reliably, and measurably learns what is required. This means a focus on relevance. I offer a variation of my quote from a business perspective: "If the courses that our clients purchase do not get results, they have no value and we will get no future business."

As our job impact study has pointed out, training also needs to address more complex learning outcomes and environments. It is no longer just about feature/function instruction or if/then decision-making skills. Training is about preparing the learner to function in the complexity of today's workplace. After the kind of instruction described in our study, learners should be able to immediately begin to contribute to the success of the company. That can only happen with training that takes place within a work context familiar to the learner and that follows a set of key fundamental principles that are the bedrock of Merrill's research.

In closing, and in the spirit of this *festschrift,* it is not only appropriate for me to take off my hat to Dave Merrill in appreciation for providing a rich body of research to draw on. I also want to publicly thank him for his direct support being my instructional design conscience; he is always there to tell me that our products could be better and to help to provide the ideas to make them better. In that same spirit I also recognize the web of other researchers in our field who have influenced me, the teams of which I have been a part, and the products that became real-world manifestations as a result of their contributions. Currently, these products touch over a million people per day in more than 11 languages—with both of these numbers growing.

I would like to leave you with one final insight that came out of the Thomson Job Impact Study, in which Dave and his students played such a significant role. Media makes no difference in learner outcomes. In case you did not hear me, let me repeat this in a louder voice: *Media makes no difference in learner outcomes.* The lovers and believers in technology and its potential to deliver effective training should post this on their mirrors and read it every morning before going to work. If Dave has taught us anything, it is that effective learning comes from the application of best practices premised on the research in the field of instructional design. That is the message in *A Pebble-in-the-Pond Model for Instructional Design* (Merrill, 2002) and *First Principles of Instruction* (Merrill, 2000). For that message, and the ripples it has caused and will continue to create, we all owe Dave our gratitude.

Now let's all turn those ripples into a tsunami.

REFERENCES

Bloom, B. S. (1976). *Human characteristics and school learning*. New York: McGraw-Hill.

Boyle, S. L. T., & Merrill, M. D. (2003). *Thomson job impact study (phases I & II): The next generation of corporate learning*. Naperville, IL: Thomson Learning.

Blumenthal, J. C. (1994). *English 2300 with writing applications: A programmed course in grammar and usage* (6th ed.). Boston: Heinle & Heinle.

Cronbach, L. J., & Snow, R. E. (1976). *Aptitudes and instructional methods: A handbook of research on interactions*. New York: Irvington.

Dunn, R., & Dunn, K. (1993). *Teaching secondary students through their individual learning styles*. Boston: Allyn and Bacon.

Eislzer, C. F. (1983). Perceptual preferences as an aspect of adolescent learning styles. *Education, 103*(3), 231–242.

Hemphill, L. S. (2000). *Development of a learner profile for computer-based training*. Unpublished doctoral dissertation, Utah State University, Logan.

Keller, J. M., & Kopp, T. W. (1987). An application of the ARCS model of motivational design. In C. M. Reigeluth (Ed.), *Instructional theories in action: Lessons illustrating selected theories and models* (pp. 289–320). Hillsdale, NJ: Lawrence Erlbaum Associates.

Kirkpatrick, D. L. (1998). *Evaluating training programs*. San Francisco: Berrett-Koehler.

L'Allier, J. J. (1980). *An evaluation study of a computer-based lesson that adjusts reading level by monitoring on-task reader characteristics*. (Doctoral dissertation, University of Minnesota, 1980). *Dissertation Abstracts International, 41/07-A*.

Landa, L. N. (1974). *Algorithmization in learning and instruction*. Englewood Cliffs, NJ: Educational Technology Publications.

Mager, R. F. (1997). *Preparing instructional objectives: A critical tool in the development of effective instruction* (3rd ed.). Atlanta, GA: Center for Effective Performance.

McLuhan, M. (1964). *Understanding media: The extensions of man*. Boston: MIT Press.

Merrill, M. D. (1987). A lesson based on the component display theory. In C. M. Reigeluth (Ed.), *Instructional theories in action: Lessons illustrating selected theories and models* (pp. 201–244). Hillsdale, NJ: Lawrence Erlbaum Associates.

Merrill, M. D. (2000, October). *First principles of instruction*. Paper presented at the meeting of Association for Educational Communications and Technology, Denver, CO.

Merrill, M. D. (2002). A pebble-in-the-pond for instructional design. *Performance Improvement, 41*(7), 39–44.

Merrill, M. D., Drake, L., Lacy, M. J., & Pratt, J. A. (1996). Reclaiming instructional design. *Educational Technology, 36*(5), 5–7.

Merrill, M. D., & Tennyson, R. D. (1977). *Teaching concepts: An instructional design guide*. Englewood Cliffs, NJ: Educational Technology Publications.

Snow, R., & Farr, M. (1987). Cognitive-conative-affective processes in aptitude, learning, and instruction: An introduction. In R. Snow & M. Farr (Eds.), *Conative and affective process analysis* (pp. 1–10). Hillsdale, NJ: Lawrence Erlbaum Associates.

Taylor, D. A. (1991). *Object technology: A manager's guide*. Boston: Addison-Wesley.

Tennyson, R. D., & L'Allier, J. J. (1980). Breaking out of the Skinner box. *NSPI Journal*, *19*(2), 28–43.

Tennyson, R. D., & Park, O. (1980). The teaching of concepts: A review of instructional design literature. *Review of Educational Research, 50*, 55–70.

Tennyson, R. D., & Rothen, W. (1977). Pre-task and on-task adaptive design strategies for selecting number of instances in concept acquisition. *Journal of Educational Psychology, 69*(5), 586–592.

Tennyson, R. D., & Schott, F. (1997). Instructional design theory, research, and models. In R. D. Tennyson, F. Schott, N. Seel, & S. Dijkstra (Eds.), *Instructional design, international perspective* (Vol. 1). Mahwah, NJ: Lawrence Erlbaum Associates.

Tennyson, R. D., Tennyson, C. L., & Rothen, W. (1977). *A review of computer based instructional control strategies: Application toward an adaptive model.* Minneapolis: University of Minnesota, Instructional Systems Laboratory.

Thomson Learning. (2003). The Thomson learning learner profile [online]. Retrieved April 9, 2004, from http://www.netg.com/research/lp/cgi/survey.exe

TLC. (2003). The Library of Congress [online]. Retrieved April 9, 2004, from http://www.tlcdelivers.com/tlc/crs/Bib0590.htm

Weinstein, C. E., & Mayer, R. E. (1983). The teaching of learning strategies. In M.C. Wittrock (Ed.), *Handbook of research on teaching* (3rd ed., pp. 315–327). New York: Macmillan.

Wilson Learning. (1984). *The versatile organization.* Eden Prairie, MN: Wilson Learning Corporation.

Witkin, H. A., & Goodenough, D. R. (1976). *Field dependence revisited* (RB 76-39). Princeton, NJ: Educational Testing Service.

The Role of Mentoring: Slaying Dragons— An Interview With Dr. Merrill

Andy Van Schaack
Vanderbilt University

Celestia Ohrazda
Syracuse University

"I would never read a book if it were possible for me to talk half an hour with the man who wrote it."

—*Woodrow Wilson*

Rather than ask Dr. Merrill to write a book (or a chapter) on his philosophy of mentoring, we spoke with him directly about it. Dr. Merrill has had a significant influence on the field of instructional technology—this book, and the distinguished authors who contributed to it, are a testament to that. He has also had a personal influence on countless graduate students, including the authors of this chapter, through one-on-one as well as indirect mentoring. We asked him about his mentors and what he learned from them. We also talked about successful and unsuccessful mentor–protégé relationships—how he enters into them and what he does when they occasionally go awry. He went on to identify the key responsibility of a mentor (which influenced the title of this chapter), and he described the most important characteristics he looks for in a protégé. The interview concluded with Dr. Merrill sharing his "secret of good mentoring."

The interview was recorded and transcribed by one of the editors of this volume (Andy Van Schaack). Dave Merrill was then given an opportunity to edit the interview for coherence. We have indicated our questions in italics in the discussion section, which consists mostly of Dr. Merrill's replies to our queries. Dr. Merrill began this interview, as he does so many of his classes, with his usual challenge.

DISCUSSION

Ask me a question.

Let's start with a little history. Who was your mentor, and what influence did he or she have on your career?

My major professor was Larry Stolurow and he was my first mentor. He was very busy and had a lot of research contracts. At the time, I didn't feel like I was getting any mentoring. I felt like that he was very busy doing his own thing. In retrospect, however, I learned a lot from Dr. Stolurow. He certainly modeled how to get sponsored research. I had an NDEA fellowship; I was a full-time student, and I didn't have to work as a graduate assistant—I wasn't on anybody's project. This allowed me to do my own research using the equipment and resources provided by Dr. Stolurow's research. In subtle ways, Stolurow provided a nurturing environment that encouraged entrepreneurship. As a result, I learned to be independent, to define my own problems, and to direct my own research efforts with minimal supervision. Although I was frustrated at the time by his laissez-faire mentoring, he nevertheless provided a rich research environment, which was a significant contribution to my later research work.

My most influential conceptual mentor was Bob Gagné. His mentoring was very indirect—mentoring through ideas rather than mentoring on a personal basis. Over the years I had several opportunities to discuss our mutual interests and the significant influence he had on my thinking. We corresponded on several occasions about our ideas. This culminated in two once-in-a-lifetime experiences for me. The first was an all-day (four 90-minute sessions) discussion on instructional design held July 10, 1988, at Utah State University. This event was videotaped and subsequently published as seven installments in a series in *Educational Technology* (Twitchell, 1990a, 1990b, 1990c, 1990d, 1990e, 1990f, 1991). The second, a year later, was a 4-day, 6 hours per day, discussion held at the National Academy of Science in Washington, DC, between Gagné and myself with only two other folks present to record the session. This was a life-changing experience for me. Unfortunately, the recordings have never been transcribed. Subsequent to this event, Gagné and I did write a paper together based on some of our discussion (Gagné & Merrill, 1990).

Probably the greatest personal mentor I had was Darrel Monson at Brigham Young University. I characterize his mentoring as "*no* is not the right answer." I learned from Darrel never to give up. Here's the story. We were working together on a proposal for a church-funded project. He mentored me through the proposal-writing process: I'd write a draft; he'd edit it; I'd write another draft; he'd edit it. Finally, he said, "Okay, it's ready. I'll take it to the vice-president of the university who's in charge of making the decision."

I was very anxious to know what was going to happen. I went into his office for our regular Thursday morning meeting and anxiously asked, "What did he say? What did he say?" Darrel said, "He said, *no.*" So I put my tail between my legs and said, "Oh darn, I worked so hard on that." When I turned to leave, he asked, "Where are you going?" "Well, what's to do?" "I didn't say we weren't going to do it. I just said he said *no.*" And I questioned, "Well, if he said *no* then how are we going to do it?" Darrel's life-changing response was, "Well, you and I both know that *no is not the right answer.*" That became my slogan for the rest of my career.

Darrel sat me down and said, "Okay, we obviously didn't think about this appropriately. We didn't think about it from his point of view, and therefore, if we redo this proposal from his point of view and how it's going to solve problems that he has, we'll probably get the money." I rewrote the proposal, trying to take into consideration what the vice-president might have in mind. We resubmitted it. It had exactly the same statement of work and exactly the same budget—everything was the same except for the reason why we were doing the study. The vice-president came back and said, "This is a much better idea—a much better proposal. I like this. We'll do this." I learned a great lesson.

Jack Adams, a professor at the University of Illinois, provided some important academic mentoring. For his class in experimental psychology I wrote a report of a research study I had conducted for his class. Adams said, "This is a fabulous paper. You should publish it." He gave me an *A.* I thought that this was very nice and put it in my file. Three years later, somebody else did the same study, and it generated a whole series of follow-on studies. I realized, after the fact, that if it's worth writing, it's worth publishing. I am still upset that I didn't publish that paper, although it was not an area of research I would have pursued.

In your examples of the influence others have had on your career, both academically and administratively, you seemed to show quite a bit of initiative, and what you looked to your mentor for was to "slay the dragon"—to take out a bureaucratic roadblock.

Darrel Monson used to tell me all the time, "My role is to knock down anything that prevents you from doing what you need to do." In my experience, too many administrators see their role as gatekeeping, putting barriers in your way that keep you from doing what you want to do. I learned that an effective academic career takes a lot of initiative, and I probably learned that from my major professor, who sort of forced me to be on my own and still get things done.

What are the characteristics of a great protégé, or at least a great person you're mentoring?

There are two things that I look for. Number one is initiative. If a person doesn't have initiative, I don't want to work with him. If they say, "Tell me what to do," then I don't want to talk to them. If they come to me and say, "I've got this whole list of things I'm going to try to do," then I can respond, "Okay, great! My role is to help you get it done, to inspire you, and to get things out of your way."

The other thing I look for is new ideas and people that push my thinking. The reason I'm at a university after all these years instead of in business is because I love to work with really bright graduate students who are constantly challenging what I'm thinking—that's my favorite thing. Just the other day, a student came to me and said, "I've just read your papers on knowledge objects, and I have a question." "What is it?" I asked. He said, "You're wrong!" Well, that started a great conversation, and he and I are now working on papers together on that subject. And he was right from his perspective. He made the point that we could do a whole bunch of things with computer science that I hadn't been able to do before. And now I'm having a hard time even keeping up with where he's going with it. But for me, that's my favorite thing—that's what keeps me at a university. When people come in with bright ideas, my job is to encourage them, help them, and maybe direct them a little bit.

In other words, slay some dragons?

Yeah, slay some dragons. And let me tell you a dragon slaying story. Many years ago, before the days of word processors, I had a student that did a dissertation in the research group that I was heading. One day, he came in and asked, "Can the secretary of the group type my dissertation?" And I said, "It's big, you know." It was almost 200 pages. "It's really going to take her a while." "Well," he pleaded, "I don't have any other resources." "Okay," I agreed, "we can use your paper as a tech report for part of what we're doing."

So, every morning, the secretary is laboriously typing this report. I'm trying to get her to do other work, but she's typing the dissertation. Every time I ask her to do something, she can't because she's typing this dissertation. It's going on and on and on and it's driving me crazy because things are not getting done that I need to have done. Finally, she finishes it and we have a celebration. We buy donuts and sing songs and say, "Yes, yes, yes!" and, "We're out of here!"

That was on a Thursday or Friday. The next Monday, I came into the office to find her laboriously typing again. "What are we doing?" I almost yelled. "We have to retype the last 70 pages of the dissertation," she meekly explained. "Why!?!" She patiently explained that when it went to the format checker, one page had four hyphens on it, and we were only allowed to have three hyphenated words per page—and that meant that everything rippled. So we had to retype all of it, because it all rippled. Now in this day and age, with computers and word processors, it would be a piece of cake to eliminate a hyphen, but not in 1969.

"This is crazy," I exclaimed. "There is no way we're retyping this [expletive deleted] dissertation." I called the hyphen checker and suggested, "Hey, retyping a dissertation for one hyphen is ridiculous." "We have rules, and we have to enforce them," he firmly explained. "If we make exceptions for your student, we'll have to make exceptions for all students, and our formats would get sloppy." "Oh, this is too much! Thank you." I hung up on him.

I called the graduate dean and asked, "Can I have an appointment with you?" "Sure," he agreed. I went to his office and explained my visit. "Dr. Riddle, I'm here about a hyphen." He looked really puzzled: "I beg your pardon." I repeated, "I'm here about a hyphen. We have an extra hyphen." The Dean was baffled. "I don't understand where you're going." "Well, one of your people checks for format. One of the rules ..." and I pulled out the little book "... is that you can only have three hyphenated words on a page." "That is the most ridiculous thing I ever heard," he muttered. I went on, "As a result, we're in the process of retyping 70 pages of a dissertation because of an extra hyphen." "That is absurd! That is the dumbest thing I've ever heard!" he said in disgust. Enthusiastically I replied, "Great, I prepared a letter for you to sign here making an exception to the hyphen." And so it was taken care of.

Slaying dragons is one of the roles of a mentor. And I think you have to be gutsy to do it, because it'd be easier to just say, "Okay, we're going to retype it." In my experience, universities are basically inane, dumb organizations that make volumes of rules that are often not in their own best interest. As a professor, one of my roles is to help my students identify these kinds of rules and teach them how to get around them. I can't always overturn them—I was very lucky in that particular case. Sometimes I run into stone walls, but as a mentor I will continue to tilt at windmills if it is in the best interest of my students.

Andy Van Schaack can tell you the same thing. He called me several years ago with an interesting proposal: "I want to come and get a PhD with you." I was delighted because we had previously worked together. "There's only one little problem," he continued. "I don't have an undergraduate degree." "That could be a slight problem," I admitted, "because there are some gatekeeping clerks in the university that won't understand that your experience is far better than a bachelor's or master's degree." But I went on, "*No* is not the right answer, we'll do it." Here he sits in this interview today, finishing up his PhD.

What's the difference between a mentor and an advisor?

I am definitely not an advisor. I refuse to learn dates for final exams, how many days after the semester starts can you drop a class, and the hundred and one other rules that control graduate study. An advisor helps a student navigate this maze of regulations. I refuse to learn all these arbitrary regulations that change from minute to minute. I advise my students to get the pamphlet and to figure out and abide by the dates. I caution them to never come to me and say, "Dr. Merrill, you forgot to tell me I had to have my plan of study in by such and such a date," because I'm just going to shrug my shoulders.

On the other hand, when it comes to helping students with the contents of their dissertation, or knocking illogical barriers out of the way—I'll be happy to do that. But I caution them not to expect me to request exceptions to things that they should have known and then after the fact say, "Oh, I forgot to turn this in. Will you help me?" because I'll say *no*.

When it comes to mentoring, how do you choose people to mentor? Or do they come to you?

Most of the time, they choose me. I can think of at least two exceptions. One was Charlie Reigeluth. When I was at Brigham Young University, the applications for PhDs came across our desks as faculty members. I took one look at this Harvard cum laude and thought, "I don't care if this guy has warts, I want to work with him. He's an exceptional person."

And this before you even had met him?

Yes. All I saw was his resumé, but it jumped out at me. It was a standard deviation above anybody else we had in the stack or had had in the stack for some time. He had put on his cover letter that his reason for coming to BYU was to work on the TICCIT project. There was a team of people on the project and he may have had someone else in mind, but the day he arrived I immediately called him on the phone and scheduled an interview with him. And, of course, I pointed out to him that I was really the key player on the TICCIT system, and he really should work with me. He ended up working with both Vic Bunderson and myself, but I got to be his advisor. Charlie and I became, and still are, the best of friends and we did a lot of writing together.

Another person I sought out was a student that had just finished his master's degree in our program. I observed his work and said to my administrative assistant, "Hire Leston Drake. I don't care where we get the money, just hire him." He was a brilliant person with whom I wanted to work and I encouraged him to do a PhD. As it turned out, Leston did the development of the electronic simulator, which had been a goal of mine for several years. His implementation of these ideas was way beyond what I could have done without his contribution.

What happens when someone approaches you? How do you determine whether you're the right person for them? And let's say you begin a relationship with them, but it falls apart. How do you handle that?

Yes, I've had a couple of situations like that. One student came to the university and said, "I came to work with you." He was an older student—a bright guy with a lot of good ideas. I arranged for him to work on one of our projects. It turns out that he had worked with the sponsoring agency and was good friends with our project monitor. Unbeknownst to me, at one point he went to the agency and told his friend that he felt like we had been dishonest and that the project was not what it really appeared to be—that it didn't work the way that we had represented it would in our presentation. This essentially undermined the project, and we lost the contract. Of course, I was very upset.

When he got back, I called him in, and spelled out the rules: "First, when you're working on our team, if you want to talk to our project monitor, you tell me, and then we talk about what you're going to say, so we speak with one voice. And second, you don't go tell somebody that we're being dishonest, especially when I don't agree with you that we are. I know the product doesn't work exactly the way you thought it should, but you know that it works very well. And to say that we're being dishonest and misrepresenting it is really bad." His response was, "Well, I have to be honest. You know, I have to be honest with myself." "Well, that's fine, you can be honest with yourself," I agreed. "I'm not demanding you to be dishonest, but I do expect at least a minimum amount of courtesy and loyalty." I suggested that perhaps he should consider working with someone else. "But I came to work with you," he pleaded. "If you came to work with me, why the heck did you do this?"

He pleaded for me to keep him on, and I reluctantly agreed but told him that if it ever happened again, that's it. And it did, just a few months later—he did the exact same thing. He told our client that nothing was the way it was supposed to be. And again, when I called him in, he was absolutely shocked that I would be upset. And I just said, "Look, I think our relationship is over. I think what you've done is unethical, but I'm not going to make an issue out of it. It's between you and me. However, I don't want to be on your committee. I certainly won't chair your committee. If you can find somebody else in the program to work with you, that's great, but don't ask me to be on the committee."

"Well," he pleaded once again, "oh, my gosh, I came to work with you. I wanted a degree with you." "You're not going to have a degree with me," I assured him. That's one case where the relationship fell apart, but that's a rare, rare, situation.

What about problem situations with dissertation committees? Do you ever find yourself working with someone on their dissertation, and it turns out that their approach or their methodological rigor is not what you expect and you have to remove yourself?

Yes, that happens all the time, of course. And generally, I find people very responsive. I like to be the chair; it's good to be the king. It's hard to be on a committee, because when you're on a committee, you find out you're not just helping the student; you end up arguing with another faculty member of the committee, and I don't like to do that.

Because that other faculty member defends the student's approach?

Yes, they defend the approach. So I'm generally very upfront with students. I just say, "Here's what I expect." And so, most of the time, students self-select.

And what would you say? Give us your lecture.

The lecture varies depending on what kind of a study that they're doing, but there are certain things that I say right upfront. For the last 10 years, I've always said to students, "Write your dissertation first. Go write me a draft of your dissertation, and I'll tell you if I'll be on your committee ... whether I'll chair your committee or not." You know, "Come back with what you think. Why are you here as a PhD student? How do you want to change the world? What's your question?" If they reply, "I don't know," I say, "Well, then, go think about it, because it's hard for me to tell you if I'm going to help you if I don't know where you're going or if you don't know where you're going. So try to decide."

Right now, we have a PhD program that I helped to architect, which has practicums as a major feature of the program. So I say to my students, "Now, look, I don't want you to go shopping for practicums. I don't want you to take a proposal over here and a study over there and a development project somewhere else. I want you to tie them all together. That's what I expect, and if you're not comfortable with that, then you and I will probably have some problems." Then I explain, "There are certain things I don't like. I don't like survey research. For the most part, I'm not equipped to do it. I don't think we do very good survey research in our field. Most of the dissertations I see in education that are surveys, I think, are a waste of the paper they're written on. And, therefore, if you're going to do survey research, you probably don't want to do it with me. Now, if you're going to do experimental research, fine, or I'll work with you on a theoretical dissertation, or I'll work with you on tool development. But I do have very strong, rigorous standards."

Let me tell you another story. When I got to USC, they asked, "Have you chaired dissertations?" I answered, "Yeah, sure, four or five." And they said, "Oh, good." Then they handed me 30 folders and said, "You're going to chair these." I said, "You can't chair 30 people! This is ridiculous!" And they replied, "Well, everybody has 30, and this is your list."

The first thing I did was call all of those people and found out that two-thirds of them were no longer even interested in getting a PhD or had dropped out of the program long-since. So I got the list down to about 10 or 12. When I called one woman, I said, "It looks like you're all done but the dissertation, and you've been here for about 2 years or 3 years at that stage. What's happening?"

She indicated that she had gone through four chairs so far. I suggested that we talk because I had just been assigned as her latest chairperson. She'd come into the program as a public school teacher and she'd done this fabulous program in discipline—working with parents to set up a whole communication system. However, she was doing her dissertation on some simple survey of discipline situations. I said, "Wait a minute, you handed me a book that you've written that's fabulous. You know, really interesting stuff. I thought it was very impressive. Why don't you use this for your dissertation?" Her reply was, "Oh, they said I had to gather data." "Nonsense. This is crazy. You don't know anything about data analysis. You did poorly in your stat classes, which you had to take, but you did a great job developing this discipline program. Why don't we just use this?" She did and she completed her PhD ... after 4 or 5 years of getting pushed around. All I did was to sit down with her and help her realize how to make it happen.

The other thing I try to do when I work with a student is to ask, "What's their passion?" and let them follow their passion. If it isn't doing an experimental study, then why force them to do that? Or if they've got some other really great idea that doesn't fit the mold of what an education dissertation ought to be, then I say, "Okay, let's make it work." But I demand rigor, but let's have the rigor in a different area. So I've chaired some really unusual dissertations. I've had committee members get upset with me, but I believe that "*no* is not the right answer," and I become the defender of the student.

You often mention the necessity of passion in research. How important do you think it is for doctoral students beginning their studies to have a passion? And, as a mentor, do you think it's part of your responsibility to help them find it?

Absolutely, if you don't have a passion, you ought to go do something else. Why are you getting a PhD? Getting a PhD is way too much work to not have a passion. So if they don't have a passion, I try to help them find a passion or create a passion. Because if you don't think you're going to change the world in some way, then why are you getting a PhD? If you're getting a PhD just to get a bigger salary or because you need it for advancement, then go work with somebody else. I only want to deal with people who want to change the world. I don't know if that's over-stated, but you know, if you don't really believe that you have something to con-tribute, why are you getting a PhD? The whole purpose of a PhD is to contribute knowledge. And so, I try to really push passion with my students, and if they don't grasp it within the first half hour, you can bet that they're never going to grasp it. At that point, I encourage them to go work with somebody else.

Let's say you meet with a student who wants to get a PhD and she knows she wants to change the world, but she doesn't know what it is she can do. She has pas-sion but no direction. How can you help her?

Well, I think there are several things that can happen. Obviously, the most pro-ductive relationships between a mentor and a student happen when they're both working on a project that they both have a passion about. So if I get a student that says, "You know, I really want to work with you," then my first question usually is, "Why?" If they don't have an answer to that and say, "Well, I just heard about you." or "I think you're important," then I say, "Okay, let me tell you what I'm interested in." And so, I lay out two or three different paths that I would be happy to pursue, and I ask, "Do any of these appeal to you?" If they answer, "Well, I don't know," then I say, "Then go think about it, and here's some things to read. If any of these appeal to you, come back, and we'll talk some more."

So, if a person doesn't know where he is going, then I try to direct him a little and say, "Here's what I'm interested in. Do any of these grab you? And if you can get turned on by some of these, then great, we'll have a great relationship. But if none interest you, you might want to go somewhere else."

I've actually turned away students who have come in and said, "I really want to work on this and this and this." And I say, "Well, I don't have any skill in that," or "That's not my area of interest." They might say, "Well, I know, but I really want to work with you." And I say, "But it doesn't make sense, because I'm not going to be of much help to you, but here's so-and-so on the faculty—this is his area. I think you'd be much better with him … and maybe if you want, I'll serve on your committee."

Looking at the big picture, do you feel that you've had a role in mentoring the field of instructional design and instructional technology?

Well, that's a hard question to answer humbly. Obviously, I've had some influ-ence, but I can honestly say that was never my intent. From the very beginning, I never set out to get tenure. I never set out to be well known. None of those were on my goal list. I entered the field because I wanted to know how to make instruction maximally effective and efficient and appealing. That was my question the day I started and it's my question today. It never changed. I pursued that question in a lot of different ways, with and without technology. So, I suppose I've had a significant influence on the field—at least idea-wise. I've never been an organization person, though. I've only held office once in my entire career. I've never run for an AERA or AECT or ISPI office. So my influence, if it's there, has been strictly conceptual. And for me, that's great. I'm just sorry that everybody didn't adopt component display theory as the standard [big smile].

Well, I certainly believe that the chapters in this book will reflect the influence that you've had on the field, directly and indirectly. And inasmuch as people have been influenced by your ideas, like component display theory, at least that, perhaps, planted a seed, allowing them to take off in a different direction.

I facetiously said that I wished everybody had adopted component display theory, but that wasn't the reason I wrote it in the first place. I think that the role of a scholar is to stimulate discussion. I see publication not as an archive but as a discussion—and I've always seen it that way. As a result, I've sometimes rushed articles into print prematurely. I've been criticized for that, because some of my articles aren't polished. But I didn't care, because it seemed to me that getting the ideas out there and getting people talking about them was what it was all about. And stimulating ideas and thought is what it's all about, and that's been my intent from the very beginning.

Dr. Merrill, can you leave us with one final piece of advice on how to work successfully as a mentor?

Let me tell you a story. I had a colleague who came to me once and said, "I don't know why, but students don't seem to like to work with me very much." And he went on, "You have all these students that are always around you, and you've got a lot of things going on, and they're all writing papers with you." And he continued, "I just don't seem to do that very much. How can I change so that could happen with me?"

I explained my approach: "First of all, I think you have to treat students as equals. I don't see myself as a professor and them as students. Most of them have had all kinds of experiences in life." And I added, "Most of them are smarter than I am. And I like to work in a way that they get as much credit as I do. Or, sometimes when I don't need the credit, let them have all or most of the credit. Put their name on a paper, even though they maybe only collected the data."

He exclaimed, "Oh, I could never allow that! A student must earn my respect before I could ever treat them as an equal." I questioned him, "And you wonder why you have a problem? That's your problem." He went away, saying, "No way." And to this day, he's still arrogant and students still don't like to work with him.

But for me, I've always had fun. I don't think that early in my career when I was working with Charlie Reigeluth, Bob Tennyson, and the whole group of people that were with them, anybody could have told who was a professor and who was a student. We were just one big group having fun together. It's a little more difficult now, because the age gap between me and students is so much greater that they don't quite see me as a colleague anymore, even though I try to treat them that way. I see the same thing happening with David Wiley here at Utah State; he's got a group of young students that are about the same age, and they all are collegial. And that, to me, is the essence of good mentoring—recognizing that here's a group of bright people who are all in this together and that I just happen to have a little different role than the rest, but we're all working together. So if there's any secret of good mentoring, I think that's it.

CONCLUSION

We would like to add, by way of conclusion, that this interview with Dr. Merrill took place via teleconferencing. The discussion section is a transcription of that interview. If you are not satisfied with this approach that was inspired by Woodrow Wilson and would like to read the "book" as well, Dr. Merrill has posted several essays on graduate education, including "Write Your Dissertation First" (Merrill, 2000). These essays and others can be found at the Utah State University ID-2 Web site (see http://www.id2.usu.edu/Papers/Contents.html).

REFERENCES

Gagné, R. M., & Merrill, M. D. (1990). Integrative goals for instructional design. *Educational Technology Research and Development, 38*(1), 23–30.

Merrill, M. D. (2000). *Write your dissertation first and other essays on a graduate education.* Retrieved March 30, 2004, from http://www.id2.usu.edu/Papers/Graduate Education.pdf

Twitchell, D. E. (1990a). Robert M. Gagné and M. David Merrill in conversation: No. 1: Reviewing the main points of Robert M. Gagné's learning theory. *Educational Technology, 30*(7), 34-39.

Twitchell, D. E. (1990b). Robert M. Gagné and M. David Merrill in conversation: No 2: Reviewing the main points of M. David Merrill's learning theory. *Educational Technology, 30*(8), 36–41.

Twitchell, D. E. (1990c). Robert M. Gagné and M. David Merrill in conversation: No 3: An overview of M. David Merrill's new component display theory. *Educational Technology, 30*(9), 36–42.

Twitchell, D. E. (1990d). Robert M. Gagné and M. David Merrill in conversation: No 4: A look at the differences between the theories of Robert M. Gagné and M. David Merrill. *Educational Technology, 30*(10), 37–45.

Twitchell, D. E. (1990e). Robert M. Gagné and M. David Merrill in conversation: No. 5: A comparison of Robert M. Gagné's events of instruction and M. David Merrill's component display theory. *Educational Technology, 30*(11), 35–39.

Twitchell, D. E. (1990f). Robert M. Gagné and M. David Merrill in conversation: No. 6: The cognitive psychological basis for instructional design. *Educational Technology, 30*(12), 35–46.

Twitchell, D. E. (1991). Robert M. Gagné and M. David Merrill in conversation: No. 7: ICAI, computers in schools, an instructional design expert system. *Educational Technology, 31*(1), 34-40.

Epilogue:
Questioning Merrill

M. David Merrill and Colleagues

Utah State University/The Universe

The 2003 AECT Presidential Panel Session entitled "Questioning Merrill: Constructing the Future of Instructional Science and Technology" was held on October 23, 2003, and consisted of 10 panelists, each of whom posed a question or comment about Dave Merrill's work to which Merrill replied. Most of the panelists had provided their questions and comments to Dave prior to the session in order to give Dave a chance to prepare appropriately focused remarks. The session was moderated by one of the editors of this volume (Spector), and the other three were among the panelists asking questions. Celestia Ohrazda transcribed the session and Dave Merrill was given an opportunity to edit the transcription. The remainder of this chapter represents that session. Comments are attributed to individual participants and represent their remarks at the 2003 AECT Presidential Session.

THE SESSION

Panelists in order of appearance:

* Michael Spector—Professor and Chair, Instructional Design, Development & Evaluation, Syracuse University—session moderator.
* Celestia Ohrazda—doctoral student, Instructional Design, Development & Evaluation, Syracuse University.

- Charles Reigeluth—Professor of Instructional Systems Technology, Indiana University.
- Paul Kirschner—Professor, Educational Technology Expertise Center, The Open University of the Netherlands.
- Jim L'Allier—Chief Learning Officer, Thompson NetG.
- Michael Farris—Director, Educational Technology Center, Texas State University.
- David Jonassen—Professor, Information Science and Learning Technologies and Program in Educational Psychology, University of Missouri–Columbia.
- Kinshuk—Associate Professor and Director, Advanced Learning Technologies Research Centre, Massey University, New Zealand.
- Bob Reiser—Professor and Program Coordinator, Instructional Systems, Florida State University.
- Andy Van Schaack—Doctoral Student, Instructional Technology, Utah State University.
- David Wiley—Assistant Professor of Instructional Technology, Utah State University.

Michael Spector:

The proceedings of this panel form the epilogue of the volume entitled *Innovations in Instructional Technology: Essays in Honor of M. David Merrill* that will be published by Lawrence Erlbaum Associates in 2005. The publisher's editor for this volume, Lori Hawver, is here, and we thank her and Lawrence Erlbaum Associates for their support. The editors of the book are myself, Dave Wiley, Andy Van Schaak, and Celestia Ohrazda. The panel is comprised of some of the people who have contributed chapters to the book and others who are not represented in the book but who represent the scope and depth of Merrill's influence. There will be about 20 chapters in the book. We are going to tape-record this session. What transpires this hour will form the epilogue of the book. Of course, Dave will have an opportunity to review and edit the transcribed version of this session. Panel participants were invited to pose questions, make a comment or present an issue about some aspect of Merrill's work and then give Dave an opportunity to respond. Most of the panelists provided their comments and questions in advance so as to give Dave some chance to prepare a response. We have 11 people who are going to take the advantage of this opportunity. Each will have about 2 or 3 minutes to make a comment or pose a question. I'm not going to take any time to introduce anybody, so the individual panelists can say who they are and what their connection with Dave is, and then make a comment or pose a challenge. And Dave, in his typical manner, will enlighten us with a response. I'm going to be ruthless with regard to timekeeping—just to let the panelists know in advance. So, if I start jumping up and down and ranting and raving—this includes you too, Dave—it's time to move along. I want to just add one word. When Dave Wiley and I talked about doing this book, we decided we wanted to emulate what we consider to be one of Dave Merrill's most significant contributions—namely, the mentoring of students. We each picked a doctoral student to assist in the process of editing the book and with this session. That's the reason why Andy and Celestia have been involved, and they've been extremely helpful thus far. Celestia has the honor of posing the first question or comment to Dave.

Celestia Ohrazda:

Okay. Dr. Merrill, first I have to express my delight in being here and having the opportunity to sit among everybody here.

I agonized in trying to find a question that would be both representative of the student population along the lines of mentoring and at the same time not be repetitive of something you had already written. On the flight here, I finished reading your collection of essays on graduate education and most of the questions that I had previously formulated in my mind were already answered. At the end of that book, you restated your original research question. I believe you have been working on this question for 40 years. You said that you seek to understand the role of instruction in human learning. How close are you to coming to answering that question?

Dave Merrill:

Well, we've got all the answers; okay, let's go home ☺. This is probably the question that drives all of us. Personally, I know a little more than I did before, but I think there's still a big issue and for me the big issue is, what is our fundamental role in society as instructional technologists? For me, the fundamental question is and has been: How do we make learning maximally efficient, effective, and appealing?

Celestia Ohrazda: Is it still a burning concern?

Dave Merrill: Yes, it's still burning.

Celestia Ohrazda: Passionately?

Dave Merrill: People keep asking me, "When are you going to retire?" I tell them I haven't answered that first research question yet.

Charles Reigeluth:

I believe a major feature of the information-age paradigm of instruction will be providing the learner with much greater control over both what to learn and how to learn it. Dave, you have long been an advocate of learner control and were instrumental in designing the TICCIT system to provide some measure of both kinds of control. As the capabilities of technology continue to grow, it seems it could become possible to design a personal tutoring system that could provide choices to a learner about both what to learn next within any area of the learner's interest and what methods to use to learn it. The keynote by Wayne Hodgins last night reinforced that notion. By keeping track of both what a particular learner knows and what methods work best with that learner, a personal tutor system could impose some constraints on what options it presents or it could provide advice about whether a learner makes a choice that seems inappropriate. So Dave, what vision do you have for such a personal tutor system and what are the most important contributions—such as within the transaction theory or ID Expert—that you've made to realize that?

Dave Merrill:

As you can see, Charlie's question requires only a very short answer . First I wouldn't call it a personal tutor, I'd call it a personal instructor because I don't want to eliminate experiential instruction, nor do I want to eliminate personalized team instruction—so "tutor" is the wrong word.

There are some current practices that might be confused with a personalized instructional system. Let me first suggest some things that such is system is not: (a) Providing only information is neither personalized nor instruction; (b) content selection is not personalized instruction; (c) constructivist-collaborative problem solving is neither personalized nor instruction; (d) digital content repositories are neither personalized nor instruction.

My vision is a system that combines learner control and system control: (a) a system that engages the learner in whole task or problems as well as teaching component knowledge and skills required to solve that problem or task; (b) a system that activates prior knowledge and skills and builds on what a student already knows; (c) a system that demonstrates and allows a student to apply knowledge and skills, providing necessary guidance and coaching early in instruction but gradually shifting the responsibility to the student as the instruction progresses; (d) a system that includes appropriate strategies for instructing different kinds of knowledge and skills; (e) a system that adapts these strategies to individual students based on prior knowledge using a combination of system and advisor control, not just of content, but also of strategy; and (f) a system that allows a student to apply or adapt new knowledge and skills to their own problems, in real-world settings.

Some of the principles we've previously identified for such a system are these: (a) uncoupling content from strategy—seeing them as separate things; (b) using content components (knowledge objects); (c) using strategy components that can be combined in different ways for different kinds of instructional outcomes; (d) an advisor function; and (e) guided learner control (Merrill, 1998, 2001a, 2001b,

2002c; Merrill & ID2 Research Group, 1993, 1996; Merrill, Jones, & Li, 1992; Merrill, Li, & Jones, 1990a, 1990b, 1991, 1992; Merrill, Schneider, & Fletcher, 1980; Merrill, Tennyson, & Posey, 1992).

Our most significant contribution to this task is our work on knowledge objects, which are not the same as learning objects and our work on strategy components. The TICCIT system (Merrill et al., 1980) involved learner control of strategies. The Electronic Text Book designed primarily by Mark Lacy elaborated our work on strategy components or transaction shells (Merrill & Thompson, 1999). The Instructional Simulator designed primarily by Leston Drake instantiated dynamic simulationlike transactions (Merrill, 1999). Currently, some work with Dave Wiley, Brent Lambert, and Del Roy Brinkerhoff is taking some of the ideas we had before and trying to build very robust computer-based representations of knowledge and instructional strategies.

Paul Kirschner:

I'm here actually as a substitute for Jeroen van Merriënboer, who is on sabbatical. I am honored that I can now ask a question of conscience and a question of clarification. David was recently honored at the Open University of the Netherlands, where he participated as an opponent (external examiner) in a PhD defense. If there was one thing that came out clearly both from his opponent's defense and from his acceptance speech, it was one simple question. The simple question was this: "But does it work?" The one question Dave asked was, "But Burt, does it work?" You are possibly the father of evidence-based research and the leading educational researcher in the United States and even in Europe. Evidence-based research is the determinant as to what we can study and what we can introduce as innovation in the schools. I know that you didn't have a chance to think about this beforehand, so let me provide some clarification.

Evidence-based research started in medicine and pharmacology, where you have this very simply defined and well-defined group. You have a person who is incredibly obese and has diabetes C and other things. They try something out, and, based on the evidence they get, they can see if it works or if it doesn't. But that methodology can't be translated and transformed to education because we're dealing with a room full of people. Yesterday Wayne said that if you gave everybody a piece of paper and a highlighter that they'd highlight different things. So what's the evidence? How do you determine if it works in educational settings? Can you really use that as the ultimate criterion?

Dave Merrill:

Number one, I think Wayne was wrong. Everyone doesn't come out differently. People learn pretty much the same now as they did 200 years ago and a thousand years ago. Evolution doesn't take place in decades; it takes place in millions of years. The argument that people are very different now or very different from one setting to another just plain doesn't hold. Basically people are human beings, no matter what culture they are in or where they are located; the underlying learning mechanisms have not changed in many, many years, and probably won't change in many years—at least not in our lifetimes. So, it's possible to have evidence-based research; it's possible to find out if people have learned and how they have learned. It's possible to find out if people have accomplished the objectives. The problem we have in education is that frequently we are so vague about what the objectives are that we have no idea what the evidence is and we don't know whether students have met those objectives or not. If we are clear what the objectives are, the evidence can be collected. If the objective is to learn something from some so-called constructivist experience, but we don't know what it is, then we don't know what the evidence is either. But this is not instruction. Instruction is when there is some specific goal to acquire some specific skill, and if you have that, then you can decide how to measure that skill—but that doesn't mean it's easy. That doesn't mean we don't have a lot of work to do in finding out how to measure complex things. How to measure adequate problem solving is not an easy thing. Most of the measures we've had in the past are really remember-type measurements and have not been measurements of high-level skills. The measurement and techniques we have to measure high-level skills are not very good.

Classical reliability theory, which is the basic theory underlying most measurement, is probably not adequate for the kind of measures we need for high-level skills. If we have any lack in this field in general it is that we are not studying measurement and assessment. We seem to have given up and thrown the baby out with the bathwater, saying, "We can't do it; so, therefore, let's not do it." So, my argument is very strong. I think it's possible; we can do it; we've got a lot of work to do; and I see very few people working on the problem.

James L'Allier:

Dave, as my academic grandfather [Merrill—Tennyson—L'Allier], I want to publicly thank you for being my instructional design conscience—always there to remind me that our products could be better and to help provide the research and best practices to make it so.

If you've taught me anything, it is that effective learning comes from the application of a set of best practices, which provides the premise of research—rigorous research. For me, that's the message in "A Pebble-in-the-Pond Model for Instructional Design" and "First Principles of Instruction." My question has two parts:

These two articles ("Pebble-in-the-Pond" and "First Principles") seem—we get to the word "conscience" again and this is a hallmark of Dave—seem to have been written as a matter of professional conscience. There is something underlying [as] the reason you wrote these two articles. Could you tell me what prompted you to write those articles, which seem very basic for the audience of performance improvement? That is the first part. For the second part, what are your thoughts and concerns for the ISD field as a whole as we look at a new generation of practitioners and researchers?

Dave Merrill:

You know that 95% of instructional design is done by designers-by-assignment. You know who they are—I am an engineer today, a designer tomorrow; I'm a tank driver today, an instructor tomorrow.

We are not, and our graduates are not, developing most of the instruction, and yet we're training them to develop instruction. We are suffering from the "ice man problem" that Wayne talked about. We're still delivering ice and we need to decide on our real value. Our real value proposition is not training developers; it's studying the process of instruction. It's not using technology that is here today and gone tomorrow. Delivering instruction is not our value proposition. Our value is making instruction more effective and more efficient no matter how we deliver it or what instructional architecture we use. We ought to be studying the underlying process of instruction.

In the Netherlands and at our Utah State University Instructional Technology Institute I delivered a paper titled "The Proper Study of Instruction." There are five things that every doctoral student in this area, and maybe master's students too, ought to study: (a) instructional theory, (b) instructional research, (c) the building of instructional design tools, (d) the development of instruction using such tools, and (e) the assessment of the instructional products thus developed.

Theory. By theory I do not mean some doctrine or specific approach that follows an "ism." Theory is an explanation of an instructional proposition, an explanation that answers the question "why?" Why is that prescription useful? What happens? What's the learning underlying what happens when we use a particular instructional prescription? I really liked Bob Gagné's book *The Conditions of Learning* (Gagné, 1985), where he laid out how learning takes place cognitively and then identified the instructional prescriptions that follow. Van Merriënboer (1997) also followed this approach to identify the cognitive processes first and then derive prescriptions from these processes. I don't see this model being followed in much of the writing in the field, including [by] myself. We lay out our prescriptions, but we either don't understand why or we fail to provide our explanation for why. So the first thing students ought to study is not only the propositions or prescriptions for effective and efficient instruction but the underlying explanations of these prescriptions. Further, students need more opportunity to develop theory, to provide explanations of why.

Research. Second, graduate students ought to study instructional research. They should first ask the question why and then find out who says so and how do they know—prove it. Find the evidence. I don't mean case studies; I don't mean testimonials; and I don't mean ethnographic or other qualitative observations. I apologize to those of you who are involved in these new research methodologies. But they just plain don't provide the data that we need. Testimonials are not research. Neither does surveying a group of teachers provide the data we need. We need hard data about how particular instructional strategies and approaches work. We need to return to the empirical support of instructional methods. Occasional case studies and personal testimonies do not provide the support that is required.

Tools.   I really think that the role of our students ought not to be to design instruction, but to design tools for building instruction for designers-by-assignment. We have all kinds of authoring tools which aren't [authoring tools]. Most are merely programming tools that have nothing to do with authoring and that have nothing to do with instructional design. We need instructional design tools. Most of the folks who are designing instruction are not you (our instructional design students), they are people who work for you after you get out on the job. We (you) need tools to help them do their job better.

One of the problems is that many designers-by-assignment don't think they need what we have. Too many designers-by-assignment don't know instructional design—and worse, they don't know that they don't know instructional design. Therefore they're happy with what they are doing, creating instruction that doesn't work. We need to help them know a little more about instructional design. You aren't going to do it by sitting in school to get a master's degree. You're going to do it by creating tools that make their job easier, and then we need to demonstrate that those tools really create instruction and that the resulting instruction really teaches. We need to get back to empirical data and then use this research base to design easy-to-use instructional design tools.

We need to return to our primary mission—the study of instruction and how to design effective and efficient instruction that works. Information is not instruction; unstructured collaborative problem solving is not instruction; learning communities are too often not instruction; and digital content repositories are not instruction. Although these activities are useful, I hope we can get back to our real value proposition—the study of and the design of effective instruction. Let's learn how to design effective instruction and let's create the instructional design tools to help designers-by-assignment create instruction that works.

Michael Farris:

I had the opportunity of working with Dave on the TICCIT project in the late 1960s and early 1970s, and one of the first major tasks on the TICCIT project was to build a comprehensive hardware and software system that was to be based on instructional principles, constructs, and strategies. What were the major ups and downs, arguments, and enlightenments from those early design discussions? And, after 30 years, what still holds true today?

Dave Merrill:

Most people here today have never heard of TICCIT, and it would be to their benefit if they learned about TICCIT, because it was one of those great innovative systems (Merrill et al., 1980). It was a great opportunity to be involved on that team. TICCIT is the longest surviving CBT system in the world. It's still running at Brigham Young University; I haven't checked, but up until a few years ago it was still running at a community college in Phoenix. And what is really amazing is that after 30 plus years, the same software is still working.

Component Display Theory (CDT) (Merrill, 1994), which is one of the things I took forward, was developed simultaneously with TICCIT. We tried to implement Component Display Theory in hardware; that is, we had a learner control strategy that consisted of buttons: rule, example, practice, easy, medium, and hard. When a student was presented with some content, the system would present an objective and then present learner control options to the student. Do you want to see a definition or rule? Do you want to see an example? Do you want to see a practice problem? Do you want to go back and see another example? Do you want to see the rule again? Do you want to see a harder example? Do you want to see an easier example? Each of these options was available by the touch of a button using the learner control keys.

This is still an excellent approach. I've not seen a system since that has learner control of strategies. When we talk about learner control nowadays, we usually refer to content control. The learner is essentially told, "Here are all the content units and you can read them in any order you want"; of course, if you do that it won't make any sense. That's not learner control. It's certainly not learner control of strategy. Learner control is difficult for students. Students don't know how to control their own strategies without considerable coaching.

TICCIT also anticipated many major computer developments. It was the first system that I know of that had colored text on the screen; today of course we all think color is supposed to be there. It was one of the very first systems that had integrated graphics, even though the graphics were pretty primitive compared to today. It was the first system that used windows long before windows were invented. And it had transaction shells that used the same information from a database both to present information and to practice information. The displays were all generated "on the fly" as they were requested by the student. These are still very good ideas. Later the TICCIT system was taken over by the commercial world, and they decided they wanted it to be like every other authoring system so they got rid of many of its innovations.

The other innovation that was unique to TICCIT was an advisor. It was one of the very first expert systems that used an overlay model of ideal student performance. We defined what we thought was the all-American strategy for a student. When students pressed the advice button, we compared where they were in their strategy with the all-American strategy and advised them the next thing they should do. I haven't seen a system since that gives advice about learner control based on their choice of strategy. These are all innovative, far-reaching ideas that have still never reached fruition in any other system that I am aware of.

So what did we learn from TICCIT? We learned a great deal about instruction. We learned a great deal about learner control. Following the TICCIT project we conducted some NSF [National Science Foundation]-funded research on learner control and we found out that students can't do it very well. But those data have long since been buried because no one believes it any more; everyone now says learners need to have learner control. But if you want to know what the facts are, most students do not use learner control very effectively. What happens is the *girlfriend-on-the-lawn* syndrome. You know what that is? The girlfriend is on the lawn waiting for me; give me the test and I'm out of here. Students take the easiest path, not the best path. And unless you train students how to use strategy control, they use it to their disadvantage, not to their advantage. And yet today, there is not a system that doesn't advocate learner control. There's little or no data that shows a student learns better from learner control. The only data we find is that learner control can be used well if students already know the subject matter, and if they have a high degree of self-direction; those are the only students who benefit from learner control and that's not the majority of our population. (Clark, 2003; Clark & Mayer, 2003).

David Jonassen:

I didn't know we were supposed to propose a question. I thought we were supposed to revise our chapters in the book, so that's what I did with a little bit of a philosophical twist; so let's talk about ontologies. Ontologies are systems based on what we perceive as reality. Dave's ontologies include the CDT and transaction theory, and I have studied them a great deal. In fact, we've built transaction generators—a couple of them. This is a representation of a particular kind of a relational transaction; when you actually use that transaction you can represent "stuff"—you can represent the knowledge or the content that you are trying to convey. This is a little eyeball of instructional knowledge representation—structural knowledge is absolutely an essential part of understanding. The rudiments are the basis for conceptual change, but there are many ways of knowing. I can probably list, if we had time, 40 or 50 different ways that we know things. We know ontologically, epistemologically, phenomenologically, et cetera. Yet all of these ontologies—curriculum ontologies, authority ontologies, representational ontologies, information access systems, library catalogues—are based on a single form of ontology: namely, a topic/subject-based ontology. And that's not the way we think about the world. Humans don't understand things and don't represent them in their own minds based on or according to a simple topic or subject ontology.

With content, that's not true. What content needs is activity. Activity systems are required in order to make sense, and this will result in instruction of different types of knowledge. It needs an intention because all activity is goal driven—I'm talking about problem-solving activity in particular. Dave and I may disagree on that; the problem is essential to the first principles of instruction. And I would argue that the concept of problem-centered learning is not specific enough. Most of my research now is focusing on different kinds of problems. I've developed specific theories of instructional design models for story problems, troubleshooting problems, case analysis problems, and I am working on designing more complex kinds of problem-solving instructional models. What we need and what I propose in the book is a kind of transaction elaboration by problem type. I would suggest different kinds of transactions can be used to solve different kinds of problems. The result is of course that the knowledge becomes activity based, because we are actually using the content rather than learning about the content.

Dave Merrill: I have just two comments. First, our ontology is based on problems—not topics, as David correctly noted. Second, to paraphrase David at an AECT session year ago, I find myself agreeing with David Jonassen, and it makes me feel extremely uncomfortable ☺.

Kinshuk:

Instructional systems have long employed adaptivity mechanisms based on student modeling components. Although sophisticated student modeling techniques are available in the area of competence-based modeling, little work is done in profiling the cognitive attributes of the student, with perhaps the exception of some shallow modeling of student's behavioral preferences. The research in cognitive psychology now permits the formalization of cognitive profiling approaches.

With your background in educational psychology, what are your views toward the need for formalization of cognitive profiling? Did you ever think about such formalization in your own research? Do you think that the computational expenses in such profiling are worth the benefits achieved? Do you think the day is near when the learners will really benefit from the adaptation mechanisms based on cognitive profiling?

Dave Merrill:

Larry Stolurow, my major professor at the University of Illinois many years ago, was one of the early pioneers in computer-based learning and probably wrote one of the very first monographs, called *Teaching by Machine* (Stolurow, 1961), that outlined what computer-based learning would be like. You have to remember, in those days there were only mainframes. So we sat around and debated whether computer-based learning would ever be cost-effective; will we ever be able to get it below $150 dollars an hour for computer-based instruction? Of course we all laugh now because you can go to Wal-Mart and buy a computer. Larry gave a lecture that really affected my life a great deal, and is directly related to this question. He drew the following diagram on the blackboard (Fig. 1).

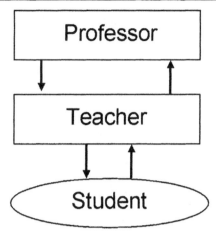

FIG. 1.   An adaptive teaching system.

He said, "Here's my view of what the teaching machine of the future will be like. There will be a student who's interacting with a virtual teacher on the system and the teacher is interacting with the student. But the student is not learning very well and the teacher's behavior is being watched by the virtual professor; as the learning goes on and the student is not acquiring the skills that they would hope, the professor would intervene and suggest to the teacher a change of strategy that would enable the student to learn more effectively." Now you've got to remember this was 1964; this is a long time ago. When I heard this lecture I thought, "Great, this is what I'll do for my dissertation." I didn't, and we are still a long way from creating a system that learns how to teach. But this idea, a system that would figure out exactly what the students need, and then give them exactly what they need to learn, is an ideal that many people have expressed.

However, I worry about the silver spoon argument—that is, if we were able to determine exactly what we need to know about the student and then give the student instruction that is exactly tailored to help him or her learn optimally, would it be like the rich kid who gets everything he ever wants, and therefore when he gets into the real world he is unable to adapt? If we adapted instruction exactly to fit what the student wanted, would we cause problems later on in his or her life by making learning too easy?

Let me jump forward to the TICCIT system that we've already discussed. In the TICCIT system we had a self-adapting instructional language—rule, example, practice, easy, hard—that allows students to adjust their strategy. Our argument was that we don't know how to determine exactly what the student needs, but students ought to be able determine what they need for themselves. We talked about a construct we called the *momentary comprehension index*. The student has in mind this little index that either says "I'm getting it" or "I'm not getting it." And the student ought to be able to say, "I'm not getting it; show me another example." This argument is what led to the TICCIT learner control of strategy. The idea was we don't know how to find out what the student needs, but perhaps the students know what they need. We can help the students by giving them the capability of controlling the instruction and giving them the next instructional component they want. "I need another rule, definition, or generality. I need another example. Show me a practice problem. Show me a harder problem, an easier problem," and so forth. The idea was that they would be able to adapt instruction to themselves.

As I've already indicated, our research on learner control shows that they are not very good at using strategy control when we gave them that capability. So we probably need some kind of advised learner control. When we have advised learner control, what do we need to know in order to advise the student? The system could say, "You ought to try this," or "You might try this," but how does the system decide what the student ought to try? What variables do we use for adaptation? I wrote an article (Merrill, 2002b) entitled "Instructional Strategies and Learning Styles: Which Takes Precedence?" I argued that content-by-strategy interaction was first. That is, everyone needs the same strategy to learn a concept, but within that strategy there may be differences, like how many examples does a student need or how many times does a student need to look up the definition or does the student need multiple forms of representation, and so forth. But there isn't one strategy for some person learning a concept and a different strategy for somebody else. I argued that content-by-strategy interaction took precedence.

Maggie Martinez has a Web site located at http://www.trainingplace.com [see the section on learning orientations research at this Web site]. Maggie argues for motivational aptitude. She talks about four kinds of learners: transforming learners, performing learners, conforming learners, and resisting learners. She argues that the type of learner and motivation is what makes the real difference. It's really the self-direction capability of the student that is critical. If students are transforming learners, they like to try things on their own. If they are performing learners, they say, "How do I get the A?" I have a lot of performing learners in my graduate classes. The conforming learner says, "How do I pass this class? I don't care about the A; I just want to get past this class and out of here." Or the resistant learner, who says, "Try to teach me something." I'm sure that these attitudes make a difference. But I don't know whether I agree with her argument that these are somewhat stable characteristics of people. Perhaps students demonstrate different self-direction within different domains. Are these aptitudes on which we as instructors or designers ought to adapt?

Then there are the Cronbach and Snow (1977) findings about aptitude–treatment interactions—that there are no aptitude–treatment interactions, except maybe verbal and visual. On the other hand, Dave Jonassen and Barbara Grabowski (1993) compiled a book on individual differences. They identified probably a hundred different variables that have been studied. And on some days or in some cases, it seems that some of these aptitudes make a difference. We obviously need more study of this issue.

Then there's the *treatment-C* argument. If you find an aptitude treatment interaction where you get a cross-over effect, you will always be able to find a treatment-C which will be better for both low- and high-ability students. If that's the case, there are no real aptitude–treatment interactions. This raises a lot of issues about how much do we want to invest in adapting and how much do we want to invest in cognitive profiling, if we won't make much of a difference in instructional effectiveness.

Adaptive instruction is such a logical argument, but it is still a wide-open question that needs more investigation. If I had to bet, I'd bet on advised-learner-control versus system-learner-control. I'd bet that previous learning and self-direction—the ability to direct your own work—are probably the key variables, rather than cognitive abilities.

Bob Reiser:

I'm Bob Reiser from the Instructional Systems Program at Florida State. Dave has been a guest speaker at Florida State so many times that we've awarded him the title of Assistant Professor, without tenure. I'm going to focus my attention on the "First Principles of Instruction" (Merrill, 2002a), a paper that appeared in the 2002 issue of *ETR&D [Education Technology Research and Development],* and I have three questions that I have given to Dave previously.

For the most part, the principles you have derived from recent instructional design theories and models appear to be similar to the principles espoused by some of the pioneers in our field, particularly Gagné and your earlier work. Would you agree with this assessment? What are some of the important ways in which the principles and their corollaries go beyond the earlier work in our field? Question one.

Two, last year you indicated that you were in the process of examining whether there was adequate empirical support for the principles you identified. What empirical research have you examined since then, and what does that research indicate about the validity of each of the principles you described?

Finally, what implications do the "first principles" have in terms of (a) the skills that we should be teaching to future instructional designers, and (b) the instructional strategies we should use to teach them those skills?

So, in summary: One—Is there anything new among the principles? Two—What research exists in support of the principles? And, three—What implications do the principles have for instructional designers and how we teach instructional designers?

Dave Merrill:

I'm really pleased to have made the rank of assistant professor at FSU. Once again Bob poses an easy set of questions to answer ☺. First of all, are these pretty much the same principles that Gagné and I put forth years ago? The answer is yes. I need to confess that I started with the principles Gagné and I had identified and then read the literature to see who agreed or disagreed with us. Then someone pointed out to me that 200 years ago Johan Herbart, who is often identified as the father of scientific education, listed the first principles pretty much the same way as I did. These are not new ideas; they've been around for a long time. What is extremely amazing is that all or some of these principles are so often not applied in the instruction that we find publicly available.

There are a couple of things that go beyond Component Display Theory. I speak for myself; Bob Gagné I won't try to speak for. It became very clear to me, as I got into the literature and struggled with the theories, that problem-centered instruction was an idea that I had not addressed in Component Display Theory (Merrill, 1994), and Gagné had not addressed [it] in his *Conditions of Learning* (Gagné, 1985). He and I did write a paper together about enterprises, in which we started down this path (Gagné & Merrill, 1990). As I studied the literature, it became very clear to me that building instruction centered around real-world problems was a key to effective content organization and contrasted with the usual topic-oriented approach.

The other change is in the ISD model. I would replace that second *D* in the ADDIE model with a *P*—namely, production—and I would move the development way up front. What we need is a content-first approach to ISD. One of the problems we've had in the past is that we try to write our objectives without knowing the content. We try to outline instructional strategies without knowing the content. And then we start writing the content. This is backward. By going problem-centered we are required to identify the entire content first. The first step in design, following front-end analysis, is to go out and find a problem; then find a series of problems; then analyze each of these problems to see what component knowledge is needed in order to solve each of these problems. Get all of this content specified in detail; don't only talk about it; get the actual problem. Get all the input, the output, the solution. Do that right up front—that's part of your content analysis. Don't try to write objectives first. Don't try to draw hierarchy diagrams first. Get the actual content. Then it's much easier to lay that into a strategy and an interface design (Merrill, 2002d; van Merriënboer, 1997).

The second question is research support for the first principles. I still do not have the research base that I would like to have for first principles. There are several recent reports that do cite research support for some of the first principles (Clark & Mayer, 2003; Mayer, 2001; O'Neil, 2003). None of these organize the first principles as we have done, nor does any one of these sources cite all of the first principles we have identified. We do have a first principles synthesis in preparation, which should be available when this discussion is published (Merrill, in press). In these sources there is some empirical support for each of the principles. It is important to note that we have not yet found any research that contradicts any of these principles.

We did do a test of first principles and the pebble-in-the-pond approach to instructional design (Merrill, 2002d) with NetG. I suggested to Jim L'Allier that their instruction might not be as effective as it could be. He said, "Let's find out." We lined up a company and identified employees that used Excel. We asked these folks how they used Excel. We got them to identify some real world problems that they used in their company. Then we put some new people through the existing NETg course.

This first study didn't go that well, but it had a happy ending. We used a four-group design consisting of a pretest/posttest plus a posttest only. We found that most subjects who took the pretest, which was a real-world task, before they took the training, didn't come back and take the posttest. Those that didn't take the pretest did come back and do the posttest, and they scored about 60 to 65%. Some thought that our study was ruined because folks were "too busy" to come back and finish the experiment. But these were randomly assigned people. It doesn't make sense that the people that took the pretest were too busy and the people that didn't have the pretest were not too busy. I suspect that those who took the pretest felt that they had not learned enough to pass the test, whereas those who did not have the pretest did not know what to expect on the test.

I suggested to NETg that I had a project class where we wanted to develop an instructional product for a real client. I said, "Why don't you let us develop a sample lesson with a problem-centered approach to teaching Excel?" So we did. NETg liked it. They took their developers and developed a professional version. There were five training scenarios and three test scenarios using real-world Excel problems.

With NETg, we conducted an experiment (Thomson, 2002) where we had three groups. These were spread out in different companies. One group used the scenario-based course implementing first principles. Another group used the existing NETg Excel course. The third group was the control group who did the real-world tasks without instruction. The scenario-based group scored 89% on the real-world test; the existing NETg course scored about 68% on the real-world test; the control group scored about 30% percent on the real-world tasks. But what was even more interesting was that the scenario-based group completed all three tests in less than 30 minutes, whereas the regular NETg took an hour to do all three tests. All of the differences were significant. NETg has developed some return on investment studies that go beyond our research that demonstrates a significant savings when instruction is based on first principles.

The third question was, "What skills do designers need?" My first comment is, to quote Bob Mager, "Most subject-matter experts aren't." For content analysis, we've often neglected our responsibility by saying, "We'll get a subject-matter expert." I don't think that works; SMEs know what to do, but they don't know how to teach it, how to organize it, or how to sequence it. Doing it is not teaching it. We need a lot more attention on content analysis. We need to know how to represent knowledge; skills hierarchies are not sufficient. Problem-centered analysis, identifying problems, sequence of problems, and identifying the components in those problems are required. This type of analysis seemed so simple until I tried to teach it and then realized that this type of analysis also takes considerable skill. However, my value proposition from earlier is that being training designers should not be our primary role. We ought to be studying the process of instruction. We should be building ID tools, not programming tools; and instructional principles should be captured in these tools for those who are designers-by-assignment.

Andy Van Schaack:

Why are there so many theories of instructional design that are supported by little or no evidence, and what responsibility do researchers in instructional design, including you, have to perform empirical studies to validate your theories?

Dave Merrill:

This is a tough question. If I knew why there was so little research, I'd probably invest in the stock market. Many are not interested in research because they love the technology. Playing with the toys is lots more fun than doing research. So I have the feeling that playing with the toys gets in the way of doing research. We're spending so much time learning the latest and greatest technology, we don't have time to do research.

One of the other problems is that there has been a huge disenchantment over the past several years with the slow progress of experimental research and scientific method. One study doesn't answer a lot of questions and is a lot of work. There are thousands of questions we need answered and people get disenchanted. People are looking for a quick answer. But I don't think there is a quick answer. As a result, we are not doing as much research as we could be doing, and we are not making as much progress as we could be making.

The third reason is the proliferation of new theories. Everybody feels like if they're going to get promoted they'd better create a new theory. Creating theories seems to be the popular thing to do these days. Everybody has their new ideas, their new wrinkles, instead of trying to build on what we already know. We need to get off this ego-centered approach to instructional technology. We need to back up and find out if there's a set of principles we can agree to and then build on those principles. Let's build on what's there instead of starting over and reinventing the wheel every single time. Our graduate students go crazy because they are taught this theory, that theory, and then are told that you've got to integrate and create your own theory. They often ask, "What does everybody agree to?" And we shrug our collective shoulders and say, "We don't know."

I already talked about the proper study of ID and what we ought to do.

The other thing that would really help is certification. I know this is a naughty word for some people. I built a kitchen in my house a couple of years ago. It took me five contractors to get a simple little kitchen put in a closet. The electrician came; then the plumber came; then the cabinet guy came; then the guy to install the countertops, and then the guy that did the painting. So I said to the last guy that came, "You'd make a fortune if you just put out a shingle that says we install kitchens." And he said, "We can't." I said, "What do you mean, you can't?" "Well, first of all it takes four years as an apprentice and four years as a journeyman to get your electrical license. It takes four plus four to get your plumbing license; it takes four plus four to get your carpentry license. That's 24 years before we can be a one-stop contractor and by then we'd be retired." This is incredible. For $25 I can go downtown and buy a license. In Logan, Utah, I can open up an instructional development shop, and I can corrupt people's minds with no experience whatever. I need no training, no internship, no apprenticeship—just a license from the city. We care more about our toilets then we do about people's minds. We ought to have a certification program, such that before a product can be put on the market the developers ought to be required to have data that shows that the product works. Developers ought to be required to field test their products, and they ought be required to publish the data. And if the product does not have data, then we ought to say no certification. No data, no support, no certification. ASTD [American Society for Training & Development] tried to develop a set of standards for certification, but it was like the fox watching the chickens. I was on that committee, and I went crazy. After we got some really good standards we reviewed some courses, and we refused to certify about 90% of them. The folks at ASTD said, "You can't do that." And we said, "What do you mean, we can't do that?" "Well, the developers of these courses are our supporters; these are the members of our organization, and we've got to approve at least 50% of their courses or we will lose their support. We've got to modify the standards to approve 50%." And I thought the purpose of the certification was to find out if these courses teach—not to make money for the organization. We need an independent organization to certify products—one that doesn't have its own ax to grind.

Dave Wiley:

I am Dave's [academic] great-grandson [Merrill—Reigeluth—Nelson—Wiley]. A lot of your career has been spent in automated instructional design. The Summer Institute at Utah State (we just held the 15th annual meeting) for the first 10 years focused on automated instructional design. At the 10th annual conference the question was asked: "Automated instructional design—can we? Should we? Will we?" And the answers that were presented by the esteemed panelists and people there were "yes, yes, and no." In your mind, are these still the right answers? That's the first question.

The second question is this: In thinking about automated instructional design, as much time as you've spent thinking about it, is there something about a social interaction and relationship with another human being that's important to learning that we won't ever be able to replicate in one of these automated systems? Is there always going to be a place for the human being to be in place in the education process?

Dave Merrill:

The answer to the first question, by key players from Allen Communication, Asymeterics (Click-2-Learn), and Macromedia, was: "We could, we should, but we won't." The reasons given were: "First, we can't make money selling authoring systems, especially automated authoring systems; there won't be enough people buying them so it's not worth our time. Second, there is a lack of interest on the part of consumers." We proposed a series of workshops showing Macromedia customers how to use Dreamweaver objects to teach concepts, procedures, and processes. Their customers indicated that they already knew how to teach; they just wanted to know how to use the tools. Unfortunately, most of the instructional products I have reviewed indicate that their customers are wrong—they don't know how to teach concepts, procedures, and processes. But "customer driven" is the order of the day. If you can't sell it, why develop it? We need another Watson (IBM) who develops products that customers need, but don't know they need, and then sells the customer on the product. Most developers are designers-by-assignment. They need all the intellectual leverage they can get if they are to ever create products that really teach. If we continue to let these designers believe that they know how to design instruction that works—when it doesn't—then we will continue to have ineffective instructional products that do not teach.

The second question concerned the role of real people in automated instructional design systems. The work of the ID2 Research Group was often misunderstood. Automated instructional design was not about designing systems that automatically teach students but rather systems that provided built-in instructional design expertise for designers who lacked sufficient skill to design effective instructional products without this intellectual leverage. Our systems were really designed to help people design better instruction, not systems to merely automate the delivery of instruction. We were not trying to replace humans. It was all about providing skill leverage—how to help designers-by-assignment to do a better job.

It is clear that students learn from each other. There is considerable interest in online communities of learners. My concern is the possibility of inefficient or even inappropriate instruction in these situations. Merely providing information or finding information may not be sufficient except for the most self-directed learners. Most learners require more than information—they require instruction. Instruction involves appropriate selection of content, appropriate sequence of content, appropriate guidance to relate generalities to specific cases, practice consistent with the objectives of the instruction, gradually diminished coaching during practice, and activation of previously learned knowledge so that the new knowledge can be built on what is already known. Professional designers frequently neglect these important aspects of effective and efficient instruction. Why would we expect that these important instructional functions will occur spontaneously in a community of learners?

Too many of the problem-based communities of learners and other open-ended learning environments provide information and rely on the learners to acquire the desired knowledge and skill. This approach is appropriate for learners already experienced in the content area who have a high degree of self-motivation. Learners inexperienced in a given content area will learn more efficiently and effectively if they are provided the instructional functions identified above. Providing these functions is possible in open-ended learning environments but requires far more sophisticated instructional design than is required for more conventional forms of instruction. Too many of these open-learning environments suffer from insufficient instructional design and hence result in ineffective and inefficient learning.

Michael Spector:

I want to thank everyone: the panelists for their questions and comments; the audience; and especially Dave. We unfortunately do not have time for questions from the audience as we had hoped. Thanks again.

CONCLUSION

It is our sincere hope that the conversations initiated at AECT 2003 will continue. That dialogue, along with the various chapters in this book and Merrill's many contributions, may well push us forward toward of a set of evidence-based first principles to guide instructional design.

REFERENCES

Clark, R. C., & Mayer, R. E. (2003). *E-learning and the science of instruction: Proven guidelines for consumers and designers of multimedia learning*. San Francisco: Jossey-Bass/Pfieffer.

Clark, R. E. (2003). What works in distance learning: Instructional strategies. In H. F. O'Neil (Ed.), *What works in distance learning* (pp. 13–31). Los Angeles: National Center for Research on Evaluation Standards and Student Testing.

Cronbach, L. J., & Snow, R. (1977). *Aptitudes and instructional methods: A handbook for research on interactions*. New York: Irvington.

Gagné, R. M. (1985). *The conditions of learning and theory of instruction* (4th ed.). New York: Holt, Rinehart & Winston.

Gagné, R. M., & Merrill, M. D. (1990). Integrative goals for instructional design. *Educational Technology Research and Development, 38*(1), 23–30.

Jonassen, D. H., & Grabowski, B. L. (1993). *Handbook of individual differences: Learning and instruction*. Hillsdale, NJ: Lawrence Erlbaum Associates.

Mayer, R. E. (2001). *Multimedia learning*. Cambridge: Cambridge University Press.

Merrill, M. D. (1994). *Instructional design theory*. Englewood Cliffs, NJ: Educational Technology Publications.

Merrill, M. D. (1998, March/April). Knowledge objects. *CBT Solutions*, pp. 1–11.

Merrill, M. D. (1999). Instructional transaction theory (ITT): Instructional design based on knowledge objects. In C. M. Reigeluth (Ed.), *Instructional design theories and models: A new paradigm of instructional technology* (pp. 397–424). Mahwah, NJ: Lawrence Erlbaum Associates.

Merrill, M. D. (2001a). Components of instruction toward a theoretical tool for instructional design. *Instructional Science, 29*(4–5), 291–310.

Merrill, M. D. (2001b). A knowledge object and mental model approach to a physics lesson. *Educational Technology, 41*(1), 36–47.

Merrill, M. D. (2002a). First principles of instruction. *Educational Technology Research and Development, 50*(3), 43–59.

Merrill, M. D. (2002b). Instructional strategies and learning styles: Which takes precedence? In R. A. Reiser & J. V. Dempsey (Eds.), *Trends and issues in instructional design and technology* (pp. 99–106). Upper Saddle River, NJ: Merrill Prentice Hall.

Merrill, M. D. (2002c). Knowledge objects and mental models. In D. A. Wiley (Ed.), *The instructional use of knowledge objects* (pp. 261–280). Washington, DC: Agency for Instructional Technology and Association for Educational Communications & Technology.

Merrill, M. D. (2002d). A pebble-in-the-pond model for instructional design. *Performance Improvement, 41*(7), 39–44.

Merrill, M. D. (in press). First principles of instruction: A synthesis. In R. A. Reiser & J. V. Dempsey (Eds.), *Trends and issues in instructional design and technology* (Vol. 2). Upper Saddle River, NJ: Merrill Prentice Hall.

Merrill, M. D., & ID2 Research Group. (1993). Instructional transaction theory: Knowledge relationships among processes, entities and activities. *Educational Technology, 33*(4), 5–16.

Merrill, M. D., & ID2 Research Group. (1996). Instructional transaction theory: Instructional design based on knowledge objects. *Educational Technology, 36*(3), 30–37.

Merrill, M. D., Jones, M. K., & Li, Z. (1992). Instructional transaction theory: Classes of transactions. *Educational Technology, 32*(6), 12–26.

Merrill, M. D., Li, Z., & Jones, M. K. (1990a). Limitations of first generation instructional design (ID1). *Educational Technology, 30*(1), 7–11.

Merrill, M. D., Li, Z., & Jones, M. K. (1990b). Second generation instructional design (ID2). *Educational Technology, 30*(2), 7–14.

Merrill, M. D., Li, Z., & Jones, M. K. (1991). Instructional transaction theory: An introduction. *Educational Technology, 31*(6), 7–12.

Merrill, M. D., Li, Z., & Jones, M. K. (1992). Instructional transaction shells: Responsibilities, methods, and parameters. *Educational Technology, 32*(2), 5–27.

Merrill, M. D., Schneider, E. W., & Fletcher, K. A. (1980). *TICCIT.* Englewood Cliffs, NJ: Educational Technology Publications.

Merrill, M. D., Tennyson, R. D., & Posey, L. O. (1992). *Teaching concepts: An instructional design guide* (2nd ed.). Englewood Cliffs, NJ: Educational Technology Publications.

Merrill, M. D., & Thompson, B. M. (1999). The IDXelerator: Learning-centered instructional design. In J. van der Akker, R. M. Branch, K. Gustafson, N. Nienke, & T. Plomp (Eds.), *Design approaches and tools in education and training* (pp. 265–277). Dordrecht: Kluwer Academic.

O'Neil, H. F. (2003). *What works in distance education* (Office of Naval Research Award Number N00014-02-1-0179). Los Angeles: National Center for Research on Evaluation, Standards and Student Testing.

Stolurow, L. M. (1961). *Teaching by machine.* Washington, DC: U.S. Department of Health, Education, and Welfare.

Thomson. (2002). *Thomson job impact study: The next generation of learning.* Naperville, IL: NETg.

van Merriënboer, J. J. G. (1997). *Training complex cognitive skills: A four-component instructional design model for technical training.* Englewood Cliffs, NJ: Educational Technology Publications.

Glossary
of Merrill's Terminology

This glossary represents some of the rich terminology that can be found throughout the work of M. David Merrill. One of Merrill's contributions is a set of terms and concepts that have helped focus and clarify discussion within the field of instructional design and technology. Merrill frequently used the terminology in this glossary in his theories and writings. Merrill's terminology evolved along with his theories of instruction. The definitions of these terms have been extracted and consolidated from the papers cited at the end of the glossary, most of which are available online at Merrill's Utah State University Web site (http://www.id2.usu.edu/Papers/Contents.html). This glossary was compiled by one of the coeditors of this volume, Celestia Ohrazda.

Abstraction transaction: In Merrill's instructional transaction theory (ITT), an abstraction transaction is one of three primary classes of transactions; abstraction transactions enable learners to transfer knowledge and skills acquired for one set of instances to another set of instances.

Activity: A type of knowledge object that represents actions or procedures that the learner can take to act on objects in the world; in ID-2, activities are things that people do in contrast with processes that occur naturally or entities that are involved in activities and processes.

Adaptive instruction: The ability of a knowledge object or instructional strategy to be adapted to individual learners in real time as they interact with instructional materials.

Analogy: One of the 13 classes of instructional transactions in ITT; an analogy transaction is an association transaction intended to support learning about a process, event, or activity by likening it to a more familiar one.

Association transaction: One of the three primary classes of transactions in ITT that consists of five classes of transactions: propagate, analogize, substitute, design, and discover; an association transaction requires, as a knowledge base, two or more associated frames from the elaborated frame network.

Authoring system: A set of tools that allow an [in]experienced instructional designer to create learning environments according to established instructional prescriptions.

Classify: One of the 13 classes of transactions in ITT; classify is an abstraction transaction that enables learners to sort new instances into subclasses based on a set of discriminating properties.

Cognitive structure principle: The general purpose of instruction is to promote the development of cognitive structures that are consistent with desired learning performances.

Competency: A set of knowledge, skills, and attitudes that enables the learner to effectively perform the activities of a given task; represented in an elaborated frame network in ITT; see also the definition of competency used by the International Board of Standards for Training, Performance, and Instruction (http://www.ibstpi.org).

Component display theory (CDT): A set of prescriptive relationships intended to guide the design and development of learning activities; CDT defined several categories of objectives using a two-dimensional performance (find, use, remember) and content (fact, concept, procedure, principle) matrix. CDT began to evolve into ID-2 when four cardinal principles of instruction were added by Merrill (1987): the cognitive structure principle, the elaboration principle, the learner guidance, and the practice principle.

Component transaction: One of three primary classes of transactions in ITT that consists of three transactions classes—identify, execute, and interpret, which correspond to the three types of knowledge frames (entities, activities, and processes).

Content type: One of two dimensions of the component display theory (CDT) performance–content matrix that includes facts, concepts, procedures, and principles; an assumption behind this matrix and also found in Gagné (1985) is that the type of content to a significant extent determines the appropriate instructional approach.

Decide: One of the 13 classes of transactions in ITT; decide is an abstraction transaction that enables the learner to select one alternative over another.

Design: One of the 13 classes of transactions in ITT; design is an association transaction that enables learners to use knowledge frames to invent or create new activities or entities.

Discover: One of the 13 classes of transactions in ITT; discover is an association transaction that enables the learner to find new processes, create new instances, or identify new relationships. The learner is required to identify an abstraction model; see also the work of de Jong and van Joolingen (1998).

Evidence-based practice: The notion that instructional design is an engineering discipline that is based on an evolving set of principles that can be empirically tested, refined, and occasionally rejected.

Elaborated frame network (EFN): The knowledge representation system used in ITT that consists of three types of knowledge frames—entities, activities and processes—that are then elaborated in terms of three primary classes of transactions—components, abstractions, and associations.

Elaboration theory: Developed by Merrill and Reigeluth to extend CDT from micro-level instructional prescriptions (e.g., present an instance) to macro-level instructional prescriptions that address issues such as selection, sequencing, and systematic review.

Enterprise: A complex human performance involving an integrated set of knowledge and skills (Gagné & Merrill, 1990); an enterprise represents the typical goal of instruction.

Entity: A type of knowledge object that represents an abstract or concrete object; in ID-2, entities are things involved in processes and activities.

Execute: One of the 13 classes of transactions in ITT; execute is the component transaction associated with an activity that enables learners to acquire or perform the steps that comprise an activity.

Feedback: The notion of providing learners with information about their performance to enable them to improve—a fundamental concept in instructional design; in CDT, feedback is provided within the context of practice at every performance level, including correct performance.

First principles: A recent statement of Merrill's (2002) instructional principles that includes engaging students in meaningful problem-solving activities, activating existing and relevant knowledge, demonstrating new knowledge, requiring students to apply new knowledge, and helping students integrate new knowledge into their lives.

Frame: Used to represent knowledge objects; different types of knowledge objects (entities, activities, processes) have different types of frames or representations. An entity frame contains placeholders for parts and properties, whereas an activity frame contains placeholders for steps, conditions, consequences, and so on. Frames provide a basic building block for an instructional transaction in ITT.

Generalize: One of the 13 classes of transactions in ITT; generalize is an abstraction transaction that enables learners to identify apparently distinct instances or classes as belonging a common, more general class.

ID-2 (second generation instructional design): An extension of CDT that integrates elaboration theory with a set of instructional transactions intended to accommodate integrated sets of knowledge and skills (enterprises), generate both micro- and macro-level instructional prescriptions for a variety of learning goals, and be extensible based on evidence and new knowledge about learning and instruction.

ID Expert: A computer-based instructional development and delivery system that used expert system technology and an early version of ID-2; this system informed the development of the Experimental Advanced Instructional Design Advisor (XAIDA) developed by the Air Force Research Laboratory. ID Expert developed into a commercial system marketed by Leading Way Technology and has evolved into the Knowledge One Authoring System (see http://www.leadingway.com).

Identify: One of the 13 classes of transactions in ITT; identify is the component transaction associated with an entity that enables learners to acquire the names, properties, and locations of the parts of a concrete or abstract object.

Instance: In CDT, an instance represents a particular item or case, as opposed to a generality that is commonly expressed in a definition, principle, or rule; in ITT, an instance is the application of a transaction class to a particular item.

Instructional design (ID): The systematic development of instructional specifications using learning and instructional theory to ensure quality of instruction and achievement of desired learning goals.

Instructional design theory: A set of prescriptions for determining the appropriate instructional strategies that will enable learners to achieve the desired instructional goals; ID theory is prescriptive and founded in learning theory and related disciplines.

Instructional object: See *transaction shell.*

Instructional prescription: A statement of what should be done during instruction to achieved the desired outcome. In CDT, instructional prescriptions are derived from the primary and secondary presentation forms and interdisplay relationships; together these comprise an instructional strategy.

Instructional strategy: A macro-level or general prescriptive instructional approach used to specify the selection and sequencing of materials, types of learner interactions, frequency of reviews, and other aspects of instruction.

Instructional transaction theory (ITT): An extension of component display theory (CDT) and Gagné's *conditions of learning* intended to provide a more complete set of instructional prescriptions; ITT represents the theory underlying ID-2 and consists of three primary classes of transactions—component transactions, abstraction transactions, and association transactions—each of which contains a number of transaction classes; Merrill, Li, and Jones (1991) identified 13 instructional transaction classes and allowed for extensions.

Instructional transaction: The dynamic, real-time give-and-take between an instructor or instructional system and a student; in ITT, instructional transactions involve an instructional strategy and all of the learning interactions necessary for the acquisition of a particular knowledge or skill; related to the concepts *instructional object* and *transaction shell.*

Interdisplay relationship (IDR): In CDT, the relationships among the primary and secondary presentations used to support learning may enhance or detract from achieving desired outcomes, depending on how the primary and secondary presentation forms are used; IDR rules such as isolating the primary representation from the secondary representation minimize the chance for ambiguity.

Interpret: One of the 13 classes of transactions in ITT; interpret is the component transaction associated with a process that enables learners to acquire and identify causes for events, explain how or why something works the way it does, or predict what will happen given certain conditions.

Judge: One of the 13 classes of transactions in ITT; judge is an abstraction transaction that enables learners to order and prioritize instances of a class based on property values.

Knowledge base: In ITT, a portrayal represents the content to be taught and is represented in the form of an elaborated frame network.

Knowledge components: Discrete knowledge elements that comprise a particular subject matter; in CDT, these are facts, concepts, procedures, and principles (sometimes referred to as rules). In ID-2, the basic knowledge components are entities, activities, and processes; see *knowledge object.*

Knowledge object: In ITT, there are three kinds of knowledge components or knowledge objects—entities, processes, and activities; knowledge objects consist of descriptors appropriate to the type of object (e.g., for entities, the descriptors may include the names, locations, and functions of various parts).

Knowledge structure: The set of relationships that exist among the components of knowledge for a particular subject or learning goal; the set of components and relationships that define a knowledge object; see also *elaborated frame network*.

Learner control: A feature in CDT that allows learners the ability to pick and choose the strategy components that best fit their momentary state aptitudes and their permanent trait aptitudes.

Learning object: The combination of a knowledge object with an instructional object to support a specific learner and learning goal.

PEAnet: In ITT, the process–entity–activity network associated with an enterprise; see *elaborated frame network*.

Performance: One of two dimensions in the CDT performance–content matrix; includes finding, using, and remembering.

Primary presentation form (PPF): In CDT, a primary presentation form will involve either a generality or an instance and will be either expository or inquisitory, depending on the requirements of the instructional situation.

Presentation forms: CDT strategy components consist of primary and secondary presentation forms that can be represented in a matrix along two dimensions: generality/instance and expository/inquisitory.

Processes: A type of knowledge object that represent events and processes not directly involving the learner; in ID-2, processes include such things as the diffusion of light through a prism or the effects of the moon on tides, and so on.

Propagate: One of the 13 classes of transactions in ITT; propagate is an association transaction embedded in an EFN that is used when two or more frames are associated.

Properties: In ITT, properties are associated with knowledge object and used to represent the various qualitative or quantitative attributes associated with those objects.

Second-generation ID: See ID-2.

Substitute: One of the 13 classes of transactions in ITT; substitute is an association transaction that enables learners to take advantage of what they already know and apply that knowledge directly to an event or process.

TICCIT (Time-shared, Interactive, Computer-Controlled, Information Television): A computer-based instructional system developed in the early 1970s and currently being marketed by Hazeltine Corp.; TICCIT used CDT for its built-in instructional strategies and included the feature of learner control, which was unique at the time.

Transaction shell: A framework in ITT used to capture, represent, and deploy information about the knowledge components involved in an enterprise in an instructional context; transaction shells are a basic building block in ITT and represent the combination of knowledge objects and instructional strategies.

Transfer: One of the 13 classes transactions in ITT; transfer is an abstraction transaction that enables learners to acquire the steps of an activity or the set of events in a process and apply these to new and relevant situations.

REFERENCES

de Jong, T., & van Joolingen, W. R. (1998). Scientific discovery learning with computer simulations of conceptual domains. *Review of Educational Research, 68,* 179–202.

Gagné, R. M. (1985). *The conditions of learning* (4th ed.). New York: Holt, Rinehart & Winston.

Gagné, R. M., & Merrill, M. D. (1990). Integrative goals for instructional design. *Educational Technology Research and Development, 38*(1), 23–30.

Merrill, M. D. (1987). The new component design theory: Instructional design for courseware authoring. *Instructional Science, 16,* 19–34.

Merrill, M. D. (2002). First principles of instruction. *Educational Technology, Research, and Development, 50*(3), 43–59.

Merrill, M. D., Li, Z., & Jones, M. K. (1991). Instructional transaction theory: An introduction. *Educational Technology, 31*(6), 7–12.

Author Index

Subject Index